## Critical Praise for *Funk* by Rickey Vincent

"The first [book] to examine seriously both funk music and its accompanying culture."

—*The New York Times*

"Grooveologist Rickey Vincent writes in a style knee-deep in both sociological insight and love for the music. . . . With *Funk,* a whole new school of discourse has been kicked open—and all ya gotta do is follow the bass line."

—*Vibe*

"A monster achievement, an exuberant, exhilarating and enlightening book that should soon be standing proudly on your bookshelf next to copies of Robert Palmer's *Deep Blues* and Peter Guralnick's *Sweet Soul Music."*

—*Rap Pages*

"Comprehensive . . . the first and only definitive take on the superfreaky genre."

—*San Francisco Bay Guardian*

*"Funk* is the intellectual equivalent of a Funkadelic album: On the surface it celebrates the spirit of funk, but underneath it is a statement on black culture and the politics of getting down, i.e., it is really saying something."

—*Urb*

"Engrossing."

—*San Francisco Examiner & Chronicle*

"Certifies the cultural heritage of a Hip Hop nation."

—*Publishers Weekly*

# Funk

## The Music, The People,
## and The Rhythm of The One

## Rickey Vincent

FOREWORD BY GEORGE CLINTON

ST. MARTIN'S GRIFFIN ❦ NEW YORK

For permissions acknowledgments, please see the Sources and Notes section on page 347.

Design by Sara Stemen

Library of Congress Cataloging-in-Publication Data

Vincent, Rickey.
    Funk  :  the music, the people, and the rhythm of the one  /  Rickey
    Vincent  :  introduction by George Clinton.
        p.      c.m.
    ISBN 0–312–13499–1
    1. Funk (Music)—History and criticism.  I. Title.
  ML3527.8.V56  1995
  781.64—dc20                          95–32678
                                       CIP
                                       MN

10 9 8 7 6 5

*For Marcus*

# Contents

# Funk Dynasties from the 1960s to the 1990s

| **Predynastic** | **First Funk Dynasty** | **Second Funk Dynasty** |
|---|---|---|
| *Early Sixties* | *Late Sixties* | *Early–Mid-Seventies* |
| | UNIFICATION | THE SHINING STAR |

| | | |
|---|---|---|
| GOSPEL | SOUL | FUNKY SOUL |
| James Cleveland | James Brown > | Stevie Wonder |
| Mahalia Jackson | Aretha Franklin | Curtis Mayfield |
| The Soul Stirrers | Otis Redding | Marvin Gaye |
| | Motown Artists | Temptations |
| RHYTHM AND BLUES | Impressions | O'Jays |
| Ray Charles | Wilson Pickett | Barry White |
| James Brown > | Joe Tex | |
| Jackie Wilson | Parliaments > | UNITED FUNK BANDS |
| Booker T & the MGs > | Isaac Hayes | JBs/James Brown |
| Isley Brothers > | Stax Artists | Parliament > |
| Atlantic Artists | | Funkadelic > |
| Stax Artists | BLACK ROCK | Kool & the Gang |
| | Jimi Hendrix | Ohio Players |
| BLUES/ROCK | Sly and the Family Stone | Isley Brothers |
| Muddy Waters | Charles Wright & the | Earth, Wind & Fire > |
| Howlin Wolf |    Watts 103rd St. Band | Rufus |
| Chuck Berry | Bar-Kays > | War > |
| Little Richard | Booker T & the MGs | Graham Central Station |
| Bo Diddley | Meters | Average White Band |
| B. B. King | Buddy Miles | Mandrill |
| Johnny "Guitar" Watson | Isley Brothers > | Tower of Power |
| | War > | Commodores > |
| JAZZ | Santana > | |
| Miles Davis Quintet | | JAZZ-FUNK |
| John Coltrane | JAZZ-ROCK | Herbie Hancock |
| Sun Ra > | Miles Davis > | Miles Davis |
| Donald Byrd | Herbie Hancock > | Grover Washington, Jr. |
| Art Blakey | Donald Byrd | Donald Byrd/Blackbyrds |
| Horace Silver | Jazz Crusaders | Crusaders |
| Charles Mingus | Ramsey Lewis | Ramsey Lewis |
| | Sun Ra | Funk Inc. |
| | Art Ensemble of Chicago | |

> = Artist's influence continued into the next dynasty

## Third Funk Dynasty

*Late Seventies*
*P-FUNK*

MONSTER FUNK
Parliament
Funkadelic
Bootsy's Rubber Band
Slave >
Brick
Cameo >
Isley Brothers
Brothers Johnson
Bar-Kays >
Undisputed Truth

FUNKY SOUL BANDS
Earth, Wind & Fire
Commodores
Rufus and Chaka Khan
Heatwave
Con Funk Shun
Rose Royce
Maze

DANCE FUNK
K.C. and the Sunshine
  Band
B.T. Express
Brass Construction
Fatback
Chic

JAZZ-FUNK
Herbie Hancock
George Duke
Grover Washington, Jr.
Roy Ayers
Stanley Clarke
Pleasure

## Fourth Funk Dynasty

*Eighties*
*NAKED FUNK*

NAKED FUNK
Rick James
Prince
Zapp/Roger
Cameo
The Time
Bar-Kays
Slave
Lakeside
Gap Band
One Way
Dazz Band
Klymaxx

BLACK NOISE
Tackhead
George Clinton
Afrika Bambaataa
Herbie Hancock
Trouble Funk/Go Go
Defunkt
Fishbone
Living Colour

FUNKY POP
Michael Jackson
Janet Jackson
Kool & the Gang
Maze
Chaka Khan
Whispers
Midnight Star
Skyy
S.O.S. Band

## Fifth Funk Dynasty

*Nineties*
*HIP HOP NATION*

P-FUNK HIP HOP
Digital Underground
EPMD
De La Soul
A Tribe Called Quest
Digable Planets
Arrested Development

POLITICAL RAP
Public Enemy
KRS-One/BDP
X-Clan
Paris
Kam

GANGSTA RAP
Ice Cube
Tupac
Dr. Dre/Snoop Doggy Dogg
N.W.A./Eazy E
Too Short
Ice-T

FUNK ROCK
P-Funk All-Stars
New Rubber Band
Red Hot Chili Peppers
Praxis
MeChell NdegeOchello
Primus
O.G. Funk

NEW JACK, etc.

# Major Funk Artists by Region

**SEATTLE**
Jimi Hendrix
Ray Charles
Sir Mix-A-Lot

**PORTLAND**
Pleasure
Shock

**SAN FRANCISCO BAY AREA**
Sly and the Family Stone
Graham Central Station
Tower of Power
Santana
George Duke
Headhunters
Con Funk Shun
Sheila E
Tony!Toni!Tone!
Digital Underground
Too Short

**LOS ANGELES**
War
Charles Wright & Watts 103rd St. Band
Earth, Wind & Fire
Billy Preston
Barry White
The Whispers
Brothers Johnson
Rose Royce
Roy Ayers
Teena Marie
Klymaxx
Egyptian Lover
Red Hot Chili Peppers
Ice-T
N.W.A./Ice Cube/Eazy E/Dr. Dre

**TEXAS/OKLAHOMA**
Joe Tex
Johnny Guitar Watson
Crusaders
Gap Band

**MINNEAPOLIS**
Prince
The Time
Morris Day
Jimmy Jam & Terry Lewis

**DETROIT**
P-Funk
Stevie Wonder
Marvin Gaye
Temptations
Johnnie Taylor
ADC Band
One Way

**BUFFALO**
Rick James

**CHICAGO**
Curtis Mayfield
Herbie Hancock
Rufus/Chaka Khan
Earth, Wind & Fire
Ramsey Lewis
Faze-O
Captain Sky

**ST. LOUIS**
Miles Davis

**MEMPHIS**
Booker T & the MGs
Otis Redding
Isaac Hayes
Bar-Kays
Stax

**NEW ORLEANS**
Meters
Dr. John
Chocolate Milk
Idris Muhammad
Neville Brothers

**DAYTON/HAMILTON/CINCINNATI, OHIO**
James Brown
Bootsy Collins
Ohio Players
Slave
Roger/Zapp
Lakeside
Heatwave
Sun

**GEORGIA/CAROLINAS/ALABAMA**
James Brown/Fred Wesley/Maceo Parker/JB's
Commodores
Brick
Bohannon

**FLORIDA**
K.C. and the Sunshine Band
T-Connection
Foxy
Blowfly
2-Live Crew

**NEW YORK**
Kool & the Gang
Jimmy Castor Bunch
Mandrill
Fatback
B.T. Express
Brass Construction
Cameo
Skyy
Afrika Bambaataa
Public Enemy
De La Soul

**NEW JERSEY**
The Parliaments/George Clinton
Kool & the Gang
Isley Brothers

**PHILLY**
Maze
Grover Washington, Jr.
Stanley Clarke
MFSB
People's Choice
Instant Funk

**INDIANA/CLEVELAND**
Jacksons
O'Jays
Dazz Band
Funk Inc.

**D.C./VIRGINIA**
Donald Byrd
Blackbyrds
Chuck Brown
Mass Production
Trouble Funk
Go Go

# *Foreword*

BY GEORGE CLINTON

All too often I am confronted with the proposition to publish my life story. Agents, lawyers, accountants—you name it. They've all had that flash-of-an-idea that someone might be interested in my autobiography. At one point, every contract I was offered—no matter what it was for—included the exclusive rights to my life story "throughout the universe, known and unknown, forever and a day."

What I think motivates these suggestions is the common misconception of the creator of funk and George Clinton as being one and the same.

Therefore, it was quite a refreshing experience for me to find that this book does not center around George Clinton/P-Funk, but instead puts things in proper perspective—all the elemental factors and forces that have provided the environment and conditions for the making of this particular music.

Trying to come up with something clever or deep to say about The Funk as an introduction to such a monumental work is an assignment better suited to someone other than myself. Funk is something that one feels, and everybody has the ability to feel it. The irony is: The more one thinks about it, the harder it is to get the feel of The Funk. It's just done.

For those that still need assistance, the information presented here can help you get an understanding of what you're feeling. It can help you get the feeling by understanding what it's all about.

A familiarity with the music is not mandatory, but definitely enhances the experience. If at all possible, you want to listen to the songs and albums that are discussed on these pages. This may be the first book to need a soundtrack.

The staying power of The Funk can't be denied; something about the music provides a cross-generational and multicultural appeal. The

P-Funk clientele has always been a peculiar mix of ages, sexes, races, and nationalities, and faiths unified and collectively categorized by a common state of mind. Funk fans knew world order as "One Nation Under a Groove."

Funk has spawned a mindset of faithful individuals who get what The Funk is about sometimes better than I do! Their continual analysis and introspection has documented P-Funk as a historical, sociological, and artistically creative event. There are those who experience the delight of an appreciation of P-Funk on multiple levels, each compounding the communication exchange of the previous one.

The earliest attempt to explain The Funk that came to my attention was in 1967, about the time "(I Wanna) Testify" was at the peak of success. A co-ed came up after a show and explained that she was doing a thesis on funk. How anyone could have envisioned such importance to what we were doing back then escapes me. She was *predicting* what it would become. I learned the project was completed, as the author—now a minister with her own radio show—surfaced backstage at a recent performance. The interesting fact was that this time she brought her daughter (a fan of the Mothership era) and her granddaughter (who loved "Atomic Dog")!

Rickey Vincent is prominently positioned at the core of this cadre of individuals who spread the word and actively encourage others to access the pleasures and treasures of P-Funk. I have always known him—The Uhuru Maggot—to be in dedicated pursuit of the universal awareness, acceptance, and appreciation of funk. My earliest remembrances center around his being a radio personality. I don't remember the station, but somehow he had free reign over programming. Aside from the majority of his playlist being comprised of P-Funk, what stands out were the specials he produced that featured particular aspects of funk music. His was an articulation of the common denominators of funk.

What is delivered nicely here is a structured line of balance between the music and what it represented while it affected and reflected the social situation of the day. Vincent paints an illuminating illustration of funk music's evolution being a human event gaining importance with time. His is a simple explanation of the complex forces that allowed/caused funk to emerge as the dominant influential force over the music of the streets.

The impact and effect of this work cannot be overstated, in that it chronologically knits a strong foundation for a broadened, deeper, and prideful appreciation of all that Black Music represents. Stripped to its bare roots, all of it is funk. It is the product we produce, and no one can do it like we do it.

This book exposes the rationale behind the Harvard Study on Black Music: the idea that prospective profits of the music led the major companies to acquire as much as possible. By characterizing The Funk as a key factor in Black Music's constant evolution, the story told herein chronicles the predicament the industry faces in trying to monopolize their profiteering of Black Music.

This literary piece is of such insight and projection as to pose quite an argument for a funk aesthetic. After reading it, it's hard not to say funk *is all that!* But it's all that and *more.* With the coming of this book, it must be time for humans to get back in touch with the ancient knowledge. In the beginning, there was funk. . . .

*[signature]*

*May 30 1995*

# Preface: On The One

This book is here for anyone who has heard a kicking rap tune on the radio or in a club and realized that some hook, riff, noise, or chant was taken from some seventies' funk cut, but you *just couldn't place it*. This book is also for those who constantly hear samples of their old school favorites in new songs and realize that if you could, you would track down that original *jam* and play it for yourself.

This book is for those music lovers who were weaned on the ferocious and funky flavors of Godfather of Soul James Brown, Parliament/Funkadelic, Sly and the Family Stone, Kool & the Gang, Earth, Wind & Fire, and the Ohio Players in the 1970s and would like to know how these great bands went about making this memorable sound. Most of all, this book is for those who knew and loved the funk bands of the seventies and could never understand why they were not granted a place in history as a musical and social movement—until now.

This book is designed to once and for all fill in the blanks about a musical style and sound that spent decades in obscurity because it was considered a spinoff of soul music, yet has been sampled to death, has been tossed around as a silly pop notion, and has become perhaps the most influential sound in American culture today, without ever getting its righteous due.

Television jingles loop funky tracks like "Atomic Dog" (for the NBC sitcom *Frasier*) and "For the Love of Money" (for a popular credit card), while bands for late-night shows like Leno's and Letterman's live by the funk jam as they go to commercial breaks. Branford Marsalis, until recently the heir to *The Tonight Show* band's staple of jazz and pop standards, was dragged kicking and screaming into the funk age, performing James Brown's "Funky Drummer" and Kool & the Gang's "Jungle Boogie" nearly every night. Paul Shaffer, bandleader of the number-one late-night talk show, is a cloned funkateer and worships

George Clinton, while performing such funk standards as Funkadelic's "Knee Deep," the Average White Band's "Pick Up the Pieces," and Sly Stone's "Thank You (Falletin Me Be Mice Elf Agin)." And the former late-night host Arsenio Hall further hyped this move toward The Funk by championing that nasty groove from his band every night.

Much of this new flavor has been spawned from the streetwise impulse of Hip Hop, the godchild of The Funk. With rap records selling in the millions despite a lack of radio airplay, the beats and funky tracks have asserted themselves into every facet of media and entertainment— as theme music, sports highlight reels, movie soundtracks, and, once again, commercials. Yet with the controversies surrounding sex and violence in rap music and the alleged "criminal nature" of rappers such as Flavor Flav, Tupac, and Snoop Doggy Dogg, hard-core rap carries a deadly stigma. What surfaces into the mainstream are the funky beat tracks, the haunting echo of an inner-city experience, jazzed up and packaged for middle America. Insulated from the grim urban source of the funk groove, Americans can't get enough of The Funk.

The American mainstream is now comfortable with pop notions of a funky sound that was scoffed at, ridiculed, and even feared a generation ago. The down and dirty sounds of bands like P-Funk, Slave, Bootsy's Rubber Band, Cameo, and the Bar-Kays were avoided like the plague in the late 1970s, in favor of a more "color-blind" sound that "everyone" could dance to. The preposterous hype-dog known as disco music was invented in the 1970s to bring the hot, freaky elements of funk to the well-washed masses in sterilized form. Yet today disco is still a joke, and The Funk has become the musical backdrop to America's modern moods: aggressive, jazzy, fresh, and delectably *nastay*.

### THOSE FUNKY SEVENTIES

Today, a new generation of music fans looks to the seventies as a Golden Age, in which dance music was played by live performers using real drums, horns were blown by real people, and vocalists impressed audiences with their time-tested soulful inflections, rather than their new body parts. Can it be that there was indeed something essential about the 1970s—that decade *after* the sixties, the decade of "no protests" of "no leaders," and of "integration"?

The timing of the seventies' decade bears close resemblance to other creative periods of black American history. If we look at other epochs that followed radical movements, we find that the storied

"Harlem Renaissance" of the 1920s was preceded by a profound black power movement inspired by Marcus Garvey and his Universal Negro Improvement Association. A similar surge followed World War II among blacks in America, as the "color line" was broken in the military, public schools, and sports, and was reflected (and interpreted) by the jazz set, and writers such as Richard Wright and Ralph Ellison, prompting claims of a "Black Renaissance" in the 1950s. Could it be possible that in between the 1967 Newark riots (a high point of equal opportunity for blacks) and the Bakke decision in 1977 (a low point) there was actually another cultural renaissance in black America?

What's clear is that there was something special, something essential about the music of that period, whether it was the attitude, the rhythm, the cadence, the color, or the instruments, it can best be identified as The Funk, and that is what will be explored in this book.

## ORIGINS OF THIS BOOK

This book is a result of many years of broadcasting a radio show called *The History of Funk* on a local college station in Berkeley, California. Long before the onslaught of Hip Hoppers' sampling of funk oldies, *The Uhuru Maggot* was pumping an old-school retrospective that asserted the grand intellectual aspects and furious jam factors of The Funk. Through a combination of academic study and interaction with my East Bay funk audience, a clear focus emerged: that The Funk was more than merely a groovy musical flavor, but instead was and is a viable musical movement that has altered the lives of millions of people around the world.

*The History of Funk* began on radio as an *oral* history that reflected what seemed like all the homeboys already knew, but was nowhere to be seen in print. As the history of each band was reiterated in special retrospectives and theme shows like the "Tenth Anniversary of the Landing of the Mothership" and the "James Brown Payback Marathon," it became clear that the memory banks of the "soul brothas and sistas" were intact and that the *community* became the ultimate authority of the music. This book is a retelling of many "Tales of the Funky" that occurred over years of radio jamming, interviewing, and vibing with listeners, performers, and guests.

To back up this oral history, I developed the idea into a semischolarly treatise for Professor Roy Thomas at UC Berkeley in 1987. He returned my enthusiasm for the project and pushed me ever forward. Yet I found few academic outlets for such a ridiculous proposition. What professor in their right mind would agree that George Clinton, the Ohio Players, and Kool & the Gang deserved scholarly attention in Afro-American Studies? After my undergraduate years at Cal, I moved on to the Master's program in Ethnic Studies at San Francisco State University. There, on my first day, I spoke of uniting politics with culture through the history of funk in a black studies class, and the instructor, Oba T'Shaka, understood and directed my vision from that first day. His vision of *black essence* was mine at that point and the book was then all but written. Within two years, the Master's thesis "The History of Funk: Funk as a Paradigm of Black Consciousness" was submitted and approved, and it served as the basis for *Funk: The Music, the People, and the Rhythm of The One.*

## PROPS

This book required the help of many people from far walks of life. First and foremost, the musicians and artists who produced the music deserve their props, and hopefully this book does them justice. As constant inspiration were the many "funkateers" that I have associated with over the years, beginning with my brother, Teo Barry Vincent, who brought home a 45 of Parliament's "Up for the Down Stroke" in 1974, and changed my life forever. Also, all of the Berkeley Funk Fans who knew The Bomb when they heard it, and didn't waste their time with pop notions.

My KALX radio work has served as a beacon for all those twisted enough to step through and provide their own particular flavor to this funk mission: Marlon "Dr. Illinstine" Kemp, Anthony "Dave-Id K-OS" Bryant, Ashem "The Funky Man" Neru-Mesit, Greg "Shock G" Jacobs, Jimi "Chopmaster J" Dright, David "The Cosmic Rooster" Organ, Yvonne "The L.A. Playgirl" Smith, Anca "Princess P" Bujes, Darryl "Liquid" McCane, Gary "The G Spot" Baca, Billy "Billy Jam" Kiernan, and William "Last Will" Smith. Props must also go to those occasional contributors whom I know only by their funk handles: "Neon Leon," "Sir Noise," "Puppy Breath," "Poochie," "Daddy Dog," "Dr. Watt," "Big Dave DDP (Double Dose of P)," "Satellite," "Zoot-Zilla," "The Subliminal Seducer," and Sam "The Conceptual Nuisance" Cooper. Other funkateers who gave their wizened maggot-brained advice include Sir Lleb of Funkadelia himself, Pedro Bell, Joe Keyes, Mark "Mr. P" Stewart, Jon Carvallo, Calvin Lincoln, and Tim Kinley.

Many other friends and allies within radio gave their time and love when it was needed: Jeff "DJ Zen" Chang, Dave "Davey D" Cook, Clay Ordona, Michael "Too Dread" Finnie, Jonathan Wafer, Michael Berry, Heather Parish, Tamu Du Ewa, Carol Baker; and, from KPFA, Bari Scott, Walter Turner, Peja Peja, Chuy Varela, Jim Bennett, and Michelle Flannery. A special thanks to all of the other creative radio personalities at KALX who shared their insights, information, energies, and attitudes with me over the years. A special no-thanks to the White Noise Supremacists who tried their best to squelch all of the African-Rooted Music at KALX. Have a Nice Day. You will be judged by a Higher Order.

Nothing would have happened with this project without the conceptual support from my well-grounded homies, Chris Williams, Kevin Foster, De Angelo "D Mo Chill" Stearnes, Doug Briscoe, Jonathan Seale, Lawrence Komo, Skay Davidson, Stefi Barna, Margot Pepper, and the indubitable Patrick "Sledhicket" Norwood.

Props to the editorial staff at Berkeley's *Daily Californian* from 1986 to 1991, which supported and tolerated my fonkey attitude; as well as Danyel Smith and Ann Powers for taking my writing seriously at the *SF Weekly*; the editors at *Mondo 2000* for laying out my articles with exotic flare, and Ben Mapp at *Vibe* for taking in my whole rap; Todd and Jeff at *URB* for giving me the juice when I needed it; and David McLees at Rhino Records for everything. Thanks to David Mills and *Uncut Funk* for doing what was needed for The Funk.

Industry professionals and associates that have given generous advice and expertise include Harry Weinger, Sharon Davis, Charles Blass, Tony Greene, Sarath Fernando, Jr., David Henderson, Jason Chervokas, Pete Weatherbee, Brian Cross, Cleveland Brown, Tom Vickers, Robert Middleman, Greg Tate, David Kapralik, John Morthland, Sarah Brown, Arnie Passman, Ethan Byxbe, Jimmy Douglass, Bill Murphy at Axiom, Aris "The Air Child" Wilson, Jack "Jack The Rapper" Gibson, Alan Leeds, Lee Hildebrand, and Ishmael Reed.

An extra special thanks to the musicians Fred Wesley, Bootsy Collins, George Clinton, James Brown, Roger Troutman, Jerome Brailey, Billy Nelson, Curtis Mayfield, Marshall Jones, James "Diamond" Williams, Nathan Leftenant, Larry Dotson, James Alexander, Stevie Washington, Alan Gorrie, Greg Errico, Benny Latimore, Rudy Ray Moore, Gary "Mudd Bone" Cooper, George Porter, Greg "Shock G" Jacobs, Afrikka Bambaataa, Claude "Paradise" Gray, Chuck D, and Dewayne Wiggins for the extra time they spent on the phone with me.

Special props to Gary "The G-Spot" Baca of KPFA for access to his vast interview archives of old-school musicians.

Academic support has been in my corner since 1978 from Professor Roy Thomas of UC Berkeley, the only person I have ever seen teach "soul" in a classroom. He was the first to open my eyes to the possibility of this project. Thanks to Music Professor Olly Wilson, who always kept me to rigorous task, for all the right reasons. Also, thanks to Oba T'Shaka, chair of Black Studies at San Francisco State University, a man with the most all-encompassing and undiluted vision for his people that I have ever seen. Thanks also to Professor Jose "Dr. Loco" Cuellar, Chair of La Raza Studies, and the entire Ethnic Studies Department at San Francisco State University. You got it goin' on.

To the many good friends and family that gave me the lane and passed the ball when I was open for this shot, thanks for believing.

Thanks to my mother, Toni, for your wisdom, clarity, love, and support for me and this project. To my father, Ted Vincent; our many far-reaching conversations and detailed editing have developed into so many articles, columns, and now music books for both of us.

Thanks to my editor, Marian Lizzi; and special thanks to Archie Ivy, and Stephanie and George Clinton, who came through with the intro, like the cavalry coming *over the hump.*

Extra special thanks to my wife, secretary, editor, life, and love, Tess, and our little one, Frederick Marcus.

This book is in memory of my grandmother, Eugenia Goff Hickman (1901–1995), who was always wise enough to judge, and loving enough not to pass judgment; and Charles "Natty Prep" Douglass. A great man who did much more than just give me my first break on radio. He was the embodiment of beliefs turned into action. He elevated us all.

PART 1

# Introduction to Funk: The Bomb

# ONE

# *Introduction to Funk: The Bomb*

"If you got funk, you got class,
you're out on the floor movin' your ass."
*Funkadelic*

## WHAT IS FUNK?

Funk is a many splendored thing. Funk is a nasty vibe, and a sweet sexy feeling; Funk is *funkiness,* a natural release of the essence within. Funk is a high, but it is also down at the bottom, the low-down earthy essence, the bass elements. Funk is at the extremes of everything. Funk is hot, but funk can be cool. Funk is primitive, yet funk can be sophisticated. Funk is a way out, and a way in. Funk is all over the place. Funk is a means of release that cannot be denied. . . . *Village Voice* writer Barry Walters explained The Funk as well as anyone could: "Trying to put that *thang* called funk into words is like trying to write down your orgasm. Both thrive in that gap in time when words fall away, leaving nothing but sensation."

Funk is impossible to completely describe in words, yet we know the funk vibe when we see it. Funk is that low-down dirty dog feeling that pops up when a *baad* funk jam gets to the heated part, and you forget about that contrived dance you were trying, and you *get off your ass and jam.* Funk is that geeked feeling that comes over you when a *superstar* steps into the room—or onto the stage—and everyone is *hyped;* The Funk hits you in competition, when that last shot you made was your best, yet you still dig down for that extra level for the over-drive that you didn't know was there; you know The Funk when you're on a date and *it's time to make your move*—The Funk is a rush that comes all over your body. Scientists have yet to discover that particular funk gland, but rest assured there are plenty of bodily excretions associated with it.

Funk is that nitty-gritty *thang* that affects people when things get heavy. Funk can be out of control, like the chaos of a rebellion, or instinctively elegant, like that extended round of lovemaking that hits overdrive. Funk is what you say when nothing else will do. When you've done all you can and there's nothing else: "Funk it!" George "Dr. Funkenstein" Clinton, the most heralded authority of funk philosophy, reduced The Funk to its barest essence: "Funk is whatever it needs to be, at the time that it is."

Someone "funky-looking" is generally thought of as someone colorful and amusing, yet unkempt, undisciplined, somewhere between exotic and ridiculous. Whether or not "funky" is in style, there are funky-looking people everywhere. Quite often, these funky people are self-styled, creative, and in touch with themselves. Funkiness, then, is an earthy sense of self that is free of inhibitions and capable of tapping instincts and celebrating the human condition in all its forms. Funkiness is a way of life.

Funkiness in a person's behavior or attitudes can mean anything from an ego trip, to a protest, to escapism. Funkiness is much more than a style, it is a *means* to a style. While baggy pants, nose rings, and a Hip Hop swagger are often little more than fashion statements, the combination of "far out" and "all in," the juxtaposition of what is in and what is not yet in, that original ensemble that is the postmodern person (particularly the postmodern African-American) is how people use funkiness as a guide to their uniqueness.

Funkiness for our purposes is an aesthetic of deliberate confusion, of uninhibited, soulful behavior that remains viable because of a faith in instinct, a joy of self, and a joy of life, particularly unassimilated black American life. The black popular music of the early 1970s was a consistent reminder of this new affirming, colorful, ethnic aesthetic, and the Hip Hop culture of the 1990s has spawned a return to this less formalized foundation of life.

## WHY A BOOK ABOUT FUNK?

There are many aspects of The Funk that are intimately tied to an African value system that has been propagated through black culture since the Middle Passage. Funk is deeply rooted in African cosmology— the idea that people are created in harmony with the rhythms of nature and that free expression is tantamount to spiritual and mental health. If we were to look into this African philosophy, the African roots of rhythm, spiritual oneness with the cosmos, and a comfort zone with sex and aspects of the body, we would find that funkiness is an ancient and worthy aspect of life. Thus, funk in its modern sense is a deliberate reaction to—and a rejection of—the traditional Western world's predilection for formality, pretense, and self-repression.

In traditional Western society, the maintenance of rationality, civility, and pomp, with deliberate disregard and disdain for the natural urges of the body and soul, has become a goal unto itself. The influx of technology has in many ways provided a further impetus for most Westerners to obsess with the aesthetics of curbing their instincts. One of Toni Morrison's characters in *The Bluest Eye* looks at the situation facing upstanding "white" Americans:

> They learn . . . how to behave. The careful development of thrift, patience, high morals, and good manners. In short, how to get rid of the funkiness. The dreadful funkiness of passion, the funkiness of nature, the funkiness of the wide range of human emotion. Wherever it erupts, this funk, they wipe it away; where it crests, they dissolve it, wherever it drips, flowers or clings, they find it and fight it until it dies. They fight this battle all the way to the grave.

This vengeance against nature is also manifest in the obsessively cruel and sexually violent treatment of blacks by whites throughout American history. The thousands of public lynchings, castrations, whippings, burnings, and Klan terrorism are grounded in the planet's most hysterical legacy of race hate. This has, of course, perpetuated the social repression of blacks and their self-expressive virtues, among them jazz, the Caribbean Carnival, be-bop, and The Funk. It is The Funk which has provided the modern musical backdrop and forum for explicit confrontations of the vicious racial legacy in America.

In addition, the implicit nature of The Funk, its inherent *nastayness,* which cannot help but drive people closer to their funky soul, peels off the veneer of pretense and exposes the unpackaged self for all to see. Just as rock and roll began the sexual liberation of America in the 1950s, it is The Funk that drives the soundtrack for the American sexuality of the 1990s. Part of the affirmation of the human condition in America is the acceptance of The Funk as a music, as a lifestyle, and as a grassroots philosophy of self-development.

Aspects of black folks' funkiness are ultimately what has fueled mainstream American culture and made it distinct from the culture in any other Western nation. One might even claim that it is the funky nature of black Americans that is the salvation of this nation. The psychologists Alfred Pasteur and Ivory L. Toldston thusly position The Funk in its proper place:

> Thus we could say that "funk" rests at the root and stem of popular culture in America. From beneath the arms, the crotch, a sensuously fragrant, musky perfume has arisen, activating an affective force that provides for life, enjoyment, enrichment and regeneration. It is the most natural force in the universe.

## WHO HAS THE FUNK?

Funk exists on an instinctive level that none of us can control, though some may try. With every new dance on a sweaty dance floor, with every extra dose of cheap cologne, with every swoop of loud lipstick on thick red lips, funk exists. With every new 360 dunk, beaded braids, and "African" fashion statement, with every swaggering pimp-strut and hood ornament on a pink Cadillac, with every black child's natty hairdo, with every country-fried remnant of black folk life seeping into integrated American culture, funk is the channel for this creative flow. Funk is the means by which black folks confirm identity through rhythm, dance, bodily fluids, and attitude. But *every booty is funky*.

Things first got funky in the late 1960s. The militant surge of black America ripped open the existing formulation of community—as whites could no longer determine or control the priorities of black America. No longer marginalized, no longer entering through the rear door, entertaining onstage, and cleaning up afterward, black folks could go anywhere (almost) in America by 1970, and in doing so, would transform that once stale environment into one that is rhythmic, spontaneous, sensual, and stylish. From raucous, revival-style local elections to a bum-rush of blacks into state-mandated jobs, the wild rides on enforced school busing, the rush of blacks moving into white neighborhoods, a tripling of the interracial marriage rate, and a black entertainment overload, the presence of African-Americans turned the social fabric upside down. As a result, the fundamental essence of community—of nation—was all of a sudden mutated by the earthy ways of black folk.

The idea and the importance of funk comes from the depths of black American life, particularly that aspect of black America which never got around to integrating. Funk and funkiness was a part of the lifestyle of those whom Malcolm X described as the "Field Negroes," those black Americans who toiled in the fields as sharecroppers and slaves and to this day struggle in the urban centers to eke out an existence. This is the population that lived in the "ghettos" in the 1960s and now lives in the "inner city." This is the population that torched Watts in 1965, Newark and Detroit in 1967, South-Central Los Angeles in 1992, and is still just as pissed off today. These are the young black Americans whom the poet Etheridge Knight refers to as "the wild guys, like me."

When Malcolm X died in 1965, there were no members of the civil rights movement who could speak to the dispossessed black masses in the meaningful ways that Malcolm had. There emerged Stokely Carmichael, H. Rap Brown, Eldridge Cleaver, Huey P. Newton, Angela Davis, and a host of black revolutionaries ready to continue the struggle, but the one person who captured and *personified* the attitudes and aspirations of the "wild guys" was the Godfather of Soul, James Brown. James Brown spoke to that group and identified their world. He understood and mastered that special process needed to inspire the dispossessed. He came up from the poorest of the poor, and while his politics were not of the militant variety, his *manhood* was. It was James who captured the rage of black America after the death of Malcolm with a "New Bag," and helped to contain the rage after the assassination of Martin Luther King, Jr. in 1968. It was James who articulated the grim yet determined response to Marvin Gaye's question, "What's Goin' On." It was James and his band who provided the musical backdrop for the authentic musical reflection of black America in the 1970s, in all its hope, despair, charm, style, and nasty, unforgiving truths.

### THE BOMB

The Godfather of Soul, James Brown, dropped *The Bomb* on America in an aesthetic fashion that many irate African-Americans were wishing that they could do in real terms. The force, the flavor, and the funkiness of the James Brown experience affirmed and validated the African-American experience at the dawn of the 1970s. The politicians and activists had largely been killed and co-opted, and the burden of capturing and maintaining the vision of a black nation fell on the Godfather, and he did not disappoint. Later, artists like Stevie Wonder and

George Clinton assumed the role of the avatar of a black nation's dreams, but the central locus of all funk, the representation of the total and complete *black man,* was James Brown. Brown represented the political black man, the successful black man, the sexual black man, the relentless black warrior that was "Black and Proud," and as the song says, "ready to die on our feet, rather than be livin' on our knees." Brown grabbed hold of the jugular vein of black aspirations and would not let go.

His band backed up this no-nonsense message with a furious and unrelenting barrage of stripped-down rhythmic R&B, the primordial funk groove that had a gravitational pull so strong that, like a black hole, it moved the music of the world toward its core. By turning rhythmic structure on its head, emphasizing the downbeat—the "one" in a four-beat bar—the Godfather kick-started a new pop trend and made a rhythmic connection with Africa at the same time. James Brown songs hit their accents in "On the One," yet drove the furious bluesy fatback drumbeats all around the twos and fours to fill up the rhythms, never leaving any blank space. The necessary change was made all the more convincing as Soul Brother #1 delivered the screaming, screeching centerpiece of soulfulness onstage, making his every action essential.

When Sly Stone and others hooked up a fuzz guitar and bass-plucking layer on top of this rhythmic madness, a whole new thang was developed, and the music world would never be the same. Off in Jamaica, the grooving, side-to-side syncopated ska sound began to change—emphasizing the fat note on the downbeat *(DOOM chick chicka chick, DOOM . . .)*—and reggae was born. All of a sudden African conga players became essential to jazz and soul performances around the world, as the one-count emphasis fit with African drum meters better than the old two-four thang. Jazz giants Miles Davis, Cannonball Adderley, Herbie Hancock, and Donald Byrd disposed of their "modern jazz" fare and got busy with bass guitars, electric pianos, and James Brown rhythms, fusing an entirely new concept of jazz, all because of the Godfather of Soul, James Brown, and The Bomb.

The James Brown Bomb was an explosion of such atomic proportions that its echoes can still be heard lingering today, just like the electromagnetic remnants of the Big Bang. Soul music took a radical turn down south, as the one-count could be heard on songs like Stevie Wonder's "Superstition," Marvin Gaye's "Inner City Blues," and the Temptations' "Cloud Nine." What began as an effect became a standard, as the funk jam became an essential aspect of any black artist's ability to reach the people in the 1970s.

James Brown–based R&B/funk dance music swept across the world in trendy discotheques from Europe to Japan. Gradually, a simplified form of this dance music began to gain popularity and ultimately sweep across mainstream America. While the "disco craze" swept the country, in malls, in movies, in fashions, and in dances, there was always a deep, grounded black anchor of unassimilated music played by "funk bands"—echoes of The Bomb—which maintained a street connection despite the pressures of record producers to change. Funk music survived, a black aesthetic in music endured the decade of integration known as the 1970s, and the music is being remembered today in glorious fashion in reconstituted form on popular rap music records.

## THE FUNK REVIVAL

The legacy of the funk tradition can be found in the function of The Funk in modern rap music. The modern incarnation of rap music was always understood to be, as rap writer David Toop put it, "syncopated speaking over a funk beat." Mixing old records on turntables has always been an integral element of Hip Hop (rap) culture. However, with the advent of sampling technology, the ability to digitally "splice" pieces of older music into new tracks, the true revival of funk began in earnest. Since the late 1980s, rap music producers have used "samples" of older black music to enhance their beats. Around 1990, during the zenith of the sampling era, the most popular rap stars sampled Funk Era music almost exclusively, and without exception every original funk artist referred to in this book can be found reincarnated in some modern rap song. This cannot be said for Motown soul music artists, earlier rhythm and blues artists, pop soul artists, disco artists, or mainstream (i.e. white) rock artists.

Rather than loop music from out of the tradition, rap samplers are uncanny in their integrity about the records they choose to pillage. Most of the "greatest hits" of the Funk Era have been stripped of all usable parts like an abandoned car. *Vibe* magazine called James Brown's 1974 recording of "The Payback" as the sample of the year for 1992, naming a half dozen raps that use the old loop. Rap superstar M. C. Hammer's first national hit, "Turn This Mutha Out," featured a chant that was taken verbatim from the chorus of Parliament's 1975 number-one soul hit, "Tear the Roof Off the Sucker." Hammer's biggest hit ever, "You Can't Touch This," used the basic riff from Rick James' 1981 hit "Super Freak" repeated endlessly. The rap group Digital Underground looped the number-one 1979 Funkadelic single "(Not Just) Knee Deep" on three separate songs of their 1991 gold record LP, *Sons of the P,* and it goes on and on.

Another intriguing aspect of the sampling revolution is the concurrent "Afro-centric" movement, in which young people have begun exploring an African-centered perspective of the world and its history. Thoughtful rappers have begun to make explicit references to issues of race, black/African pride, black American history, and the works of scholars such as Yosef ben-Jochanan, Cheikh Anta Diop, and Francis Cress Wesling, while maintaining the emphasis on dance rhythm in their music.

Recent legal developments have made it more difficult to legally sample old songs, but what is clear is that any cursory listen to the latest rap music reveals another past world of music beneath the high-tech crashing beats—the world of funk that gave birth to rap in so many ways.

### THE HISTORY OF FUNK

This book follows the thrust of the entire Funk Age, from the James Brown Bomb through the Hip Hop Nation, which is all connected by an irresistible, nasty groove. The book is broken down into seven parts, dealing with crucial aspects of what we know as The Funk: The Bomb, what funk *is,* what it *isn't,* and what its roots are.

The Funk is then discussed in terms of the funk dynasties. The idea of funk dynasties was originated by Bay Area rap producer Ashem "The Funky Man" Neru-Mesit, who wanted to make sure that funk history is told on its own terms, not in terms of other genres like rock and roll and soul music. Like the Egyptian dynasties or the dynasties in China, their histories are told on their own timeline.

The First Funk Dynasty (1965–72) was the period of unification. Funk music was just being developed, first by James Brown, then Sly and the Family Stone, and many other artists who reflected the times by breaking formalized styles and generating a synthesis. This grooving synthesis occurred within the wide-open reaches of rock music, underneath the pop glitter of soul music, and throughout the innovative furor in jazz, as these once separate and segregated sounds all began to "Come Together."

Then, with the many social and musical developments of the 1970s, we got the United Funk Dynasty (1972–76). The many often ridiculous efforts to put the ideas of "Power to the People" to use often created very funky situations, and funky music as well. As seen in everything, from blaxploitation movies to "Soul Train," it was a great time to be funky, as Chapter thirteen (*Those Funky Seventies*) discusses. Perhaps the greatest legacy of the United Funk Dynasty was the United Funk Bands that dominated: musically diverse groups that had men and women, blacks and whites, delivering hard funk and tender moods, high-tech equipment and traditional sounds, and spiritual issues without dogmatic preaching, all wrapped into self-contained units.

Next came the "golden age of dance music," the period when dance music became an institution in America, and despite the dominance of the simplistic imitation of funk known as disco, some of the greatest dance funk ever produced came from this scene. Regrettably, there were the musical changes that compromised the diversity of earlier groups and put a premium on dance beats. But The Funk that resulted was vicious and unrelenting, as Chapter sixteen: *Dance Funk: Do You Wanna Get Funky with Me?* details. The *most* vicious and unrelenting act on the scene was, of course, The P-Funk Mob, George Clinton's Parliament/Funkadelic. Their story, from the barbershop singing in Plainfield, New Jersey, to an intergalactic funk movement, is detailed here. The lasting legacy of The P can be found in the unique spiritual and philosophical themes of P-Funk music, which are explored in Chapter eighteen: *The Metaphysics of P: The Mothership Connection.*

By the 1980s, The Funk as a higher force was almost forgotten, as a number of factors conspired to strip down the essential funk impulse into *Naked Funk.* Beneath the hype of pop funk, a seething underground funk scene flourished nationwide, and emerged in Hip Hop and the black rock of the times.

To bring things up to date: It was clear to many in the early 1980s that there was much more to Hip Hop than a trend of silly rhymes and machine beats. The underground culture of rap music served to rekindle the black pride movements of the 1960s—often by sampling the funky beats of that same period. By 1988, Hip Hop had evolved into what was rightly being called the Hip Hop Nation. And it was clear to anyone listening to rap from a funk perspective that the same values and ideals in modern rap had their genesis in The Funk. Thus, the Hip Hop Nation can be thought of as the "fifth funk dynasty."

As a study of music, as a study of society, and as simply a study of the way *black folks be,* an understanding of The Funk can help explain the continuity of the black folk experience in America since the 1960s. With the many changes within black America since the mid-1960s, it can be helpful to find a reference point from which to interpret the results we are witness to today. The Funk brings it all together.

# TWO

# *Funk Music: Dance Wit Me*

*"You see we are scientists of sound.*
*We are mathematically puttin' it down."*
Kool & the Gang

Funk is a musical mixture. Its most popular form is dance-tempo rhythm and blues–style music with the rhythmic interplay of instruments stretched to a dramatic level of complexity. Any number of different instruments or sound layers can be on various meters, but then suddenly all could tighten up and blurt one synchronized note or phrase, and then just as suddenly swing back into rhythmic interplay. Complex syncopations of instruments are frequent. Some funk songs are constructed tightly, with just one "bridge" in which instruments take deliberate, crisscrossing paths before returning together. Others are free-form grooves, pulsing along as each musician communicates with the other. The bass drives the music, throbbing, thumping, or popping. The tempo can be a slow, sexual gyration, or a high-energy fist-in-the-air romp. As long as there is rhythm, as long as there is togetherness, as long as there is a vibe—it's funk. As George Clinton puts it: "If it makes you shake your rump, it's The Funk."

Trombonist Fred Wesley, one of the most important creators of funk music during the fertile period of James Brown's bands in the early seventies, was an architect of funk arrangements for George Clinton, James Brown, and Bootsy's Rubber Band, and was Brown's bandleader for many years. In a 1992 interview with British TV show host Lenny Henry, Wesley described the basic method of construction for a funk song:

> If you have a syncopated bass line, a strong, strong, heavy back beat from the drummer, a counter-line from the guitar, or the keyboard, and someone soul-singing on top of that, in a gospel style, then you have funk. So that if you put all of these ingredients together, and vary it in different ways, you can write it down, you can construct The Funk.

Wesley maintains, however, that performing The Funk is a "spiritual thing," and that it takes a special type of artist to play it just right. To generate a tight, whipping funk groove that swings so hard it *swangs,* it takes a special vibe. It takes musicians in complete command of their instruments, completely in touch with each other, hip, and well-versed in musical traditions.

Every instrument contributes to this sound. Rhythm instruments often create melodic lines, and melodic instruments often pulse with percussive strength. The bass line, the guitar line, the horn lines in funk often deliver such complete melodic phrases that each could be the primary melody of a simpler soul or R&B tune. (Soul and R&B grooves are generally composed of one primary melody, which is simply accented by the other instruments, not "countered," as in funk.) This complexity is yet another reason why funk music is so readily sampled by producers in the 1990s. Separate lines in funk grooves can now be deconstructed and replicated by digital instruments in dehydrated form.

Another reason why much of modern dance music is so heavily laden with funk samples is that the riffs that were invented by playing funk in the 1970s were created by *bands,* in an interactive process that cannot be duplicated with digital equipment. In a funk jam session, the bass line would lump along, a guitar would fall in, the drummer would kick a funky march, a horn player would devise an adventurous riff along the funky foundation, and the process would build and build. The chops that resulted took an accumulation of ideas, effects, and talents, as each element complemented the other. To jump in twenty years later and extract one tone, riff, or bar in a surgical procedure is a completely different aspect of creation.

Funk music was and is always played together, and for best results, funk should be played continuously, so that the musical energy can generate among players and listeners. Not everyone can lock into a wicked rhythmic lick and keep it tight. As one story goes, Fred Wesley was auditioning a guitar player for James Brown's band and asked him, "Can you play an E ninth chord, 'chicka ta chicka ta chicka ta chicka chick'?" The guitar player replied, "Well, sure." Wesley would respond, "Yeah, but can you do it with feeling, *all night long?*" If the player said yes, then he got the gig.

Funk music can be very difficult to play for those attempting it from a technical point of view, because it requires a freedom of mind, a relaxed and intuitive state in which one devises the appropriate back-beat and counter-line from whatever musical root (jazz, pop, blues, and so on) that the musician feels is fitting for the moment. Ideally, if one attempts to feel the changes, the vibe, the blues, then the melodies and changes come simply and naturally. This is the musical link to jazz and blues. In his book *The Complete Book of Improvisation, Composition and Funk Techniques,* Howard C. Harris describes the essence of funk music:

> Funk is a style of music in which elements of jazz, pop, rock, gospel and the Blues are fused to create a rhythmic, soulful sound. Funk thrives on rhythm, and the art of it depends on the level of togetherness between the performers. It is, in essence, togetherness in motion.

This "togetherness" of funk is different from other jazz forms because of the prevailing ethos of "liberation," which pervaded American society in the late 1960s and 1970s, particularly in black America, and particularly among the artists. A synthesis of the entire black tradition, sacred and secular, peaceful and confrontational, was the framework of black art, concurrent with the "Black Revolution" of the same period. A new threshold of access, acceptance, urgency, and involvement drew black musicians together, and they created, with others, a new sound of unity.

### FUNK BANDS

At the dawn of the 1970s a large number of black acts developed their styles toward the wide-open improvisations and soulful grooving associated with funk music, and occasional acts defined their music as funk, such as the Bar-Kays at Wattstax calling themselves "Black Rock Funk" in 1972, and James Brown naming himself the "Minister of New New Super Heavy Funk" in 1974, but overall, there were no interested critics to coin a definitive term for the sounds, so they were called "soul groups," "dance bands," "black rock," "jazz-funk," and even "super-groups," and, only occasionally, funk bands. The people called them what they wanted. Nevertheless, acts like War, the Blackbyrds, Earth, Wind & Fire, and Kool & the Gang were constantly referred to by critics as groups that utilized a "fusion" of styles, as a "synthesis," and so on. It was so common with so many acts that a mix of styles eventually became the style itself.

In the mid-1970s teenagers who listened for the funky dance singles referred to these groups as "funk bands." It would be a measure of any hip black act in the seventies to come with a *funk bomb* to get respect. With the rise of "P-Funk" the cosmic scope of funk as a model that embodied a philosophy began to take shape, and the diverse, musically rich, very funky "dance bands," "black rock groups," and "jazz-funk" acts all began to fit into a congruent musical movement, much of which was based on the philosophies and aesthetics of funk. Thus, the funk band. The funk beat gradually took over the black music sound, as 1980s R&B fell into the funk pocket and never left, and club freaks and Hip Hoppers made their obsession with the funky beat into a counterculture all its own. Yet it is the funk band that made it all possible.

Just about every funk band would begin as a small core of musicians, often brought together by one leader. Jam sessions would provide the opportunity for musicians to feel out each other's musical styles. Unlike the typical jazz band, the horn players were not necessarily the primary bandleaders or soloists. Unlike the rock or blues band, the lead guitarist or singer was not considered any more significant than the rhythm section. A soul singer in a funk band was one of many players, not the focus as in much of soul or rhythm and blues. Equality was the basis of the funk band, both in music and in attitude. This opened the doors for far-reaching improvisations and broad landscapes of rhythm for the many new ideas of the times.

The bass guitar was key, and with the popularity of Larry Graham and Bootsy Collins, the bassist was free to pursue any number of influences and was expected to provide rhythmic direction, either from percussive thumps or entire melodic phrases. The lead guitar became centralized in seventies black music as a result of Jimi Hendrix, and thus there were similarly few limitations on guitarists, although fluency in the choppy, percussive form of rhythm guitar pioneered by James Brown's guitarists Jimmy Nolen and Cheese Martin was crucial to a successful soul or funk band. Michael O'Neal described the crucial musical fusion created by Funkadelic:

> Funkadelic conceived the notion of being in the stratosphere and at the same time being right here. In other words, the guitar, so much influenced by Jimi Hendrix, is played so as to take the listener to a space beyond the self, and the

bass is played in such a way as to keep the listener (and the dancer, too) grounded in reality with a bottom beat, thus establishing polyrhythmic structure and foundation.

Horns were given a new responsibility as melodic and percussive components of the sound, thanks to the arrangements of Alfred "Pee Wee" Ellis, Fred Wesley, and Maceo Parker, who had developed the JBs' sound. Horn solos tended to emphasize an involved interplay with the prevailing rhythm, rather than the abstraction and introspection of modern jazz. Horn riffs could dominate the swing of the jam, or they could give understated counterpoint to the primary melody. If the jam kicked, everything would fit. Former *Rolling Stone* editor Alan Light describes the role of Earth, Wind & Fire and other groups responsible for further elevating the use of horns (while inexplicably avoiding the idea that these were all funk bands):

> Rather than incorporate the horns primarily for emphasis or punctuation, as James Brown or the Stax bands had done, EW&F wove them into the arrangements, playing fluid secondary melodic lines and then unexpectedly leaping into the foreground. Along with the early recordings of such EW&F contemporaries as Kool & the Gang and the Commodores, this sound would spawn an entire school of horn-based R&B pre- and proto-disco groups, including Slave and Brass Construction.

The drums and bass had their traditional roles as organizers of the rhythmic pattern, but the advent of new keyboards gave the pianist a dual role as rhythm and lead instrument, depending on the situation. The goal was for every player to improvise at his or her best, while staying "locked" with the others. The instruments would provide different "meters" that would exchange roles as the dominant rhythm signature of the music.

Syncopation was the center, as numerous instruments would drive along a groove, and melodic lines from one instrument would often swing right into another's. A tight band could cook up a stew of separate melodic lines playing simultaneously. (Check out the Ohio Players' "Who'd She Coo" or James Brown's "Get on the Good Foot.") Their spacing and their symmetry were determined by the dexterity of the musicians, yet for the groove to flow, each player must be making sense with the overall jam.

Collective improvisation is a part of the African music tradition, from open-air jam sessions in Congo Square of New Orleans to the frenetic fusion workouts of Earth, Wind & Fire onstage at Madison Square Garden. Many funk bands would simply feel each other out and determine when and how the "change" would come in and out as they wrote each song. This is where the predominance of feel and unity comes into play in funk.

Many bands wrote and arranged songs collectively. James "Diamond" Williams of the Ohio Players explained in a 1992 interview that "we went into the studio to create, while most people go into the studio to duplicate, which means they already have in mind what they want to record. We used to go in there and *jam groove,* the best of which we would turn into a song." Maurice White of Earth, Wind & Fire used the same process: "We'd have skeletons of songs, but there was a lot of improvisation in the studio. We were very free, very spontaneous." Clyde Stubblefield said the same of James Brown's band: "Nobody in the studio knew what was going on except the horn players."

In the studio, everyone just felt each other out on the rhythms, and to an extent that there was a leader, that person encouraged and orchestrated the ideas of the others. George Clinton refereed the P-Funk sound, James Brown with the JBs, Ronald Bell/Khalis Bayyan with Kool & the Gang, Maurice White with Earth, Wind & Fire. Even rap superstar Dr. Dre, whose famous funky Hip Hop beats have that old-school lively funk feel, was the referee as studio players at his Track Records studios in North Hollywood would kick the jams, and he would take it from there. Dr. Dre explained it to S. H. Fernando, Jr., in *The New Beats*: " 'Cause a lot of times I'm in the studio, and somebody hits some shit, and I'm like, 'Yo, what was that?' And they don't remember what the fuck it was. So we'll just rewind the tape and get something out of that."

Funk bands exercised an understanding of creative diversity that to this day stands as an example of egalitarianism. Dance hits, love ballads, blues-inflected laments, dirty rock "sleaze," silly gibberish, inspirational chants, revolutionary anthems were all fair game for the funk band. On some albums one could find all of the above, such as the Ohio Players' "Fire" and the Isley Brothers' "The Heat Is On." Music scholar

Portia Maultsby asserted in an interview that "the seventies provided the freedom for black performers to interpret and present music that was based on their own understanding of the music." For black Americans to operate and create "based on their own understanding of the music" was and is a perpetual struggle, and the music of the Funk Age, particularly the United Funk Dynasty of the early 1970s, shines as a victorious moment.

Funk music combines aspects of a wide range of black musical traditions. The blues, rhythm and blues, soul music, progressive jazz, African percussion, psychedelics, and synthesizers all find a place in the rich structure of The Funk. Funk music is a direct offspring of the blues in terms of its intimacy, intensity, and meaning for "common" black folks in the decade of integration. Funk music, with its nonstop, sweaty dance appeal, is also the no-nonsense form of dance entertainment most directly related to the rhythm and blues tradition. Good, loud dance music has always been the antidote to black America's troubles, and The Funk has served this purpose honorably.

Funk music is also the successor to the soul music of the 1960s in terms of its representations of popular black values—particularly those ideals of social, spiritual, and political redemption. While soul was the original music of black unity, funk took it one step further: Funk maintained its ties to the black underclass while, as we shall see, soul did not. Funk was also the medium by which many traditional African instruments and arrangements, many brand-new sound technologies, and far-out forms of psychedelics were channeled creatively through black music. Funk comprised all of these elements into a thriving, diverse sound and style in the 1970s.

Funk returned to the ideals of the African ensemble just as technology began to push American music toward artificiality. Just as the electric Fender Rhodes piano, the Moog synthesizer, Hohner clavinet, and ARP ensemble synthesizer were introduced into black popular music, the conga player, percussion section, Kalimba, and the extended jam were also incorporated. Funk became the medium by which electronic sound effects never before heard on synthesizers of the future could be channeled through a black aesthetic, complemented by traditional sounds of the past, creating a better understanding of the present. From the extremes of a simple drumbeat, to orchestrated polyphonic arrangements played by multiple musicians in unison, to a celebration of deep individual expression, funk music was arranged to bring "soul" to the people through the new formulas of popular music.

## MUSICAL MODEL OF FUNK EVOLUTION

Funk music is worth studying because it has a place in popular culture as one more in a long line of black musical styles—ragtime, swing, blues, and rock—that are often borrowed but not acknowledged. One purpose of this book is to acknowledge The Funk as another chapter in America's legacy of acquisition and assimilation of black music and culture. Each time a new and fresh musical/cultural development comes from the black community, such as jazz, rock and roll, or funk, it gets taken and eventually loses its original flavor, forcing its originators to develop something new. The cycle of artistic appropriation by the white mainstream and subsequent revitalization by black folk culture into other forms was defined by Charles Keil in *Urban Blues* as the "Appropriation-Revitalization Syndrome."

The history of black musical development can be thought of as a process of constant creation and adaptation to restricted circumstances. The restrictions inevitably allowed whites to produce imitations, and formalize various musical styles for popular consumption. The devious nature of this phenomenon was explained by writer and activist De Angelo Stearnes:

> To prevent black musical innovation from becoming "dangerous," it was co-opted, diluted, re-packaged and sold off as "refined" and "improved" pop music. Check it out, New Orleans street music was chumped by Dixieland. Bebop was watered down by Cool Jazz. Rock and Roll was pushed out by white rock and rockabilly. Disco thumped Funk. Now, gangster/buffoon rap preaching negativity has duped everyone into thinking that it is Black culture under the guise of Hip-Hop. In each instance, the strength of the music has been destroyed because it lost its purpose and musical integrity.

Black music has continued to innovate; from the first slave songs, to the latest street-corner raps, the mission has been the same: to tell it like it is. The Funk is no exception, yet it hasn't been placed in its proper context in music history. With an understanding of the black music evolution from West African music, to slave songs, blues, spirituals, and later jazz and soul, a framework can be organized for the inevitable convergence of styles which led to the birth of The Funk:

---

### *Musical Model of Funk Evolution*

*(see chart on page x for more detail)*

| | | SIXTIES | SEVENTIES | EIGHTIES–NINETIES |
|---|---|---|---|---|
| | gospel | | | |
| - | | > soul | | disco |
| - | R&B | > | | |
| blues | | > black rock > | **FUNK BOMB** > | Hip Hop > |
| - | rock | > | | |
| - | | > jazz fusion | | |
| - | jazz | | | |

---

While the musical evolution is more complex than illustrated here, the basic historical, structural analysis is consistent with the majority of other music histories. For example, soul music is often regarded as a blend of rhythm and blues and gospel music, with a large number of crossover gospel artists moving into soul music, such as Aretha Franklin, Sam Cooke, and Al Green. This is the fundamental theme in the birth of soul music in the 1960s.

Black rock exists as a hybrid genre consisting of black artists reinterpreting the psychedelic scene of the 1960s. These acts include the Isley Brothers, Sly and the Family Stone, the Bar-Kays, Funkadelic, and Jimi Hendrix. While the term *black rock* is somewhat anachronistic, it was developed to help the American public understand the difference between the stereotypical black artist (Motown-style soul singer) and the atypical "hippie-looking" acts like Sly Stone, Hendrix, and Funkadelic. The real story is, of course, much more complex. The relationships of these artists to their R&B roots will be made clear in Chapter nine.

The "jazz fusion" category belongs largely to the work of Miles Davis and is often described as a fusion of jazz and rock. Many of the innovations of Miles Davis, however, were influenced by the original funk of the Godfather of Soul, James Brown. As he described in his autobiography, Miles was taken by The Funk. The evolution from modern jazz into newer forms of fusion and funk is a story unto itself, and will be explored in Chapter eleven.

This period of fusion, in which jazz fused with rock and gospel fused with rhythm and blues, occurred just as black America was flexing its collective muscle and beginning a period of unprecedented creative freedom. It was no coincidence, then, that the period that followed the early 1970s was fraught with layers of fusions of all types. These artistic convergences required larger ensembles of musicians, with members that were trained in jazz, versed in the blues, and forward-thinking and experimental (and, in many cases, drug-influenced) enough to expand the existing formulas for musical expression. This is one more reason why funk bands became the focal point of black music by the mid-1970s.

There were, of course, many other musical trends in the 1970s, but to understand the fundamental role of The Funk in the music of today, the fat, funky foundation of the sound must be understood on its own terms. The outrageous craze of disco music that spread across the nation like a locust swarm in 1975 was actually a popularization of the urgent and irresistible black dance music of the early 1970s—The Funk. With black style, black soul, and black funk saturating radio and television in the early 1970s, white America needed a means to get in on the fun, and sterilized simulations of *Soul Train* across the nation— known as discos—were the ticket.

It is the funk beat that now pulses through modern music more than any other. That tasty tension in the groove, combining a sexy grind with a rigid backbeat, is the meat of MTV. Perhaps the most influential sound in America today, The Funk has been misunderstood too long, and it deserves its due among all the others *in the tradition*.

# THREE

# Myths About Funk:
# All That Is Good Is Nasty

"Funk used to be a bad word."
*Funkadelic*

Until the surge in popularity of rap music and its resuscitation of seventies funk, there has been no common notion of a history of funk, let alone a deep appreciation of the nastay folk ways of African-Americans. Due to ignorance, many people, black and white, simply dispose of the notion that funk can be taken seriously, because it sounds silly (funk often is designed to be "metafoolish"), and also because there are no legitimate icons or references to funk in mainstream American culture. In an attempt to catch and dispel some common misunderstandings about funk, it's time to unravel some of the myths.

*MYTH #1: I'VE HEARD OF SOUL AND R&B, BUT NEVER HEARD OF FUNK MUSIC, SO IT ISN'T IMPORTANT*
The lack of a coherent reference point in the record store may have led many to assume that funk is a minor genre. Any style of music can be played in a "funky" way. Grooving, funky jam sessions were scattered across black popular music, from Miles Davis to Motown, but the record companies often categorized the artists in an all too limited fashion. Earth, Wind & Fire, for example, was a jazz-funk group that "became" a soul group due to Columbia's thoughtful record management. Their funky rhythms were heard on long, scorching instrumentals as well as perky dance singles. Funky dance music was simply part of their repertoire.

Isaac Hayes was a deep blues-rooted soul singer, but because of the inventive work of his backup funk band, the Bar-Kays, his records featured long, sexy instrumentals and wound up selling thousands in the jazz category. Herbie Hancock began his career as a "jazz" artist, whose pop sales were constantly minimized because his amazing funk records were ghettoized in the jazz listings. The unifying essence of funk music, which was in reality a celebration of the entire spectrum of the black music tradition, was not appreciated by the music industry. The industry, in fact, made a killing by separating black acts into Motown-style soul, pop-jazz or jazz-funk, and token rock or pop acts. Unless you were living at the bottom of America's class structure and feeling the funk (or playing it), you may have missed the funk movement altogether. The rappers of today are the offspring of people who lived during the era of funk, played The Funk, felt The Funk, and kept their funk records for their children to play, and it's largely thanks to them that The Funk has survived.

*MYTH #2: FUNK IS NASTY MUSIC PLAYED BY NASTY PEOPLE*
Funk is stigmatized in the same way that the "hot jazz" of Louis Armstrong was considered "sex music." Funk is, of course, linked with sex, and difficulties with the word abound because of its auditory proximity to the word *fuck,* and the many potential implications of the words. This is in fact one of the very legitimizations of the music, for black culture in its unassimilated form is not burdened by Western distinctions of what is nasty or crude. Funk—and even "fuck music"—is therefore quite legitimate if one considers that music is a part of life and sex is a shameless and special part of life. James Brown's classic recording of "Sex Machine" is a celebration of the strength and vitality of the black man's sexuality. Barry White's seemingly infinite capacity for anticipation and romantic begging was a gift that many young people born around 1974 should be grateful for. George Clinton's use of "dirty" words is part of a rebellious repudiation of the West's concept of formality. The childlike, "dirty" nature of some funk lyrics is also a deliberate return to an uninhibited state of mind, a state of childlike innocence and wonder, as a part of an adult state of sexual release and a state of African-rooted balance between Western and African opposites. Comedian Richard Pryor's phenomenal success in the early 1970s as a stand-up comic was precisely due to his use of vulgar language and imagery, which black folks found hilarious because of its pungent truth in their lives. Whether it is a symbol, metaphor, or the real thing, there is no reason why funk should not be associated with "dirtiness" and sex.

> "Nasty? I didn't make the rules."
>           Funkadelic, "Mommy What's a Funkadelic?" (1970)

The "hard-core" entertainment in question is actually a part of a risqué tradition that has thrived for generations in back rooms, burlesque halls, speakeasys, and red light district casinos throughout America. Most of the participants in such "obscene" behavior are well-to-do, well-groomed, and respectful citizens, and, for what it's worth, have stable family lives.

A more serious issue affecting the acceptance of funk music is that many blacks have historically looked down upon "roots" black music such as the blues and The Funk. Negative, "primitive" images of black people were so prevalent during the first half of this century that it was considered disastrous by many intellectuals to celebrate the "funkiness" of black folks. The perils of "double-consciousness" and black self-hate rear their ugly heads when dealing with funk.

## MYTH #3: FUNK IS DISCO MUSIC, NOTHING MORE

Disco is the simplified form of nonethnic, electronic-sounding dance music that swept the country in the mid- to late 1970s. The essence of disco is a repetitive simulation of the rawness of black funk, with music extended by machines and not by grooving, improvising musicians. Disco dancing was popularized in clubs in Europe in the late 1960s, playing records of black dance music—the original funk tracks. It later spread to the United States and by 1974 was the hottest dance trend on the East Coast. The mechanical aspects of disco music production swept the popular music industry, and accelerated the destruction of the live recording session, live bands, and the soulful recording experience. As a result, black music in general became less soulful, more mechanical, and less meaningful. While the ideals of disco were to dance interminably to monorhythmic beats, the ideals of funk were to get off your ass and jam. Funkadelic explains this distinction best as they describe the funky needs of the affectionately described "Freak of the Week":

> She's a dance interpretation, of the meaning of syncopation
> She's a big freak, got to be a freak of the week
> Don't give her that one move groovalistic
> That disco sadistic
> That one beat up and down it just won't do
> Don't give her that forever and ever foreplay
> She's not looking for the short way
> She got to reach the point where she gets off.
>                     Funkadelic, "Freak of the Week" (1979)

Funk bands often challenged the low standards of disco, recording such titles as "The Undisco Kidd" by Funkadelic, and "Anti-Disco" by Mutiny. Most, of course, went along with the charade and made the best of a sad situation. Brilliant bands sold out before our eyes as James Brown proclaimed himself the "Original Disco Man," the Ohio Players jumped in with "(Feel the Beat) Everybody Disco," the Isley Brothers wasted our time with "It's a Disco Night (Rock Don't Stop)," and the Earth, Wind & Fire debacle "Boogie Wonderland" speaks for itself. When pop music fans began to relish in the chant "Disco sucks," a subtle racial classification brought together all of black dance music, despite the fact that late-seventies funk bands had declared war on disco, too.

The average listener bombarded by disposable pop music on the radio is always at the mercy of the radio programmer, who is in turn accountable to corporate interests that mandate certain records (usually the lousy ones) to be played, despite the tastes of the audience. Ignorance, therefore, allowed one to assume that a simplistic song by the Ohio Players, for example, and a song by the disco act Silver Convention heard on the radio meant that they basically played the same music. The Ohio Players, like many other funk bands, explored the entire spectrum of music, including disco, while Silver Convention was a disco dance music trio that sang over synthesized music, which by design had the same beat on every song, and was produced by one person. Both artists were judged by the popularity of their single sales, and the demise of most funk groups was a result of their failure to sell as disco acts.

The assumption of radio throughout the 1970s was the same as that in the 1960s: that an artist's best work was on the single, to be heard on the radio. Rock radio circumvented this by developing the A.O.R. (Album-Oriented Rock) format. Black artists were similarly album-oriented, but black radio was not. Funk bands generated dance songs, hybrid ballads, jazz fusion, semi-religious chants, and many other originals that were neither heard nor understood because of black radio. Often a funk artist would happily make a fool of himself on a disco-dance single and be deathly serious on the other album cuts. This was consistent with the artists' ideas of thematic range, but served to reinforce the mistaken reputation of funk as irresponsible and silly.

This is why the *entire album* is an important listening experience for funk bands. Unfortunately, many of the new compilations and tributes to the great funk artists are simply hit parades that do not expose a band's political consciousness, the breadth of their musical talents, or their spiritual beliefs. One must look closer to find the rich musical roots found in funk, and the artists' original rendering is your best bet.

*MYTH #4: JAZZ IS REAL MUSIC, WHILE FUNK IS NOT*
In the late 1960s the jazz scene was undergoing a radical change that was difficult for the jazz "purist" to understand. John Coltrane died in 1967, leaving a void at the seat of the jazz throne, while other long-time greats explored other musical territory for their own interests. Miles Davis, Cannonball Adderley, Donald Byrd, Ramsey Lewis, Wayne Shorter, Chick Corea, and Herbie Hancock were all put on record and put to task for moving beyond the realm of what others' expectations of traditional jazz were. Most decided to go electric, incorporating the bass guitar, the electric lead guitar, electronic keyboards, and rhythmic influences from James Brown. All of this made some new jazz bands look conspicuously like rhythm and blues bands. Other artists chose to follow the iconoclastic road of Ornette Coleman, the saxophonist who began to do away with formal melodic structures in the music. Coleman's influence, along with Miles Davis's, led to the development of a "technical" form of jazz known as fusion, which had its own detractors but nevertheless sold millions to a multiracial audience.

Miles Davis, one of the pillars of the jazz community, was vilified by jazz critics for going electric and embracing the musical styles of Jimi Hendrix, James Brown, and Sly Stone. He responded to these critics in his 1989 autobiography:

> Musicians have to play the instruments that best reflect the times we're in, play the technology that will give you what you want to hear. All these purists are walking around talking about how electrical instruments will ruin music. Bad music is what will ruin music, not the instruments musicians choose to play. I don't see nothing wrong with electrical instruments as long as you get great musicians who will play them right.

By 1970 jazz was evolving into funk. A number of acts began playing a new form of instrumental music that sometimes resembled pop jazz, sometimes resembled jazz-rock fusion, and sometimes featured vocalists. Forward-thinking—and often hungry-for-cash—musicians trained in jazz were willing and ready to drive a groove and yet still improvise. Thus, a music born of a funky bottom and jazzy top, often called acid jazz, rare groove, or jazz-funk, was born. The selections featured covers of pop and soul standards, as well as rock, blues, gospel, and jazz traditionals. These groups indeed had an electronic rhythm section, and the performers, while they had few straight-ahead jazz recording credits, were nevertheless well trained in jazz music, and it showed in their arrangements. The best of these groups were the funk bands Kool & the Gang; Earth, Wind & Fire; the Ohio Players; the Meters; Funk Inc.; Mandrill; War; Tower of Power; the Crusaders; the Headhunters; and most importantly, the JBs. Funk is actually the *last* form of black popular music played by musicians trained in the jazz arena.

> "Jazz is the teacher, Funk is the preacher."
>
> James "Blood" Ulmer, 1980

## MYTH #5: THERE ARE NO BOOKS ABOUT FUNK, SO IT MUST NOT BE THAT IMPORTANT

In the 1960s there was an avalanche of music books discussing the coming of age of black music in jazz, soul, and the blues. The decade of the 1970s was such a musically diffuse period that it defies the concise treatment given to such previous popular musical movements as soul, rock, or jazz. Furthermore, to understand the black music of the 1970s, the essential links between the work of James Brown, Sly Stone, Jimi Hendrix, and Miles Davis required a sophisticated understanding of the black music scene that few established writers possessed.

Yet today's retrograde rap music has exposed the direct musical lineage of The Funk of James Brown, Sly Stone, and George Clinton with great clarity. Each of these men has stood at the pinnacle of stardom and success, yet there is no book that identifies their creative locus or their connections. There are plenty of books about other artists, but there is no well-known American-produced history of James Brown—the central figure in soul music as well as funk—outside of his own autobiography, published in 1986. There are plenty of books about blacks that interested whites, such as those about Motown Records and Jimi Hendrix, yet no author has connected Motown, Jimi Hendrix, P-Funk, and rap music, which were arguably the most influential elements in American music since the mid-1960s. The concept and the legacy of The Funk ties all of these aspects together.

However, while the affectation of funk in literature surfaced occasionally in the early 1970s in magazine articles, it was not associated with the black struggle, nor was it embraced by the black mainstream writers as acceptable black behavior. The musical movement developed among musicians and the black teenage audience without mainstream interest, although record sales alone could prove that something was happening. By the 1970s many established authors abandoned popular black music as a topic of discussion. As former *Rolling Stone* writer John Morthland told me in 1994, "Most music writers of my generation are white, like I am, and sort of gave up on [black] music after soul music, and they really didn't follow it into the early seventies and the funk era. A lot of them just kind of lost interest when the soul music era ended."

The primary published attempt to discuss the period of the 1970s music scene from a black music perspective is *The Death of Rhythm and Blues* by Nelson George, published in 1988. George discusses the corporate machinery involved in the exploitation of black talent with lucidity and authority, but treats the black aesthetic in the music of the 1970s somewhat secondarily. The writer with the breadth and insight of LeRoi Jones's earlier work is Greg Tate, who until now has only published articles, and one compilation of writings in 1992. His analyses of black culture from a "funk prism" are powerful, iconoclastic, and intellectual, if somewhat meandering. Tate's work is clearly distinct from George because Tate has internalized funk as part of his understanding of black culture, as the first page of his 1992 book *Flyboy in the Buttermilk* reveals:

> Funk used to be a bad word. Now everybody's trying to get knee deep. These days there's a lot of funk-ploitation going down. But don't get me wrong, 'cause pimping The Funk ain't bad per se—truth is, pimping it's always been half the game-plan. Besides giving funk mass appeal and liquid assets. Uncle Jam [George Clinton] also gave it a metaphysic, proposing that the bottom of the human soul, its base elements one might say, are what makes life a song worth singing. So contrary to the funky-come-latelies, it's always been possible to have your funk low in the saddle and eat-it-cum-intellectualize-it too. I mean, conceptualizing the

funk as mind, body, and soul music ain't no new type thang—just listen to your "Loose Booty."

There are thousands of rappers and funkateers who subscribe to Tate's approach to black culture, and it is only a matter of time before The Funk is written and understood in systematic, historical context. If one stops to think about the distortions in black history, from the history of African civilization to modern militant struggles, it is clear that the established historical tradition cannot be relied upon to make accurate assessments of the black experience.

Despite the logic of the arguments, the problem remains that most people do not realize that a significant musical movement occurred during the 1970s, generated primarily by outcast musicians from the black underclass in America. The music of funk spoke directly to those people, while others simply danced to it. The fact that The Funk is a nonlogical concept with an assortment of coded meanings and slang terms does not help to clarify the situation. Yet today's rap music movement and its artists have nevertheless shown a phenomenal affection for funk music and its message. This is because the music is from the same class of people—dispossessed blacks with a bizarre combination of poverty, hope, bitterness, and humanity. The Funk rests at the core of hard-hitting urban dance music of today, and is the missing link for a lost generation of funky people to find their place in history.

# FOUR

# Roots: Where'd You Get Your Funk From?

"In the beginning there was Funk."

*George Clinton*

The best way to understand the development of funk music is to understand the evolutionary process of black (African) culture as it propagates throughout the world. From the word and meaning of funk to the necessary process of communal music-making, dancing, worshiping, and truth-telling, Africans have provided Americans of all colors with vital aspects of their American cultural life. And through The Funk, even integrated black Americans are able to do the same. What follows is a discussion of the original elements of black folk culture that evolved into funk.

## THE ORIGIN OF *FUNKY*

Funk music can be traced back in time from the rap music of today, to the work of James Brown in the 1960s, to funk-jazz in the 1950s. Before that, funk was simply an adjective, a description of the earthy style of black folks. Recent scholars, such as Philip Morehead in his *1992 New International Dictionary of Music,* conclude that funk is "a term of uncertain origin indicating a style of African-American popular music." Some musicians will claim that they invented it, and George Clinton has wryly prophesied that The Funk is an eternal force that was "placed among the secrets of the pyramids, along with kings and pharaohs . . . until a more positive attitude towards this most sacred phenomenon, cloned funk, could be acquired" (from Parliament's "Prelude to Dr. Funkenstein," 1976). Clinton, however, maintains that his point of view should not be taken too seriously. What, then, is the origin of funk?

The earliest English language dictionaries refer to the term *funk* as a "cowering fear," a "somber emotional state," or a depressed mood. This concept derived from the Flemish word *fonck,* a term for fear or dismay (I looked that one up in my *Funk & Wagnall's Standard Dictio-*

*nary).* The use of the word *funk* in this context has been used in English literature as early as Shakespeare's period in the seventeenth century. Considering the situation facing black Americans at the turn of the twentieth century, the somber state of funk, even in its oldest European definition, could apply to black Americans as a form of melancholy not unlike the blues.

Older linguistic references to *funky* come from the word root *fumet,* a French word for a musty smell, which is also clearly derived from the Latin root of fume, *fumus,* which means "smoke." Old English definitions of the term involve a "strong smell" or "big stink," which has been the most common vernacular use. The 1970 edition of the *Webster's New International Dictionary* quotes a seventeenth century seaman describing the stench on board a ship in 1623: "Betwixt decks there can hardlie a man catch his breathe by reason there ariseth such a funke in the night that it causes putrefaction of blood." (The writer may indeed have been describing the "funke" of a slave ship.) This use of *funky* is clearly associated with black people today, and often with black music. *Webster's* defined the modern use of *funk* as follows:

> Originally Negro argot, literally smelly, hence musty, earthy, from obsolete funk to smell, or smoke; probably from French dialect *"funkier"*—to smoke. In jazz, having an earthy quality or style derived from early blues.

Eventually the notion of "funkiness" in terms of body odor was associated with "funky music," and the currency of the term most likely came into use among jazz musicians. This scenario is plausible if one considers the presence of French-speaking participants in the "birthplace of jazz," who congregated in the open jam sessions in Congo Square in New Orleans for centuries. This region is where French, Spanish, British, and even Filipinos all commingled with the variety of Africans, both slave and free, who engaged in open musical expression, sharing rhythms, instruments, and dialects since the early colonial period.

A significant discussion of the origins of the words *funk* and *jazz* is put forth by art historian Robert Ferris Thompson. In his 1983 book *Flash of the Spirit,* Thompson (among others) asserts that the slave trafficking in the West Indies did not decimate African linguistic patterns completely, and that "Kongo civilization and art were not obliterated in the New World: They resurfaced in the coming together, here and there, of numerous slaves from Kongo and Angola." These two regions were in fact the source of two thirds of all the Africans brought to the Americas. Thompson maintains that the black slang term *funky* always referred to "strong body odor" (never to depression or fear), which is closer in meaning to the Central African Ki-Kongo word *lu-fuki:*

> The Ki-Kongo word is closer to the jazz word "funky" in form and meaning, as both jazzmen and Bakongo use "funky" and *lu-fuki* to praise persons for the integrity of their art, for having "worked out" to achieve their aims. In Kongo today it is possible to hear an elder lauded in this way: "Like, there is a really funky person—my soul advances toward him to receive his blessing" (yati, nkwa lu-fuki! Ve miela miami ikwenda baki). . . .
>
> A leading native authority on Kongo culture explains: "Someone who is very old, I go to sit with him, in order to feel his lu-fuki, meaning, I would like to be blessed by him." For in Kongo the smell of a hardworking elder carries luck. This Kongo sign of exertion is identified with the positive energy of a person. Hence "funk" in black American jazz parlance can mean earthiness, a return to fundamentals.

Similarly, Thompson discusses the origins of jazz (as do others) as a "Creolized" term for sex that was applied to the Congo dances of New Orleans. Thompson maintains that many African-derived words described by etymologists as "origin unknown" are African in origin, and that in particular, *jazz* came from the creole *jizz,* which is related to *dinza,* the Ki-Kongo word for "ejaculation." Linguist Geneva Smitherman, in her book *Talkin' and Testifyin',* also indicates that the Mandingo term *jasi,* which means "to excite," is also a plausible root word for *jazz.*

Over the years, African slaves and their American counterparts developed a form of pidgin language that spread around the region, evolving into a hybrid, or Creole. According to Smitherman, "this lingo involved the substitution of English for West African words, but within the same basic structure and idiom that characterized West African language patterns."

Thus, the original assumption of etymologists and ethnomusicologists that words like *jazz* and *funk* derived from the interplay of musicians in the New Orleans region where jazz was born was only partially correct. The roots of the words—as was the spirit of the music—were brought into the scenario by Africans from Africa.

If indeed what Thompson suggests is true, that the "smell" of a man of integrity carries a blessing, then what is considered good in the West (no scent?) versus what is considered good in Africa (heavy scent) reveals something profound about the differing frames of reference. With The Funk clearly on the side of the expressive African value system, are we prepared to claim that George Clinton's whimsical notion about The Funk resting among the "secrets of the pyramids" is completely false?

## MUSICAL ROOTS
### *African Retention in Modern Black Music*

Despite centuries of slavery and acculturation, and decades of integration, black Americans have propagated the African musical experience in remarkably coherent form. UC Berkeley Music Professor Olly Wilson, in a 1992 essay titled "The Heterogenous Sound Ideal in African American Music," asserts that all of black American music stems from an "African conceptual approach" to music and its making. These fundamental structural qualities include the following characteristics which I have excerpted from Wilson's essay and adapted to The Funk:

• *The tendency to approach the organization of rhythm based on the principle of rhythmic and implied metrical contrast.* That is, the tendency to generate a "swing." Whether it is the sway of the blues, the head-bopping of cool jazz, the high-stepping of boogie-woogie, or the lean-to-the-side foot-stomping of funk, it's the same *thang.* Beyond mere melodies and beats, grooving dance music generates a life of its own: a groove. There is no way to transcribe or translate this effect. A jam either has it or it doesn't. As Duke Ellington put it, "It don't mean a thing, if it ain't got that swing." The often dense structure of funk music was such that many instruments could develop independent melodic lines that grooved simultaneously, with their accents in different yet complementing places in the count. The funk music of the late sixties generated a groove so wicked it should be called a "swang."

• *The tendency to approach singing or the playing of any instrument in a percussive manner.* This was an innovation that James Brown brought into soul music, particularly with the rhythm guitar, a style that he learned years later was African in origin. Brown utilized the rhythm guitar in such a fashion that its role changed from a secondary or primary melodic instrument to an almost totally percussive sound. From a strum, to a plink, to a *chank*—the tighter the rhythm chop, the more contrast could be developed with the bass and drums that were splashing around the rhythm count in percussive ways. Even Brown's vocals were arranged highly rhythmically, often ad-libbed like scat-singing, while many song lyrics were arranged in repeating syncopated chants, like "I got ants in my pants/and I need to dance," or "I'm payin' taxes, what am I buyin' . . ."

• *Antiphony, or call-and-response musical structure that emphasizes audience participation and involvement.* From the Sunday congregation rhythmic chants of "Hallelujah Jeesus" to Hip Hop deejays exhorting "Everybody say Ho!" the purpose is the same: Performer and audience become one, united by the music. Sly Stone can still be heard on the hillside of Woodstock, reaching half a million people to chant "Higher!" James Brown exhorted his audiences to "Get up/Get into it/Get involved!" As the crowd repeated each chant, they were drawn into its meaning. P-Funk drove the notion even further, using the chant "Think! Think! It Ain't Illegal Yet!" and drawing the audience (through active participation) into the P-Funk mind set, which, in turn, was a means toward reclaiming one's individuality. The large ensembles of the funk bands created a further symbiosis in which both the audience and the performers were *collectives.*

• *The tendency to create a high density of musical events within a relatively short time frame.* That is, a tendency to fill up all the musical space. This was one of the colonial era carryovers from the famed New Orleans *second line,* as a parade (often a funeral march) band would pass by, only to be followed by other performers with instruments of their own, each playing on individual rhythm patterns, yet working within the dominant one. Funk bands were large ensembles for this primary reason, yet the emphasis was on variety and complexity of sounds rather than mere quantity of instrumentation. Good funk music (and much of jazz) is designed to allow the listener to focus on any one instrument and hear a complete musical statement, yet the instrument still remains viable within the group. While rock artists were content to drive power trios, funk bands were consistently large—even Jimi Hendrix performed with a six-piece band at Woodstock—and whenever the opportunities were there, funk bands grew in size until the 1980s.

• *A tendency to incorporate physical body motion as an integral part of the music-making process.* With an emphasis on individual expression over formulation, essential experience over repetition, and interaction over isolation, black/African music links the mind and body through the rhythms. Music, motion, and dance become synonymous. This is expressed by George Clinton on the 1978 recording of "Mr. Wiggles": "From the looking comes the seen/one with real eyes realize/the rhythm of vision is a dancer/and when he dance it's always on the one." According to UC Professor Roy Thomas, there is no distinction between the concepts of music and dance in many African languages.

Another fundamental aspect of music from the motherland has been a predilection for making musical instruments come to life by imitating the sound of the human voice. The wicked and wild atonal scales played by Louis Armstrong in his *Hot Five* in the 1920s were meant to drive past the conscious mind and hit the soul in a language all its own. From Lester Young through John Coltrane, Bird, and, yes, Jimi Hendrix, there has been a tradition as well as a trail of legends capable of accomplishing this. In the blues, the "bent" notes in a guitar solo are meant to accent and in many ways imitate the moaning sounds of a melancholy mood. When Herbie Hancock soars on his synthesizer in his classic solo on "Chameleon," he is launching from the jazz saxophone tradition of wailing, rhythmic crescendos, yet he is taking it the next step beyond. When Bootsy Collins works out his orgiastic finale to "Munchies for Your Love" on the bass guitar, he comes closer than anyone to a musical replication of the male orgasm. The Funk brought to life the musical soul of black America in the 1970s by keeping it connected to the past, the present, and the future.

## THE ONE

Perhaps the most important retention from Africa has been the spiritual element of music-making, the necessity to bring about trance, to raise rhythm to a cosmic level. African music, gospel music, and jazz were designed to accomplish this, and with The Funk the tradition has continued. Traditionally, West African music did not emphasize melodies that meandered along the rhythms; the music emphasized *rhythm itself,* and in doing so, it ventilated around The One. Pulsing waves of drumbeats designed to suspend the listener/participant on a crest of percolating tension *compelled* one to dance. The dancer then provides yet another rhythmic contribution to the overall group experience. In the African musical experience, everyone is included, for everyone's individual rhythms are essential to the total vibe. Thus, all participate as part of a greater whole. A locked, happening rhythm brings everybody together grooving *as one.* Ultimately, to be "on the one," the musical performance is not only emphasizing an ancient rhythmic pattern, it is emphasizing the essential openness toward all participants to the groove. Locked, yet fluid, when everything is "on the one," a harmony among all people is achieved. When George Clinton is heard chanting onstage "On the one, everybody on the one," he isn't trying to get his band on the beat (they are already there), he is savoring the rhythmic lock that has brought the entire house together, as one.

The liveliness, the creativity, the innovation, and the inevitable spontaneity were and are the crucial elements of black music, and the degree to which each black American generation pursues these aesthetics represents the relative state of health of that generation. While the 1970s have been long since considered musically dead, it is interesting to note that the funk movement was a deliberate movement toward larger ensemble bands, the simultaneous rhythms of James Brown's bands, the use of layered acoustic and electronic musical effects to fill up the musical space, and an adherence to the traditional aspects of dance, performance, and call-and-response collective participation. When seen in full view, The Funk is a music that incorporates *and accumulates* the best of its preceding traditions, and was perhaps the last black music style to do so.

Unfortunately, by the 1980s, as we shall see, the economics of large ensembles discouraged big bands, and the musical restrictions of disco compelled bands to downsize and further dissipate their soulful (that is, African) characteristics. The Funk waged an all-out battle against this conformist phenomenon, by using age-old aspects of black folk culture as its weapon.

### FUNKY BLUES

From the days of slave shouts and hollers to the rowdy activities of church revivals, torrid after-hours jam sessions, and Hip Hop freestyle (rapping) challenges, black folks have perpetuated their funky behavior, letting it all hang out. Black Americans, once freed from slavery, began to develop their own idioms of music from the scraps of instruments available to them. Beginning with the mouth harp, fiddle, and guitar and the earliest blues, to the brass instruments and the earliest jazz, black folks played and personalized their music to represent their time, their place, their era.

The sweaty Saturday night ritual of early blues was designed to produce essentially the same effect as African music thousands of miles to the east. Even without the prominent use of the drum, the African vocabulary, and the idols and ritual dances, Africans in America continued their traditions, and ritualized their down-and-dirty lifestyle in this country, because it was all they had.

After the country blues literally grew from the ground in southern cotton-field Saturday-night parties, and the instrumental blues known as jazz music was developed as reeds and brass got into the hands of black musicians in towns at the turn of the century, the urbanization of blacks during World War I led to the creation of a dense music marketplace in cities like New York, Kansas City, Chicago, and St. Louis. The first commercially recorded black music, the "classic blues" of Bessie Smith, Mamie Smith, and a number of other black female singers, was a risqué treat for the sexually uninitiated. While Bessie Smith had made her name with more melancholy downhearted blues laments, she could still deliver the sultry goods on songs like "Need a Little Sugar in My Bowl," "Sweet Jelly Roll Like Mine," and "My Daddy Rocks Me with a Steady Roll." Innuendo was the name of the game, as a "jelly roll" of the time had the same meaning as "coochie" would today. The hot Delta-rooted jazz of Louis Armstrong was one of the first to scare the critics and turn people on to the potential of race music. The hot jazz combos got the white Cotton Club audience going, while the soulful classic blues recordings generated the black music marketplace for records and sparked the interest of the common folk, "those who accepted and lived close to their folk experience," as Ralph Ellison described them.

## JAZZ AGE

The culturally rich "Harlem Renaissance" of the 1920s was a financial and social boon for many blacks who migrated to Harlem and thrived in a lush, urban, yet segregated environment. Black singers, dancers, and musicians stepped in style onstage performing for voyeuristic whites and, after the whites went home, made their own reputations performing for each other, helping to make Harlem the cultural center of the world.

Inspired a great deal by the black nationalism of Marcus Garvey and his powerful rhetoric, which expounded the glories of Africa and self-reliance of blacks around the world—as well as the obvious flaws of Europeans who had just decimated themselves in World War I— many blacks began to declare with Garvey, *"Up you mighty race!"* Economic independence and cultural pride were fostered amid the white patron/black performer nightclubs like the Cotton Club, Connie's Inn, and the Shuffle Inn, long before that small burlesque dive on 125th Street became the Apollo.

The positive imagery of the Harlem Renaissance of the 1920s and 1930s fostered a movement toward sophistication in black culture— as a deliberate counter to the "Sambo" and savage stereotypes that were spread through white entertainment and media, such as the Tarzan movies. Classy, orchestral jazz arrangements were performed (though usually for whites-only audiences), while the arts, sculpture, drama, and literature were also cultivated extensively. Country folk were looked down upon, and the celebrities who identified with them, such as Zora Neale Hurston and Claude McKay (not to mention Marcus Garvey himself) were rejected at the time by W. E. B. Du Bois and a majority of intellectuals.

With the rise of a black middle class came a racial caste system, particularly in Harlem. Garvey's race-pride rap worked wonders with the downtrodden masses, the blues people, and it certainly inspired the black establishment to action on the part of the race, but inevitably a code of status emerged among the haves and the have-nots, between the city folks and the country types, even between the light-skinned versus dark. The down-home rural country (read: funky) blues was out of step with the high-style pinstripe set, and the nappy-headed po' folks were a reminder of bleaker times.

While most black folks around the country were content to sweat up a storm at the local juke joint, the cats in Harlem were starting to take the showcase to a level of style with their suits, the swagger, the wit, the gleaming smile, and the smooth stepping. The zoot suits, loud two-toned shoes, fair-skinned, straight-haired black *ladies,* and scat-rhythm-talking emcees like Cab Calloway and later Louis Jordan were the ideal showtime image of the day. Calloway and Jordan were the quintessential image of a bandleader; like drum majors in a marching band, their every motion signified aspects of the songs. Their bodies pulsated in cadence with the high-energy grooves, and their percussive raps jumped along the rhythms: "Eee diddy op/oh I'm a jock/and I'm back on the scene/with a wreckin' machine/sayin' oooh papa do, how y'all do."

The finger-snappin' swing of the Jazz Age was captured in the 1930s by swing bands that produced strong, crisp, danceable music, often with a huge horn section and an interracial cast of performers. The orchestrated, highly structured nature of swing jazz led to a gradual detachment from its funky blues roots, to the point where it became a music that whites could play as efficiently as blacks. Despite the huge success of Duke Ellington and Count Basie, white bandleaders like Benny Goodman and Paul Whiteman collected the most money and recording opportunities. Historian Ted Vincent describes swing music contemptuously as "the disco music of the 1930s."

### RHYTHM AND BLUES

Rhythm and blues music was the prevailing popular music in black America by the 1940s. Swing bands were hard to keep up, so stripped-down urban "jump combos" like Louis Jordan's Tympany Five concentrated on their performance—dance, rhythm, scat, rhythm, tap, rhythm, horn solo, rhythm, and on and on. The high energy and low overhead of small black dance bands, particularly in rural areas, led them to the center of black folks' entertainment nationwide. The louder, rowdier southern style of R&B came from the same bittersweet wellspring as the funk bands would a generation later.

People who worked hard all day needed good, hard, loud, soulful music to get them through a rough night of dancing and carousing. A virtuoso wasn't important; a heartfelt scream, a billowing saxophone, or a rocking guitar would do the trick. As long as the rhythm pulsed and the singer was sincere, the function of the music would be served, and the hard, black troubles of the day would go away. As LeRoi Jones explained it: "Its very vulgarity assured its meaningful emotional connection with people's lives."

The very vulgarity of rhythm and blues became the main ingredient of The Funk, as R&B eventually gave way to a more politically charged and rhythmically sophisticated form of grassroots dance entertainment. The process of unification of the music had begun, as the southern R&B of James Brown gradually grew both more appreciated in its raw power and more polished and sophisticated. When James Brown recorded his first *Live at the Apollo* album in 1962 (which went gold—an astonishing feat for a live R&B album), rhythm and blues had come of age.

But just like The Funk and Hip Hop of today, rhythm and blues was not taken seriously by intellectuals. It was a music for the blues people, those with little money and supposedly little to offer of intellectual value. While most black intellectual activity in music criticism after World War II was spent defending the aesthetics of jazz, an almost universal chauvinism against rhythm and blues persisted throughout the music scene. Considered a performers' medium rather than an art form, and a music for the uneducated and unrefined, R&B was and is universally assailed from a musical standpoint. Even legendary trombonist and bandleader Fred Wesley admitted that he was a "frustrated jazz man" who wanted to join Count Basie's big band and "only took the job with James for the money. Later on I realized that what I was doing was something special, after so many people told me that what I was doing changed their lives." As jazz critic Bob Porter wrote in 1971:

> For too many years R&B has been dismissed as bad jazz . . . the difference comes because seemingly all intellectual resources have been devoted to the study of modern jazz. . . . In a sense this is all right because R&B, whether it be the New Orleans, Chicago or California variety, is meant to be enjoyed rather than analyzed. You'll never enjoy R&B if you need a pencil and a scorecard.

Despite the fact that it afforded the freedom of expression for the wilder, almost hysterical workings of dynamos like Chuck Berry, Little Richard, and Bo Diddley—which in turn started something that inspired the entire nation to "rock and roll"—the genius of these black originators was largely ignored. Despite the fact that the entire so-called British Invasion of rock and roll bands in the 1960s payed homage to the original black rhythm and blues performers, the image, the reputation, and the tradition of rhythm and blues remained for years on the margins of America's consciousness. Despite the fact the rhythm and blues "chitlin circuit" of small-time nightclubs across the South and Midwest was the womb from which The Funk was born, rhythm and blues lives on as an anachronism, too often discussed in terms of other styles, not at the center of the black tradition. Nevertheless, the musical developments of R&B in the fifties and sixties captured the spirit of black America, and with a heavy influence from gospel and jazz, became the basis for soul music and later funk, as the "Invisible Man" of the 1950s became the genius of Ray Charles, the Godfather James Brown, and the Queen of Soul, Aretha Franklin.

### FUNK AND SOUL BE-BOP

While funk and soul developed musically most directly from rhythm and blues, the *ideals* of funk and soul came from jazz. The war years had given rise to a deeper, more intellectual and iconoclastic music played primarily by blacks called be-bop. The sounds were not smooth in this music. In fact, they were jagged, bouncing from one tone to the next in unexpected ways; like its name, be-*bop,* there was an eccentric, spontaneous sensibility to it. This was in fact the mission of bop, as an antidote to the sameness of swing, and the theatrics of jump combos and rhythm and blues; a truly intellectual African-American expression was fermenting late at night in the city.

Serious, methodical musicians played bop, determined to make a music that could not be co-opted by whites. Within a few years, however, smoother jazz incarnations from the West Coast tempered the jazz impulse, calling it "cool," a sound more accessible, more hummable, and easier for whites to play.

"Cool" was countered by incarnations of "hard bop," which were often called by the names "soul" and "funk." This music was noisy, working around one chord, and often teasing with gospel and blues styles to signify on the homespun black experience. Drummer Art Blakey and pianist Horace Silver are associated with the "funk" movement in jazz, a movement back toward black roots. Others, such as saxophonist Archie Shepp, were known for their onstage vocal diatribes about the down-home elements of black life and culture.

By the late 1950s the jazz musician had replaced the blues singer as protest leader in the music. Compositions with political messages such as Sonny Rollins's "Freedom Suite," Max Roach's forward-thinking "Garvey's Ghost," his work with his wife, Abbey Lincoln, on "We Insist—The Freedom Now Suite," and Archie Shepp's "Malcolm Malcolm, Semper Malcolm" were all part of the trend. A down-home flavor also went into tunes such as "Black Groove," "Filet of Soul," and "Ribs and Chips," which were all part of this new back-to-back impulse in jazz. It was a constant movement to re-create jazz as an unmistakably black idiom.

Thus, the hot term for *hard* bop became *funky*. With funk as their weapon, black jazz musicians finally had something that was their own. "Barrel of Funk," "Big Hunk of Funk," "Waltz de Funk," "Funk Underneath," "Opus de Funk," and other songs spoke of a uniquely black perspective. Frank Kofsky explained the circumstance:

> . . . funky was a uniquely black idiom; like many "foreign" words and phrases (*chozzerei, shlemeil, mensh, mazel tov,* and others in Yiddish) it has no precise equivalent in standard English. Hence, to call a composition, a passage, or a player "funky" was not only to offer praise in general, but a means of lauding the object of praise for its specifically black qualities.

Funk was so prevalent that it became an overused gimmick rather quickly and was replaced by "soul." Compositions such as Charles Mingus's "Better Git It in Your Soul" made clear where the sound was coming from. The "soul brother" was styling at jazz clubs in the late 1950s and early 1960s, long before the pop trend of soul music hit the radios.

It was actually quite radical in the 1950s for black artists to use an intellectual form of music such as be-bop to celebrate their roots. The prevailing wisdom concerning high culture was that it was separate from "low life," and the high art of jazz had no business with the common flavors of blues that were used by the common folk. Fusing the two aesthetics represented a revolution in black consciousness. According to LeRoi Jones, the hard bop movement may have been decisive in setting the foundation for the "Black Revolution." Jones explains:

> It is as much of a "move" within the black psyche as was the move north in the beginning of the century. The idea of the

Negro's having "roots" and that they are a valuable possession, rather than the source of ineradicable shame, is perhaps the profoundest change within the Negro consciousness
since the early part of the century.

It is also significant that this major change in the aesthetic point
of view of jazz occurred at the dawn of the civil rights movement, in
the late 1950s. As if the dubious merits of integration were foreseen
by Blakey, Silver, and others, they began to signify on their folk roots
just as the specter of assimilation reached this threshold. If this is indeed the case, then the formula worked to a greater extent in the 1960s
as the bulk of America's segregated institutions were dismantled, and
the popular incarnation of The Funk took place.

It is no mere coincidence that the ideology of hard bop, driven
by its technical fury as well as its affirmation of black roots, had such a
direct impact on what was to come in the 1960s. Rather, The Funk was
an integral part of the jazz musicians' progression toward "black consciousness"—the consciousness that came to define the Black Revolution.

The 1960s began to bring together black people from across political, regional, and economic barriers to contribute to the rapidly
changing black struggle, and the symbolic forms of black unity and race
pride can be illustrated through the music of the times. The Funk, in
particular, reflects the spirit of great comings together—the growing
unity amid diversity and change.

# PART TWO

# The Original Funk Dynasty (1965–72): Slippin' into Darkness

# FIVE

# The 1960s: If 6 Was 9

*"You can't talk about funk
without talking about the Black Revolution."*
Greg "Shock G" Jacobs

## CIVIL RIGHTS AND THE DREAM

The 1960s was a decade of transformation across America—the decade in which the youth of America awakened into their brave new world and dared to take a stand against an establishment that was oppressing its people in the most brazen fashion. The nation endured a "generation gap," as the youth of the time rejected the uptight middle class values their parents had been infected with. The cozy illusions of America's lofty ideals collided with the naked truth of the country's vicious, racist, violent reality, and there was little if any middle ground. The music followed the people, as both matured and grew to new levels of independence and meaning.

Inspired by Dr. Martin Luther King, Jr.'s visionary moral challenges to the racial segregation of the South, and the black students' lunch counter sit-in in Greensboro, South Carolina, in 1960, students of all races flocked to the early civil rights marches and "Freedom Rides" of 1961. Chants from the gospel standard "Don't Let Nobody Turn Me Round" resonated on the buses. Led by churchgoing blacks, challenges to southern segregation spread like wildfire in the form of boycotts, sit-ins, legal challenges, marches, and speeches. As the small victories accumulated, a cross-section of young people, artists, iconoclasts, labor activists, communists, and others joined the church-rooted (and typically middle-class) black activists to form a movement, and grew more politically mature in the process. The zenith of these efforts was the 1963 March on Washington, in which Dr. King summoned "the words of the old Negro spiritual," for the climax of his "I Have a Dream" speech: "Free at last, free at last, thank God almighty, I'm free at last!"

With a radical new movement being led by churchgoing blacks, the new music on the streets was influenced by the music of the church. Civil rights songs began to hit the streets, often as updated gospel tunes. Sam Cooke's magnificent "A Change Is Gonna Come," the Impressions' "Keep on Pushing," and Stevie Wonder's "Heaven Help Us All" were early examples of popular black music that went beyond the personal issues, dealt with a higher force, and spoke of the *society*. Rhythm and blues music as "statement" music would grow into soul music and eventually take on more explicit themes of protest, particularly after the changes promised during the civil rights movement failed to materialize.

Despite the passage of Civil Rights Acts in 1957, 1960, and 1964, a Voting Rights Act in 1965, and housing discrimination legislation in 1969, each allowing for channels for redress of grievances, the masses of black people in the country felt little change. Within one generation of World War II the average black workers were living in overcrowded urban tenements, suffering twice the unemployment of whites, and sending children to inferior schools that, despite the School Desegregation Act of 1954, were still underfunded and all-black. The frustration of this reality was not addressed publicly until a CBS news report discussing the Chicago-based Nation of Islam, "The Hate that Hate Produced," was aired, which featured NOI spokesman Malcolm X. It was Malcolm X who had taken the point of view of the dispossessed black Americans and affirmed their nonintegrated reality. He writes in his autobiography:

> It takes no one to stir up the sociological dynamite that stems from the unemployment, bad housing, and inferior education already in the ghettoes. This explosively criminal condition has existed for so long, it needs no fuse; it fuses itself; it spontaneously combusts from within itself. . . .
> (1965)

The symbolic debate between Dr. King and Malcolm X seemed to mirror an age-old dilemma about the "Negro question": whether or not there really *was* a place for blacks in America. Being an "integrationist" or a "separatist" was never a clear choice for black Americans. Dr. King had a dream that blacks and whites could work together, while Malcolm X was adamant that blacks take care of their own business. The two leaders balanced each other, fed off of each other's roles, and provided the strongest leadership core black Americans had enjoyed since the Harlem Renaissance.

Malcolm X had an appeal that reached that sleeping giant of the black nation, the dispossessed black youth, who by any objective analysis had the most potential for rebellion. Growing up a dirt-poor country boy in Michigan, spending years as a hustler on the streets of Harlem before his transformation in prison to the Nation of Islam, and ultimately leaving the Nation to travel his own path enamored him to the poorest of the world's people as a role model that had come from their own ranks.

But the situation got much heavier after Malcolm's death. Malcolm's assassination left a void in the heart of a people that had been touched—perhaps for the first time since the demise of Marcus Garvey—with hope. Contemporary poet Etheridge Knight explored Malcolm's hold on his people in the poem "It Was a Funky Deal":

> It was a funky deal
> The only thing real was red
> Red blood around his red, red beard.
>
> It was a funky deal
>
> In the beginning was the word
> And in the end the deed
> Judas did it to jesus
> For the same herd. Same reason
> You made them mad, Malcolm. Same reason
>
> It was a funky deal
>
> You rocked too many boats, man
> Pulled too many coats, man
> Saw through the jive
> You reached the wild guys
> Like me . . .
>
> It was a funky deal.

Things became very funky indeed after the focal point of Malcolm X was no longer there. It appeared that the movement was heading toward a more intense, nitty-gritty level. It was getting funky out there. At the time of the assassination of Malcolm X in February 1965, the black American population had a number of nonviolent organizational resources to fight racism and advocate for resources, such as the Congress of Racial Equality (CORE), the Student Nonviolent Coordinating Committee (SNCC), and Dr. King's organization, the Southern Christian Leadership Conference. But the death of Malcolm signified a dramatic new direction in the movement. For many young blacks, the hypocrisy of nonviolence in the face of a violent system was affirmed by Malcolm's murder. The presumption of tolerance was wearing thin on an entire generation. Later that year, in August, the first of many large-scale riots to sweep the nation throughout the remainder of the decade hit Los Angeles and lasted for three weeks, burning block after block and killing thirty-nine people. (The Los Angeles radio deejay Magnificent Montague stirred up the controversy by playing the pop tune "Burn, Baby Burn" by the Creators regularly as the city was consumed.) The Watts Riots were a tragedy to some and a battle call to others, but nobody thought they would be the last. The requisite shock and outrage were heard, a federal commission was appointed to "study" the causes of the riot, and the pressure mounted. Ultimately, rebellion became the method of choice for protest across black America.

### BLACK POWER

Born as a slogan on the dirty Mississippi roads during James Meredith's "Freedom from Fear" march in 1966, a weary marchers' chant of "Black Power!" developed into a political manifesto. By the time state troopers raided the overnight camp of the marchers, "Black Power" was their rallying cry. Shortly thereafter, Stokely Carmichael openly challenged the leadership of SNCC to abandon its ties to white benefactors and take on a philosophy of "Black Power." Carmichael and Charles Hamilton described "Black Power" in their 1967 book of the same name:

> It is a call for black people in this country to unite, to recognize their heritage, to build a sense of community. It is a call for black people to begin to define their own goals, to lead their own organizations and to support those organizations. It is a call to reject the racist institutions and values of this country.

By 1966, SNCC had expelled whites from its leadership and was advocating separate institutions in the fight for what was no longer called civil rights. "Black Power" meant something different to each person who used the term. Musicians such as Curtis Mayfield and James Brown were lobbying for their own separate resources to make their music on their own terms. The Black Power movement found the most sympathetic followers among the dispossessed and among the radical intellectuals, including Marxists of all persuasions. So-called Marxist revolutions occurred in the Third World nations of Ghana, Algeria, Vietnam, and Cuba, and it was the poor, the "wretched of the earth," that drove those liberation efforts. Their inspiration for a revolution in America was far-reaching, and terribly appealing to a people in search of a new vision.

### THE BLACK PANTHER PARTY

The "Black Panther Party for Self-Defense" was founded in Oakland, California, in 1966 by Merritt College students Huey P. Newton and Bobby Seale. Their plans involved community policing, active community centers with health and education services, and a far-reaching plan for black liberation that included an inevitable revolution led by black Americans. After months of following the police, reading the penal code out loud to arresting officers, and developing a small following in the Oakland area, the group took their case to the nation. In full view of the national media, the Panthers walked into the California State Legislature in 1967 wearing dark leather jackets and dark shades, and, armed with rifles, demanding an audience. Their address concluded with a startling challenge:

> Vicious police dogs, cattle prods, and increased patrols have become familiar sights in Black communities. City Hall turns a deaf ear to the pleas of Black people for relief from this increasing terror. *The Black Panther Party for Self Defense believes that the time has come for Black people to arm themselves against this terror before it's too late.*

The idea of armed black people came as a total shock to America's social system. While Black Panther Party chapters sprung up in over thirty cities nationwide, FBI chief J. Edgar Hoover labeled the group "America's No. 1 threat to national security" in 1969. The party quickly wound up in numerous violent clashes with police, the organization was infiltrated by FBI informants, and many leaders were double-crossed, ambushed, or imprisoned.

Nevertheless, their essential message was clear as day: The black warriors were on the scene. One did not have to agree with their politics or their program, but their *strength* was indisputable, and hypnotic. For perhaps the first time since the slave rebellions of Nat Turner in 1831, there was a place where blacks—particularly black men—could fight for their own people, as the backbone of their own black nation. The Black Panthers became the reference point from which all of black America was judged. Questions abounded in integrated settings, like "What do you think of Black Power?" which really meant, Are you one of *them?*

The legacy of the Black Panthers can be seen on the cover of Funkadelic's 1979 *Uncle Jam Wants You* album, designed in the same format as the famous Black Panther publicity poster of Huey P. Newton—with George Clinton as Uncle Jam in Newton's place. Rap producer Claude "Paradise" Gray of X-Clan put the Panthers in perspective: "The same environment that created *funk* created the Black Panthers to start with. The Black Panthers were created out of the same idea. It was a rebellion."

The Panthers were not alone in their confrontational stance toward the American establishment. There were dozens of urban riots in 1966, over a hundred more in 1967, including one in Newark that was at one point a shootout between the National Guard and armed blacks, and another in Detroit in which forty-three people died, and many more in over a hundred cities after the assassination of Martin Luther King, Jr., in April 1968. The nation was reeling from the Vietnam War, the assassination of popular Democratic party presidential candidate Robert Kennedy in June, and the urban unrest. Even Dr. King had moved beyond topics of integration and come out in opposition to the Vietnam War and economic injustice, issues that alienated portions of his so-called "liberal" following and made it clear to most blacks that his days were numbered. After the death of Dr. King, the void in black leadership was filled on the nightly news by avowed black revolutionaries like H. Rap Brown, Eldridge Cleaver, and Angela Davis. The conciliatory rhetoric of Dr. King was nowhere to be heard.

An upheaval was in full swing in America, and the entire world was now aware of it. In October 1968, black athletes organized a boy-

cott of the Olympic Games scheduled in Mexico City. While the boycott had mixed results, the political nature of exploitation of blacks was
made vividly clear after the 200-meter dash, as gold and bronze medal-
ists Tommie Smith and John Carlos raised gloved fists on the victory
stand, as the American National Anthem played. (They were expelled
the next day.) Heavyweight boxing champion Muhammad Ali had already shocked the country by taking a Muslim name, uprooting the
image of the silent black boxer with his unrelenting boasts of "I'm the
greatest, I'm pretty, I'm a baad man!" and stood tall against the U.S.
government by refusing to go to war in Vietnam. His public boasting
and self-affirming style were revolutionary for a race of servants, and
his classic anti-war line "No Viet Cong ever called me a Nigger" mocked
the system he was challenging.

By 1969 the black radical movement had developed to the point
where all Americans were aware of the potential of an organized black
uprising, a mythic confrontation that has dwelled in the psyches of
white and black Americans since the days of the Civil War. For a brief
moment, blacks could tell whitey what they really thought. (This was
made clear on Sly and the Family Stone's classic 1969 instrumental
blues/funk jam "Don't Call Me Nigger, Whitey.")

Street-savvy musicians were caught up in the fervor of the time
as well. Many of the musicians who would later play roles in the growth
of The Funk were members of the very same group on the front lines:
poor, black, young, and male. Marshall Jones, bass player of the Ohio
Players and a close follower of Malcolm X, remembers stepping off a
bus with the band in Lexington, Kentucky, in the middle of a riot and
finding himself in the mix: "The next thing I know, I'm caught up in it,
I'm throwing rocks, anything I can get my hands on." Bootsy Collins
recalled a similar situation: "We was goin' for *all* of it," he said as he
described the riots that happened "right outside" his house in Cincinnati. In Baltimore, Rubber Band vocalist Gary "Mudbone" Cooper had
the same experience: "I was a part of it—I got up there and was riotin'
just like everybody else. . . . I identified easy and I fell right into it because I'm from the streets. . . . When you're from the street, everything is a gamble." And in Plainfield, New Jersey, the hometown of
George Clinton and the Parliaments, the National Guard moved in on
teams of black youths, who fired back. The city's business district was
torched, but Clinton's barbershop was left unscathed. What was important about these events was not only the wild hearts of the youths,

but the antithetical references in their world. It was the university of the streets that was giving out degrees. This is yet another reason why the grim, dark spirit in so much heavy funk is resonant in the hard-core rap music of the 1990s—many of the same urban dramas are being played and replayed.

Ironically, the urban underworld that was causing destruction nationwide was gaining sympathy from liberals and intellectuals who were feeling similarly detached from the American establishment. Many of the most respected artists in the country sympathized with the "Black Power" movement, as vague as its goals were. The distinguished author and humorist Langston Hughes, in one of his last works, published *The Panther and The Lash* in 1967. The poem "Black Panther" captured the romance of the turbulent times: "The Panther in his desperate boldness/wears no disguise/motivated by the truest/of the oldest/lies." Distinguished author and poet Nikki Giovanni captured the galvanized mood of the times with a poem published in 1968 entitled "The True Import of Present Dialogue, Black vs. Negro," which begins:

> Nigger
> Can you kill
> Can you kill
> Can a nigger kill
> Can a nigger kill a honkie
> Can a nigger kill the Man
> Can you kill nigger
> Huh? nigger can you kill . . .
> Can you kill a white man
> Can you kill the nigger
> in you . . .

Written into the violent imagery is the notion of freedom—and a willingness to make the ultimate sacrifices for it. These sentiments were echoed throughout the black arts. H. Rap Brown, Eldridge Cleaver, Dick Gregory, Nikki Giovanni, Amiri Baraka, and many other celebrities preached black revolution in their works. Artists, writers, and orators turned the artistic world upside down by attempting to affirm the destiny of the black uprising and denouncing all things European in vivid texts. Playwright Baraka's *The Slave* was set in the home of an interracial family in the midst of a national race war. The novel-

ist Sam Greenlee's *The Spook Who Sat by the Door* was a fictionalized account of a black CIA agent who leaves his government job to secretly
train black guerrillas to cripple the U.S. system. Jazz musicians soaked
in the black nationalism and expressed their views in instrumental fashion. Titles such as "Justice," "Now's the Time," and "Black Revolution"
were typical.

Carmichael's use of the phrase "Black Power" began to take hold
with the movement and exposed the legal term *Negro* as an outmoded
term that was created by their oppressors. "Black Power" was chanted
in the marches, on the streets, and finally in a song, "Say it Loud, I'm
Black and I'm Proud" by the Godfather of Soul, James Brown. His refrain, "Say it *loud,*" was returned (in traditional call-and-response fashion) by a chorus of children—the future of America—"I'm black and
I'm *proud!*" Brown's ability to place the emphasis where it was needed
by a black nation cannot be underestimated.

> Now we're people
> We're like the birds and the bees
> We'd rather die on our feet
> Than be living on our knees
> Say it loud!
> > I'm black and I'm proud!
> > James Brown, "Say it Loud, (I'm Black and I'm Proud)" (1968)

*Black* quickly became a word of praise, a superlative, an icon.
From marchers, to soul singers, to the mainstream of the black population, and finally as a legal definition of African-Americans, the celebration of "black" was the cornerstone of the newest Negro, now a
liberated being, free to express anger, rage, and compassion, and finally
free to love.

## BLACK IS BEAUTIFUL

What was really happening was the realization of the complete humanity of black people. The revolution in black America had as much
to do with *identity* as it did with one's political or social status. Beyond
the "New Negro," beyond the discovery of a new black iconography,
beyond the opportunistic use by all sides of the idea of integration,
came the potential for a completely defined African-American, a break
from the crushing yoke of white acceptance, and a move toward true

self-determination. "Black Is Beautiful" was the theme, as the de-meaning language of European culture was finally, ultimately, being dissolved.

Inverting the meanings of the term *black* was a monumental task, for the entire religious/linguistic orientation of the West has associations of darkness and blackness with evil, and conversely, goodness with whiteness. "Black magic," black markets, black sheep, blackmail, and black lists have been with us since the "Dark Ages." Even the negative, offensive terms *funk* and *funky* were being reclaimed as something worthwhile, if only because—or especially because—of their centrality to the black experience.

The innovative nature of funky music fit into the same rebellious attitude of the times. The freedom to redefine *black* meant the freedom to redefine black *music,* and if putting bongos and violins together was happening, then it was all right. The experimental, avant-garde, psychedelic, tribal consciousness in black music and art was a direct result of the political freedom found in the 1960s.

The affirmation that black is actually *beautiful* was as total as a transformation could be. It was the essence of the Black Revolution, it was the incubator of The Funk, and it was the inspiration for the overall social revolution of the 1960s.

### HIPPIES AND THE COUNTERCULTURE

The transformation of the black community in the 1960s generated a similar upheaval in white America. This change was felt among white youth for many reasons, among which were the moral quagmire of civil rights, their own uptight and racist family backgrounds, their personal attractions to black culture, the life-threatening fear of the Vietnam War draft, and the influence of mind-altering drugs.

Rock and roll music began to reflect the newer and more serious needs of American youth, beginning with Bob Dylan's grim and insightful "folk" songs like "Pawn in the Game" and "The Times They Are a Changin'." Rock music matured into a lifestyle, with an iconography and philosophy all its own. As harder drugs, violent street clashes over civil rights and The War, and ultimately the draft made white males experience the vulnerability of oppression, the poets, artists, and rock musicians became their saviors. What began as a primitive teenage youth movement in the 1950s, preoccupied with sex and abandon, evolved into a global belief system with an ethos of peace and love, and

a collective vision of redemption that piggybacked on the ideals of the
civil rights movement.

### SGT. PEPPER

With John Lennon and the Beatles paving the way with their psyche-
delics-influenced *Sgt. Pepper's Lonely Hearts Club Band* recording in 1967,
rock music began to explore more liberated ideals of freedom. *Sgt. Pepper* was an opus work from the decade's most popular and influential rock
band. The self-contained quartet from Liverpool, England, had started
out performing covers of R&B classics such as Chuck Berry's "Roll Over
Beethoven" and "Johnny B. Goode," and brought the past traditions into
a mutated new age. The Beatles were weaned on the intimacies of
black music, having absorbed Berry's audacity for cultural insurrection,
as they sold a million copies of "Roll Over Beethoven," a record with
the blasphemous lyrics that challenged the hegemony of European cultural doctrine: "Roll over Beethoven/and dig these rhythm and blues."
(Bandleader John Lennon told *Jet* magazine in 1972 that "to me nothing
has really happened to me since 1958 when I heard black rock and roll
. . . that changed my life completely. . . . I got me a guitar . . . and that
was the end of it. So black music was my life and still is.")

The Beatles would challenge many more doctrines with their
own songs, and with *Sgt. Pepper,* recorded in the spring of 1967, they
were determined to be different. The Beatles' fantasy landscape of performing as *another group,* in fluorescent marching band uniforms, helped
to open the listener's mind to a new flavor of rock. Layered levels of
consciousness in the lyrics floated in and out about the many sound effects: "I'm fixing a hole/where the rain gets in/and stops my mind
from wandering/where will it go." Years ahead of their time (their innovative hands-on studio trickery is now achieved by other artists via
computer), the Beatles introduced a new psychedelic era in popular
recordings, one which would have a profound effect on Jimi Hendrix
(check out *Electric Ladyland*) and George Clinton's Funkadelic (listen
to the *Free Your Mind and Your Ass Will Follow* album), as well as many
others. The Beatles inspired a generation of irreverent art, as the band's
bright, "psychedelic," yet formal uniforms and absurd new name toyed
with the standards of forthright production and presentation. Within
two years of *Sgt. Pepper,* Sly Stone could be seen on *The Ed Sullivan Show*
in a bright red velvet band uniform as well, and that purple outfit on
Prince can also be traced to *Sgt. Pepper.*

The group went on to claim a reputation as social outcasts, and despite their 1970 breakup, the Beatles became pied pipers of the anti-establishment generation. When John Lennon and his wife Yoko Ono recorded a video from their bedroom for "Give Peace a Chance" in 1969, they celebrated the intimately felt possibilities of change for a beleaguered generation.

As the release of *Sgt. Pepper* and the celebrated flower children and hippies of the 1967 "Summer of Love" in San Francisco captured the imagination of the world, the rock-based counterculture grew from simply a rebellion *away* from the establishment, to a movement *toward* a new society. This society presumably could be reached through the new drugs, free love, long hair, a love of the earth, and, of course, an end to racism. Grounded by a certain faith in the power of youth, and structured often only by symbols, the counterculture symbolized the dawning of a new age, although no one knew what that really meant.

Musically, the effects of the counterculture on the pop-rock scene would be longer lasting. The great rock cultural transformation of the late sixties took a variety of forms: Musically, all the separate musical traditions in jazz, R&B, pop, rock, and folk music were brought together as rock artists worked toward an eclectic synthesis; the arrangements developed highly complex and elaborate extended forms, while the music became a multimedia experience with light shows, smoke, incense, and dancing. Technically, bands began to use the full range of electronic instruments and the technology of electronic amplifiers. Musicians and audiences developed new relationships as groups and their listeners shared the same lifestyle and the same drugs. Perhaps more important, the new music achieved a height of knowledge, understanding, insight, and truth concerning the world and people's feelings that was far greater that what any other media had been able to express. These new elements were also incorporated by black rock acts (Hendrix, Sly Stone, Funkadelic, War, Ohio Players, Isley Brothers, Bar-Kays) and quickly became aspects of The Funk.

With the rock and roll universe opening up a new approach to communal living based on shared values, the rock concert-as-tribal-gathering took on greater significance. Larger and larger shows were performed—outdoors—and their zenith was the Woodstock Festival in August of 1969. (Unlike the white-bread mudfest of Woodstock '94, the original concert was the showcase for the era's most groundbreaking black music artists as well: Jimi Hendrix, Sly and the Family Stone, and Santana.) The scope of Woodstock and other large gatherings gave millions of Americans the idea that politically, socially, and spiritually, society could *change*. And despite the incredible scope of this idea, in the 1960s anything seemed possible—even a six could be nine—if the people believed.

The 1970 and 1971 deaths of Hendrix, Janis Joplin, and Jim Morrison; the murder in full view at the Rolling Stones Altamont rock concert; the police killings at student protests at Jackson State and Kent State; and the sound defeat of Democratic presidential hopeful George McGovern in 1972 put an end to the idea that rock and roll could change the world. But the ideals still remained—and in black music, it would be The Funk that would keep those ideals fresh, and keep the possibilities infinite.

# SIX

# The Rhythm Revolution:
# Tighten Up

"You see, I invented that thing, Get on The One."

*James Brown*

## THE RHYTHM REVOLUTION

A black *music* revolution spread across the country just as the social up-heavals of the sixties were taking center stage. Changes took place in the people's dance music, and the themes expressed within their entertainment began to take on much more meaning. With soul music capturing the hearts of the mainstream media and the nationalism within jazz causing controversies among the critics, the real black rhythm revolution was taking place right under their noses. The loud, electric blues shouters; the well-produced hit makers in Motown, Memphis, and the Fame recording studio in Muscle Shoals, Alabama; the West Coast soul innovators; and country funkers from across the nation, were all experimenting with a new groove, a wild new upside down rhythmic chop that was first worked on the public by the James Brown Revue and was spreading everywhere fast.

The Godfather himself broke down the breakthrough song, the 1965 "Papa's Got a Brand New Bag": "That was the turnaround song. It turned everybody around. Because I went on one and three as opposed to the music (count) bein' written on two and four. But I also took gospel and jazz and defied all the laws." The jerky guitar, absurdly offbeat bass line, and sharp bursts of brass and guitars had a percussive feel that was never heard before. By calling out the latest dances and his central chant "It ain't no drag/Papa's got a brand new bag," the God-father had erased all doubt about what this record was here for.

While a series of later works developed a James Brown sound closer to The Funk we now know, "Papa's Got a Brand New Bag" may indeed have been the original funk fossil. With the help of his new and very talkative (jazz-trained) bandleader Alfred "Pee Wee" Ellis, who influenced the new licks, Brown turned out top-heavy, polyrhythmic

grooves like "Bring it Up," "Let Yourself Go," "Licking Stick," and finally "Cold Sweat." These were more than simply R&B hits. These were
jams that took on a whole new rhythmic dimension, where horns and
drums could be heard accenting where downbeats were supposed to
go, and the bass popped in places that were complete confrontations
with the drums, guitars, or keyboards; the guitar was played in percussive spurts like a drum, and James's wicked vocal authority kept
smoking through the confusion. Only James Brown was capable of
surfing the waves of contrasting rhythms without wiping out. Yet he
inspired a universe of musicians to "give it up, or turn it a loose." With
the live energy, musical reputation, and authority in the black community that James Brown possessed in 1965, the innovations from his
band would resonate throughout the black community and, eventually,
the world.

The Godfather's New Bag was already known to rhythm and
blues stalwarts who had heard the basic ingredients of "Bag" on "Out
of Sight" in 1964. By the summer of 1965, the monster groove was already in full swing, as a burning new energy could be heard in rhythm
and blues from Otis Redding's "Respect," Jackie Wilson's "No Pity (in
the Naked City)," Stevie Wonder's "Uptight," and Junior Walker and
the All Stars' very symbolic "Shotgun."

The *rhythm* in rhythm and blues was getting a shakedown. "The
real important thing that changed," writer and drummer Lee Hildebrand said in 1995, "was that the high hat pattern was no longer a
'shuffle.' " Since at least World War II, the standard rhythmic structure of R&B drumming had been a *shuffle,* a skipping kind of rhythm in
which drummers double-timed their counts, as in *da dat, da dat, da dat,
da dat,* that came from the swing rhythm in jazz. The "new thing" developed by the Godfather went toward the even, pulsing hi-hat pattern
of *domp domp domp domp—domp domp domp domp.* The "even" hi-hat
opened the door for the stomping funk beat, with open holes of anticipation extending the rhythmic tension on each beat. With The Funk,
a hard-hitting stomp came along with roots as far back as the French
Quarter marching bands of New Orleans, and the "shuffle beat" was rendered obsolete.

The demise of the shuffle had a unique irony to it. While the shuffle *rhythm* was a part of many great forties and fifties dance steps like
the jitterbug and lindy hops (which were going out of style), the shuffle *step* continued to be a cruel aspect of the negative imagery of the

"Negro." The shuffle originally developed during colonial times as a caricature of African dance styles that had always employed skipping, hopping steps. The distorted blackface characters in the minstrel shows of the 1800s exaggerated the shuffle to ridicule blacks for whites' entertainment. Segregation determined that blacks never stand tall, look whites in the eye, or talk back—just shuffle along, head down, with their dignity gone. The symbolism of the shuffle was one of many negatives of "Negroness" that were being done away with in the 1960s: Just like the civil rights marching song said, "Ain't gonna shuffle no more."

### PROTO-FUNK

It was the *social* revolution in America that inspired the *rhythm* revolution. The desegregated mobility of black performers, their well-trained versatility, the playfulness and optimism of the times, and a profound sense of mission drew black musicians in the 1960s to combine and interrelate the many strands of their musical traditions, affirming them all, while creating still others. The inevitable musical cross-pollenation led to a celebration of the depth and breadth of the music—a music one was no longer ashamed to admit was rooted in Mother Africa. Sarah Brown and John Morthland describe the burgeoning proto-funk phenomenon in the liner notes to the 1994 compilation CD *The Roots of Funk:*

> Essentially, James [Brown] demonstrated that it was possible to use an entire band as a drum kit, creating polyrhythms that took the music back to Africa. . . . In retrospect, the whole thing seems like a gigantic experiment in role reversal, leading to a pronounced sense of playfulness and liberation: It's as though the musicians who had provided the dance tracks of the earlier sixties were now free to dance themselves.

All of a sudden, from bands throughout the South and Midwest, a unifying groove swept the country in the mid-sixties—one with style, togetherness, and moral authority. Up it came, like a voodoo spell over America, spawning new flavors of rhythm and blues, rock and roll, soul, and, finally, The Funk.

The Phoenix-based Dyke and the Blazers kick-started the funky dance fad in early 1967, with "Funky Broadway—Part I." A heaving, lumpy groove with a jumping bass and percussive organ, "Funky Broadway" was the first black dance record to call itself *funky*—and it *was*. Dyke's scratchy lyrics celebrated the ubiquity of Broadways everywhere, as the gritty grimy feel of nightlife on the boulevard came to life. Originating in Buffalo, Dyke's band was backing the O'Jays on a tour, but was stranded by the yet unsuccessful singers in Phoenix. (The group made the best of their funky situation until Arlester "Dyke" Christian was shot to death in Phoenix in 1971.)

The "dirty, filthy Broadway" that appealed to Dyke and the Blazers also worked for Atlantic Records' soul superstar Wilson Pickett. Pickett's richer, smoother remake captured the funky flavors of the original, and smoothed it out for the radio audience and national distribution. The Pickett version, released in the fall of 1967, went to No. 1 R&B, and No. 8 pop on the *Billboard* charts—one of the best-selling funky titles ever. Pickett put to good use the session players at Atlantic's recording mecca in Muscle Shoals, Alabama, which included the likes of David Hood on bass, Roger Hawkins on drums, Spooner Oldham on piano, and Chips Moman on guitar. The team grooved some of the era's classic soul hits for Aretha Franklin, Pickett, Joe Tex, and others.

Joe Tex was one of the quintessential transitional singers who made the leap from easygoing ballads in the fifties, to hot and heavy sixties rhythm and blues, right into nastay, swanging seventies fonk. Developing a reputation for story songs about relationships, Joe Tex delivered the saucy goods with cuts like "Show Me," "Skinny Legs and All," and "Give the Baby Anything the Baby Wants," Tex's flavor was actually so funky that he had to get with musicians that were a little wilder, and recorded his most potent hit—the throbbing, lecherous, and hilarious "I Gotcha"—with musicians in Memphis. Tex managed to keep his funky image through the next decade, recording one of the funniest records of the disco era, "Ain't Gonna Bump No More (With No Big Fat Woman)," in 1977 (for Epic) and toying with themes of The Funk with his comical 1978 Dial album *He Who Is Without Funk Cast the First Stone*.

## STAX

The Memphis-based Stax Records was a cornerstone of the rhythm and blues to funk evolution. The home of Otis Redding, Booker T & the MGs, Johnnie Taylor, the Mar-Keys, the Bar-Kays, Rufus Thomas,

Carla Thomas, the Staple Singers, Isaac Hayes, Albert King, and others, Stax Records was a musical empire of the 1960s that could rival Motown in total record sales. Its down-home country-fried sound made it distinct, and probably not as completely appealing to the middle-class set, both black and white. Founded by the siblings Jim Stewart and Estelle Axton in 1960, the company exuded the easygoing demeanor of its bosses. Unlike their northern rhythm and blues counterparts, Stax producers welcomed performers, producers, custodians, secretaries, and executives to play important roles in developing a finished product. This cooperation and spontaneity contributed to the flavor of the Stax sound. Otis Redding explained the differences between Stax and the music-making corporation at Motown in an interview printed in *Rolling Stone* in 1968:

> Motown does a lot of overdubbing. It's mechanically done. At Stax the rule is: Whatever you feel, play it. We cut everything together, horns, rhythms, and vocal. We'll do it over three or four times and listen to the results and pick the best one. If somebody doesn't like a line in the song we'll go back and cut the whole song over. Until last year, we didn't even have a four-track tape recorder. You can't overdub on a one-track machine.

Stax producers were interested in producing an intimate, blues- and gospel-rooted feel in their music, and appealing to *blacks* first—almost the direct opposite of their counterparts at Motown. More important, the improvisational nature of the label's arrangements allowed artists to take more chances—and by the late 1960s there were a lot of chances taken in black music.

Otis Redding's best-known foray into the funk was the rhythm and blues classic "Tramp," recorded with Carla Thomas in 1967. Picking up on Lowell Fulson's earlier hit of the same name, Otis and Carla went after each other in a comic way, with Carla dogging Otis for being "too country" and Otis treating the jibes as words of praise. With the MGs pumping one of the loudest, low-down bass lines ever heard on the radio, the stuttering drumbeat, swaggering piano, and swooping bass groove made "Tramp" one of the catchiest R&B/proto-funk tracks of all time. (Rappers Salt 'N Pepa picked up on the flavor with their 1986 remake, turning up the bass volume even higher, but keeping that insatiable *swang*.)

The most outrageous R&B singers at Stax found themselves eminently qualified to kick it with the funkier tracks backing them up. Johnnie Taylor's spicy and risqué "Who's Making Love" in 1968 spoke of a nasty side of life rarely exposed: "Who's making love to your old lady/while you're out making love?" His use of the hot and heavy session players at Stax betrayed the seething funk that was prevalent there. In 1969 Taylor scored an R&B Top 5 hit recording of George Clinton's Parliaments' hit "(I Wanna) Testify." The easygoing flow of the song can't mask the oozing funk of Taylor's feel of Clinton's composition. Taylor followed with the mysogynist funk/blues classic "Cheaper to Keep Her" in 1973, and mastered the disco-funk formulas with the biggest-selling soul hit of 1976, "Disco Lady" (which featured Bootsy Collins on the bass). Taylor's teasing, guiltless sexual imagery made him one of the best vocalists in the funky R&B vein. His 1976 platinum album *Eargasm* was one of many titles that stretched the limits of "decency" in the seventies. Johnnie Taylor survived longer than any other Stax veteran after the label's demise in 1975 and challenged the slick soul superstars of the seventies with his undiluted flavor of funky soul.

The elder statesman of the proto-funk trend was Rufus Thomas. A former Memphis deejay at WDIA in the fifties, the raspy-voiced jokester-turned-singer found his niche at Stax Records with a string of funky joke records, starting with "Walking the Dog" in 1963, and taking the country by storm in 1970 with "Do the Funky Chicken." Sporting a hilarious knee-wobbling "funky chicken" dance, and a wild and loose dialogue about smearing chicken gravy on yourself, Rufus Thomas helped to define funkiness as the seventies began. The "funky chicken" was as significant as it was stupid. Hitting the Top 40 charts (at No. 28), it made being funky just a little more acceptable. His 1971 follow-ups, "(Do the) Push and Pull," "Do the Funky Penguin," and "The Breakdown," were actually strong attempts at James Brown funk, rather than the gimmicky riffs of "Funky Chicken," but none saw the same popularity.

Out West the uniquely smoothed-out funkiness of Charles Wright and his Watts 103rd Street Rhythm Band brought a sweet elegance to tender yet trippy tunes. Wright's lazy, almost stoned vocal flow disarmed the listener to his many witty insights, and his scatting, wailing ad-libs brought new meaning to his biggest hit in 1970, "Express Yourself." (This was the song looped by rappers N.W.A. in 1989.) The band's distinctive guitar counterrhythms (played at times by Al McKay and Bobby Womack, among others) can be traced directly to the James Brown rhythm chop, yet the Watts Rhythm Band's sound is utterly *West Coast*. Exquisitely delicate funk numbers like "What Can You Bring Me," "Do Your Thing," "High as Apple Pie," " 'Til You Get Enough," and "I Got Love" had an irresistible, understated tug on the heart and soul. Based in Los Angeles, and bringing as much of a synthesis of styles as Sly Stone (albeit slightly more mellow), Charles Wright was a consistent player in the organic unification of styles that epitomized The Funk from 1967 to 1973.

While nobody was calling it The Funk at the time, instrumental groups and R&B backing bands in the late sixties began to take more chances with their grooves, improvise, and *get funky*. In New York City a band of jazz-trained youngsters known as the Jazziacs were staking out some territory as instrumental groove bands, putting down James Brown grooves with jazzy horn patterns and snazzy dance steps on top. They would soon change their name and become Kool & the Gang. The Ohio Untouchables moved on from gigs backing the Falcons and Wilson Pickett, and struck out as a self-contained act, changing their name to the Ohio Players. Out West, the laid-back rhythmic feel of Compton's Creators were combining Latin jazz, R&B, and proto-funk when they met up with British rocker Eric Burdon, and Burdon's producer Jerry Goldstein renamed the band War.

The most prominent instrumental band of the late sixties era was Booker T & the MGs. Their smooth, soulful grooves were kept tight through Steve Cropper's fluid guitar chops, Al Jackson, Jr.'s drums, the bass playing of Donald "Duck" Dunn, and Booker T. Jones's fluid organ playing. Their rolling rhythm and blues feel delivered a full sound without a lead vocalist—as their first hit "Green Onions" confirmed. The band's tight, fluid style strengthened dozens of hits recorded by the Stax stars Otis Redding, Rufus Thomas, Sam and Dave, and others. They rarely came with the funk bomb, however, as their passion was groove; a fluid sound in which all instruments cruise along a melodic roadway with an interesting background, but take straight-ahead lines. With a penchant for tasty pop melodies delivered by Jones's organ playing, the MGs delivered instrumental pop tunes uniquely tuned to finger-snapping hipster styles like the grooves on James Bond movie soundtracks (the band did score the soundtrack for the British film *Uptight* in 1969).

The late sixties grooves "Hip Hug Her" and "Melting Pot" delivered perhaps the strongest funk chops from the MGs. Some of their heaviest competition was still in Memphis at the time, including the original Bar-Kays, whose 1967 "Soul Finger" instrumental was a scorcher of rhythmic counterpoint and funky party jam flavors. The original Bar-Kays would have taken the Memphis funk crown if they had not perished with Otis Redding in that fateful plane crash into Lake Winono, Wisconsin, in December of 1967.

### THE METERS

Indeed, when the Memphis bands hit their funkiest hooks—the ones that *kicked,* with chopping, bouncing humps that opened big holes in the groove—they began to sound more like their New Orleans counterparts, the Meters. The quintessential rhythm band of the sixties, the Meters redefined the simplicity of the funk riff, while subtly developing an inimitable style all their own. Guitarist Leo Nocentelli, keyboardist Art Neville, bassist George Porter, Jr., and drummer Zigaboo Modeliste perfected the funk lock for a generation of rhythm bands.

While the Meters never gained the notoriety of the MGs, their pedigree was just as outstanding. After starting out backing R&B stalwart Lee Dorsey, kicking his most lively hits "Ride Your Pony" and "Working in the Coal Mine" in the mid-sixties, the quartet played on the first smash hit for Aaron Neville ("Tell It Like It Is" in 1966), produced the biggest hit for New Orleans "swamp rock" guru Dr. John ("Right Place, Wrong Time"—a seething funk monster!) in 1973, and played the worldwide smash "Lady Marmalade" for Patti LaBelle in 1975 (another funk bomb!). Meanwhile the group recorded their own records for nearly a decade, beginning in 1969.

The Meters' solo singles told the whole story of the New Orleans funk sound. "Sophisticated Cissy," "Cissy Strut," "Cardova," "Stretch Your Rubber Band," "Doodle Oop," "Chicken Strut," and other cuts delivered a full, melodic R&B sound, but were swarming with subtle counterrhythms, and fell into open holes of groove at the tightest points in the jam. The seasoned communication between drummer Modeliste and bassist Porter created the flow of anticipation onto each riff, leaving the expected note unstated, implied, improvised, *experienced* in a unique fashion. "There was holes in the music, there was always space. . . . I always believed that it's not what you say, but what you don't say," George Porter observed of his approach in 1994. Many of the Meters' grooves have been devoured by Hip Hop samplers searching for that elusive tangy lick. Indeed, most of their early songs were "rhythm tracks waiting for something to happen," as Porter put it. It is unfortunate, however, that younger music lovers born in the digital age may never experience the intimacies of communication between like-minded musicians that brought about the fertile and flavorful chops found in The Funk.

The Meters went on to produce a series of stellar albums for Warner/Reprise Records, beginning with the strong *Cabbage Alley* in 1972, the tragically underrated *Rejuvenation* in 1974, and quite tasty *Fire on the Bayou* in 1975. The band's lack of exposure led to an ill-fated stab at disco music on their 1976 *Trick Bag* album, and the group cashed it in. Their reputation, however, remained intact. The Meters' funk was a bright beacon shining from the New Orleans/Delta region, the cradle of all black American music. Their effortless fusion of polyrhythms, pop melodies, new ideas, and traditional instruments kept strong the legacy of the New Orleans sound.

New Orleans R&B spawned the equally underrated Chocolate Milk during the mid-seventies as well. This versatile nine-member set delivered the Delta's strongest late seventies funk with fierce cuts like "Action Speaks Louder Than Words" (1975), "Girl Callin' " (1978), and "Say Wontcha" (1979), and a remarkably fluid variety and mix on their early albums. Like the Meters, Chocolate Milk also cashed in their roots by going for the disco hooks, hitting once with "Blue Jeans" in 1981, but wasting away their preponderance of talent in the effort.

It would not be until the rise of the Neville Brothers (including brother Art from the Meters) in the mid-1980s that the New Orleans funky rhythm and blues tradition would be given the national attention it deserves.

### NEW ORLEANS HEART AND SOUL

Deep South R&B soaked in the Delta rhythms like a white shirt soaking up bayou sweat. As the New Orleans polyrhythmic drumbeats informed the Muscle Shoals, Memphis, and Cincinnati rhythm players, a deep, rhythmic lock from New Orleans drummers capable of kicking layers of contrasting meters was brought up the river in juke joints and dance halls across the Southeast, spreading The Funk of a thousand swamp dives.

Like its African predecessors, New Orleans music has always been built from the bottom up: drums first, bass second, followed by the guitar, horns, and other goodies. As the New Orleans showman and pianist Mac "Dr. John" Rebennack wrote in his autobiography, "In New Orleans roots music, the drummer is crucial, chronic to our thing because he lays down the foundation of what New Orleans music is all about: The Funk." The New Orleans session drummer Earl Palmer is regularly given credit for being not only the number one drummer in the fifties (heard on nearly all of Little Richard's hits) but perhaps the original funk drummer. Palmer's ability to lock a beat, maintain a high-energy pulse with both tight snares and heavy backbeat throughout a song, and groove tightly with his session cohorts made him the man. Palmer influenced other local drummers, such as Leo Morris (later known as Idris Muhammad), Charles "Honey Boy" Otis, and Joe "Smokey" Johnson, whose caretaking influence on young drummer Joe "Zigaboo" Modeliste was instrumental in the growth of the Meters.

The New Orleans style of drumming was a busy sound, one in which layers of subtle counterrhythms were maintained simultaneously with the primary beat. The polyrhythmic emphasis of New Orleans drumming was a specialty of the region—the only region in the United States where black slaves were allowed to play the drums from day one. The endless drumming and rhythmic interplay of the slaves at Congo Square (now named Louis Armstrong Plaza) is still visible among the storied "second line" of musicians that has followed parades and funeral marches throughout New Orleans for generations, playing cowbells, tambourines, and other percussive instruments. The very African quality of performing with multiple rhythms playing simultaneously—in a lively syncopation—was retained by the people in the region and has spread through New Orleans Dixieland jazz (featuring cornets and trumpets in a syncopated manner), ragtime (syncopation on the piano), rhythm and blues (guitars), and, ultimately, The (bass-driven) Funk. According to Meters' bassist George Porter, "The New Orleans funk scene had a lot to do with the combination of street music and traditional music, and the space that happens with the two meeting."

The timeless rhythmic feel and the intimate, on-time street vibe of New Orleans music are the main ingredients of an ancient essence that can be traced all the way to Africa. It is interesting that the irrepressible influences of The Funk have come full circle, from the Deep

South, with its Caribbean and African rhythms and rituals, upriver to the midwestern urban centers, across the nation, and ultimately back to the Motherland.

## AFRICA (TAKE ME BACK)

New Orleans music opened the vast rhythmic chasm of African music for practitioners of The Funk. It should come as no surprise, then, that across the Atlantic Ocean, from South Africa to Morocco, African musicians with their ears to the West heard The Funk and internalized it as their own. Multifaceted saxophonist Manu Dibango was one of the first Africans to incorporate The Funk into his sound, recording the influential "Soul Makossa" in 1972. A fast-paced club scorcher with smart, African congas, a phased-out, funky rhythm guitar, and Dibango's percussive ad-libs on top, "Soul Makossa" kicked The Funk and brought African music to black radio. (His work was the inspiration for Kool & the Gang's smash hit "Jungle Boogie" in 1973.) With a groove that ranged from High Life—electrified traditional rhythms—to the wicked grooves of James Brown funk, Dibango became the ambassador to the African music sound for many American soul music fans.

An even more compelling influence was associated with Fela Anikulapo Kuti, the Nigerian bandleader and activist who internalized the James Brown funk edge into all of his extended play Afro-beat grooves, particularly after meeting with Brown during his tour of Africa in 1970. A chopping, distorted rhythm guitar held down an urban flavor to Kuti's Nigerian-produced grooves, as numerous horn and keyboard solos highlighted his often twenty-minute-plus selections. Kuti took on an extremely hard political edge, preaching "music is the weapon," and writing songs such as "Black President," "Colonial Mentality," and "Teacher Don't Teach Me Nonsense." Kuti took his political music mission to another level, challenging the established Nigerian government (which resulted in a murderous assault on Kuti's compound in 1977) and running for president in 1983. In his autobiography, Brown described Kuti as "the African James Brown," and if one considers the pulsing funk grooves, the fearless political stands, and subsequent state repression, the two are very similar. Yet there is something about The Funk that remains uniquely American.

Funk has always been part of a deep southern stew of rhythms and bluesy incarnations that bounced around the urban midwestern cities, growing more complex and meaningful with each stop of the James

Brown Revue. As James Brown biographer Cynthia Rose put it, "Funk is not a reconciliation of opposite rhythmic impulses, but the fusion and transcending of their essential *conflict*." The incredible pressure of the social climate of the 1960s created external conflicts, while the ego and insistent energy of the Godfather generated internal conflicts in a band that ultimately led to an explosion, a rhythmic explosion of total groove—the James Brown sound—The Bomb.

# *The Godfather: Soul Power*

> "When we get through with this session,
> they'll know where the funk come from."
>
> *James Brown*

### JAMES BROWN

James Brown was born on May 3, 1933, in a one-room shack in the pine woods outside Barnwell, South Carolina. His parents split up when he was four years old, leaving young James to fend for himself as his father worked long hours. Brown grew up in a series of shacks until he was six years old, when he moved into a brothel run by an aunt in Augusta, Georgia. There he was raised among the "gambling, moonshine liquor, and prostitution." As a youth he danced for pennies, shined shoes, picked cotton, played sports, sang in church, and eventually began stealing. He was sent home from school more than once for "insufficient clothes." Brown was sent to prison for eight to sixteen years for breaking into a car—to steal a coat—at the age of fifteen. He put together a gospel choir while in prison, and when he left prison on parole after three years, it was to perform as an entertainer.

Brown paid his dues as a struggling musician, often living house to house by gaining the trust of churchgoers or neighbors simply because of his good manners, charming demeanor, and workaholic attitude. Most of Brown's trials were a result of the harsh American social system, and his survival was due to the sympathetic networks of the black community. Fresh out of jail, he was taken in by the mother of his first bandleader, Bobby Byrd. The Byrds' generous support at the outset and loyal support later on were central to the stability of Brown's musical empire.

After joining Bobby Byrd's gospel/doo-wop singing group in 1952, he eventually took center stage because of his lightning-quick moves, his splits, slides, and camel walks, and soon developed the group into the Flames. The Flames met up with Ralph Bass, who signed them to the Cincinnati-based King subsidiary, Federal Records, and the group languished as one of many struggling acts, relentlessly touring, performing, and persevering. His 1956 recording of "Please, Please,

Please" grew slowly and eventually caught on as an R&B classic, while his 1958 follow-up "Try Me" rocketed him to national stardom, and four years later he was headlining the Apollo Theater for a live concert to be recorded and released—the first successful black concert album. It soared to the top of the pop charts. By 1963 Brown was a leading black popular music figure, with many dance hits and ballads in his repertoire. His appeal spread across racial lines. From hotel lounges and frat houses to swanky R&B juke joints and city auditoriums, James Brown caused a minor stir whenever he came to town. "When you heard James Brown was coming to town, you stopped what you're doin' and started saving your money," Pee Wee Ellis told writer Cynthia Rose unboastfully. "We were it, you see, and *everybody went.*"

Brown was beginning to arrange his music in different, jazzier ways. He was bringing instruments in and out where they had never been before. Like the process of jazz, the *jam sessions* (onstage and in the studio) were the central places of his creativity. James squeezed the soul out of his band, then arranged the output as he saw fit. "You had to think quick to keep up," sax player Maceo Parker told Rose in 1990. "A lot of solos, for instance, were just impromptu. He calls out your name, you just had to throat it, then hope it's kinda relative to what is goin' on." It was *improvisation,* under the influence of the Godfather, that drove the engine of James Brown music. Contrary to popular assumptions, his reputation as an R&B act was too narrow for his tastes. "I've never been an R&B act, but I've been classed as one," he told journalist Chuy Varela in 1986. "My music always came from gospel and jazz, which is called funk and soul. You see funk and soul is really jazz." Not surprisingly, Brown's bandleaders were accomplished jazzmen. The band's leader during the funk genesis period, Alfred "Pee Wee" Ellis, had been studying the great saxophonist Sonny Rollins when he joined the group in 1965. Fred Wesley, bandleader off and on from 1969 to 1974, always claimed to be a "frustrated be-bop trombonist" who went on to play with Count Basie shortly after his funk sessions in the seventies. Brown had figured out how to orchestrate a drum set, and make everything in the band work around a groove, rather than a melody. It was a revolution that still impacts us today.

## A NEW BAG

Aware of his strengths, and uncompromising about his work, Brown was insulted by his label's lack of support and jumped to another label, the Mercury subsidiary Smash Records. (The proto-funk smash "Out of Sight" was recorded on Smash.) Injunctions were served, effectively splitting his catalog in half—instrumentals only on Smash, vocals on King!—and leaving Brown in a quagmire. He stuck it out, however, and returned to King after demanding changes in his contract. "You need power to get freedom . . ." he remarked about the incident, "[and] you need freedom to create."

After resolving the legal problems with his labels, Brown hit the studios with a vengeance. His past management problems, his live tours, the addition of the seasoned guitarist Jimmy Nolen (a veteran of Johnny Otis's R&B band), a young North Carolina drummer named Melvin Parker, and his saxophone-playing brother, Maceo, helped Brown to find a clearer focus on his sound:

> I had discovered that my strength was not in the horns, it was in the rhythm. I was hearing everything, even the guitars, like they were drums. I had found out how to make it happen. On playbacks, when I saw the speakers jumping, vibrating a certain way, I knew that was it: deliverance. I could tell from looking at the speakers that the rhythm was right.

In that early February 1965 session, James Brown recorded "Papa's Got a Brand New Bag," and began the string of his many patented "comebacks." The verses were chopping and tight, his screams were piercing, and the bass line counterpunched the dominating, marchlike rhythm. Jimmy Nolen's chopping guitar break was something never heard before, yet the wicked tension was unmistakably familiar. It was a song that changed soul music forever. "New Bag" paved the way for the funk era. The song was recorded during the month that Malcolm X was assassinated. It was released on July 17, 1965, three weeks before the Watts Riots. Papa had a new bag indeed.

The new music was more immediate and intense. It was vivid, urgent, and dignified. It was a scorching expression of the black man's soul, just when the entire world was listening in anticipation. Brown began to record a series of records with powerful, socially relevant themes. Early in 1966 he released the classic ballad "It's a Man's Man's Man's World," which brought the blues text where it had never gone before; he took on the towering reality of male power and the way the world works:

Man made the cars, to take us over the road
Man made the train to carry the heavy load
Man made the electric light to take us out of the dark
Man made the boat for the water like Noah made the ark . . .
And after man make everything, everything he can
You know that man makes *money,* to buy from other man
This is a man's man's *man's* world
But it wouldn't be nothing, without a woman or a girl.

James Brown, "It's a Man's Man's Man's World" (1966)

Brown recorded the up-tempo tunes "Money Won't Change You" and "Don't Be a Drop Out" later that year, and his formula for tense, tight polyrhythms countered by his frantic vocal style brought home the urgency of their messages. Almost instantly, there was a naked intuition between Maceo and James when they performed. Brown was capable of exhorting, screeching, scatting, and literally spazzing out to the energy of Maceo's inspired cadence. The very core of funk as we know it was spawned from that uninhibited flow. Brown was putting so much meaning into his music that the vibe was taking the whole thing to another level. The raw power and the relevance of this type of rhythm and blues make it funk. LeRoi Jones brought the energy of Brown's music into perspective in a 1967 essay:

> The "whitened" Negro and white man want a different content from the people James Brown "describes." They are different peoples. . . . If you play James Brown (say, "Money Won't Change You") in a bank, the total environment is changed. Not only by the sardonic comment of the lyrics, but the total emotional placement of the rhythm, instrumentation and sound. An energy is released in the bank, a summoning of images that take the bank, and everybody in it, on a trip. That is, they visit another place. A place where black people live. . . . But dig, not only is it a place where black people live, it is a place, in the spiritual precincts of its emotional telling, where black people move in almost absolute openness and strength.

James Brown in fact was and *is* taking people back, back to a place of primitive, visceral emotional truth. This has always been the pur-

pose of black music. In the case of funk the circumstances are dramatized because of the proximity of black America to the stifling aspects
of "whiteness" that LeRoi Jones refers to. Questions of black music in
a bank gained a new level of irony, because black people as of 1967 were
going everywhere in America they were never found before, and they
took their funk with them.

The funk just kept on coming. Night after night of touring, with
days off for recording, earned Brown the reputation of "the hardest
working man in show business," and made his music indisputably in
touch with the audience. James Brown took his success as a black role
model very seriously. He purchased radio stations in Knoxville, Tennessee; Baltimore, Maryland; and Augusta, Georgia. He volunteered
to play in Vietnam, well aware that a greater proportion of the ser-
vicemen in Asia were blacks who deserved a good show. James became the archetype of the black man's contradictory success in white
America.

Brown was touring in April 1968 when Martin Luther King, Jr.,
was assassinated. In one of the most memorable moments of his career,
Brown convinced the mayor of Boston to go ahead with a concert that
had been scheduled for that evening, and even *televise* it, so people
would have something else on their minds. Brown and the mayor of
Boston shared the stage, and the sparse crowd (it had earlier been an-
nounced that the show would be canceled) enjoyed an intimate audience with the Godfather of Soul, as did many viewers. This was
probably the first televised James Brown concert in the country. Damage to the Boston streets was kept to a minimum.

Brown then crisscrossed the nation preaching his message of "Stay
cool" and "Learn, don't burn." He told people, "Get an education,
work hard, and try to get in a position of owning things. That's Black
Power." He was later praised by Vice President Hubert Humphrey and
wound up endorsing and campaigning with him in the summer of 1968
in Watts. Brown felt the pressure from that relationship. This was a
time in which every black person in the public eye was compelled to
take a political stand on the Black Revolution. Brown recalls in his autobiography a discussion with the black nationalist activist H. Rap
Brown, who had openly advocated a violent Black Revolution and was
by this time the leader of SNCC. James recounted the "cordial but direct" conversation that followed:

JB: Rap, I know what you're trying to do. I'm trying to do the same thing. But y'all got to find another way to do it. You got to put down the guns, you got to put away the violence.

RAP: You don't understand. . . . You just travel from town to town without staying long enough in one place to find out what's really going on. I'm out in the neighborhoods, working with people. All you know is what you can see from the stage.

JB: Maybe, but I can see pretty good from there. I know what's happening, and I understand why. I probably come from a much poorer background than you do.

RAP: Then you should understand how people feel. You have an enormous following in the ghettos. You ought to get them to take action.

JB: I'm not going to tell anybody to pick up a gun. . . . Besides, even if we did start a revolution, our people couldn't do nothing but lose. We're outgunned and we're outnumbered.

The disagreement between the two leaders mirrored the conflicts swarming in and around the black community. Brown was a fixture among blacks, and everyone knew of his power with the people. According to his manager, Alan Leeds, "He had spent night after night holding court in his dressing room sharing ideas about the black community and their ongoing plight in America." By 1968 the situation had become so severe and violent in black communities nationwide that even the Godfather had to do something.

### SAY IT LOUD

During the hot summer of 1968 James Brown and his band toured California. He had yet to write an explicitly "militant" song, but he was under pressure to take a stronger stand as the death of King was followed by the assassination of the popular presidential candidate Senator Robert Kennedy in June, and the FBI's all-out raids on the Black Panthers in Oakland riled large numbers of blacks. In June of 1968 Brown recorded the sentimental "America Is My Home"—a softspoken tune that he would later claim was misunderstood—and he toured Vietnam, an action that was resolutely condemned by anti-war activists. By the time he returned from Vietnam in July, he was in need of yet another "comeback," this one to prove that he was politically "down." According to one account by sideman Hank Ballard, "machine gun toting Black Panthers" intimidated James into taking a more direct approach to black liberation in his music, and shortly thereafter the group wrote three solidly socially conscious pieces—"Blackenized," "How You Gonna Get Respect (When You Haven't Cut Your Process Yet)," and the No. 1 hit "Say It Loud (I'm Black and I'm Proud)." While it is unlikely that anyone intimidated James Brown, the tenor of the times was indeed serious. What Brown did as a result had perhaps the greatest impact on the black nation since the deaths of King and Malcolm.

"Say It Loud" was a turning point in black music. Never before had black popular music explicitly reflected the bitterness of blacks toward the white man—and here it was done with ferocious funk. Classic works such as Billie Holiday's "Strange Fruit" and John Coltrane's "Alabama" were powerful indictments of racism, and Martha and the Vandellas' "Dancing in the Streets" may indeed have been a symbolic call to protest, but "Say It Loud" was a call to *action*, whether James intended it to be one or not:

> Now we demand a chance to do things for ourself
> We're tired of beatin' our head against the wall
> And workin' for someone else
> We're people, we're just like the birds and the bees
> We'd rather die on our feet
> Than be livin' on our knees
> Say it loud, I'm black and I'm proud!
> 
> James Brown "Say It Loud (I'm Black<br>and I'm Proud)" (1968)

To a generation of frustrated blacks who understood Malcolm X when he called for freedom "by any means necessary," Brown had touched a nerve. He inspired the poets to dream of Black Revolution, to speak of killing whitey (though not his point of view), and to prepare for redemption on this earth, not the next. Brown had entered the movement. He influenced everyone, from revolutionary poets Umar Ben Hassan and Gil Scott-Heron to balladeers Marvin Gaye and Stevie Wonder. Brown even reached the intellectuals. Sixties poet and activist

Larry Neal recalls the Harlem study groups that were moved from poetry and revolutionary theory to a place closer to the people:

> We began to listen to the music of the rhythm and blues peo-
> ple, soul music. . . . The big hero for the poets was James
> Brown. We all thought that James Brown was a magnificent
> poet, and we all envied him and wished we could do what
> he did. If the poets could do that, we would just take over
> America. Suppose James Brown had consciousness. We
> used to have big arguments like that. It was like saying,
> "Suppose James Brown read Fanon."*

By the end of the 1960s, a number of intellectuals came out and
joined the struggle in the community. The poet and playwright Amiri
Baraka immersed himself in the Black Power movement of Newark,
New Jersey, and the political organizing of Mayor Kenneth Gibson. San
Jose State graduate student Harry Edwards organized a boycott of black
athletes from the 1968 Mexico City Olympic Games. Intellectuals
were accepting the people, and in turn direct political statement had
found acceptance in the black musical mainstream.

James Brown was one of only a few performers who could have
released a record like "Say It Loud" and have it aired, because he was
one of the few black recording artists with complete control over the
production of his music. Perhaps more important, he remained in
touch with the people on a daily basis.

The white population did not quite figure it out. "Say It Loud"
went to No. 1 soul and No. 10 pop, and Brown was trotted out on the
pop circuit to play his latest hit; nothing could have looked more ridiculous than to see the video of James Brown lip-synching "Say It Loud"
on Hugh Hefner's *Playboy After Dark* to a mostly white and mostly female audience. Brown would not crack the pop Top 10 again until
1986—but he had no regrets about the stand he'd taken:

> The song cost me a lot of my crossover audience. The racial
> makeup of my concerts was mostly black after that. I don't
> regret recording it, though, even if it was misunderstood.
> It was badly needed at the time. It helped Afro-Americans

---

*Influential Algerian revolutionary and scholar, Frantz Fanon.

in general and the dark-skinned man in particular. I'm proud
of that.

"Say It Loud" initiated the discussion of racial consciousness in
popular music that could be heard on the Temptations' 1969 "Message
from a Black Man," Sly Stone's "Don't Call Me Nigger, Whitey," and
Curtis Mayfield's "Mighty, Mighty, Spade and Whitey." Ironically, this
transformation was brought about by a man with decidedly conservative politics. Brown spoke constantly to people about not burning their
cities and the futility of violence. He was adamant about black capitalism, and wound up endorsing Hubert Humphrey in 1968 and Richard
Nixon for reelection in 1972 because of it.

### THE JBS

Onstage and on record James was still unquestionably Soul Brother
Number One. James Brown drilled his band like a military unit, dis-
pensing fines for notes missed, and screeching out demands for ever
higher levels of performance. Brown could write a song on a napkin,
hum it to the horn players, and record it that night. Often an old song
would become the foundation of a new one, as a new lyric or riff would
be added, and the jam would take shape. The combination of inspiration and discipline was at its peak in the band, and the tireless work of
Alfred "Pee Wee" Ellis, Fred Wesley, Maceo Parker; guitarists Jimmy
"Chank" Nolen and Alphonso "Country" Kellum; "Sweet Charles" Sher-
rell and Bernard Odum on bass; workhorse drummers John "Jabo"
Starks, Clyde Stubbefield (the "funky drummer"), and others kept the
sound tight as a drum.

After a confrontation over tough working conditions and low pay
one night in March 1970 in Columbus, Georgia, James called his players' bluff and flew in (on his private jet) a group of studio musicians
from Cincinnati. They called themselves the Pacesetters, and they were
led by eighteen-year-old bass player William "Bootsy" Collins and his
twenty-five-year-old brother "Catfish," who played guitar. As crazy as
the setting was, without rehearsals, they knew the repertoire. They
walked onstage and pulled the gig off, as well as many others after that.

The new band, called The JBs, smoked. Bootsy's bass playing
licked all around the rhythm, stretching out Brown's sound. Bandleader
Fred Wesley later remarked of Bootsy: "The kind of energy he brought
to the funk was infectious. It would bring everybody's funk level up a

notch. You just had to fall in *with* it, or get run over *by* it!" Drummer
Clyde Stubbefield said of Bootsy's playing, "When he started playing,
man, when you set in the groove, *everything* moved." With trombonist, bandleader, and arranger Wesley gone for nine months to try his
thang in California, the James Brown sound concentrated on rhythm—
bass and guitar—the effect of the Collins brothers. For their part,
Bootsy and Catfish managed to maintain the all-powerful James Brown
funk groove and turn it inside out (as they would George Clinton's band
a few years later), interpreting James's impulses into incendiary fonk
that created a breathless, animated, nastay hype-dog feel.

The James Brown Revue invented The Funk, and the JBs perfected it. Their first recording with James Brown was the No. 1 hit "Sex
Machine." Bootsy remembers that the process of writing the music was
not a pen-and-paper type of thang:

> Musically speaking, my brother and I were pretty much in-
> volved with the writing of the music. James wrote the lyrics
> on a paper bag, on the bus, and I never will forget that. . . .
> He felt everything that he wanted to feel, and he would use
> *us* to "write it down." We were kind of like the interpreters
> of what he was trying to say. You look at his body move-
> ments, [he would go] "uh, ah, aaaa, aaah." It wasn't no
> notes, it wasn't no melody . . . nobody would sit us down
> and say it goes like this . . . you just had to figure it out.

James himself brought Bootsy forward onstage to perform bass
solos during their brief coexistence, exhorting Bootsy to "do the lean"—
a wild, hang-to-the-side gangsta-lean Bootsy was known to do while
girl-watching on the corner—James had Bootsy leaning, and jamming
*up front,* giving the Boot his first taste of stardom. Bootsy said "the lean"
got him "all the chicks." "James used to call me 'young and single and
loves to mingle,' " Bootsy recalled in 1994. Brown became a sort of
father figure to Bootsy, and explained to him the significance of the one-
beat in music:

> I think Bootsy learned a lot from me. When I met him he
> was playing a lot of bass—the ifs, the ands, and the buts. I
> got him to see the importance of the *one* in funk—the down-
> beat at the beginning of every bar. I got him to key in on the

dynamic parts of the one instead of playing all around it. Then he could do all his other stuff in the right places—*after the one*. . . .

It was hard to discipline him and keep him in line; I couldn't spank him, so I lectured him. He wasn't bad or anything; he was just determined to be wrong. I saw a lot of spunk in Bootsy. A lot of life.

As Fred Wesley and other crucial members came back into the fold, the band became stronger than ever. Brown recorded some of his hottest and most legendary music with the band that became the JBs: "Sex Machine," "Soul Power," "Superbad," and "Talkin' Loud & Sayin' Nothin'," as well as the furious studio sides of the *Sex Machine* album and the very nasty *Love, Power, Peace* live concert recorded in Paris in early 1971. By the time Bootsy and Catfish left the band in March 1971, the JBs sound had elevated The Funk to an essential level of *stanky groove*. While out on the West Coast Larry Graham's thumping had elevated the bass thump into the focal point of The Funk, it was Bootsy who engineered and asserted the orgiastic primacy of the rhythmically placed bass note.

Without missing a step, Wesley replaced the Collins Brothers in the spring of 1971, and the band never looked back. The "new" band once again featured Jimmy Nolen's guitar and Fred Thomas on bass, and recorded a number of solo albums that have become the staple of rap music samplers. The first JBs album in 1972, "Food For Thought," included the much-looped tunes "Pass the Peas," "The Grunt," "Gimme Some More," and "Escapism." All of these were instrumentals that featured occasional vocal vamps from James, and slicing, playful rhythmic grooves by the rhythm section. Wesley and Maceo Parker were key players in the fantastic new style of funk horn solos, in which the rhythmic swang was maintained in solos that still took on daring melodic vamps and wicked, assertive blorts. For James Brown's anthemic 1972 double album of the same name, Wesley arranged the quintessential polyrhythmic funk masterpiece "Get on the Good Foot." "That was James' formula in its purest form," Wesley remarked of the jam. "Because none of those parts really go together." Yet it was Wesley's unique ability to make music from the mind of James Brown that made The Funk we know hit that lock so tightly: "He ran it through my brain. He hummed each one of those parts to me, and I put them together and made them work. . . . Whenever I put a new tune together, I use it as a model for just about everything I do when I want to make some funk."

With the wickedly crisscrossing rhythms on the bottom, and the high-powered big-band brass of the band commanding upper ranges, screaming as effectively as the Godfather himself, the JBs were the complete musical expression of James Brown's mind—and thus, the black man's soul. What may have been a facetious remark by emcee Danny Ray on a 1973 JBs album turned out to be quite prophetic:

> Ladies and Gentlemen, there are seven acknowledged wonders of the world, you are about to witness the eighth. Standing in the spotlight, on showcase, twelve young men, who have given you such tunes as [drum roll] "The Grunt," "Pass the Peas," "Gimme Some More." Ladies and Gentlemen, without no doubt, *these* are the JBs!

Their influence on the music of the world is staggering. African bandleaders Fela Kuti and Manu Dibango changed their music after hearing James Brown, and (according to Brown's autobiography) rock superstars Mick Jagger and Elvis Presley would swear by the Godfather. One thing was certain—black music would never be the same. One could hear the swanging, brassy riffs the JBs pioneered in the big-band funk sessions of Kool & the Gang and Tower of Power; the fusion experiments of Earth, Wind & Fire and Miles Davis; the grooving black rock of Mandrill and War; and the Afro-pop workouts of Mongo Santamaria, Hugh Masakela, and Manu Dibango.

Even the president of the African nation of Gabon, Albert Bongo, paid $160,000 for James Brown's entire entourage to come and perform at his inauguration in 1975. Brown's image was so large in the mid-1970s that in 1975 a *white* New York resident held up a restaurant, took a number of hostages, began talking about the plight of blacks, and demanded an audience with James Brown. According to *Jet* magazine, the man with the hostages told authorities, "He'll free them if he talks to James Brown." The gunman apparently felt "that no one could speak more authoritatively for blacks than James Brown." Brown was contacted in Los Angeles, and was prepared to go to New York, when the assailant fell asleep and was captured. Absurd as the event was, the idea that James Brown carried more weight than any black politician, and still commanded the moral authority of the Black nation, was right on target.

### THE PAYBACK

Yet by 1973 Brown's personal life was already coming apart. He was reeling from other pressures, such as the death of his beloved son Teddy in a June automobile accident, his inexplicable endorsement of Nixon, and an accusation from the IRS that he owed $4.5 million in taxes. (Later revelations that the IRS *spied* on Brown illegally did not help him at the time.) Brown scored two movie soundtracks *(Black Caesar* and *Slaughter's Big Rip Off)* that did not yield No. 1 hits, and produced a number of spinoff acts. When the JBs released their second LP *Doin' It to Death,* it featured Brown's biggest seller of the year, even though it was credited to "Fred Wesley and the JBs." Without his pop airplay, and with the phenomenal success of Stevie Wonder, Marvin Gaye, and others using the James Brown funk formula, the Godfather was losing the spotlight.

James signed to produce a third movie soundtrack that year, for Larry Cohen (who had directed *Black Caesar*) and with the help of Wesley, Maceo, Jimmy Nolen, and a few others, some of his strongest work ever recorded—"The Payback"—was produced. Wesley remembers that particular session:

> It was a rush job. . . . That dynamic guitar sound was Jimmy Nolen's creation, based on James' humming. Those famous horn riffs are actually the wrong notes. And James tore apart the words I'd written. His vocal was completely spontaneous. But Jabo (Starks, the drummer) played such a solid beat it made everything else work. When we were finished, the engineer offered to remix, and James shot back, "Don't *touch* this."

Incredibly, when Wesley took the title track to Cohen, he rejected the soundtrack, telling Fred, "It's not funky enough, babe, I need something more *James Brownish,* babe." James promptly released it on his own, and it went straight to No. 1 as "The Payback." This was his finest hour. The indignities of his popular rejection due to his politics, of his rejection by Cohen (one of the few times decision-making control was ever out of Brown's hands), of his abandonment by his black music peers—they were all vindicated with a vicious guitar lick, rock-hard drum track, and signature screech: *"I'm mad!"*

In the intervening years, Fred Wesley and Maceo Parker had developed the JBs sound into a high-powered artillery tank of soulful and assertive funk. Slick and snappy, yet down and dirty, the JBs were the epitome of black soul rhythm, and the spinoff projects from Fred Wesley and the JBs, Maceo and the Macks, as well as the singers Bobby Byrd, Lyn Collins, Marva Whitney, and others solidified the James Brown empire—and the genius of his band at the time.

Brown followed "The Payback" with another double album, *Hell,* in 1974, another record fraught with social commentary, and a thirteen-minute rendition of his now-classic and much-sampled "Papa Don't Take No Mess." Also released in 1974 was another project that featured Wesley's unique funk rhythm arrangements: "Reality," a brilliant, smooth yet wicked package of quintessential seventies rhythm drive. The LP featured another funk standard, "Funky President," and although the artwork, lyrics, and layout showed a strong social consciousness and a sense of *soul music mission,* the recording quality was terribly bad; it sounded as if it had been recorded in *mono,* and couldn't compete with the slick packaging of the more glamorous early seventies funk bands like the Ohio Players, the Isley Brothers, Earth, Wind & Fire, and the indomitable Stevie Wonder.

Later Brown's records became somewhat inhibited in their rhythm formulas, often generating little more than one dance single. Torrid title tracks "Get Up Offa That Thing" in 1976, "Body Heat" in 1977, and "For Goodness Sakes, Look at Those Cakes" in 1979 were supported by almost no album sales, and the monstrous dance tracks "Nature," "Jam," and "The Spank," from Brown's *Jam/1980s* (released in 1978), were lost in obscurity. The album format eluded James, as did the pop stardom enjoyed by a dozen of his imitators throughout the decade. Many funk artists were faithful to the James Brown funk sound and made millions on pop radio, while Brown—regularly hitting the soul charts—could not buy a pop hit. He broke this issue down in the vocal interlude to his 1975 jam session, "Dead On It":

> Now when we finish with this session, they'll know where the funk come from. Every time I look, listen at the radio, I hear, I hear JBs. I hear James Brown. Can't even say, "Good God." But that's alright, I don't care. They don't never give

me no royalties, and when they get on the different shows
they say, "Yeah, I put it all together by myself." Listen to
James Brown, that's all they got to ask me. But that's alright,
I can take that, yeah, cause I'm sayin' it loud. But we gonna
get on down, 'cause reality don't never lie. . . .

James Brown, "Dead On It" (1975)

With the many changes in seventies dance music, the James
Brown sound became fossilized into a raw, primitive precursor to the
complex mayhem of P-Funk–influenced late seventies dance music.
James Brown wound up underground, a caricature of the black passion
of the sixties. He appeared in the late 1970s movies *Dr. Detroit* and *The
Blues Brothers,* but it was not until the single from *Rocky IV,* "Living in
America," was a worldwide hit that people remembered that James
Brown had been recording since the 1950s nonstop.

### UNIVERSAL JAMES

In 1984 the first of the Hip Hoppers got serious about acknowledging
James Brown. The street organizer and party deejay turned Hip Hop
elder statesman Afrika Bambaataa produced an outrageous duet with
James Brown titled "Unity," which was so noisy it was years before
other works could compare to its rough edge and noisy Hip Hop production style. The record (single) cover featured Brown and Bambaataa gripping hands. Very few artists kept the same respect for the
Godfather of Soul.

By 1985 Brown was enjoying a worldwide renaissance as a result
of "Living in America," a worldwide smash hit. Yet this pop phenomenon had little to do with what was happening in da hood. By 1986 rap
acts were starting to capture James Brown riffs in selected samples of
his older music. New York rap group Eric B. & Rakim produced a version of "I Know You Got Soul," one of many James Brown–produced
songs (this one cut by Bobby Byrd in 1971). The record was a huge club
hit and Brown was given no credit on the cover. The popular 1988
dance hit "It Takes Two" by Rob Base and DJ Easy Rock featured a
catchy squeal-and-yell gimmick that was sequenced onto every beat, as
a percussion effect throughout the song, without break. The sounds were
unmistakably James Brown–era samples, and the record had an electri-
fying, breathless quality to it (the loop was a yelp from Lyn Collins's
James Brown–produced "Think [About It]"). Long Island hard-core rap-

pers Public Enemy blew onto the scene with a wicked twelve-inch single "Rebel Without a Pause," also in the summer of 1987—a track that looped the 1970 James Brown instrumental "The Funky Drummer" as a drum track, and scorched the highs with a repeating Maceo Parker saxophone screech from the 1972 JBs instrumental "The Grunt." The record was a club monster, and it was clear that there could be more where this came from. The James Brown sound was out of the bag, and James Brown was *it*. By 1988, literally every rap act with a contract recorded James Brown samples on their records.

The peculiar appeal of funk samples was that there was no legal precedent for the splicing of old music for new music, until a series of copyright infringement suits made "sample-clearing" a necessary aspect of Hip Hop publishing. James Brown finally responded to the barrage of "biters" who would nibble on his rhythms in a 1988 recording with Full Force, "I'm Real." Brown told all of the "copycats" to "get offa my tip," telling all the "biters" in the business that think they "got pull" to "take my voice off your record—until I'm paid in full!"

James Brown was imprisoned later that year after an altercation at his place of business and a police chase across state lines. For three years he was the brunt of a slew of jokes and derision, many more samples, and painfully few large-scale showcases of appreciation or support. His problems with the law and his much-publicized domestic abuse allegations have undermined Brown's leadership in a music business and black cultural landscape that is desperately in need of understanding, experienced leaders.

James Brown has since taken a public stand against the "negative" lyrics in Hip Hop and has refused to allow samples of his music to be used for such goals. He is not alone in his conviction that the negative music and a lack of positive images have undermined the self-reliance of the black community. Mr. Brown was livid in a 1993 interview:

> That self concept of "what I gotta do to make it better for me" has gotten lost somewhere with this crazy music out there. It's really detrimental to a whole culture. It's detrimental basically to the Afro-American culture right away because it denounces your women, it denounces your self, and it lets people know that you ain't got nothing on your mind. Now these young kids are being led to that music, and that's what we are supposed to be about—to lead them away

from it. Some of it makes a lot of sense if it's the kind of constructive criticism that we need—positive. Without the four-letter words it makes sense, but when you add all that, you blow the whole thing.

While James Brown is in touch, vibrant, articulate, and a *living legend,* his perspectives on issues of the day are no longer given the high profile they once had. His absence from serious public discussion is a tragic loss for a man and a people that have given so much. While imitators of his style like the Rolling Stones and Prince are making multimillion-dollar tours, the Godfather remains underground, building and rebuilding networks in the communities that have followed him since day one.

"Everything really worked around James," is what Maceo Parker said of playing with the Godfather. After twenty years of funk grooves, fusion jams, dance fads, and digitized Hip Hop tracks, everything *still* works around James.

# EIGHT

# The Family Stoned: I Wanna Take You Higher

"Stand! In the end, you'll still be you."

*Sly and the Family Stone*

## SLY AND THE FAMILY STONE

For mainstream America the ambassador of funk was Sylvester Stewart, also known as Sly Stone. His outlandish appearance, infectious smile, throaty soul-singing voice, and hyperactive rock music turned America on at a time when the nation was searching for identity.

Sly and the Family Stone was a band that defied categorization. The band's spirited screams, kicks, and hops betrayed a richly rooted gospel heritage, yet they had freaked-out colors: drummer Greg Errico's white-hippie-mashing-black-funk was a shock, as much as homegirl Cynthia Robinson's *red* trumpet, bassist and preacher Larry Graham's Moses robe, sister Rose's white wigs, and Sly's slithery, lanky frame sporting orange Robin Hood getups, spinning in style like a black Errol Flynn with lips. The incredible visual image was sustained by the powerful music and Sly's ability to fuse profound lyrical wordplay with gibberish babbles. The show was too much—yet you could never get enough of Sly. The slang term *far out* was coined for the sole purpose of identifying Sly and the Family Stone.

Barriers were *meant* to be broken by Sly and the Family Stone. They used horns and performed dance steps like their rhythm and blues contemporaries, but they could crunch guitars with the best of the rockers. Jerry Martini's shouting saxophone fired up the best of the blues vibes, yet the jagged, staccato horn rolls he and Cynthia locked into revealed a be-bop sensibility at the same time. Brother Freddie Stone's chopping guitars twanged with a freaky, lighthearted feel of James Brown's band *at the circus,* while the entire soup rode along Larry Graham's pulsing, popping, punching, never-before-heard fuzz-bass, and Sly's genius for tension at the organ. The Family Stone was the first self-contained, all-purpose band. The warmth and innocence of the pop hits "Everyday People" and "Hot Fun in the Summertime" was but a smokescreen for the assaulting lyrics and bone-crunching funk riffs of "Don't Call Me Nigger, Whitey," "Stand!" and "Thank You (for Talkin' to Me Africa)." The group had a series of pop hits and was alternately claimed by soul and rock music followers.

Sly Stone *owned* pop music from 1968 to 1970, and reached his highest point in the highest rock high of all—Woodstock—but in a few short years disappeared not only from the scene, but the *history* as well. Sly Stone somehow fell off the train of pop idolatry and vanished from the lore of rock and roll as if he had never happened. There are books about the Who, the Doors, the Stones, the Beatles, and volumes on Jimi Hendrix, but not on the Family Stone. His music is now found only in the "soul" music bins, as if his rock and roll superstardom were a fluke. John Gabre points this irony out:

> If Sly is as good as he is described, and he is, why is his name so seldom bracketed with other heavies—Lennon and McCartney, Richards and Jagger, Dylan, Townshend— when people start running down lists of the current rock giants? The reason, I fear, is simple: Sly Stone is a black man, and we have been slow to acknowledge the contributions of black performers to our music even when they are massive.

For what it's worth—and to his credit—Sly's music created such an open atmosphere of tolerance and truth that the wicked elements of racism were exposed and thrust into the pop dialogue like never before. There was more discussion of race with Sly than with James Brown, because Sly was a much more accessible figure in the racially charged pop/rock scene in America at the dawn of the 1970s. But with the demise of Sly came the end of the dialogue about race in pop music.

The impact of Sly Stone on *black* music was greater than anyone else from that era except for James Brown. Brown was identified with black ghetto folks who would *never be leaving the ghetto,* while Sly represented everyone else in the new melting pot. It was much easier for studio musicians to imitate the infectious, upbeat innocence of Sly Stone's pop sounds than to try to capture the Godfather's serious, race-conscious vibe. Following Sly's lead, dance music in the early seventies captured the soulful, funky polyrhythms and shouting riffs and shed the sixties soul sound for good. The dubious, apolitical black pop in the seventies had little to do with the Motown legacy, and was all too often the bastardized remnants of the conscious people music the Family Stone produced. Without Sly at the center, his lightweight imitators (such as the Jackson 5, Honey Cone, the Commodores, and Heatwave) could imitate only the loud colors, snappy dance steps over the top choruses, and kicking funk licks. Yet everyone tried. The massive stage spectacles of Earth, Wind & Fire, P-Funk, Michael Jackson, and Prince are all extensions of the glamorous, infectious, Sly Stone–united funk vibe.

The Family Stone did not develop at all the way James Brown did. Brown went through new musicians on nearly every tour, maintaining his act with almost military efficiency. Sly hand-picked his band from enduring personal contacts that ranged across the multiracial Northern California music scene. Sly had known trumpeter Cynthia Robinson since her stint in the Sacramento High School marching band; Jerry Martini and Gregg Errico had been toiling in cheesy pop groups; and Larry was literally "delivered" to Sly over the radio. Along with Sly's brother Freddie and sister Rose, the performers brought their respective talents in pop, jazz, R&B, and gospel music into the mix, allowing Sly to make magic come from it all.

Sylvester Stewart was born in Texas in 1945 and moved to Vallejo, California, at the age of nine. His early training in music was picking up the guitar and drums, exercising his gospel roots, and playing in various unsuccessful high school bands. Sly jumped into the pop entertainment business that was thriving in San Francisco, trying to produce small-time acts for Autumn Records (such as then-unknowns Grace Slick and Billy Preston). After a few more setbacks, he went to radio school. Sly was one of the first deejays on the new black station KSOL in 1966. His energetic style garnered a large following and fueled Sly's ideas of pop stardom. After another deejay stint at KDIA, the No. 1 soul station, he began to recruit members for a band that could play the latest rock and roll music with the energy of soul and gospel singers. Before long he was jamming with five performers—two of them were women, two were white, all were musicians, and all could sing.

Sly's brother Freddie played guitar. Larry Graham played bass, had a great bass voice, and came from gospel roots. Cynthia Robinson and Jerry Martini played trumpet and reeds (an outrageous sight for a white guy and a black woman to be onstage playing instruments together) and Gregg Errico was the relentless drummer, yet another white player who sounded black.

If it seems ridiculous to mention the race of the members of the Family Stone, it should, because if there was ever a group of people capable of sounding as one unit, it was this band. Sly's band didn't just cross racial boundaries, they *obliterated* them. Most people were blown away by the energy of the band as much as their look. The women played instruments, the men sang, and blacks were running the show (to the extent that there was any control at all). The show was so hot, there was nothing you could do but move to it, and be moved by it. Griel Marcus captured the flavor of Sly:

> There was an enormous freedom to the band's sound. It was complex, because freedom is complex; wild and anarchic, like the wish for freedom; sympathetic, affectionate, and coherent, like the reality of freedom. And it was all celebration, all affirmation, a music of endless humor and delight, like a fantasy of freedom.

Originally formed as the Stoners in 1966, when opportunities in the business called, Sly updated the band with his new lineup and got busy. He convinced CBS record executive David Kapralik that "the kids will come around" to his new sound, and CBS went for it. Sly was the first black rock star to be packaged by the corporate music industry. His ability to sell himself, to navigate the predominantly white music business, and to play on the liberal atmosphere of the times were all crucial factors in the rise of the Family Stone, for there were (and are) very few opportunities for atypical black acts to flourish in America, and Sly managed the system better than any other performer to date. James Brown, for example, was entrenched in black radio, and basically *defined* the black radio sound. After "Say It Loud" hit, he more or less disappeared from white radio and was effectively removed from access to the mainstream, despite complete control over his catalog. But Sly could play anywhere, from the Apollo in Harlem to the offbeat white rock clubs like the Avalon or the Fillmore. He could scorch the R&B venues with the best of the honkers and shouters, he would be booked with white rock acts and blow the others off the stage, and his wild act was a natural for the newest invention sweeping the country, color television. From his 1968 debut performance of "Dance to the Music" on The Ed Sullivan Show, it was clear that Sly was ready-made for the New Age of music that was coming.

"Dance to the Music" was played everywhere—in discos in London, on the streets of Memphis, and in the suburbs of Los Angeles. Steve Lake describes the effect of that record:

> . . . for a few months in 1968 Sly brought people together in the discotheques of the world with . . . "all we need is a drummer for people who only need a beat" *Thump Thump Thump.* Yet on closer examination the song is put together with an almost mosaic-like intricacy. Multilayered voices, squiggling horns, and brother Freddie Stone's guitar rocking out down low in the mix. And that bass. Always that bass. Fragmented and jerky, it's the one element that has remained constant throughout Sly's recordings, and is one of the most widely imitated of his innovations.

The record introduced each member of the Family as they came in with their instruments, played one bar out front and dropped back into the groove. The "squiggly" horns had the eccentric yet elegant sensibility of a be-bop line, but were repeated in utterly tight syncopation like the latest Motown licks. The organ sizzled with the swing of a gospel church revival, while the bass and drums stomped with the energy of a civil rights march. Musically and lyrically, this was a band that could *speak for itself.*

### STAND!

"Dance to the Music" carried the band through a tame follow-up album, but shortly thereafter, Sly had hit another peak: the *Stand!* album in early 1969. Race, sex, love, hate, and the power of the human spirit were explored on *Stand!* The wit was infectious, and the groove relentless. There was something for everyone—mindless child's play ("You Can Make It if You Try"), furious dance funk ("Sing a Simple Song"), joyous rock and roll ("I Wanna Take You Higher"), a thirteen-minute bluesy sex grind ("Sex Machine"), a pop standard ("Everyday People"), and biting black pride anthems ("Don't Call Me Nigger, Whitey," and "Stand!"). With this record, the format of the funk album had been incarnated. The album seemed to encompass the entire landscape of the black experience. It was broad in scope, yet intimate. It was joyous, but it had a dead-serious sensibility to it. It was too hot and too black to be rock, too positive to be blues, and too wild to be soul. Sly had given birth to the funk album.

And he was just getting started. In August of that year the Family Stone played Woodstock, and by most accounts was the highlight of the three-day-long event. As Steve Lake put it on the *Small Talk* liner notes: "What could be a better antidote to three days of mud, rain, and dysentery than Sly's ecstatic exuberance? Half a million clenched fists and peace signs rising into the air in a massive human tidal wave of approval."

Bassist Larry Graham spoke of the awesome thrill he experienced on stage at Woodstock, as the band was hit with that overwhelming scream of praise, and called back for more, so deep into that August night:

> We got this encore from a half a million people. I had never heard anything like that, or close to that, in my life. That was beyond my wildest imagination. . . . Man, every hair on my body was standing on edge . . . it was like electricity was just running all through our bodies. Then, that had us so pumped up when we went back out for the encore, that was when we shifted into a gear that none of us had ever shifted into. . . .

When Sly and the Family Stone hit high gear, there was nothing like it. Sly's magnetism onstage was incredible. Often wearing a bright white sequined leather combo, Sly was the white-hot focal point of energy that brought the entire history of black music through his live wire. His vivacious banter and infectious positivity complemented a strikingly deep voice that could soar and scorch your soul in an instant. He was at his best with frolicking dance numbers, as there was nothing sad or bluesy about his presence. Sly had transcended the blues, yet captured its intimate essence.

Despite the lack of a follow-up to the *Stand!* album in 1970, he produced two singles that only sparked a hunger for more. "Hot Fun in the Summertime" was a mesmerizing ballad that was the first of many heartrending gentler tones from the Family Stone. Released in August of 1969, the record captured the late summer haze with an atmospheric swing, as gentle side-to-side syncopations rocked you through Sly's dreamy lyrics. But it was the January 1970 release of

"Thank You (Falettin Me Be Mice Elf Agin)" that altered the Family Stone legend forever. Perhaps more than any other record, "Thank You" introduced the Decade of Funk.

Always daring to innovate, the band pulsed with an outrageous thumping masterpiece—funk of the highest order. With bassist Larry Graham popping the bass on every note, Sly and Larry drove home a new force in funk, a punishing new standard of the nasty rhythm force that funk alone claims. The song was literally the swan song to the group as it was known, as Sly again packaged magnitudes of meaning into the simplest of words. One refrain summed up his past hits, his present genius, and future impact as he asked the people to "Dance to the music all night long" because "Everyday people—sing a simple song."

## LARRY GRAHAM

Larry Graham solidified himself as one of the originators of street funk with "Thank You." Although the chopping, popping, and plucking bass sounds could be heard here and there in earlier works of many bands, typically as an accent to the basic riff, "Thank You" used the popping bass as the primary melody—a syncopated melodic phrase from the bass, which turned the bass guitar from a background rhythm instrument into the driving force of the song. After "Thank You," both rhythm and melody became the territory of the bass.

Despite the presence of Bootsy Collins in James Brown's band at the time, even the JBs had to step back and give it up for Larry Graham's inventiveness. While the time meter of "Thank You" shows the strong JBs influence—the rhythm pulse on the one count—none of the JBs were popping their bass strings. As *Bass Player* magazine describes it: "probably the single most important factor in establishing funk as an idiom unto itself was the thumb of Larry Graham."

Graham, of course, fell into the formula by accident. Born in Texas and raised in the East Bay (like Sly), Graham learned to play on his own. Playing music at local East Bay clubs in a trio with his mother, Larry played guitar and sang, and for a percussive, bass effect, he pumped the foot pedals of an organ on the stage. When the organ broke down, he rented a bass, and was so adept at playing both lead and bass riffs, Graham and his mother worked as a duo, without a drummer. According to Graham, "That was when I started to thump the strings with my thumb to make up for not having a bass drum." Sly Stone was told of Graham by a relentless caller on Sly's KSOL radio program, and when he went to see Graham's act, he decided to add Graham to the Family Stone, even though Sly had planned to play the bass himself.

Desperate for more of this new heavy funk, by late 1970 the audience was constantly let down. The paradoxical genius of Sly turned a new chapter in what amounts to the archetypal funk melodrama. Sly began to miss concerts and perform late or in an uninterested fashion. Just as his status skyrocketed, Sly turned inward and away from his celebrity, leaving millions wondering how someone so positive and appealing could disappear from the scene so quickly. It would be another year and a half before anything was released by the Family Stone, now reconstituted, but this new thang was even more compelling. The albums *There's a Riot Going On* and *Fresh* are still being talked about as breakthroughs twenty years after the fact.

## RIOT

Sly had always been good copy for rock critics, but *Riot* caught them completely off guard. The critics lamented, "there's no joy here," "a brooding masterpiece," or that he had simply "blown it." Sly performed nearly every instrument, and the music was completely different from anything he had released before. The ironies Sly refers to in his texts were insoluble, without the innocent faith of previous work. There *was* faith, however—the faith of a blues singer, believing in the power of catharsis and truth. There was nothing depressing about this work in the context of funk; Sly Stone was perhaps speaking to someone besides the rock music establishment, to an aesthetic from within, which was based on his identity as a black American, and not a white pop icon.

From the lyrical content to the gurgling, bass-driven sound, regardless of where this record is placed among rock fans, it is a funk masterpiece.

Sly had a new sound, and it was a smash hit. He took on topics of life that were not based on naivete, or on privilege, aggression, or self-destruction—the typical rock lyric catalog. His topics were swimming in contradictions, but the faith continued to penetrate. The single "Family Affair" was perhaps the most coherent, as it captured the melancholy and joy of life with a sublime elegance. Songs like "Just Like a Baby," "Luv & Haight," and "Poet" oozed in a stew of murky rhythms, overlaying a relentless bass, splatters of clavinet, obliquely audible choruses, and Sly's sparse, unpredictable, and yet utterly stirring vocals.

Sly reworks "Thank You (Falettin Me Be Mice Elf Agin)" into a slow, murky, bass-driven thump titled "Thank You (for Talkin' to Me Africa)," a song with meanings that eluded white critics. Sly might have been acknowledging his source of strength as he survived the onslaught of media hype and unrealistic demands of himself. Griel Marcus explored the racial contradiction of *Riot*: "With *Riot,* Sly gave his audience—particularly his white audience—exactly what they didn't want. What they wanted was an upper, not a portrait of what lay behind the big freaky black superstar grin that decorated the cover of the album." It was clear that Sly's reclusiveness was a reaction to the demands of the audience, but his artistic response relied on a deeper soul level of his self-concept, and the introspection invariably came closer to the black man's true heart and soul.

Once the damage was done, Sly was grudgingly accepted on the margins of the rock mainstream, and his music made its way to the soul music bins. His follow-up to *Riot*, called *Fresh,* was by all accounts even stronger than *Riot* and somewhat more upbeat, but just as dissonant, with lyrics slipping in and out between heavy bass thumps and webs of horn lines. The single "If You Want Me to Stay" was another gourmet selection of innuendo, this one also symbolically asking the public for acceptance as Sly asks for the chance to stay among us—with one condition: "I've got to be me."

### TIME FOR LIVIN'

By 1973 Sly had settled down, had a child, had recovered from the blizzard of hype and expectations, but never quite found his recording niche again. The interesting 1974 release of the *Small Talk* album featured a cover of his girlfriend Kathy Silva and their child (an interracial family in a vibrant pose), and among many surprises was the song "Time for Livin'," which explored Sly's peaceful resignation from the musical battlefront. After Sly's much-publicized 1975 wedding and concert at Madison Square Garden, he seemed to disappear, producing records that never hit the charts, and only occasionally playing with his loyal Family members, Martini, sister Rose, and Robinson.

In 1977 a "disco" remix of "Dance to the Music" was released, which did nothing more than solidify Sly's image as an over-the-hill act. In 1979 Sly hooked up with George Clinton, the great funk bandleader. Sly went on tour with Clinton's entourage in many cities, with Sly often suffering from stagefright. Show after show found Sly peeking his head onstage, singing a few bars, and retreating. He began to record with Clinton, and appeared on a few choice cuts of the 1980s P-Funk repertoire, such as Funkadelic's "Funk Gets Stronger" and the P-Funk All Stars' "Hydraulic Pump."

In 1981 Sly and Clinton were arrested for cocaine possession and went their separate ways after that. It was heard that Prince was interested in producing work with Sly Stone in the mid-1980s; one of the Prince protégés, Jesse Johnson, the guitarist from the Time and a successful solo act from 1984 to 1987, signed up Sly to perform a "duet" entitled "Crazy," which was successful. Sly's 1989 collaboration with the Bar-Kays, "Just Like a Teeter Totter," was a sign that when he's ready Sly can deliver the goods. He can now be heard on many rap songs that sample the music of the Family Stone, particularly Digital Underground's "Humpty Dance," Janet Jackson's "Rhythm Nation," and, perhaps most visibly, Arrested Development's "People Everyday."

The impact of Sly Stone was felt immediately within black music. Sly had made it clear that one could come as hard as James Brown's funk and still be fresh and accessible. Motown Records capitalized almost immediately on the "Dance to the Music" formula, with the release of the Temptations' "Cloud Nine" by the end of 1968. Other funk bands followed Sly's rhythm arrangements that featured lighter guitars and more keyboards than James Brown, and more "universal" topics. Kool & the Gang, Earth, Wind & Fire, and War produced rhythm arrangements and topical choices that reflected Sly Stone's influence. The joyous, colorful, rhythmic spectacle of Earth, Wind & Fire on stage in the 1970s can easily be seen as an extension of Sly's spirit. Herbie Hancock, the jazz-funk giant, produced a tribute to Sly on his landmark *Headhunters* album. The record was as bizarre as Sly's ebullient personality. The disco-funk craze was based more on the Sly Stone brand of fun-loving funk, as K.C. and the Sunshine Band, the Commodores, and the Ohio Players all made millions in the mid-seventies with the Sly Stone formula of dance funk. What the artists did or did not do lyrically, or conceptually, with the remainder of their album sides should also be kept in mind, however.

Sly was the first to incorporate women into his self-contained musical unit as performers. His band was unique in this respect, and while the musical themes of equality were followed zealously by other artists, few developed such strong professional relationships with women. Lead singers in funky music bands like Chaka Khan and Rufus, Patti La-

Belle, and Minnie Riperton developed a great degree of creative control of their music in the 1970s, but too few female *instrumentalists* found their way through the door. For all of its universality and freedom, funk and the era of black bands were still a movement led by black *men*.

The funk band nevertheless owes much of its identity to Sly and the Family Stone. He was the catalyst for a culture of musical and social unity not known before or since. Were he born into a spiritual society, Sly may have been a prophet; instead he exists on the margins of musical categories, misunderstood as a central player in the funk assault. The Godfather broke the door open, but Sly let everyone in. The standard by which togetherness is measured is Sylvester Stewart's richest gift to music.

# PART THREE

# Searching for The Funk: Come Together

# NINE

# Black Rock: Givin' It Back

"Funk is just speeded-up blues."
*George Clinton*

## THE BLUES, ROCK, AND FUNK

The story of blues, black rock, and funk has yet to be told without the intrusion of white rock as a reference point, yet the continuity is as fluid as a Hendrix guitar solo. Despite the efforts of the great black rock and rollers Chuck Berry, Little Richard, Bo Diddley, and Fats Domino, by the time of the rise of Elvis Presley in the early 1960s, rock music had become a white form. The mid-sixties' so-called "British Invasion" of rock bands from Europe, led by the Beatles, the Rolling Stones, and the Animals reinforced this myth, despite the fact that the groups were all profoundly influenced by the blues and black R&B of the 1950s. The musical dominance of Sly Stone and Jimi Hendrix in the latter part of the 1960s finally served to uproot the myth of rock as a white phenomenon. But in only a few short years rock music was resegregated by a shrewd music industry. It was not until the phenomenal crossover success of Prince in 1984 that the popular white image of rock and roll came under scrutiny once again.

The perpetual overdose of white rock icons continues to obfuscate the rich, if misnamed, musical tradition of black rock that continues in the 1990s in the form of the black rock bands like Living Colour, Body Count, Bad Brains, Fishbone, the P-Funk All-Stars, and many others. Rock bands of the 1960s, both black and white, were all based in the blues. Rock bands of the 1990s, both black and white, are now based in The Funk. But it all comes from the same source.

## BLUES TO ROCK

The blues comes in many forms. LeRoi Jones wrote in *Blues People* that the blues began as soon as the Africans in America realized they were not leaving. The blues is the singer's means of release—the singer's vindication and salvation found in the expression of the truth. Often mournful and melancholy, it always had threads of irreverence and humor to balance the laments. And there was always a swing, a slow and low swaying march that seemed to emphasize the fact that despite all the problems, life will go on.

The melancholy and the *music* of the blues seem to go hand in hand. Polyrhythms, call-and-response, and unconventional, atonal scales were all utilized by blues performers to bring their sound closer to the tones of a human voice, closer to a fuller, ensemble sound, and ultimately closer to its ancient spiritual and rhythmic foundations. Muddy Waters was one of the many down-home bluesmen who took the sound to the city and opened the scene up for all kinds of changes. Yet his vibe was as traditional as a Sunday church revival:

> But you see blues, its tone—deep tone with a heavy beat . . .
> I think the best blues singers came from the church. I even
> thought of being a preacher myself, the blues is so close to
> preaching. I got all my good moaning and trembling going
> for me right out of church.

Waters was a Mississippi-born, heavy-throated blues singer who was discovered by Alan Lomax in his search for the legendary blues composer Robert Johnson. Waters adapted well to electrified guitars, and influenced rock and later funk with his heavy emphasis on back-beat. "The big drop after the beat on the drum formed the foundation of my blues. Nothing fancy—just a straight and heavy beat with it," he once told David Henderson. (Just listen to "Electric Mud.")

Waters thrived in the electric blues revival of the late 1960s, along with artists such as B. B. King, Bobby (Blue) Bland, and Howlin' Wolf. In a peculiar social development—based in part on the integrationist impulses of that generation, as well as what Nelson George described as "the praise of white guitar heroes"—the blues giants found themselves being booked into the largest clubs, walking in the *front* door, and "getting paid better than at any time in their lengthy careers because they had suddenly started reaching that elusive white audience."

The West Coast was the happening place for that "elusive" white audience to soak in the soulful sounds of sixties black performers. The area was ripe with multiracial coalitions, in politics, in jazz, and in the many multiracial bands in the area, like Sly and the Family Stone, Tower of Power, and Santana. The diversity, relative tolerance, and hybrid cultural mixing of people lent itself to new ideas in music. The distance from the entrenched problems of the urban North and the segregated South most likely helped, too, making fertile ground for those bold and imaginative enough to elaborate on their dreams of a new society. (It's no coincidence that black rock innovator Jimi Hendrix grew up in the integrated [black, white, Asian] West Coast city of Seattle, and Sly Stone in the integrated [black, white, Latino] Bay Area city of Vallejo, California.)

While Hendrix remained loyal to the blues idiom throughout his career, and Sly mastered the dance music of the times, both men defied stereotypes and created organic syntheses of sound and style to produce some of the most important black rock and some of the earliest funk. It would be the psychedelic rock influence on The Funk that served to move the style from simply a wicked brand of R&B into something universal and inclusive. Uprooting racial (and musical) stereotypes with each new release, Jimi and Sly utilized the freedom inherent in rock and roll to expose thriving new visions of society— visions induced by the social revolution of the *black man in America,* and articulated by these black men. Symbolically, it was their time, as Jimi and Sly blew open the minds of popular music listeners and created a legacy only the funk bands have righteously followed up on.

## JIMI HENDRIX

The legacy of Jimi Hendrix has been completely misunderstood. Hendrix was and continues to be a part of the rock tradition of music (which really means "white" tradition), despite his black American heritage, his black American musical training, and his work in all-black bands. And while his life as a black musician was central to his identity and his legacy, most rock histories discuss Hendrix exclusively in terms of rock.

Jimi was born in 1942 in Seattle to parents with musical backgrounds. Jimi learned to explore and enjoy music at an early age. His father encouraged this and bought him his first guitar. Jimi was surrounded by mixed races of kids, and musical influences from the jazz guitarist Charlie Christian (often heralded as the first to electrify the guitar and "send the banjo back to folk music" in the forties) to the rock and roll staples Bill Haley, Bo Diddley, Chuck Berry, and Fats Domino. His first high school band was a black R&B/rock group called the Rocking Kings. His wild guitar antics caused problems with jealous band members—and sent the girls crazy even then.

After a few aborted efforts in the local scene in Seattle, Jimi joined the military at the age of seventeen (following in the footsteps of his father), and eventually wound up stationed in Kentucky. The sounds of the country blues impacted Jimi greatly, and he spent many off hours in the black parts of nearby Nashville, soaking up the urban yet down-home sounds of the blues singers, and hip urban bands like the Mar-Keys and Booker T & the MGs, the storied Memphis sound. In the army he started a trio with fellow black enlisted men, with drummer Gary Ferguson and Billy Cox on bass. Cox became close with Jimi and would figure in Jimi's life after he gained his fame. Jimi could navigate the world of musicians wherever he went; though he didn't say much, his sincerity was evident whenever he hung out, and people would only have to hear him play once to be convinced.

Hendrix left the army and later was picked up by Little Richard in 1963. He jumped ship in St. Louis and met up with Albert King, another left-handed guitarist with funky down-home roots. King showed Jimi T-Bone Walker's style of "squeezing strings" to make sounds without a pick, and shared his ear for horns. Hendrix wound up in Harlem in late 1963 looking for lead guitarist gigs in an R&B act. He was picked up when Ronnie Isley went to the Palm Café looking for a lead guitarist for an upcoming Isley Brothers tour of Bermuda.

Hendrix thrived in the Isley Brothers band, performing his wild stage show, licking the air, biting his guitar, wearing loud bandannas, and getting the most out of his solos. He made $30 a night and didn't complain. Jimi became a popular session guitarist in Harlem, recording sides for Curtis Knight and the Isley Brothers in 1964 and 1965 (check out the Isley Brothers' "Testify Parts 1 & 2"). Jimi's girlfriend at the time was Fayne Pridgeon, a black woman who constantly had to defend him in public because of his outrageous appearance. She took him in to live with two friends and her young child. Like James Brown's years fresh out of prison, Jimi survived in the care of a black social network that still survived in Harlem. Once he left it, however, he was *alone*.

Jimi began to hang out in Greenwich Village, where the hippies dressed as outrageously as he did. There were other black artists that hung out in the bohemian set, such as the Chambers Brothers, blues singer Taj Mahal, and spiritual folk singer Richie Havens, but none developed the mainstream popularity and public scorn of Hendrix. He was "discovered" playing in a grungy club one night by Chas Chandler, one-

(George Livingston Collection)

## The Godfather of Soul: James Brown

*Above:* The Godfather in full effect. *Right:* James Brown works out in front of Fred Wesley and his ultra-tight band.

(Copyright © Paul Roberson / George Livingston Collection)

## *Sly and the Family Stone*

*Above:* Sly Stone takes you higher. *Below:* The Family Stone (l-r): Freddie Stone, Sly, Rose Stone, Larry Graham, Cynthia Robinson, Jerry Martini, Greg Errico (rear).

## Great Funk-Fusion Innovators

*Top to bottom:* Jimi Hendrix, father of psychedelic rock and key inspiration for The Funk; Funky Soul genius Stevie Wonder; Jazz-Funk pioneer Miles Davis.

*(Bill Nitopi Collection)*

*(Mastahn Fanaka/Ace of Shades)*

*(Mastahn Fanaka/Ace of Shades)*

## *Funk Bands in Action*

*Above:* Kool & the Gang, from their "Light of Worlds" years, 1975. *Below:* The Bar-Kays working out at Wattstax, 1972. Opposite page *(top to bottom):* The Earth, Wind & Fire stage experience; The Isley Brothers dominating the stage; The Commodores keeping in step.

*Top to bottom:* Chaka Khan puts it all into her singing, 1974; Curtis Mayfield delivering funky soul with authority, 1975; Herbie Hancock during his Headhunter years, 1974.

## Great Funk Performers

*Above:* Larry Graham, bassist for Sly and the Family Stone and Graham Central Station; *Left:* Lead singer and guitarist Leroy "Sugarfoot" Bonner of the Ohio Players.

*Left:* Key architects in The Funk: Fred Wesley (l) and Maceo Parker of the JBs.

*(Copyright © Kwame Brathwaite)*

Funkadelic, 1971 (l-r): Eddie "Maggot Brain" Hazel, William "Billy Bass" Nelson, keyboard wizard Bernie Worrell, drummer Tiki Fulwood, rhythm guitarist Tawl Ross.

time bass player for the Animals, and wound up on a flight to London, with Chandler in charge of all of his affairs. He was given a band, venues to play, and a recording contract. The Jimi Hendrix Experience hit the roof. He blew away everyone else in rock and roll (and by the time he died in 1970, it was just called rock).

He returned to the United States to play the Monterey Pop Festival in June 1967, and upstaged the headliners, the Who. Anyone who's seen the tape of this performance has witnessed a new age of music being born. His wild bush of hair couldn't conceal his hypnotic gaze, his large-boned face with slightly Asiatic, sharp-angled features accented by a thin goatee and mustache, his distorted mouth with tongue darting out as he worked his guitar strings and effect levers with blistering dexterity. His outfits were always splashes of color, bizarre crochet, mutant lapels, sequined bellbottoms, and, of course, the red bandanna, all combined with his *backward* guitar to make for an unbelievable effect.

Displaying an ability to explore the aural landscapes of the subconscious—with a guitar—and yet still rock the blues hooks, the Jimi Hendrix Experience stormed onto the rock scene in the spring of 1967 with the debut album *Are You Experienced?*—but Jimi was just getting started. On "If 6 was 9," from his second album, *Axis: Bold as Love,* Hendrix was able to articulate the social and cultural dichotomies he was helping to confront:

> White collared, conservative flashing down the street,
> Pointing their plastic finger at me.
> They're hoping soon my kind will drop and die,
> But I'm gonna wave my freak flag high, high,
> Wave on, wave on,
> Fall mountains, just don't fall on me,
> Go ahead on Mr. Business man, you can't dress like me.
> > Jimi Hendrix Experience, "If 6 Was 9" (1967)

The dialogue is set along a spacey, free-form groove, transcending the blues riffs that begin the jam. The spacey sounds were only the backdrop for an existentialism never experienced in rock before. As the jam expands further, Jimi can be heard whispering, "I'm the one that's got to die when it's time for me to die/so let me live *my* life/the way I want to."

When Jimi played Woodstock in August 1969, it was with a six-piece multiracial band, with Jimi, his old army buddy Billy Cox on bass, *two* Afro-Latino percussionists (Jerry Velez and Juma Sultan), a black rhythm guitarist named Larry Lee, and Mitch Mitchell, his drummer from his first hit group, the Experience. The performance, the finale of the three-day ultimate rock event to end the ultimate rock decade, actually had a distinctive African polyrhythmic energy to it. However, the engineers effectively mixed out the percussionists and much of the work of the other guitarists, leaving the sound of Jimi and Mitch Mitchell, the sound of the old Experience.

Jimi's African ensemble, exposed to the world, vanished with a sweep of the mixing board. As biographer Dave Henderson wrote, "The sound the African drums made was lost, an entire acoustical realm lost in the air." This may be a small point, but careers are made at significant points in history, as James Brown's was solidified after Dr. King's death. The best-selling Woodstock soundtrack featured only "Purple Haze" and Jimi's solo performance of "The Star Spangled Banner," the subtleties of which, the ironies of which—the *knowledge* of which—evaded the typical black listener, who was not even exposed to Hendrix on black radio. While the ultimate concert was a showcase for the propulsive Latin rock of the then-unknown act Santana, and Sly Stone's triumphant rendition of "Higher" is legendary, Jimi's efforts to flow musically in that same direction were sadly missed.

After Woodstock Hendrix performed with black musicians regularly until his death on September 18, 1970. The Band of Gypsys—veteran R&B drummer Buddy Miles, Hendrix, and Cox—recorded on New Year's Eve 1969 at the Fillmore East, their only recording available to the public. Jimi also recorded with Alafia Pudim (a.k.a. Lightnin' Rod) of the Last Poets, a funky rhythm track to a rap written by some black prison inmates entitled "Doriella du Fontaine." He played the 1969 Harlem Arts Festival in the heart of his old stomping ground, and offered to participate in a benefit concert for the Black Panther Party but was talked out of it by his management.

With Jimi's group reluctantly touring in Europe to pay off endless legal bills, Billy Cox was apparently given some "bad acid" after the Isle of Feherman Festival, and he wound up catatonic. Jimi had to postpone his return to the States because of Billy's health. Two weeks later Jimi sat in with Eric Burdon and War in London—his last performance. He died the next night of complications from sleeping pills, vomit, and suffocation.

Musicians from all walks of life came to his funeral, but his *image* remained: He was a rock star, and died that way. The passage of time has not helped. The essential musical connections that were reflected deeply by other artists like Miles Davis, Prince, Bootsy Collins, George Clinton, Norman Whitfield, Ernie Isley, Eddie Hazel, Stevie Wonder, and Marvin Gaye were apparently missed by the music establishment. Jimi was as much a part of black music as any artist who ever lived. But his history has been written from a rock (read: white) perspective, not a funk (read: black) perspective. The true story of Jimi Hendrix as a *black musician* has been obfuscated, and twisted by myth like the black roots of the Egyptians.

Jimi was swept up in the pantheon of rock music so quickly that his popularity among blacks was not an issue in his many public appearances. Part of the myopic mythology of rock music is the process by which artists whose roots are in black music—such as Hendrix, the Rolling Stones, Elvis Presley, and the Beatles—are heralded as innovators and originators of their sounds, while their black mentors languish in obscurity.

Nevertheless, there were still plenty of opportunities for Jimi to catch on with the bruthas and sistas. Sly Stone played rock but was accepted as a hero at the time. Certainly one reason was the type of venues Hendrix played (musty, drug-infested rock clubs packed with long-haired hippies), and the all-white backup players in his band, yet there was perhaps more. Nelson George explained one reason for the difference:

> Jimi Hendrix used blues and R&B as his building blocks, and Sly Stone worked from gospel and soul. . . . The difference was that Hendrix drew from a style blacks had already disposed of; Sly shrewdly stayed just a few steps ahead of the crowd. . . . Sly never worked the chitlin circuit like Hendrix . . . but Sly always gave up The Funk. . . . Sly brought [James] Brown's funk to the rock masses almost uncut.

In his autobiography, Miles Davis was less diplomatic when he summed up the misconceptions about his good friend Jimi Hendrix:

He used to play 6/8 all the time when he was with them white English guys and that's what made him sound like a hillbilly to me. But when he started playing with Buddy and Billy in the Band of Gypsys, I think he brought what he was doing all the way out. But the record companies and white people liked him better when he had the white guys in his band. . . . But Jimi Hendrix came from the blues, like me. We understood each other right away because of that. He was a great blues guitarist. Both him and Sly were great natural musicians; they played what they heard.

One thing that eluded Hendrix was dance music, which would have gained him an R&B reputation. Jimi *tried* at Woodstock, but with the flick of an engineer's wrist, it was wiped from history. *The Band of Gypsys* album featured one bona fide funk cut titled "Who Knows," which features Buddy Miles's ferocious backbeat and Jimi's twisted scatting and patented guitar distortion. (This record was "sampled" and reworked in 1989 by the platinum rap group Digital Underground on "The Way We Swing," which was arranged clearly as a tribute to Hendrix.)

Jimi worked toward more kicking funky grooves in his later works, which were released as *Cry of Love* and *Rainbow Bridge,* but he was never able to complete them. Without accessible dance music, an accessible lyrical base in Jimi's music could have helped, but his lyrics were so fantastic and far out that he could not get a foothold on black radio formats. There was, of course, plenty of Hendrix's music that was structured enough for black radio, such as "Foxey Lady," "Crosstown Traffic," and "Castles Made of Sand," but there was no marketing interest in the black crowd, as Hendrix's image was being carefully tuned toward whites. So with only musicians and rock critics to maintain his legacy, the father of psychedelic rock was claimed by a white music establishment.

Yet the impact of Jimi Hendrix on black musicians was nevertheless profound. Drummer Buddy Miles accelerated his rise to seventies superstardom, driving a train of rhythm into a string of grooving, thick rock albums as "The Buddy Miles Express." The Isley Brothers, for another, were pumping out rhythm and blues that was conspicuously close to rock and roll, thanks in part to Hendrix's presence. The band developed a taste for leathers, and the grand decorations of rock, after leaving Motown in 1969. Their 1973 release of "That Lady" includes a guitar solo by Ernie that is one of the longest and loudest ever heard in dance music. The arrangement is cleaner, more coherent, and more danceable than any of Hendrix's work, but the links are obvious. The Isley Brothers went on to become one of the heavyweights of funk music, uniting their R&B roots and strong rock background (and following), to produce some powerful fonk—and paying homage to Hendrix along the way.

## BLACK ROCK BANDS

It became something of an organic process for rhythm and blues bands to step forward and "become" black rock bands by the 1970s. These bands fused the wide-open impulse of rock with the rhythms of James Brown and Sly, and turned into funk bands by the mid-seventies. George Clinton's Parliafunkadelicment Thang captured perhaps the most authentic replication of the Hendrix legacy, recording as Funkadelic. The band recorded loud, freakish, bluesy versions of the polished records they had performed as the Parliaments, and steadfastly maintained the hard guitar-driven edge in their music even after most black acts began to polish their sounds. The impact of Hendrix on P-Funk can be heard on the 1971 Funkadelic classic "Maggot Brain," and on the 1994 compilation: *P-Funk Guitar Army Tributes to Jimi Hendrix*.

Similarly, the Ohio Players had toiled in Dayton as the Ohio Untouchables for years in the early sixties, spending time as the backup group to the Falcons, who featured Wilson Pickett for a while. When they replaced guitarist Robert Ward in 1965, the group matured with the lyrical talents of their brilliant blues guitarist Leroy "Sugarfoot" Bonner, changing their name to the Players. In 1970 they signed to the same Detroit label (Westbound) as Funkadelic, and made a name for themselves with outrageous, blues-jazz-rock that dabbled in strange time changes, with bridges coming and going, and segments of songs in one style, only to leap to another, while the lyrics always remained standard-fare blues text. The interesting combination of accessible lyrics and outrageous rhythmic arrangements was overshadowed by their album covers, which featured a baldheaded black woman (Pat Evans) in leather in various positions for each of their five Westbound LPs. In 1972 the group scored a huge national hit "Funky Worm" (a record often used by rap music samplers), which led to their move from small-time Westbound to Mercury Records in 1973.

## MANDRILL

Creating a bizarre blend of African-based rhythms, scorching rock riffs, country fonk, bop jazz, Latin riffs, and one-chord guitar rock operas, the New York–bred Mandrill was a mind-blower from the outset. Led by brothers "Dr. Ric," Louis, and Carlos Wilson, and including Omar Mesa on guitar, keyboardist Claude "Coffee" Cave, drummer Neftali Santiago, and bassist Fudgie Kae, the multiethnic long-haired band was a visual feast, and a musical history lesson. Driving out jazz chords, spiritual chants, Caribbean festival rhythms, and throbbing guitar rock hooks, all worked in and out with a flair for the unpredictable, Mandrill was the quintessential fusion band. Thick, punishing, bass-heavy grooves like "Fencewalk," "Hang Loose," and "Mango Meat" grounded the outrageous act in The Funk. With the success of the band's first *Mandrill* LP for Polydor Records in 1970, and their following workouts *Mandrill Is, Mandrilland,* and *Just Outside of Town,* Mandrill was poised for superstardom—in the rollicking cross-cultural vein of Earth, Wind & Fire. But the group failed to deliver the catchy radio-friendly hooks and melodies as the years went by, and despite a move to Los Angeles in 1975, the fantastic African-tribe black rock extravaganza of Mandrill was out of the picture by 1976.

## WAR

Out West, the wide-open music landscape spawned some of the most powerful rhythm-rock sessions of the era. One such band was War. The seven-member rhythm section with roots in the Long Beach–Compton area of Southern California was "discovered" by British rocker Eric Burdon, who brought Danish-born harmonica player Lee Oskar to front the band, along with mainstay Howard Scott's sparse rhythm guitar, Lonnie Jordan's mastery of Afro-Latin–flavored keyboards, B. B. Dickerson's rugged bass thumps, Charles Miller's tireless drumming, rotund Papa Dee Allen's gripping percussion, and Harold Brown's well-toned saxophone. War was just breaking out from second billing, and their particularly Latin-tinged strong, bluesy rhythms hit stride in 1971 on their second RCA solo LP *All Day Music.* They swept the country with unforgettable singles "Slippin' into Darkness" (1971), "Cisco Kid" (1972), "Low Rider" (1975), and "Why Can't We Be Friends" (1975), and showed an effortless ability to make good music in almost any style. The grim, earthy feel of jams like "Four Cornered Room," "The World Is a Ghetto," and "Slippin' into Darkness" affirmed life in the bleak urban landscape of Los Angeles (just as fellow Compton natives N.W.A. would do twenty years later). On their live tours (captured on *War Live* in 1974), the band seemed to relish their ability to create anticipation and build rhythmic tension before releasing it. Despite the band's brilliant lyrical quality and unique harmonica and saxophone brass tones, the essence of the group was rhythm—a wide-open, earthy dance rhythm, and an innate ability to incorporate the heaviest of funk chops in everything they played. (It's ironic that such a dance-rhythm-oriented band would be the one Jimi Hendrix played with in his last performance, the night before he died.)

War's sound represented the focal point in the Latino influence on the fonk, as the band generated anthems of streetwise Southwestern culture, including the all-time cruising jam "Low Rider," the springtime party favorite "Cinco De Mayo," the richly rhythmic "Leroy's Latin Lament," and the dramatized folktale of a Mexican bandit turned freedom fighter, the "Cisco Kid."

The thriving Mexican-American culture of the Southwest was enjoying its own renaissance of "Chicano Pride" and brilliant fusions of Mexican folk, Texas blues, and American soul that can be heard from groups like El Chicano, Tierra, and Los Lobos.

Chicanos embraced as their own the funky West Coast vibes of War, Tower of Power, Santana, and a variety of soul stylists.

### SANTANA

Another brilliant band with cross-cultural roots was Santana, the multiracial, percussion-charged thrill ride of a band that took the world by storm at Woodstock in 1969. Growing out of San Francisco's Latin Mission District garage jam sessions, the Santana Blues Band was a musical feast, led by the founding core of Carlos Santana on guitar, Gregg Rollie on organ and piano, Dave Brown on bass, and a slew of percussionists, starting out with Mike Shrieve's set drums, and Jose Areas and Mike Carabello on congas. With the help of promoter Bill Graham, the band secured the gig at Woodstock and left the mesmerized audience screaming for more. Within three months they had signed a deal with Columbia Records and had their first million-selling album in the stores. Many more would follow. With a unique ability to transmit his soul through a guitar, Carlos Santana could grind and splatter with the ferocity of his percussion-rich band, yet he could soar beyond the beat, floating to new horizons by holding and extending single notes with stirring effects. Santana thrived on the Latin rhythms and used the rich traditions of Mexican folk music and Afro-Cuban jazz as source materials for their songs, lyrics, and themes. Deeply spiritual about his music, his blessings, and the traditions from which he came, Carlos Santana turned quickly to experimental efforts in jazz and rock, recording with jazz giants Chick Corea and John McLaughlin, unaffected by his time in the rock spotlight.

### STAX

Perhaps the most important result of the black rock musical trend was the activity in Memphis, Tennessee, at the Stax recording company. The entire industry was given a jolt in late 1967 when Otis Redding and four members of his band, the Bar-Kays (Jimmy King, Ronnie Caldwell, Phalon Jones, and Carl Cunningham), died in a plane crash on December 10 in Lake Winono, Wisconsin. Stax was particularly hit because of the rising popularity of Redding and the work of the Bar-Kays as a studio band. As a result of the crash, Stax Records literally panicked and was ready to try anything to stay in the black, including making a deal with Gulf Western to produce more than two dozen albums in one month.

The one player not on the plane, bassist James Alexander, reconstituted the Bar-Kays and took them in the direction of black rock in the Sly Stone–Jimi Hendrix mold. Their most notable postcrash work was on the 1969 solo LP of Isaac Hayes, another staff writer pushed into work with Stax's new managers. Despite a string of writing credits that included Sam and Dave's "Soul Man" and "When Something Is Wrong with My Baby," Hayes was an afterthought as a performer at Stax. Yet to stay alive, the label put its entire roster to work and released twenty-seven albums in one big splash in the spring of 1969.

### ISAAC HAYES

Hayes's work was stunning. "Hot Buttered Soul" changed the popular definitions of black music. His ten-minute cover of the Dionne Warwick ballad "Walk On By" begins with slow, brooding strings, and when the rolling blues count hits the peak, a loud fuzz-toned guitar breaks out—where one might have expected a sax solo in earlier soul music. After a lengthy guitar solo, Hayes's voice creeps in slow and breathy, mutating the Dionne Warwick standard into an anthem of masculine torment. The four songs on the album were long, extended renditions of Hayes's cheesy, breathy nightclub act. His long dialogues about how love can make you laugh, and can make you cry, were cadenced effortlessly by the band. The Bar-Kays could shift from sweetened Sinatra-style sentimentality to soaring soulsville screeches, right along with the versatile voice of Isaac Hayes. Hayes's powerful yet deceptively tender voicings spread out along a vast landscape of mood and musical tone, setting a new standard for soul music. It was blues in its melancholy, inevitable mood. There was a clearly fresh, authentic southern sincerity in Hayes's delivery.

The record stayed on the jazz charts for two months, and while it was clearly in the pocket with rock music, there was not yet a category for it. Stax was primarily interested in reaching black listeners, but Hayes and the Bar-Kays had put Stax and black rock on the map. Hayes followed the formula closely with *To Be Continued* and *The Isaac Hayes Movement* before his landmark *Shaft* soundtrack broke the door right down, with the band sweating out sixteen minutes of "Do Your Thing."

*Soul Music* was supposed to have three-and-a-half-minute songs, ready-made for radio airplay. This black rock thing was messing up the program. Recording loose, long jams that flow in and out was not only a way to produce albums quickly, it was also a way of returning to an African aesthetic of extended ensemble performing. Nelson George wrote that "with *Shaft* and *Black Moses*, Isaac Hayes broadened the commercial impact of black records. To appreciate fully his long sultry tempos, listeners had to purchase the LP, which turned black music fans from singles to album buyers."

### THE BAR-KAYS

The rise of Hayes to a soul superstar did not reflect on the unknown players backing his work. But the Memphis funk scene was too strong, and the new Bar-Kays were determined to be a self-contained act that backed up no one.

In 1971, the same year of the *Shaft* soundtrack release, the new Bar-Kays released a record entitled *Black Rock* on Stax, featuring a picture of the band wearing everything from purple suede vests and flower sequin necklaces to white afro wigs, *Sgt. Pepper*-style blazers, capes, a boa constrictor, and an assortment of leather streamers. Visually the band resembled Sly and the Family Stone, yet the sound was influenced more by Funkadelic; the record was raunchy, sloppily mixed, derivative, and loud. It delivered the goods, though. In fact, everything the Bar-Kays have recorded over their twenty-five-year career has delivered—no matter what style was hitting. From their precrash solo hit "Soul Finger" in 1967, through their own "Son of Shaft" follow-up in 1972, their P-Funk days with "Shake Your Rump to the Funk" in 1976, their disco-funk sounds with "Move Your Boogie Body" in 1979, and their naked funk noise with "She Talks to Me with Her Body" in 1982, the Bar-Kays have been an amazingly accurate barometer of the latest hard black dance music styles.

What distinguished the band from weaker sets is that the Bar-Kays never diluted their music, always remained creative despite their obvious adherence to pop formulas, and made every show a guaranteed foot-stomping sweat-fest. The Bar-Kays possessed the primary ingredients of any up-and-coming band at the time: They could put on a show, and they could *jam*.

## GRAHAM CENTRAL STATION

While Sly Stone wrote the book on the elevating jam session—kicking horn breaks, over-the-top drumming, screaming organ tones, and screaming voices well arranged to create the impression of hysteria— some of the best workouts on record are from Sly's imitators: Earth, Wind & Fire's *Gratitude* double live album; War's 1974 *War Live* double album; Tower of Power's 1976 *Live and in Living Color;* and the 1977 *P-Funk Earth Tour* double album. With the slow and distressing demise of Sly Stone, the inaugural impulse of West Coast fonk was in danger of disappearing altogether, if not for the wild and wicked antics of the horn band Tower of Power, and Sly's protégé and original bass player, Larry Graham, and his band Graham Central Station, who continued the hit-making tradition of Sly and the Family Stone.

As the bass player on the many frenetic hits of the Family Stone, Graham provided an integral spark that was sorely missed when he left the group in 1970. His fuzz-bass can be heard on "Dance to the Music," and "I Wanna Take You Higher"; his nasty pops can be heard on Sly's thirteen-minute "Sex Machine" and "Stand!"; and Graham's own syncopated plucking on "Thank You (Falletin Me Be Mice Elf Agin)" became the cornerstone of funk for the decade. Yet Graham continued to expand. He recruited a band called Hot Chocolate that he was planning to produce, but once the group hit the stage, Graham couldn't resist. He joined the act himself, renaming it Graham Central Station. Delivering a stirring depth of soul, rock and roll, and thick, funky groove, the self-titled *Graham Central Station* album plummeted to the depths of bass, and soared along Graham's four-octave vocal range into the falsetto. Perhaps pre-dating Bootsy Collins' psychedelic bass works, Larry Graham expanded his bass effects with the guitar distortion techniques of Jimi Hendrix, and redefined the instrument once again. The wide-open range of the group was further tapped on *Release Yourself*, recorded in late 1974. Freakish, thumping funk workouts ("I Believe You," "'Tis Your Kind of Music"), exotic gospel rock anthems ("Today"), and high-stepping rockabilly ("Release Yourself") marked the album's fantastic musical landscape. The title cut and the hyperactive "Feel the Need in Me" took church revival into the Funk Age with Graham's breathless plucking speed and the band's spirited energy.

### THE JAM

But Graham Central Station was a West Coast secret until "The Jam" hit in 1975. Brilliantly capturing the apocalyptic scope of the funk bomb, "The Jam" was the meatiest, manliest, monster of a funk jam—a fire-breathing Godzilla in a land of hefty funk dinosaurs. Billowing in surging bass crescendos, "The Jam" begins in a stew of bass sounds, raises up, and drops into the thickest dance track anyone had heard since Sly. In a play on the intros heard on "Dance to the Music" in 1968, Graham's band members introduce themselves, each taking a measure to kick their flavor. Robert Sam's sticky, gooey organ playing is delectable; Hershall "Hershall Happiness" Kennedy stirs up the clavinet, a forgotten instrument that was the staple of healthy funk bands; the tasty lead vocalist Patryce "Chocolate" Banks played the "funk box," an early form of a drum machine; David "Dynamite" Vega slapped his guitar around; and Willie "Wild" Sparks played drums as a (stereotypical) mock Asian drummer "Wonyuwul," all leading to the point when the Godzilla bass takes over and "The Jam" climbs a funk mountain where few have tread, reaching that rarefied level of total groove.

Pulsing, spinning, churning, and burning, "The Jam" created new horizons and leaped over them with each riff, cooking up a groove that ascended until it ended—and never leaves your feet. "The Jam" was the quintessential funk workout—a jam session in which every player made a statement, the band smoked together, reached a peak, splashed down—and unlike the album cuts from those art-rock space cadets, this jam was eminently danceable, in the hardest funk sense. "The Jam" was one of the high points in the development of The Funk: For years the Godfather directed the flow of ultra-tight bands with jazz and blues roots to foster heavy groove sessions, and the Stax session players locked tight grooves for ten minutes at a time, but the new upcoming funk masters had developed a collective groove thang that took on a transcendent musical life of its own.

Graham Central Station continued their own transcendent musical life with their brilliant, topical albums *Mirror, Now Do U Wanta Dance,* and *My Radio Sure Sounds Good to Me,* further pushing traditional blues, soul, and R&B into the background.

## JOHNNY "GUITAR" WATSON

The blues impulse in black popular music was being cast aside in favor of The Funk and was in danger of being forgotten until Johnny "Guitar" Watson connected the blues with soul and funk. Watson had been delivering a wild West Coast electric blues act since the early fifties, but when he got hold of the latest electronic keyboards (recording tracks by himself, like Prince) and combined with his humorous drawls and brilliant blues guitar scales, Johnny "Guitar" Watson crossed from blues to soul (with "I Don't Wanna Be a Lone Ranger" in 1975) and worked his way into hard-core fonk. His opus work is the *Ain't That a Bitch* album in 1976. Flowing along slick, state-of-the-art soul arrangements, Watson's swanky, gold-toothed grin and down-home vocalizing threw listeners into a time warp. His ability to bring the symbolism and simile of blues dialogue into the modern era on tunes like "Superman Lover," "I Want to Ta-Ta You Baby," and "Telephone Bill" set him apart from his old-school peers.

With *Ain't That a Bitch* (the title toying with a well-known street saying) Watson enamored himself to the hipsters and captured a new pop ideal of the cool, stylish blues artist with *money*. The cultural crossbreeding prompted *Soul Train* host Don Cornelius to ask Watson on his lively 1976 appearance outright, "Are you blues, or are you funk?" Watson didn't answer Cornelius directly, but on his following works, "A Real Mutha 4 Ya," "Funk Beyond the Call of Duty," and "What the Hell Is This?" he answered the question quite clearly. Watson's fluid incorporation of blues with The Funk, along with similar transitions made by the Ohio Players and blues-rooted singers such as Benny Latimore, moved the blues once and for all to the margins of black popular music.

The "Black Rock" of the mid-1970s basically became funk. The ubiquity of radio airplay compelled black acts to dispose of their rock riffs and guitar solos, and most bands conformed. Only a few acts challenged this formula. Funkadelic took a proud stance, recording "Who Says a Funk Band Can't Play Rock" in 1978, and a series of monster cuts from Slave, Mother's Finest, and the Isley Brothers also made their point. It would take the rock and roll sound of Prince in 1982, and the direct political action of Vernon Reid's Black Rock Coalition in 1985 to assert the independence and "equal rights" of black rockers to get heard, to give up The Funk, and get paid.

# TEN

# *Funky Soul: Express Yourself*

"People get up, and drive your funky soul."

*James Brown*

## SOUL AND FUNK

The legend of soul music stands on its own in the pantheon of rock folk-lore and in the scores of books on the subject. Yet the soul music phe-nomenon in the 1960s and early 1970s was a crucial element in the development of The Funk, from a wicked groove thang to a polished, purposeful sound with an entire people's ideals transmitted through it. Without the musical mastery of the soul music performers and pro-ducers, and the strong (if segregated) infrastructure of black radio to promote it, hard funky music would never have developed the tight, accessible, meaningful level it ultimately reached.

When we think of soul music, images of the 1960s pop up, with Aretha Franklin's majestic voice, the Temptations' smooth stepping, Otis Redding's heartfelt laments, and the glitz and glamour of the Supremes. The Horatio Algier story of Motown Records, the spirited sweaty singing of Jackie Wilson, Wilson Pickett, and, of course, the Godfather of Soul James Brown, all represented some aspects of soul. There was, in fact, a soul culture that came to reflect the catchy and coordinated new styles, the warmth and optimism, and newfound pride emanating from black America. Many writers went so far as to claim that soul was the music of the Black Power movement. To the degree that the black community was united in the 1960s, soul music was a celebration of that fact.

In many ways soul music represented the beginning of the syn-thesis of black America—the synthesis of popular R&B styles with the moral overtones of gospel music. Musical barriers were coming down; there was finally *empowerment* in the unification of the sacred and the secular—Saturday night swing and Sunday morning salvation all in one.

## RAY CHARLES

Soul singers were coming closer and closer to the complete musical experience by the mid-sixties, and when funky bands came along to enrich the grooves, soul singing became an essential aspect of classic seventies funk. Throughout the chronology of soul music, it has been the slick, sharp packaging of the *essential funkiness* of the artists that has made it so successful. This pattern was originated in the fifties by the ever so funky Ray Charles.

Charles is a musical giant of the ages, whose expressive, jubilant, soulful persona defined the essence of black expression for generations. Hailing from the Deep South, Charles lost his sight at the age of six, and after rugged beginnings as a performer he escaped all the way to Seattle, Washington, in 1947 to develop his own fresh, funky feel. This young, blind, black, gravelly-voiced singer brought together the most engaging aspects of black music into one form and began the process of synthesis that led to soul and, ultimately, funk a decade later. He would turn around gospel standards like "My Jesus Is All the World to Me," re-creating it as "I Got a Woman"; "This Little Light of Mine" became "This Little Girl of Mine," and so on—bringing gospel to the heart and the soul.

Charles's persona was the most convincing aspect of his funky soul style. He was (and *is*) a living celebration of the soulful, moral, spiritual man, with a sassy, funky, *nastay* side. His jazzy improvisations took his style beyond the typical R&B fare, and the enthusiasm he brought to the music made it accessible to anyone, and instantly identifiable to black folks. His impact on funk pioneer Maceo Parker was crucial: "What I think I got from Ray Charles was the soul, the sweetness, the depth and meaning of what it was he was doing, which in a sense to me is soul—the feeling of his style." George Clinton adds that Charles was the original "funky man," and that his first notions of what was funky came from Ray Charles. *"What I Say* probably got to be the most funky record ever made—it had to be the epitome . . . I just didn't know what I was calling it."

Following Charles's lead, Godfather of Soul James Brown expanded the tradition of using the gospel style of music-making to produce engaging, "secular" dance music. The "strained, full-throated use of the voice" was the backbone of any gospel singer's power, and the complex rhythm and melodic arrangements were at the foundation of

Brown's music. Brown admits in his autobiography that he literally learned music from those roots:

> Singing gospel's a good way to learn about music in general. There's a format for gospel; you learn the different parts, and then you start putting them together: first tenor, second tenor, baritone, bass. Instrumental music's put together the same way. That's how I knew the chords before I ever got to the piano. I had sung so much gospel . . . in Augusta that all I had to do was to go to the piano and pick out the chords.

Black church choirs and performances offered an enriching spiritual, unifying environment for young singers and players, as well as hours and hours of practice time. While technique is often important, a gospel singer's strength is his or her sincerity and spirit. The simple transition from "testifyin' " about the Lord to "testifyin' " about love is what gave soul music so much substance. By the mid-1960s a slew of black stars had moved out of their gospel roots and began careers as rhythm and blues, a.k.a. soul singers. This list included Aretha Franklin, Sam Cooke, Al Green, Johnnie Taylor, Joe Tex, the Staple Singers, Donny Hathaway, and Larry Graham.

### ARETHA FRANKLIN

The popularity of soul music swept the nation with the emergence of Motown Records, the power and style of the James Brown Revue, and the stirring breakthrough of Aretha Franklin. With a trumpet of a voice, and a unique ability to "leap two octaves in a single bound," Aretha was the quintessential soul singer. Raised in her father's church, spirited yet disciplined, Aretha had all the gifts a singer could ask for.

Aretha grudgingly entered the soul music business in 1960, and after a few misguided attempts by Columbia Records to mold her into a crooner in the Nat "King" Cole vein, Atlantic Records executive Jerry Wexler took her to Alabama and recorded songs of her choice, letting her loose to perform her own arrangements on piano with the Muscle Shoals session players, and everything changed.

Her first Atlantic album, *I Never Loved a Man* (1967), was a smash hit, producing perhaps the most important soul song of all time: "Respect." While the lyrics implied a song about relationships, it nevertheless carried an emotional backlog that symbolized the yearnings of oppressed peoples everywhere. R-E-S-P-E-C-T blew through the spirits of people young and old yearning to be free. As a metaphor for an entire people's frustrations and dreams, "Respect" was *it.*

Franklin became the "Queen of Soul" almost overnight, for she could deliver a wailing, begging, brooding stew of emotions that seemed to carry more truth, more low-down funkiness, and more strength than the loudest of the shouting *male* singers—Otis Redding, James Brown, and Wilson Pickett. Aretha's music brought with it so much meaning that her very presence on the scene served to elevate all of black popular music. Songs like "(You Make Me Feel Like) A Natural Woman," "Chain of Fools," "Think," and "Respect" were more than just hits; they were *anthems.* Aretha Franklin—as an accomplished musician *and* singer—brought a new era of meaningful music with a groove to America, one that would expand beyond the realm of what was called soul. It would be the *funk* players (beginning with James Brown) that would maintain that meaningful musical function through the 1970s.

The same year of the release of "Respect," 1967, was the year of James Brown's "Cold Sweat," often acknowledged as the closest thing to the first funk groove. " 'Cold Sweat' deeply affected the musicians I knew," Atlantic Records producer Jerry Wexler told Harry Weinger. "It just freaked them out. No one could get a handle on what to do next." Nineteen sixty-seven was also the year of the largest and most violent riots in the country. It was the year of the deaths of Otis Redding and John Coltrane. It seemed like black America had found its musical voice, even if everything else was falling apart. The times they were a changin', and soul music made the best of it. Curtis Mayfield and the Impressions summed up the positive mood of black music with their late 1967 hit "We're a Winner":

> We're a winner
> And everybody knows the truth
> We just keep on pushin'
> Like your leaders tell you to . . .
> At last that blessed day has come
> And I don't care where you came from
> 'Cause we're movin' on up.
>
>    The Impressions, "We're a Winner" (1967)

Black musicians, and soul singers in particular, occupied an exhalted place in the lives of black folks, especially as political leaders began to disappear. Soul music was bringing into focus the essential unity and strength in the black community that had been exercised on the streets in so many marches and demonstrations. Concerts were showcases of style, substance, fashion, and funk. The many crafty and charming singers and dancers reflected and expressed the pride and passion that went along with the exhilarating social changes. The poet Nikki Giovanni elaborated on the special reverence that was held for the "Revolutionary Music":

> you've just got to dig sly
> and the family stone
> damn the words
> you gotta be dancing to the music
> james brown can go to
> viet nam
> or sing about whatever he
> has to
> since he already told
> the honkie
> "although you happy you better try
> to get along
> money won't change you
> but time is taking you on"
>
> While the mighty mighty impressions have told the
> world
> for once and for all
> "We're a Winner"
> even our names—le roi has said—are together
> impressions
> temptations
> supremes
> delfonics
> miracles
> intruders (i mean intruders?)
> not beatles and animals and white bad things like
> young rascals and shit

> we be digging all
> our revolutionary music consciously or un
> cause sam cooke said "a change is gonna come"

Soul music had managed to exemplify the broad unity within black America until 1968, when James Brown released "Say It Loud (I'm Black and I'm Proud)" in September. James initiated a more militant direction for black music, and other forms began to speak to the permanently dispossessed. There were soon "revolutionary poets" coming out of coffeehouses, making records, and appearing across the nation, such as the "Watts Prophets" in Los Angeles, Gil Scott-Heron, and the Last Poets from New York City. Black rock stars such as Jimi Hendrix and Sly Stone also provided new directions for the music fan that left the soul music formula a smaller piece of the black music pie. Even Motown's "sound of young America" had to change and get funky with the times.

## MOTOWN

Berry Gordy's storied Motown empire, built from scratch in a Detroit warehouse and designed to provide the populist entertainment that guaranteed record sales, was a phenomenon of black capitalism and an uplifting symbol of black success in America. By 1968 Gordy's empire boasted a stable of the most successful acts in the country: Martha and the Vandellas, Smokey Robinson and the Miracles, Diana Ross and the Supremes, Jr. Walker & the All Stars, the Temptations, the Four Tops, the Jackson 5 (in the wings), Marvin Gaye, and Little Stevie Wonder. The hit-making writers, aptly dubbed "The Corporation," managed to keep the sound coming from all ends of the label. Time would tell on the organization, however, and despite shrewd business practices, the label would decline, move to Los Angeles, and lose its black ownership. More significant for the purposes of The Funk is the fact that the only acts that survived into the 1970s were artists who were writers themselves, who developed some autonomy from the Motown pop music machinery. With perhaps the one exception of Diana Ross, the superstars Michael Jackson, Stevie Wonder, Marvin Gaye, and Smokey Robinson survived beyond the 1960s Motown era because they could write their own material and keep up with the times.

One in-house writer named Norman Whitfield took some chances with the Motown formula that paid off huge funk dividends for Motown records, particularly with the Temptations. Working his way up from paper pusher to producer at the label, Norman Whitfield injected a rougher edge into Motown's hit machine, an edge that can be heard on the Temptations' "Ain't Too Proud to Beg," "Can't Get Next to You," and clearly on Gladys Knight's rendition of "I Heard It Through the Grapevine." In 1968, as Sly and the Family Stone was scorching the charts, Whitfield completely changed the Temptations' sound and recorded wild, extended songs and topical themes such as "Psychedelic Shack," "Ball of Confusion," and "Cloud Nine." There were rock-style guitars, spacey sound effects, and references to psychedelic drugs. The George Clinton, Sly Stone, and Jimi Hendrix influences were obvious, as was the drug-oriented subject matter. Temptations' lead singer Eddie Kendricks can be heard on "Take a Stroll Through Your Mind" singing "one drag was all it took/and I was hooked." The chorus to the Temptations' No. 2 pop hit "Cloud Nine" went, "I'm doing fine/on cloud nine." Perhaps even more significant was the strident black pride themes, heard on tunes like "Message from a Black Man," and "Slave."

Beginning with the *Cloud Nine* album in 1968, the Temptations took on a decidedly psychedelic look. Gone were the coordinated blazers and matching slacks. Each singer wore his own boots, flared pants, sweaters, leather vests, and widely cut shirts of all colors, with bandannas, fedoras, and scarves worn in the wide-open vein of Jimi Hendrix. The look and sound on *Psychedelic Shack* in 1970 and *Puzzle People* in 1971 continued this theme, and the 1972 *All Directions* album was an appropriate title for an act that managed to experiment radically with sounds and textures while stringing No. 1 hits at a steady rate. Each album release was a strange mix of grooving monster funk and remnants of the sixties Motown format, such as "It's Summer" and "Just My Imagination." Whitfield had a keen eye for pop trends. When "Papa Was a Rolling Stone" surged to the top of the national charts in late 1972, the flowing, moralizing street tale both affirmed and expanded the growing style of grooving soul music with a message: *funky soul.*

The P-Funk influence was heavy on the Temps. The classic Funkadelic chant "wo ha hey" heard at so many P-Funk concerts can be heard at the end of the nine-minute long "Runaway Child, Running Wild" from the *Cloud Nine* LP. Original P-Funkers Eddie Hazel and Billy Nelson performed on the Temptations' 1975 No. 1 R&B hit "Shakey Ground."

Later in the seventies, Whitfield reincarnated the Undisputed

Truth, a vocal trio, into a black rock band complete with silver face-paint and white Afro wigs in the mold of Funkadelic. Many Motown session players regularly attended P-Funk jam sessions. Perhaps the most underrated player in the Motown sound, and responsible for the core of late sixties funk arrangements that can be found there, is Norman Whitfield.

The musicians at Motown were similarly underrated. Many were brilliant innovators in their own right, but were only paid by the session, and almost *never* credited on album liner notes. They were known around town as the "funk brothers," but unlike the JBs, or the Bar-Kays, the Mar-Keys or the MGs at Stax Records in Memphis (backup bands with well-deserved moments in the spotlight), the Motown session band toiled in obscurity for years. Drummers Benny Benjamin and Uriel Jones kept the bottom intact for the entire Motown family, while Robert White's guitar and Earl Van Dykes's keyboards smoothed out the feel, and Jack Ashford's relentlessly loud and tight tambourine playing was perhaps the best-known effect of the Motown instrumental sound.

Bassist James Jamerson was the best-known musician and had perhaps the strongest impact of any single player in the Motown family. His ability to cook a groove, skipping, stopping, and swinging while still hanging tight (listen to Stevie Wonder's "For Once in My Life" or "Uptight"), influenced musicians everywhere, and made it difficult for live acts to replicate his sound. Jamerson recounted some of his methods to Nelson George in 1983:

> My feel was always an Eastern feel. A spiritual thing. Take "Standing in the Shadows of Love." The bass line has an Arabic feel. I've been around a whole lot of people from the East, from China and Japan. Then I studied the African, Cuban, and Indian scales. I brought all that with me to Motown.

Contrary to the myth of Motown as a mechanized music factory, much of Jamerson's bass chops were developed on his own, in that magically inspired method musicians have:

> I picked things up from listening to people speak. From the intonation of their voices, I could capture a line. I look at people walking and get a beat from their movement. . . .

> There was one of them heavy, funky tunes the Temptations
> did. . . . I can't remember the name, but there was this big,
> fat woman walking around. She couldn't keep still. I wrote
> it by watching her move.

One reason (among many) why Motown failed to continue its success through the 1970s was the fact that the core of the studio band remained in Detroit when the label moved to Los Angeles, and their magic
could not be reconstructed. The exits of the Holland-Dozier writers,
the Four Tops, the Isley Brothers, and Gladys Knight within two years
also undoubtedly contributed to the label's downfall. The real changes
hit in 1971, as Stevie Wonder and Marvin Gaye took to their own directions, interpreting the changing times with radically different music
as the seventies unfolded.

### WHAT'S GOIN' ON

Marvin Gaye was a troubled man. One of many frustrated pop crooners on the Motown label, he released dimensions within himself that
his followers are still just beginning to comprehend. The death of his
sparkling duet partner Tammi Terrell in March 1970 devastated him,
along with constant problems with drugs, his father, and Motown
brass. After a period of mourning, depression, and creation, Gaye produced a masterpiece of mood, melody, and bitter reality. This was the
most important work of Gaye's life, and the beginning of a new era for
Motown. Gaye described the genesis of *What's Goin' On* to writer David
Ritz in *Divided Soul*:

> I looked at what was happening at Woodstock and thought
> to myself, Here's a whole generation of people about to
> travel a new path. I understood that musically I'd have to
> go on a path of my own. The Motown corporate attitude
> didn't give me much room to breathe, but I was starting to
> feel strong enough to start down my own path. When my
> brother Frankie came home from Vietnam and began telling
> me stories, my blood started to boil. I knew I had some-
> thing—an anger, an energy, an artistic point of view. It was
> time to stop playing games.

A number of breakthroughs in recording occurred for Marvin as he visualized the record as a musical whole. Inspired by listening to the fluid lines of jazz great Lester Young, the seamless flow of the album made sense to him, and he worked up the courage to do it.

When Gaye delivered the record, Berry Gordy couldn't stand it. He called the title song "the worst record I've ever heard" and refused to release it. Gaye had to threaten to leave the label to defend his album. The publicity department put it out with very little fanfare. The record shot into the Top 10, and was No. 1 soul for five weeks.

Every song on *What's Goin' On* melded together. It was an endlessly elegant, blue mood put to music; there were episodes of bitter melancholy and despair, and few emotional highs. But it was beautiful. The relaxed string ensemble, the wispy drums, and the velvet moans of Marvin Gaye were irresistibly moving. No one had ever recorded music like this before.

The record sleeve featured lengthy liner notes penned by Gaye himself, as well as a "family photo album" collage. Gaye had single-handedly redefined the structure of black popular music from a singles format to an album format, and opened up the parameters of personal exploration and revelation on a popular record. Almost overnight the sound of young America had matured, and reality became more important than fluffy feel-good sounds. *What's Goin' On* opened the door for the graphic realism of The Funk to get on the radio.

Whitfield and others at Motown picked up on the formula, producing "Papa Was a Rolling Stone" for the Temptations and "Smiling Faces" by the Undisputed Truth shortly after Gaye's release. Other artists produced deep, melancholy works that begged for redemption, such as the O'Jays' "Back Stabbers," The Chi-Lites' "For God Sakes (Give More Power to the People)," War's "Slippin' into Darkness," and of course Sly Stone's "There's a Riot Goin' On" (was Sly perhaps answering Marvin's question?). Nelson George described this period, from 1971 to 1975, as "Redemption Songs in the Age of Corporations." It was redemption indeed.

Marvin Gaye, for his part, retreated from social commentary to a series of records exploring his sexual fantasies, and went on to produce some of the era's most erotic mood music. When his "Let's Get It On" broke in 1973, black music as *erotica* rose to a new level. An explicit sexual fantasy if there ever was one, Marvin Gaye rewrote the book on sultry singing. The balls-out begging of the title cut, the serious sex music of "You Sure Love to Ball," and the sincere sentiments of "Distant Lover" moved Marvin's music toward a realm of moods so intimate and personal—yet universal—that the record helped make it cool to be sexual in public. Not lewd, and not necessarily nasty, but open about one's flow of sexual energy. Marvin Gaye had liberated his listeners on a level that transcended his *What's Goin' On* album, which had been considered an insurmountable breakthrough in and of itself. Gaye's hypnotic, erotic grasp on the souls of his listeners can be heard in its fullest effect on the 1973 recording *Marvin Gaye Live,* performed in Oakland, California. The deafening female screams heard on his rendition of "Distant Lover" tell the whole story of perhaps the most *loved* man in the world.

Gaye remained the hottest black male singer in the world late into the 1970s, and after a number of personal problems returned in 1982 with the international hit "Sexual Healing." His career was full of promise once again when he was shot by his father in an argument in 1984. As a performer, as a musician, as a dreamer, as a lover, as a man, Marvin Gaye stood tall, and was a crucial player in the unification of black music.

### SWEET FUNK

On the heels of "Let's Get It On" and other lush yet down-to-earth soul arrangements like Billy Paul's exquisite "Me and Mrs. Jones," and Al Green's funky pop breakthrough "Let's Stay Together" in 1971, a new breed of sultry soul crooners hit the scene. Los Angeles producer Barry White brought his huge frame and deep, low voice to dark bedroom musings that captured the nation's imagination, and scored consecutive pop Top 10 sweet funk sides in 1973 with "I'm Gonna Love You Just a Little More, Baby" and "Never Gonna Give You Up." Using a vast collection of studio musicians he dubbed an orchestra along with a standard R&B rhythm section, White's plush layers and grooving, soulful swinging brought about an incredible synthesis—Western elegance with breathy black sexiness. White had found a new level of black *luxury*—a lifestyle never even *considered* ten years earlier.

A daring brand of psychedelic flavors, smooth, catchy melodies, gritty funk riffs, and dog-nasty sound effects made the airwaves from *soul* groups that weren't afraid to show their colors. The breathless tug of the Moments' magnificent 1973 "Sexy Mama," the Main Ingredient's incessant pleas on "You Can Call Me Rover," the Miracles' delectable "Do It, Baby," Leon Haywood's exquisitely erotic "I Wanna Do Something Freaky to You" (which was the loop for Dr. Dre's breakthrough 1993 single, "Nothin' But a G Thang"), and the New Birth's irreverent packaging and outrageous workout "Gotta Getta Knutt" were all prime examples of sexy soul and serious funk on a collision course.

The sex music scene grew even more explicit, as the veteran singer and music producer Sylvia Robinson scored an even sultrier pop hit with the steamy "Pillow Talk" in 1974. Sylvia's whispery, flirty bedroom banter and teasing rhythms brought a new aural mood to sweet sexy style, and left even less to the imagination. What was left was removed when Major Harris (formerly of the Delphonics) scored a comeback with a classy ballad "Love Won't Let Me Wait," released in 1975. The record stood on its own merits, but an extra-sexy tease was added at the end, as studio singer Barbara Ingram performed an unforgettable simulated orgasm in sync with the breaks of the song. The explicit sex sounds that floated among the most luxurious of melodies made the song a prominent example of sexy sweet funk, as the seemingly separate worlds of "high class" and "down-home sexy ass" were brought together through the channel of The Funk.

### STEVIE WONDER

It was one man, actually, who brought together the entire black American musical tradition for the world to witness in the 1970s. Stevie Wonder (born Steveland Morris in Saginaw, Michigan, on May 13, 1950) had been waiting for his twenty-first birthday, at which point he could write his own contract and therefore produce his own music. He rewrote musical history on his own terms from that point on.

By the late sixties, Stevie was leaning toward a funkier, grooving feel in his music, as heard on "Signed, Sealed, Delivered," "For Once in My Life," and, in 1970, the spacey funk workout "Do Yourself a Favor." He spent most of his time at the storied Electric Ladyland Studios in Greenwich Village—the very studio that Jimi Hendrix worked so hard to build—on the first album of his liberated era. With the help of producers Malcolm Cecil and Robert Margouleff, who owned that fancy new gizmo called a Moog synthesizer, Stevie got busy.

What developed from his initial solo work was the iconoclastic *Music of My Mind*—a psychedelic wandering that despite its brilliant textures had no big hits and did not win him favor with Motown brass.

Stevie's second independently produced LP, *Talking Book,* released in 1972, was a powerful piece of work. It was the type of album one could get stuck with on a desert island and never get tired of. It had biting political commentary with "Big Brother," and dramatic love songs like "You and I" and "I Believe When I Fall in Love It Will Be Forever." It also changed pace and dropped furious funk bombs with "Superstition" and "Maybe Your Baby."

Clearly influenced by Billy Preston's pioneering instrumental keyboard work on the 1972 hit "Outa-Space," Stevie popularized the use of the clavinet keyboard, an instrument with a twang that sounds not unlike a guitar. The clavinet became the staple of funk music, as it often accompanied the bass line, making the bass bottom sound thicker, and often was simply played in a counter rhythm to make the entire ensemble fill with sound. The funk musicians were paying attention.

Unfairly passed over for pop awards for *Talking Book,* Stevie returned in 1973 with perhaps an even more penetrating, more balanced masterwork, *Innervisions.* This record featured the smash hit "Living for the City," a seven-minute musical *monster.*

The song builds in a relentless throb, then fades into the dialogue of a black man who steps off a bus in New York City and within thirty seconds lands in jail. The song picks up again and Stevie is hoarse at the final verse, as if the song itself represented one man's disintegration at the hands of the urban blight.

"Living for the City" is one of the most sampled songs in the rap world, with the particularly jarring prison-door slamming interlude ("C'mon, get in that cell, Nigger") appearing prominently on Public Enemy's unforgettable 1988 recording "Black Steel in the Hour of Chaos." Filmmaker Spike Lee played the entire seven-minute song as the backdrop to a visit to a crack house in his controversial 1991 film *Jungle Fever.*

Stevie Wonder's music is referred to as soul music, but the bitter truths told in "Living for the City," along with the driving, throbbing melodic riff and the daring, complex orchestration, are all elements of funk, and this record definitely would not have happened without James Brown's rhythmic foundation.

What was also significant about the *Innervisions* album is that it complemented its bittersweet moods with sly social critiques like "He's Misstra Know It All" and "Too High," and grooved with joyous vamps like "Don't You Worry 'Bout a Thing" and "Golden Lady." The thematic balance of the record created a standard for others to reach for, although few could. The album was awarded the country's highest pop music award, a Grammy as Album of the Year for 1973, as were his next *two* albums.

These four albums taken together—*Talking Book* (1972), *Innervisions* (1973), *Fulfillingness' First Finale* (1974) and *Songs in the Key of Life* (1976)—remain the high points of Stevie's career, particularly in terms of the Funk Age. His records cover the United Funk Age with a glorious glossy coat of soul, and also stand out as standards of excellence and balance in terms of range of style, musical technique, lyrical genius, and total *jam* factor. His funk sessions were and are spectacles to behold, and each album delivered the goods: "Superstition," "Maybe Your Baby," "Living for the City," "Higher Ground," "You Haven't Done Nothin'," "Black Man," "All Day Sucker," "I Wish," "Have a Talk with God," "Ordinary Pain," and more. If one uses Howard Harris's definition of funk as "togetherness in motion," Stevie brought together the entire black music legacy and served up plate after plate of exquisite soul-food gumbo, and made diverse, digestible music that funk bands far and wide aspired to.

With Stevie leading the way, soul music was bringing it all together, from masculine leads to tender feminine charms, from esoteric imagery to straight-up truth-telling. Many soul acts tried to diversify their sound in the 1970s, producing a style that I call "funky soul." The poignant, delicate voice and bold social commentary of Curtis Mayfield (see Chapter twelve) perhaps paved the way for others (while upholding the independent-minded legacy of the great Sam Cooke, Mayfield's Chicago soul mentor). There were other smooth crooners that dabbled in social commentary, like the Stylistics with "People Make the World Go Round" in 1972, the Chi-Lites with "Give More Power to the People" in 1971, Bloodstone with "This World Is Funky," and the Main Ingredient with "Shame on the World" in 1975. There was also a major contingent of strong, sincere gospel veterans who produced wholesome and not-so-wholesome message music that paid tribute to the rhythmic foundations of James Brown, and came with The Funk. These could be heard on the Staple Singers' "I'll Take You There" (1972), Al Green's "Love and Happiness" (1976), Donny Hathaway's "The Ghetto" (1970), and, of course, Aretha Franklin's "Rock Steady" (1972). (The Memphis Sound of soul music was also a key element in the evolution of funk, and is discussed in Chapters six and ten.)

### THE PHILLY SOUND

But for seventies soul strength, the Philadelphia International empire, led by Kenny Gamble and Leon Huff, were the leaders of the pack. Hooked up with and distributed by CBS Records, the Philly Sound boasted a lineup that included the O'Jays, the Intruders, Billy Paul, and Harold Melvin & the Blue Notes featuring Theodore Pendergrass, as well as the house band, MFSB (Mother, Father, Sister, Brother). Every one of these acts scored huge national hits and brought a down-home vocal style into Gamble and Huff's candy-coated string ensemble arrangements.

While the producers developed their own polished reputation as writers, the session band continued to lock tight at Sigma Sound Studios in Philadelphia, forming the foundation of the Philly hit machine. Driven by guitarists Norman Harris and Bobby Eli, with Ronnie Baker on bass and Earl Young on drums, MFSB became the most successful studio band of the seventies. Aside from their No. 1 soul hit "TSOP (The Sound of Philadelphia)" (a record picked by Don Cornelius at the recording session to be the theme for *Soul Train*), MFSB backed the Philly stable on an endless string of major hits and deceptively funky jams, particularly those made for the O'Jays.

### THE O'JAYS

Eddie Levert, Walter Williams, and William Powell (Powell was later replaced by Sammy Strain in 1977) made up a vocal group with gospel roots from Cleveland, Ohio, and named after the famed deejay Eddie O'Jay. The trio followed Gamble and Huff to Philadelphia and made a name for themselves in 1972 with "Back Stabbers," a sober, chilling single, and part of a brilliant album—one of a group of soul albums that was exploratory, diverse, visionary, and yet still accessible. With catchy hooks that everyone could identify with, "Back Stabbers" was the start of something big for the O'Jays.

The morally strong, socially conscious formula was expanded even further with *Ship Ahoy* in 1974. This album featured a ten-minute musical orchestration of life on a *slave ship,* articulating a powerful drama that every black American possesses in their historical memory. The two singles from the album were gospel-style preachings, but one had a decidedly different feel to it: "Put Your Hands Together" had a strong gospel feel, but was fairly standard musically; but "For the Love of Money" was another story. The thumping, elegantly mixed heavy bump funk bass line introduces the song, as the misty vocals flow in "money, money, money, money, MONEY!" It had become clear from "For the Love of Money" that the O'Jays were producer Kenny Gamble's primary outlet for his social commentary, and he was serious about it. (By a sad coincidence, the record scored such huge pop dividends that it became a caricature of its original purpose, reducing a grim expression of the realities of life to a joke record for mall music soundtracks.) The O'Jays followed up with the potent *Survival* album in 1975, then delivered an exhilarating anthem of unity, *Family Reunion,* followed with the uneven yet optimistic *Message in the Music* LP.

The O'Jays were a magnificent singing group that could handle the hottest funk tracks while blending smooth harmonies and tender ballads with social statements. But like most of the soul singers, after 1976 there was no longer a message in the music, and unlike Aretha Franklin's symbolic "Respect," there was no longer any mandate from black America to be made by middle-class–oriented soul artists. The message in soul music all but disappeared.

With the success of disco singers such as Gloria Gaynor and Donna Summer it was becoming difficult to make distinctions between the slicker sound of disco, the street sound of The Funk, and the once familiar sentimental sound of soul. The Four Tops' "Catfish," Harold Melvin and the Blue Notes' "Bad Luck" and "The Love I Lost," and the Spinners' "Mighty Love" were all brilliant, upbeat gospel/soul grooves that thematically fit all too easily into the disco formula.

One clear distinction between the sound of a strong soul singer and that of a funk band was the strength of the band driving the songs. A good example of this is Chaka Khan's solo work in the late seventies (standard soul singing), compared to her work with Rufus, a jam-packed band in which she collaborated, cowrote, and covered her fullest range playing The Funk. A similar thing happened with Lionel Richie. The superstar pop balladeer of the 1980s performed a greater range of styles as lead singer of the Commodores in the 1970s, including dirty swamp-dog funk. This is why there is very little conflict between the notions of funk and soul. Funk is essentially hard-core soul music, with the band in soulful, full effect along with the singers. The high standards of sixties soul had elevated The Funk into a complete genre of music—United Funk—with soul vocals and funk grooves. With the intrusion of artificial means of music making, the soul singer without a strong band inevitably wound up playing disco.

Ultimately, the 1970s witnessed the demise of the soul singer as the authentic voice of black America, and to the degree that there was a music that reflected the values and ideals of a Black Nation in the later 1970s, it was the united sound and spirit of The Funk that carried the flame of a people's passions.

# ELEVEN

# Jazz-Funk Fusion: The Chameleon

"Jazz is the teacher, Funk is the preacher."

*James "Blood" Ulmer*

## JAZZ AND FUNK

The original association of *funk* and *soul* with music came from black hard bop players of the 1950s. The terms were used in a deliberate effort to define the music and style as raw, earthy, and *non-white* (see Chapter three). While they faded away as names for jazz by the early 1960s, the terms *soul* and the *soul brother* made their way directly into the dialect of hip blacks and into the black popular music of the mid-1960s. Meanwhile, getting *funky* was not in style again until the late 1960s (after the Black Power Movement had made all things black *beautiful*). Funky music, through the works of James Brown, then took hold as a low-down, earthy, rhythmic, and percussive way to jam dance music.

While dance music was often considered "selling out" by chauvinistic jazz players, many black jazzmen interested in making money *and* exploring black consciousness through their music were drawn toward The Funk by the late 1960s. The gravitational force of the funk grooves spawned new forms of jazz-fusion music, a vast danceable jazz-funk movement, and has propagated into the 1990s as a coherent subculture of jazz chops, funk grooves, and Hip Hop raps.

The black nationalist impulse in sixties jazz had been growing in size and scope to the point where modern jazz artists were creating multimedia expressions of their ancient *tribal* identities. For example, The Art Ensemble of Chicago was a collective of artists that filled up the stage with everything from traditional jazz instruments to banjos, bike horns, gongs, and whistles, with players dressed in grass skirts, African ceremonial face paint, and worker's hard hats. The appearance and sound of the group gave an implication of chaos to the outsider, but it was actually an expression of a postmodern tribal consciousness that was infecting the jazz (and later funk) of the era.

The phenomenal jazz wizard Sun Ra created the original space-traveler imagery through his broad-ranging works spanning forty years. His indulgence in numerology, Egyptology, astrology, a variety of cosmic insights, and his unique mode of language preceded the electronic age of jazz-fusion by decades and introduced an intergalactic orientation to improvisational music. As Sun Ra put it, "I paint pictures of infinity with my music, and that's why a lot of people can't understand it." Sun Ra's visionary approach to music (not to mention his approach to existence) was picked up by Miles Davis in the seventies and, most important, was elaborated on by George Clinton's intergalactic funk movement.

Saxophonist and bandleader Ornette Coleman, inventor of the uniquely layered melodic texture he calls "harmolodics," was a controversial figure in jazz when he came to prominence in the late 1950s. Coleman's efforts increased the rumblings about this "new thing" jazz music that had dispensed of melodic lines and, as Miles Davis put it, "wasn't lyrical, and you couldn't hum it." Jazz was heading in all directions by the mid-1960s. The critics' trepidation turned to all-out confusion when the Miles Davis Quintet, featuring the young, spunky keyboardist Herbie Hancock, began to go electric.

At the same time came the infancy of pop-jazz fusion, which sought to incorporate the strengths of the traditional R&B and gospel styles (a.k.a. soul music) into an accessible form of jazz—or at least instrumental music, depending on one's definition. Ramsey Lewis provided the key breakthrough with his 1965 pop instrumental hit "The In Crowd." With a rolling, easy-to-swing rhythm and loud, prominent use of the electric piano as a melodic device, a totally new pop sound was born. In the introduction to Julie Coryell's *Jazz-Rock Fusion,* Lewis described the circumstances of his work:

> Without knowing it, we combined into an approach some of the music we had always been exposed to: black church music (chantlike figures), rhythm and blues (melodic repetitive rhythms), and jazz. Because of my classical training, in some arrangements we also showed the influence of European harmonies, musical devices, and theories. From musicians, and critics alike, there were shouts of foul play. At the time they said it was sacrilegious to involve any other kinds of music, especially R&B, with jazz.

The Ramsey Lewis trio spawned and inspired a number of "accessible" jazz groups, not the least of which were the Young-Holt Unlimited (comprised of his two former band members El Dee Young and Red Holt), who scored a huge pop instrumental hit "Soulful Strut" in 1968, and his subsequent drummer, Maurice White, who went on to produce one of the most popular bands in the world—Earth, Wind & Fire.

Another notable R&B-styled pop instrumental hit black radio in late 1966; it was Julian "Cannonball" Adderley's recording of "Mercy, Mercy, Mercy," a slowly swinging, soulful instrumental that featured heavy use of the electric piano, the Fender Rhodes (a brand name that became the only name for this type of electric piano). Adderley and his band frequented the New Orleans "funk" scene, keying in on the counterrhythms that were soulfully maintained by the local R&B players there. The keyboard was played by the Austrian-born Joe Zawinul, who went on to important work with Miles Davis and fame and fortune as the leader of the fusion band Weather Report.

Also spanning the realm of jazz styles was trumpeter Donald Byrd, himself a veteran of Art Blakey's Jazz Messengers in the 1950s. Byrd's bold experiments with a variety of black rhythms (Caribbean, African, rhythm and blues, funk) on his many late sixties and early seventies solo albums for Blue Note Records helped to draw a strong focus on the possibilities of rhythmic jazz fusion, with a jazz sensibility on top, and a tight, funky groove below. Important Byrd breakthroughs included *A New Perspective* in 1963 and the million-selling funky groove classic *Blackbyrd* in 1973.

The most successful and popular act that incorporated the energy of The Funk with the technical mastery of jazz was the Bay Area phenomenon known as Tower of Power. An almost absurd collection of performers conspired to bring the Tower of Power sound: Brilliant rhythm players—led by Francis Prestia's percussive bass, David Garibaldi's stuttering drums, Bruce Conte's bluesy guitar licks, and Chester Thompson's soulful genius at the organ—held down a spastic groove that would swing in the truest big band tradition, underneath a monster five-piece horn section of long-haired "hippies": Emilio Castillo, Lenny Pickett, Greg Adams, Mic Gillete, and the "Funky Doctor" Steve Kupka. Their fantastically complex yet grooving funk hits and ballads were all tied together by a succession of soulful black lead singers, from Rufus Miller to Lenny White and Hubert Tubbs. While their horn-heavy ballads got the band onto pop radio in the early seventies, their instrumental funk scorchers "What Is Hip?" "Knock Your-self Out," "Back on the Streets Again," "Squib Cakes," and "Soul Vac-cination" put them on the short list of swinging jazz-funk masters.

### MILES DAVIS

While pop-jazz swingers were toying with funky dance rhythms de-signed for radio airplay, Miles Davis was taking the same influences so far out of orbit that they obliterated the existing definitions of jazz. His late sixties recordings explored new rhythms, longer, extended en-semble improvisations, over-the-top electric guitars and synthesizers, and a variety of percussion effects. He often played in rock venues with a murky, brooding persona that was difficult to identify with. What most of his critics missed at the time was the fact that Miles Davis was inspired by the rhythms of the street, and James Brown in particular. Davis discussed the music he was listening to in 1967 in his autobiog-raphy:

> I was beginning to listen to a lot of James Brown, and I liked the way he used the guitar in his music. I always liked the blues and always loved to play it, so around this time I was listening to Muddy Waters and B. B. King and trying to find a way to get that kind of voicing into my music . . . see when I used to listen to Muddy Waters in Chicago down on 33rd and Michigan every Monday when he played there and I would be in town, I knew I had to get some of what he was doing up in my music. You know, the sound of the $1.50 drums and the harmonicas and the two-chord blues. I had to get back to that now because what we had been doing was just getting really abstracted.

But Miles Davis had more in mind than simply imitating James Brown rhythm arrangements. His music would find a groove, invert it, subvert it, splatter it, and simply flow on, with endless solos and only rare bridges or changes of pace. His live performances became hour-long nonstop flowing journeys through musical moods, often driven into rough, funky terrain by electric bass, guitars, or keyboards.

In August 1969 (the same weekend that his friend Jimi Hendrix was headlining Woodstock), Davis brought together more than a dozen musicians to record his electronic opus work, *Bitches Brew* (released in

1970). While his extended recording format had been in use for a few years, this record was different. It had the understated reserve of his rhythmically groundbreaking *In a Silent Way* (1969), but had the power of his monstrous rock sound of *Tribute to Jack Johnson* (1971). The visual clarity brought about from the dissonant sound was like a step into a jungle—an urban jungle, teeming with mangled life-forms. Greg Tate summed up the dilemma, the disrespect, and the genius of Electric Miles in a 1983 essay: "The trick about this music is that its textures rather than musicianship make it sound like garbage, like maggot- brained cosmic slop, or if you will, like cosmic debris. . . . Because of this, to truly love the music you have to want in on this filthy mess as a way of life."

Miles continued to take a path little traveled in his music, and took up a relationship with Jimi Hendrix a year before he died. The two discussed music and planned to record together, which would have certainly caused marketing problems for the corporate bigwigs ("Is this jazz or rock?"), but Hendrix died before they could set up a session and play together. Davis nevertheless managed to introduce the jazz-rock fusion style, and jump-start the careers of later fusion stars Chick Corea, Lenny White, Joe Zawinul, Billy Cobham, John McLaughlin, and many others, including his quintet band members Herbie Hancock, saxophonist Wayne Shorter, and the exhilarating drummer Tony Williams.

Davis recorded and performed until 1975, creating music that portrayed a torrid underworld of lush, melodic, disarming riffs, dangerous, sexy moods, and scarred sensibilities. His most remarkable set was a recording in Osaka, Japan, in February 1975—his last performance for six years—which was packaged into two double albums, *Agharta* and *Pangea*. He showcased the fractured genius of Pete Cosey to play the soaring guitars and ghoulish synthesizers, the young Michael Henderson on bass, Al Foster's throbbing drums, Sonny Fortune's saxophones, Reggie Lucas's guitar grooving, and Mtume Heath's percussion. The entire ensemble developed layers of percussion, layers of rhythms, each instrument slithering along on different time signatures, yet collectively seeping together. It was vicious. Yet the sounds were too contemporary for the older set, too complex, perhaps, for the young, and truly demanded that the listener understand James, Sly, Jimi, and Funkadelic to fully partake. His music never caught on with the "kids" as he sorely wanted, but when listened to today the session makes perfect, exquisite sense.

Many of Miles's veterans outlived the fusion era to score their own radio hits playing The Funk. Bassist Michael Henderson scored a wicked Top 5 R&B funky dance hit "Wide Receiver" in 1980, and an under-rated follow-up "Slingshot" the next year. Drummer Lenny White scored one of the year's hottest funk hits in 1979 with "Peanut Butter," and percussionist Mtume Heath scored a No. 1 funky soul hit "Juicy Fruit" in 1983. Mtume led one of the few funk-oriented R&B groups to score any success in the mid-1980s.

In 1980 Miles returned to recording and performing with clearer R&B based jazz-funk. Many sides of his eighties work were exciting, such as "You're Under Arrest" (1983) and "Fat Time" (1980), but too much of it drew on formula rhythms and did not have the propulsive quality of his mid-seventies jam sessions. In 1990 the rap group Digital Underground sampled his 1980 tune "Fat Time" and arranged it as a tribute to Miles (as well as themselves) called "Nuttin' this Funky." Before his death in 1992 Miles was working on tracks with straight Hip Hop rhythms, and the posthumous *Doo-Bop* set was his best-received in years. It helped to generate the Hip Hop/jazz phenomenon of the early 1990s, as soloists took on the rhythmic underpinnings of Hip Hop beats to produce yet another fusion.

If it seems ironic that a giant of jazz would wind up playing delib-erate Hip Hop beats, take a look at the funk concept itself and it will all make sense as an evolutionary process. The plethora of new-style jazz-rap groups such as Digable Planets, US3, Guru, and the Phar-Cyde are only now beginning to decode the impulse that connects the blues, jazz, The Funk, and Hip Hop—the impulse Miles Davis had all along.

### HERBIE HANCOCK

Perhaps the missing link in the jazz-funk continuum is Herbert Jeffrey (Mwandishi) Hancock. Hancock had been dabbling in electronics since his early days in the Miles Davis Quintet and by 1968 was ready to move on to his own things. Recording *Crossings* for David Rubinson in San Francisco, he was introduced to Pat Gleeson, who showed Herbie his first synthesizer. After that recording, he went to Los Angeles and sought out musicians who could produce the electronic funk sounds he wanted. He described what caused the change in his music:

> I listened to James Brown and Sly and said, "Look, I want
> to find out what this is, and I'm going to go as far as I can."

That's why I got some cats who can play funk, and it's really funny. I knew that I had never really heard any jazz players really play funk like the funk that I had been listening to. Instead of getting jazz cats who could play funk, I got funk cats who knew how to play jazz.

The "cats" Herbie got became the Headhunters, a band that claimed the jazz-funk turf for their own. Oakland-born Paul Jackson played the bass guitar—the *Thumpasaurus* bass guitar—and remained with Herbie throughout his funk sessions. Percussionist Bill Summers, one of many formally educated musicians in the seventies jazz fusion scene, was a student of African percussion instruments and layered an exotic, "native" feel to Herbie's stellar synthesizers. Bennie Maupin was also a veteran of Miles Davis's *Bitches Brew* set and brought his peculiar bass clarinet sound, and even more peculiar phrasings. Harvey Mason began as drummer, but was replaced by Oakland native Mike Clark on the *Thrust* LP. The group later added black psychedelic guitarist Dewayne "Blackbird" McKnight, a gifted improvisor whose guitar, according to one critic, "can become a sarod, synthesizer, melotron, and laser all at once." Blackbird later went on to join George Clinton's Parliament/Funkadelic thang in 1977.

The *Headhunters* set changed the face of jazz. The first song, "Chameleon," was the breakthrough. It featured a thumping, walking synthesized bass line that was sequenced, automatically repeating throughout the song. The fifteen-minute set begins with the synthetic bass, then the drums and bass guitar fall in and improvise around the sequenced thump track, followed by James Brown–style horn lines (thickened and accompanied by Herbie's keyboard), until a bridge briefly brings the band together. After the second bridge, Herbie begins a four-minute scissor-sharp synthesizer solo that screams, nibbles, giggles, and soars on a journey that for many was the beginning of a new musical age. By the end of the solo, the band comes crashing down, the synth-bass is gone, the timing is changed, the bass flows like a Miles Davis improv session, and the "Chameleon" has changed colors. After a five-minute free-form jam, the rhythm returns to the synth track, Bennie Maupin solos on top of it, and the record fades.

The second song on *Headhunters*, "Watermelon Man," is a cover of an earlier Hancock composition originally performed in 1963, using only the electric piano and a traditional jazz set. The new version, however, begins with Bill Summers playing a syncopated, shrill, very African-sounding flute known as a hindewhu that was played by the Ba-Benzele pygmies (the names of most African instruments sound like the noises they make; *hindewhu* is the noise a hindewhu makes, a bongo drum makes a *bongo* sound, and so on). A slow, bluesy jam fades in over the flutes, using Herbie's clavinet to imitate a guitar sound, with Maupin's melancholy brass on top. The hindewhu provides the outro to the song. Side two features a tribute to Sly Stone titled "Sly," which is a whimsical musical interpretation of the workings of Sly's mind.

The *Headhunters* album, released in late 1973, soared to No. 1 on the jazz charts, and a 45rpm single of "Chameleon" was released. The record remained at No. 1 on the jazz charts for fifteen weeks, over three months, and outsold all of Herbie's previous records combined. Herbie was *it*. Youngsters across the country who were learning acoustic jazz were now hungry for a Fender Rhodes piano, or a clavinet. R&B musicians took a second look at their instruments and spent more time with sound effects and coherent solos. The synthesizer became a staple of black dance music. Overall, the *Headhunters* album, while it was lighter compared to much of bop jazz, was the closest thing to a jazz record that maintained a street-level identification with an African aesthetic, as John Coltrane had done symbolically years earlier. Jazz purists both white and black were shocked and dismayed again, but damn if Herbie didn't give up The Funk.

Hancock never stopped playing "traditional" jazz, and played either style when he felt like it. He recorded a series of masterful, funky, electronic instrumental albums that remain part of The Funk hierarchy and are perhaps even more accessible today in this age of electronics and digital funk-rap beats. He was ahead of his time with *Headhunters*, *Thrust* (1974), *Man-Child* (1975), and *Secrets* (1976)—all available on CD. ("Chameleon" became break-beat favorite of deejays and was reissued on a twelve-inch single in 1984, and his 1975 recording of "Hang Up Your Hang Ups" became the central loop for N.W.A.'s popular 1992 rap "100 Miles and Runnin'.") Herbie also coproduced two solo projects for his band the Headhunters, the first of which contained the much-sampled funk jam "God Made Me Funky." Herbie explained the appeal of his funk in 1977:

The funk band—now that music has such strong roots in the Earth. With all the earthiness there's room for flight. The biggest reason I enjoy playing this new kind of funk is the contrast between the wide open improvisation and the funky foundation at the bottom. It gives the music a character that is broad, vast, yet in touch with the people.

## JAZZ-FUNK FUSION

On the strength of *Headhunters,* 1974 was the year that jazz-funk took over. The soft-jazz southern instrumental group the Crusaders produced their funk opus in late 1974, a two-record set entitled *Southern Comfort* on ABC Records that featured the single "Stomp and Buck Dance," a well-orchestrated musical movement that somehow maintained its gutbucket funkiness at the same time. Their strong follow-up album, *Chain Reaction,* is also worth seeking out. The fluidly locked quintet had a magical level of communication, groove, and individual talent working as one. Pianist Joe Sample, guitarist Larry Carlton, drummer "Stix" Hooper, sax players Wilton Felder and Wayne Henderson all established themselves as players, producers, and solo artists. As a backup band in the mid-seventies, the influential Crusaders scored classic funky sides for the angelic vocalist Minnie Riperton ("Inside My Love," "Adventures in Paradise"), and Michael Franks' memorable flirtatious hits "Eggplant" and "Popsicle Toes." Henderson's production credits include the workhorse Portland-based soul-jazz octet known as Pleasure, whose grooving 1977 hit "Joyus" put them on the map, and follow-up funk blowout "Glide" is a funk classic.

Donald Byrd, who had also been experimenting with R&B rhythms on his instrumental tracks, produced the first record by a group of his protégés from Howard University he called the Blackbyrds. Out of the blue, the thumping, slippery lock of "Do It, Fluid" established the Blackbyrds as a No. 1 funk act, and they followed with monster jams "Happy Music," "Rock Creek Park," and "Unfinished Business." Their first four LPs were refreshingly clean expressions of mature R&B and funk rhythms, with tight, meaningful solos and catchy hooks.

A number of jazz-trained recording artists dropped hard, radio-friendly funk tracks in 1975 and '76. Saxophonist Ronnie Laws began his solo career with the piercing "Always There"; the Brecker Brothers delivered a wicked funk-fusion debut album and single "Sneakin' Up Behind You"; Donald Byrd kicked heavy hump with "Change (Makes You Wanna Hustle)"; and Ramsey Lewis delivered the scorching "Spiderman."

Classy jazz players from Quincy Jones to Roy Ayers got into the funk groove. Jones's theme songs to the television shows "Sanford and Son," "Ironside," and the first Cosby Show were featured on a series of otherwise smoothed-out albums in the early seventies. Jones's 1976 *Mellow Madness* LP was his stankiest effort, a record that featured the debut of the Brothers Johnson plucking away on "Tryin' to Find Out 'Bout You" and "Just a Little Taste of Me." Vibrophonist Roy Ayers and his band Ubiquity captured the best in soul-jazz flavors for years, and reached their peak with the classic "Everybody Loves the Sunshine" in 1976, and followed with nastay funk chops "Running Away" and "Freaky Deaky."

There was actually a burgeoning trend of easy-listening jazz that acquired a measure of funky rhythms and interesting improvisation during the early 1970s—a style sometimes called acid jazz. A hugely popular sound today, marked by its funky bottom and jazzy top, it's an organic synthesis of the often segregated values of jazz and funk. The works of Roy Ayers, Funk Inc., the JBs, and the MGs were some of the most potent in the genre.

Philadelphia-bred saxophonist Grover Washington, Jr., was the one to take jazz-funk to the next step with his 1975 release of "Mr. Magic," a long, slow, bluesy, sexy syncopated Latin-flavored jazz riff that he licked and fondled with his saxophone. There was enough blues in the guitar work of Eric Gale to make the record a soulful standout, and Grover's ability to improvise over funk tracks is phenomenal, but the potential for imitation was dangerous: While Grover and his fluid Philadelphia-bred backup band Locksmith maintained their musical integrity throughout the decade, many jazz musicians disposed of pretense and made juvenile dance records that astonished even the most sympathetic fans. Lonnie Liston Smith, Idris Muhammad, Donald Byrd, Patrice Rushen, and even Herbie Hancock later made some simplistic music that they passed off as dance music, and it made them look foolish. The most consternating aspect of this disco-jazz phenomenon was that most of the artists made brilliant music on the same albums that featured the monorhythmic nonsense designed for disco clubs. Listeners were forced to hold their noses while scanning the latest releases by their favorite late seventies jazz-fusion artists.

By 1977 the jazz-funk field had thinned out, as a new flavor of over-the-top pop jazz was going strong, led by the likes of George Benson and Chuck Mangione. Among the true funk players still kicking were Herbie Hancock on his constant technological adventures; George Duke, whose San Francisco Bay Area roots and stint with Frank Zappa's Mothers of Invention gave him an irreverent style suited to late 1970s funk (his funk classics "Reach for It" and "Dukey Stick" are all-time monsters); Stanley Clarke, a phenomenally gifted jazz bass performer from Philadelphia who dabbled in funk grooves and made memorable entrees into the style, with his rapid-fire plucking and adventurous riffs embellishing such funk splatters as "Silly Putty," "We Supply," and "Hot Fun"; and Grover, who kept a tight, soulful, jazzy, funky band well into the 1980s and gave accessible jazz-funk its strongest proponent (his live concerts are still well worth checking out).

### THE 1980S AND BEYOND

While Grover Washington was grooving and Herbie Hancock was getting electronic in the late seventies, another wild brand of jazz-funk was developing in underground clubs in New York and other East Coast cities. There were plenty of frustrated jazz, rock, and soul musicians who were out of work as a result of new recording techniques, fewer live shows, and the demographics of discotheques replacing music clubs. New York was thriving with hungry, funky jazz-trained musicians who took the subway to gigs and played for what they could get. This culture gave rise to an intense, spastic, yet danceable type of jazz played by bands like Defunkt, Kelvynator, the Decoding Society, and Prime Time. The 1980s musical resurgence of Miles Davis also had a hand in flavoring this music.

By the late 1970s Ornette Coleman had begun to explore electronics, incorporating the talents of guitarist James "Blood" Ulmer, drummer Ronald Shannon Jackson, and scatological bass playing of Jamaldeen Tacuma in a group known as Ornette Coleman and Prime Time. Coleman's work spawned a school of irreverent and funky jazz stylings that writer Jason Chervokas describes as "Harmolodic Funk." Drummer Jackson went on to spawn the Decoding Society, which brought guitarist Vernon Reid to prominence in the 1980s. Jamaldeen Tacuma, Coleman's bassist, also ventured into his own solo work, as did the guitarist James "Blood" Ulmer, who defied categorization with the rabid riffs on his 1982 album titled *Black Rock* and his 1981 Columbia LP *Are You Glad to Be in America,* which featured the prophetic jam "Jazz Is the Teacher (Funk Is the Preacher)." Greg Tate described Ulmer in a way that was typical of the scene:

> Sure, Blood is pimping the funk, but like Miles [Davis] he's
> pimping it on his own terms. . . . Blood doesn't play sen-
> suous, explosive space-blues lines like Hendrix . . . or warp
> speed sheets of exotic scales like [John] McLaughlin. What
> he does play is shrill, disjointed fragments, nervous bits and
> rickety pieces tied together by a staggered but wryly swing-
> ing thematic sensibility. No flash-in-the-pan runs or simu-
> lated heavy-metal orgasms here. . . . Essentially, Blood's
> lead lines are almost identical; his rhythm chops are what
> kick in the accelerator.

The effort to reclaim black music from the doldrums of electronics
and rhythmic sameness leaned heavily on the funk impulse, primarily
enforced by George Clinton and his gang, and later on because of the
likes of Ulmer, Defunkt, Kelvynator, and the others.

### WHITHER JAZZ?

Jazz became a useless term for defining a coherent musical trend by the
1980s. Music with clearly pop appeal—from Angela Bofill, Hiroshima,
George Howard, and others—made the term pointless, while crossover
jazz artists George Benson, Grover Washington, Jr., Herbie Hancock, and
Miles Davis each returned to *roots* jazz styles at least once during the
1980s, rendering descriptions of their contemporary jazz styles moot.

The most successful fusion band of the decade, Weather Report,
resigned themselves to a profound sense of destiny with their 1984
album *Domino Theory,* which contained the brilliant melody "Can It Be
Done?," a maudlin lament about the end of a musical era. Weather Report, led by keyboardist Joe Zawinul and bassist Jaco Pastorious, had
spent over a decade redefining the expectations of what could be done
with jazz. But as the eighties dragged on, the spirited musical interplay
that spawned the many varieties of jazz was waning. The variety of
styles, from funky instrumental "rare grooves," to rugged jazz-rock fusion, the candy-coated "Quiet Storm" formula, the stalwarts of the dissonant "new thing" such as Pharoah Sanders and Sun Ra, and acoustic
traditionalists such as Wynton Marsalis and the ageless Dizzy Gillespie,
all called their music jazz, and left the notion of jazz without a core.
When pop superstar Prince intimated that "it's time for jazz to die" in
1983, he touched the pulse of the musical community far and wide. To
the extent that Prince was referring to be-bop, it was becoming clear

that what originated as a medium of protest and dramatic statement of musical sophistication had become removed from much of its essential purpose. Hip Hop activist Harry Allen explained the problem in 1987:

> While many hail the rebirth of so-called jazz, it appears at this late date that so-called jazz is dead, or perhaps somnambulistic, in socio-functional terms. An art form which is enshrined and worshipped by the former targets of its barbs . . . cannot be the mode of present-day black self-determinist sentiment. A music whose politics easily cater to the status quo cannot be the vehicle of Black progressive thought, either literally or symbolically.

Despite the much-publicized efforts of Wynton Marsalis to present jazz as America's "classical" music, and despite his efforts to chastise jazz musicians (including his brother Branford) who strayed from the "standard" forms, jazz music continued to go in all directions in the 1980s. How can jazz be defined? There is really no way. The function of jazz has changed over the years, leaving some to claim that it is one thing, and some to claim that it's another. The be-bop giant Dizzy Gillespie made one thing plain in his autobiography: "Jazz was invented for people to dance. So when you play jazz and people don't feel like dancing or moving the feet, you're getting away from the idea of music. . . . You want to dance when you listen to our music because it transmits that feeling of rhythm."

Yet other music giants, particularly those of the more recent generations, have had a difficult time preserving the lessons of the classic jazz sounds and have made steadfast statements denouncing electronic jazz or dance music with jazzy roots to it. "For musicians of our generation . . ." Wynton Marsalis told *Goldmine* in 1991, "for us, we grew up, we didn't play blues and all that kind of stuff. We played funk and pop music. There's a long distance between that and playing jazz. I mean *long*. And it takes a very conscientious desire to study and constantly work to learn how to swing." While Marsalis's support of classical jazz forms is admirable, there are those who discuss jazz not in terms of technique, but *attitude*. Harry Allen, the designated "Media Assassin" for the rap group Public Enemy, has maintained that "Hip Hop is the new jazz."

If this seems like a reach, funk can help explain it. In terms of the black dispossessed, Allen is expressing the continuity of black "self-determinist sentiment" that expands over four decades. The only missing link is the funk era. Bop jazz was the locus of black nationalist expression in music for many, including Malcolm X, until the mid-1960s. It was funk music—originally called soul music—that maintained the "self-determinist sentiment" through the 1970s until the growth of Hip Hop culture in the 1980s. Miles Davis understood this and changed his music accordingly. His break with "traditional" jazz was a move toward funk, toward the people. His last recordings were strictly Hip Hop, strictly for the people. Herbie Hancock made precisely the same moves, with greater commercial success. If you listen carefully, you can find that the musicians in James Brown's bands were playing jazz with a streetwise raw-rhythm attitude. That's funk.

# PART FOUR

# The United Funk Dynasty (1972–76): The Shining Star

# TWELVE

# Power to the People: It's Just Begun

> "You need power to get freedom,
> and you need freedom to create."
>
> *James Brown*

### FUNKY POWER

Perhaps the most important legacy of The Funk can be found in the assertive expressions of realism and race pride that thrived in the early seventies funky music. There was a fonky new attitude on the streets in the early seventies that was both grim and idealistic. The sad realities abounded—from the human fallout from sixties drug addictions, rampant unemployment, and the thousands of wasted Vietnam veterans that clogged the pool halls, bars, and street corners of urban America, to the trashed housing projects abandoned by absentee landlords from "across the tracks" and failed businesses still reeling from years of exploitation and the destruction wrought by upheavals and rebellions. Yet the presence of all-black institutions such as Muslim Bakeries and a variety of community centers combined with a potent new "black and proud" rhetoric on the streets, and the many new ways to hustle the system influenced a bizarre kind of idealism. Songs like "It's Just Begun" by Jimmy Castor, "Who's Gonna Take the Weight" by Kool & the Gang, and "The Revolution Will Not Be Televised" by Gil Scott-Heron kept alive subtle and not-so-subtle ideas of *total change*.

This almost absurd idealism became a consistent theme of the hard black music of the time, celebrating the possibility of a revolution, of money and success, and of a *funky black nation*. War captured the ironies on their gripping 1971 funk track "Get Down": "If you running the country/and you ain't runnin' it funky/you got to *get down!*" The Godfather of Soul James Brown was of course at the forefront of the funky power impulse, chanting "power to the people/soul power" on his 1971 live rendition of "Get Up, Get Into It, Get Involved," and delivering his outrageous spin on the resignation of Richard Nixon, and making his own case for political office with the ridiculous yet dead-serious "Funky President." And the P-Funk mob explored the black power fantasy to ridiculous levels, imagining popular black cultural leaders in *what used to be* the White House on Parliament's 1975 "Chocolate City":

> Now don't be surprised if Ali is in the White House,
> Reverend Ike, Secretary of the Treasure,
> Richard Pryor, Minister of Education,
> Stevie Wonder, Secretary of Fine Arts,
> And Miss Aretha Franklin, the first lady.
> > Parliament, "Chocolate City" (1975)

The strongest examples of black music that directly spoke of empowerment and liberation were produced by artists who possessed the greatest degree of independence and control over what they said in their music—James Brown, Stevie Wonder, Curtis Mayfield, George Clinton, and the Isley Brothers in particular. It's no coincidence that these artists were also among the strongest of the *funk bands* of the early seventies, and their social commentary was driven by the relentless funk beat. The Isley Brothers were ready to "Fight The Power," Stevie Wonder was charging to the politicians "You Haven't Done Nothin'," Curtis Mayfield was dealing with the "Future Shock," and of course Funkadelic was claiming "America Eats Its Young." By 1975, artists with the most *recording* freedom were indulging in their ideas of liberation to the point where the Isley Brothers were bold enough to urge their listeners to "Fight the Power" in no uncertain terms:

> Time is truly wastin'
> There's no guarantee
> Smile is in the makin'
> We gotta fight the powers that be.
> > The Isley Brothers, "Fight the Power" (1975)

Message music was clearly a risk. Just as "Say It Loud" was James Brown's last Top 10 pop hit for fifteen years, the Isley Brothers—at their peak—also found that "Fight the Power" was to be their last Top 40 pop hit! Because artists delivering outright message music seemed to be ignored by pop radio as the decade progressed, black popular music degenerated into senseless disco dance drivel—and the presence of strong music that adhered to high ideals and positive cultural values came only as a result of a vicious struggle with an industry that had no interest in permitting black artists (or *any* artists) to develop on their own terms.

Yet as the seventies dawned, ideals ran high. The "power to the people" movement of the late 1960s had an enormous impact on the independent-minded musical efforts of a large number of black artists. A defiantly innovative approach to their music—using different instruments, different players, and a different groove (the funk)—translated into a free-for-all with the record companies as the seventies began. A slew of established artists took matters into their own hands and rewrote their recording contracts, while many other acts—primarily funk bands—who would have been ignored three years earlier were signed up (often to major labels) with enthusiasm.

### NATRA

Part of the liberal atmosphere of the major labels toward black artists was a result of strong-arm tactics of the "Fair Play Committee," associates of an organization of black radio deejays and promoters known as the National Association of Television and Radio Announcers, or NATRA. NATRA had existed since 1956 as a forum for black radio deejays to convene, high-style, and network with each other and to schmooze with record company executives. As the clout of black deejays increased, the political rhetoric grew more militant at their annual conventions.

During the mid-1960s black deejays had played an important role in the civil rights movement, announcing marches and rallies over the air, and delivering the *important* news with a certain style that affirmed the essence of the soul music they were playing. Their enormous power was realized on the night of Martin Luther King, Jr.'s death, as many local black deejays defied FCC regulations and stayed on the air well into the night, keeping their listeners informed and "cool." Comedian Dick Gregory underscored this notion at a NATRA convention when he said, "The mike is mightier than the pen or the sword. You have more power over my seven kids than I do. But remember, after you get through with all your bullshit commercials, you've *got* to inform me." The deejays at the NATRA conferences in the late 1960s became bold enough to articulate their disagreement over white control over their product, black music—a control that continues, unabated, to this day—but with nothing but talk as their weapon, they were not taken seriously.

At their thirteenth convention, held in Miami in the summer of

1968, just months after the death of Martin Luther King, Jr. (and featuring such luminaries as King's widow, Coretta Scott King, Bill Cosby, and most of the major record executives), members of NATRA took a much more radical stand against the white-owned industry they were working for. "We are not begging the record companies for anything, but they will have to make us part of it if they wish to stay in business," NATRA executive secretary Del Shields asserted in one of many rhetorically charged speeches. Yet behind the podium and around the convention, things got nasty.

Vague threats to the "system" had escalated this time into outright assaults on the executives present. According to Peter Guralnick in his book *Sweet Soul Music,* well-known and respected Atlantic Records producer Jerry Wexler was hung in effigy; there were reports of fistfights, and people being pistol-whipped, taken away, threatened, and beaten. Veteran Atlanta-based deejay Jack "Jack the Rapper" Gibson remembers it well: "Yes sir, I was there when the nitty went down with the gritty." Guralnick quotes Isaac Hayes's recollections of the affair: "I was there when they kidnapped those people, took them out on a boat, and made demands. What [they] was saying was, 'Hey, you ripping us off, now you got to put some money back.' . . . Maybe the record companies were a little more sensitive toward black artists after that."

What the record companies did was get much more sophisticated about their treatment of black acts. While their support for NATRA and other overtly black-oriented organizations (and artists) disappeared, they hired many new black promoters and middlemen—to attend parties and diffuse touchy racial issues—and continued their business as usual. The industry "integrated," but the real power had not changed hands. "If we could have succeeded, they would have changed the entire black radio scene. But we weren't able to bring about a change because the white folks owned the record companies, and they owned the radio stations," Gibson recalled. (At the peak of the nationalistic furor in the late 1960s, blacks owned only eight of the more than three hundred R&B-oriented radio stations in the country, and three of those belonged to James Brown.)

The situation was bursting with ironies. The major labels knew that black music was a gold mine to be tapped—even though it was a result of the new maturity and racial consciousness within the music. The defiant "Black Power" attitude of the NATRA conference and at other events opened the doors for artists to get major offers for their sounds—which were then subjected to more rigid racial classifications of soul and rock, making true creative independence more difficult. While the early seventies was a watershed period of brilliant and effective black protest music, many of those influential artists suffered the same manipulation as R&B singers had endured during the days of segregation—bogus contracts, underpaid royalties, and lost publishing rights.

### RECORDING POWER

The record companies revamped their black music divisions and went after the thriving, funky talent. CBS Records, riding the success of Sly and the Family Stone, was quick to sign Santana; Earth, Wind & Fire; and Herbie Hancock as soon as they were available. They absorbed the thriving Philadelphia International label, invested in (and then undermined) Stax, and thus took a lion's share of the black music market in the 1970s. In 1970 Westbound snagged the Ohio Players and Funkadelic, and De-Lite Records came into the spotlight with Kool & the Gang. James Brown, Mandrill, and Roy Ayers' Ubiquity were picked up by Polydor. The Bar-Kays were reconstituted after the Otis Redding plane crash and developed a whole new image as a black rock band for Stax by 1970. War stepped out from under the hand of Eric Burdon in 1970, signing with United Artists, and the JBs began their string of potent solo projects on James Brown's People label in 1972. Nobody was telling these people that they had to "fit the format." For a moment in time, black artists could call the shots.

James Brown, for his part, had complete control over his production and—musically, at least—could not be compromised. Much of his race-conscious work, from "Say It Loud" on, consistently hit No. 1 on the soul charts (though he rarely crossed over onto pop radio). Already "Soul Brother Number One" by 1970, Brown was courted by a number of labels, and after the European conglomerate Polydor made him a series of lush offers, he transformed his entire catalog, gained his own production company, maintained complete artistic control, and—in a music-industry first—had his *face* printed on each record. The Godfather was runnin' thangs.

Nothing could ease the pressure from the powers that be, however. Despite his endorsement of Richard Nixon for re-election—ostensibly in support of Nixon's dubious "black capitalism" program—Brown was practically driven into the ground by the federal government. He complained bitterly in his autobiography about harassment by the I.R.S., and in a congressional scandal exposed in 1975, it became known that he was spied on by the I.R.S. "Special Services Staff" regularly from 1969 to 1973 as one of 11,000 citizens who promoted "extremist views and philosophies."

Nevertheless, as the Godfather of Soul, he wielded enormous power over the musical world, and other artists emulated his independence and merciless jam factor. A number of acts who had struggled for consistency in the soul music market during the 1960s struck out on their own in the 1970s. The Isley Brothers, Gladys Knight & the Pips, the Four Tops, the Spinners, Marvin Gaye, and Stevie Wonder all shook free of the conformist trappings of their Motown Records contracts, while the Impressions and Curtis Mayfield, the Chi-Lites, the O'Jays, the Ohio Players, the Spinners, and the Parliaments all found new life—and a new sound—on new labels at the dawn of the decade.

Eugene Record of the Chi-Lites claims to have waited for five years to record his No. 1 ballad "Have You Seen Her" because at the time "nobody was making anything over three minutes." After the 1969 success of Isaac Hayes's sixteen-minute ballads on the funky soul project *Hot Buttered Soul,* the doors were opened for longer black pop records. Eugene Record's patience and vision were rewarded as the Chicago vocal trio recorded the disc for their timely 1971 album *(For God Sakes) Give More Power to the People* for Brunswick.

The Isleys were among the first to leave Motown. They incorporated themselves as T-Neck Records and signed a distribution deal with Buddha Records. They wound up in a bitter legal battle against their old label over the No. 1 1969 hit "It's Your Thing." Motown claimed it was recorded under their contract and that Motown should be paid for the song. The Isleys were seriously opposed to this, for beyond the monetary concerns, they had deliberately left the label to produce harder, very un-Motown songs like the wickedly swinging "It's Your Thing" and the ethnically oriented "Black Berries" and "Freedom." The legal battle ensued for five years, with the Isleys eventually winning and ultimately winding up with a lucrative deal with CBS distributing T-Neck in 1973. The hard-earned freedom the band commanded allowed them to take a leading edge in soul-rock-funk innovations throughout the seventies.

Gladys Knight & the Pips began a relationship with Buddha Records in 1973 and the group accelerated their pace of No. 1 soul hits, recording the unforgettable "Midnight Train to Georgia," the pulsing "I've Got to Use My Imagination," and the major-league funk tune "On and On" after joining Buddha. The Four Tops found a better reception at ABC/Dunhill, and recorded a more masculine brand of gospel-flavored soul, scoring such righteous sides as "Keeper of the Castle" and "Are You Man Enough" as well as tasty favorites like "Ain't No Woman Like the One I Got" and "Midnight Flower."

### CURTIS MAYFIELD

Independently produced funky soul music had its brightest beacon in Curtis Mayfield. The Chicago-bred Mayfield was a serious businessman as well as a musician and was greatly inspired by the late Sam Cooke, the leading smooth soul crooner of the early 1960s and one of the first black artists to take control of his entire production. Mayfield formed his own label, Curtom, while heading the Impressions in 1968, and when he went solo in 1970 he brought the independence and social commentary that had marked many of the Impressions' big hits into his sound. Mayfield's new music grew even more intense and experimental, with long, spacey interludes and musical workouts that left behind the three-minute formula of sixties soul.

Mayfield's first solo LP *Curtis* featured a seven-minute psychedelic soul extravaganza "If There's a Hell Below, We're All Gonna Go (Don't Worry)." The jam opens with a much-sampled chant with strange echo effects that addresses: "Sisters . . . niggers . . . Whiteys . . . jews . . . crackers . . . don't worry . . . if theres hell below . . . were all gonna go . . . aaaaaahhhhhhhh." Songs like "Mighty Mighty, Spade and Whitey," "We the People Who Are Darker Than Blue," and "I Plan to Stay a Believer" were stylish soul anthems and political manifestos all in one. On "Believer," Mayfield dared to dream of solutions for his people:

> We're over twenty million strong and it wouldn't take long
> to save the ghetto child
> If we get off our ass ten dollars a man
> yearly think awhile
> Twenty million times ten would surely then
> put our brothers free
> what congregation with better relations
> would demand more respect from society?
>
> Curtis Mayfield, "I Plan to Stay a Believer" (1972)

Mayfield's ability to fuse the smoothest of soul harmonies with a militant, underground orientation was central to his contribution to The Funk. His tenderly delivered lines disarmed the listener to his piercing streetwise visions: "I don't mind leaving here, to let them know that we have no fear" was one example of his commitment to his people, portrayed with integrity and style. Mayfield's fourth solo LP, the *Superfly* soundtrack, was a turning point in black music, as his social consciousness blended in a fluid fashion with the latest hip street styles to identify the decade's ultimate street hero. The combination of shag-velvet elegance with poignant realism became the newest standard of funk—smoother, more stylish, yet just as real: the ideals of the black community in a nutshell in the early 1970s.

### STAX POWER

In perhaps the most representative tale of the rise and fall of independently produced funk, the legendary Stax Records flashed and burned as a black-owned label in a few short years in the early 1970s. After enduring a chaotic reorganization in Memphis following the death of Otis Redding in late 1967, the assassination of Martin Luther King, Jr., in Memphis in April 1968, and subsequent racial disharmony at the label, cofounder Jim Stewart was ready to quit. Selling a portion of the label in 1968, Stewart bailed out and sold the label to his (black) partner, executive Al Bell. Bell had a lot of idealistic plans, although eventually the label went under. But for a hot minute, he had Stax on top of the black music scene.

In an ambitious effort to give back to the community, the record company that had just expanded operations to Los Angeles put on a huge eight-hour concert in the Los Angeles Coliseum in August 1972 that featured the entire label's entourage. The lineup included Isaac Hayes, Rufus Thomas, Albert King, the Staple Singers, and the new Bar-Kays, who exploded on the set—calling their sound "the new, black rock funk!" The concert was called Wattstax, and with the help of a Schlitz beer sponsorship (and a $1 admission fee), it was a great success—as a fashion show as well as a concert. Stax recorded the event and packaged it in similar fashion to the Woodstock soundtrack, and enjoyed similar sales. The Reverend Jesse Jackson performed the invocation. (The prophetic opening lines "Brothers and Sisters, I don't know what this world is coming to . . ." were taken by the rap group Public Enemy for the intro to "Rebel Without a Pause," one of the most important records of the rap era, fifteen years later yet just as meaningful.)

Another shrewd move by Bell was the promotion of a trash-talking comedian named Richard Pryor, whose 1973 album *That Nigger's Crazy* made it to the black album Top 5 in the summer of 1974 with the help of a grassroots campaign that no large company would have bothered to undertake. The record sold a million copies without radio airplay and set a precedent for the funky, low-down humor of Pryor's style. The label itself was not as successful as Pryor would be, however, as the expansion increased their financial risks and a generous distribution deal with Columbia Records collapsed, stranding Stax by 1975. The company went bankrupt, but its efforts to remain in touch with the people were admirable.

The slow demise of Stax underscored a painful reality in the music business of the seventies: that the days of the flourishing independent R&B labels of the fifties and sixties were over. The major labels could either swallow up, or out-distribute their smaller competition. To survive on an independently distributed label, artists needed to be very lucky, or so radical that word-of-mouth brought them notoriety. The radical politics of the times kept a few of the most serious acts in the mix.

### GIL SCOTT-HERON

With the rhetoric of radical change and black revolution in the air at the dawn of the seventies, war poets became celebrities overnight. Gil Scott-Heron was the most notable. His ferocious social commentary became the reference point for socially conscious artists throughout the decade. After graduating from Lincoln University, Scott-Heron set about writing novels and politically charged poetry, and after some insistance by supporters he moved into jazz performance. His poetry recording, *Small Talk at 125th and Lenox,* and 1970 music album *Pieces of a Man* were brilliant collections of heartfelt sentiments and vicious realism. Tunes like "The Get Out of the Ghetto Blues" and "Whitey on the Moon" became anthems for the outcast, but none had greater impact than his seminal effort, "The Revolution Will Not Be Televised."

Expressing a critique that for many is still relevant today, "The Revolution" was in the minds of many people in 1970. Scott-Heron made a clear distinction between the society of consumerist make-believe and that of reality. The building climax from Brian Jackson's flute accented the genuine thrust of Scott-Heron's compelling anthem:

The revolution will not be back after a message about white
lightning, a white tornado, or white people . . .
The revolution will not go better with coke
The revolution will not fight germs that may cause bad
   breath
The revolution *will* put you in the driver's seat
The revolution will not be televised,
will not be televised,
will not be televised,
will not be televised
The revolution will be no re-run, brothers,
The revolution will be *live*.
  Gil Scott-Heron, "The Revolution Will Not Be Televised" (1970)

    While the upbeat tempo could almost be called a funk groove, what
stayed with the listener to Gil Scott-Heron was his revolutionary vision—a clear and tasteable vision of a new society. That theme endured
through a series of profound articulations like "Winter in America," a
poetic lament at the dark times of today, which await the springtime of
tomorrow; and more deliberate musings like "Western Sunrise" and
"Third World Revolution." Unlike the gospel-rooted soul singers who
preached a divine calling for change, Scott-Heron was grounded in the
here and now, and dealt with the realities in clear-headed, pragmatic,
nation-building fashion. His most stirring works are the long, biting jazz
poems that took on the U.S. power structure with unblinking ferocity:
"Ghetto Code," "$H_2O$ Gate Blues," "Bicentennial Blues," and "We Beg
Your Pardon (Pardon Our Analysis)" were all the closest thing yet to
the Hip Hop street commentary of the eighties. (Much of the work serves
as groundwork for sound-byte samples today as well.) Scott-Heron's
most dramatic works described the drug experience; "The Bottle" (1975)
and "Angel Dust" (1978) became some of his biggest (and funkiest) hits.
    As his music moved into the 1980s, his jazz band incorporated the
stronger street-funk sounds and regularly featured rugged, bass-driven
funk workouts as part of his act. Scott-Heron moved into the rap era
with alacrity, producing the sharpest indictments of the Reagan administration on record, the assaulting "B-Movie" in 1981, and the Hip
Hop–produced "Re-Ron" in 1984. Scott-Heron was a massive player
in shaping the political ideals of black America in the 1970s, and continues to perform and record with wit and conviction in the 1990s.

## THE LAST POETS

Another profoundly influential cadre of artists was the irrepressible Last Poets. An ever-changing trio of New York–area poets, many of whom had taken on the Black Muslim faith, began to preach the ills of American society over a drumbeat at local cafés and political events. They recorded their best-known album of street poetry for Douglas Records in 1970—and assaulted their audience with the seminal "Niggers Are Scared of Revolution":

> I love niggers
> I love niggers
> I love niggers
> because niggers are me
> And I should only love that which is me
> I love to see niggers go through changes
> love to see niggers act
> love to see niggers make them plays
> and shoot the shit
> but there is one thing about niggers I do not love
> Niggers are scared *of revolution*.
>
> The Last Poets, "Niggers Are Scared
> of Revolution" (1970)

Variously including the poets Gylan Kain, David Nelson, Felipe Jeliciano, Abiodun Obeyole, Omar Ben Hassen, Suliaman El-Hadi, and Alafia Purdin (also known as both Lightnin' Rod and Jalal-Uddin Nurridin), the Last Poets were the last word in anti-establishment sentiments.

As if a precursor to the vast popularity of the political rap of Public Enemy in 1990, the Last Poets' first album sold over three hundred thousand copies and spent one week at No. 40 on the U.S. *Billboard* album charts in 1970. The group followed with *This Is Madness,* which included the classic "Mean Machine," a rap production that was remade in 1984 by producer DST: "Automatic push button/remote control/synthetic genetics command your soul!" Lost to obscurity from the early seventies onward, the Last Poets were reissued by Celluloid Records in 1984 and brought three original members for a reunion album *Oh My People,* which featured the keyboard work of P-Funk genius Bernie Worrell, among others.

Streetwise Hip Hoppers looking for a virulent chant or classic rebel rhyme to sample need look no further than the Last Poets and Gil Scott-Heron. Despite the glitzy camouflage of the so-called seventies revival in dress and songs, what was truly visionary of the period was the revolutionary conviction of these particular artists. They dared to imagine *complete and total liberation* for their people, a theme that fueled the musical exploits of the many great soul groups and funk bands of the mid-1970s.

Another important aspect of the Last Poets that is often overlooked is that their rhyme styles were forged as much from streethustler lingo as from the Nation of Islam doctrines and other political manifestos. Alafia Purdim's (a.k.a. Lightnin' Rod) 1972 classic *Hustler's Convention* was a twelve-movement tale of a small-time thug's exploits at a mythical hustler's convention, in which he gets away with thousands of dollars, only to be captured and imprisoned. The violent, heady, hopeless underworld described in rhymes by Purdim was the archetype of today's gangsta rap, and with many of the rap tracks on *Hustler's Convention* backed up by the monster funk band Kool & the Gang, the streetwise nature of The Funk was once again placed in the center of the thang.

### PARTY AND BULLSHIT

The virulent, streetwise, yet politically sophisticated critiques of the Last Poets posed a greater question for the movement—one that had to do, ultimately, with The Funk. It boiled down to a confrontation of values: Was it possible, meaningful, or useful for blacks to be poised for revolutionary changes in America and yet still be nastay? Would a disciplined political movement accommodate the essentially funky nature of black Americans? The Funk was great for telling it like it is, but taking care of business is another matter. As one ex-Panther described the downfall of her organization, it broke down along "party" lines—too much partying: "The bloods were coming in late talkin' 'bout *colored-people-time,* while the revolutionaries were synchronizing their watches." Last Poet Abiodun Oyewole captured this theme in the rap on "When the Revolution Comes":

When the Revolution comes
Guns and rifles will be taking the place of poems and essays
Black cultural centers will be forts

Supplying the revolutionaries with food and arms
When the Revolution comes,
When the Revolution comes . . .
But until then
You know and I know
Niggers will party and bullshit and party
And bullshit and party and bullshit and party
and bullshit and party . . .
        The Last Poets, "When the Revolution Comes" (1970)

Some felt that black art was supposed to be serious, not "chocolate coated, freaked out and habit-forming." Yet not everyone, even members of the Last Poets, were capable of maintaining a lifestyle of revolutionary activity in the midst of the materialistic onslaught of American society. It was a fonky situation indeed.

    It appears that at the time nobody was prepared for the magnitude of accommodation that occurred as the seventies progressed. Yet something did survive. Some fonky essence of total *nonwhiteness* survived the 1970s and resurfaced in the rap tracks of urban America in the 1980s as Hip Hop. The funk attitude, the rebellious "Fuck America" point of view, gained its essential voice in black music and poetry of the early seventies, and persists to this day. "Funk has been what's happenin' for the past thirty years," according to funkateer Ashem "The Funky Man" Neru-Mesit. Judging from the slew of samples of the Last Poets, Gil Scott-Heron, Curtis Mayfield, and early seventies James Brown, what has survived intact to this day, despite the digitized camouflage, is the *funk attitude.*

# THIRTEEN

# *Those Funky Seventies:*
# *Livin' for the City*

"Different strokes, for different folks"
*Sly and the Family Stone*

## CHANGE

With a multitude of converging influences to draw from, black life in America was funky indeed in the early 1970s. A new, integrated world was surrounding blacks everywhere. Change was the operating principle, although not all of the change was for the better. The period from 1972 to 1976 was one of unparalleled change in the black community that, unlike during the 1960s, was not recorded on the nightly news.

With so-called equality in one hand and a government job (or handout) in another, the masses of blacks settled down to their lives as the crisis point of the 1960s was diffused. American culture soaked up the rage of black Americans and chugged along. With many political leaders entering office and most of the radical leaders reduced to shuffling in and out of the courts and jails, the many black movements withered away, and only their symbols remained. The idealistic, cathartic, and historic rhetoric of the Black Revolution had been formalized into a "style." Black action movies reinterpreted the thrust of the Black Power movement as a celebration of pimps and hustlers. By 1976, the year of the country's bicentennial, voices of dissent could barely be heard. "Black Is Beautiful" was no longer a militant gesture; it was simply cool to be black. "Power to the people" was the greeting in 1972. By 1976 it was "Have a nice day."

Black culture had finally become a "national" culture. The nationwide networks that had been developing under crises such as civil rights marches, boycotts, and rebellions developed into social networks. There was a general sense of brotherhood and sisterhood, a faith in black folks that carried across class and regional lines. Black people who had never met called each other "brother" and "sister." Black styles were no longer based on region, such as "southern," or "New York," for there was more emphasis on what black folks had in common.

The "slappin' five" handshake and sayings like "Right on" and "Can you dig it?" were heard in every state. People wore Afros and kept them up-tight or gave them "blowouts." Platform shoes, bellbottoms, loudly printed polyester shirts, dashikis, a serious affinity for astrology, and a heavy indulgence for marijuana ("weed") were all part of the stylish black American life of the early 1970s. Hoop earrings, beaded braids, incense, leather belts and vests, and peace signs were all in style as what amounted to "black hippies" thrived in popular American culture. "Far out" blacks like Sly Stone, Angela Davis, Tina Turner, and Isaac Hayes became the new ambassadors of style, while the commercial funkiness of the Jackson 5, the Temptations, and the Ohio Players showed just how far into the mainstream the funky style was heading. Blacks became mainstream consumers and bought the loudest furniture, clothing, jewelry, and cars. Black action films came out every week, playing along with karate films in loud, crowded theaters in black communities across the nation. New dances like the breakdown, the washing machine, the penguin, the robot, the boogaloo, and the camelot, along with new slang and new fashions, swept the nation *overnight* on television shows like *Soul Train* and *The Flip Wilson Show*. America had become one nation under a black aesthetic.

## THOSE FUNKY SEVENTIES

Funkiness was everywhere in the early seventies. What was a bad word in the 1960s, all of a sudden was *baaad!* What began as an affinity for "gettin' down" proliferated in black dance music in the 1970s. A series of dance singles using *funky* in the title hit the radio as the decade dawned. James Brown's instrumental "Ain't it Funky" in 1969 and "Funky Drummer" in 1970 paved the way. Within the next three years there was "Funky Chicken," "Funky Penguin," "Funky Granny," "Funky Worm," "Funky Nassau," "The Funky Man," and the Temptations' "Funky Music Sho Nuff Turns Me On." There were the dances—the funky chicken, the funky walk, the funky butt, and, as joked about on James Brown's 1972 "Escapism," the new dance "The Funky Train." It had finally become cool to be funky.

It was so cool, in fact, that funk was becoming mainstream. The not-so-funky columnist Henry Allen wrote a column for the *Washington Post* in 1971 entitled "Funk Is in the Eye of the Beholder," in which he concluded that "funk is more than just another way to get high, pregnant, united with God, or thrown in jail. Funk is a way of life that only yesterday you considered tacky, old-fashioned, obnoxious, or irrelevant." Like drinking cheap wine, dancing in the street, or lounging in one's underwear on the porch, there was satisfaction to be found in a life of funk. In so many ways, funk represented doing what you're *not* supposed to do. Like throwing a food fight at a formal dinner, there are some things that don't "belong"—but with The Funk, anything goes. With a tongue-in-cheek insight, Allen concluded that "funk is the conscious adoption of value systems previously considered antithetical to one's social position."

## TELEVISION

If anything was "antithetical" to the social position of blacks in the 1960s, it was mainstream television. But in the seventies, fonky blacks made it to the mainstream almost overnight. What began as a liberal overture to the "Negro" question with Bill Cosby's *I Spy* in 1965, *Star Trek*'s Nichelle Nichols playing Uhura, and Diahann Carroll's vapid character, Julia, in 1968 turned into a showcase for the "down and funky" and flavors of black America. Black entertainers found access to network shows such as *The Smothers Brothers Comedy Hour*, *Laugh-In*, and *The Dick Cavett Show* on a regular basis. (Sly Stone's incredible performances on *Dick Cavett* are worth searching out.)

The four-year run of *The Flip Wilson Show* on NBC starting in 1970 marked the beginning of a new era in black entertainment. Billed as a standard variety show with a nightly monologue filled with ethnic jokes and the requisite skits and guest performers, Wilson poked fun at his people with the streetwise homegirl Geraldine. With her loud-talking sass and her mythical boyfriend Killa, the dark, nasty underworld of po' blacks' relationships was turned into a caricature. Wilson's Geraldine was the precursor to Martin Lawrence's sassy and silly drag characters of today. Perhaps most memorable for fans of the seventies was the four-year run on ABC of Pete, Linc, and Julie of *The Mod Squad*, a trio of painfully hip undercover cops. The silent and very dark Linc and loud, obtrusive Geraldine became white America's prototypes of blackness as the decade began on television.

The funky image of the "dirty ole man" became a national sensation when *Sanford and Son* debuted on NBC in 1972. The show's producers extended the "tell it like it is" theme of their successful *All in the Family* and applied it to a black junkman and his son. An interesting lesson can be learned from the phenomenal success of the show, which ran for six years (and two more as a syndicated show up to Redd Foxx's death in 1991). Rather than hire an actor to play an ornery old black man, the show's producers hired a black trash-talkin' nightclub comic. Foxx's popularity skyrocketed as he played the ornery, chauvinistic, southern-bred Fred Sanford. (Foxx's real name was John Sanford.)

Like it or not, the Sanfords were a funky set. No longer attempting to appease "the race" with positive images, Fred Sanford was gutbucket funny in the finest Sambo tradition, yet there was something authentic about him. His mannerisms, his waddle, his rhythmic cadence, and his crankiness were genuine expressions from a man used to grossing people out onstage with R-rated diatribes about stanky asses and dirty prostitutes. Foxx navigated from his low-down comedy to the mainstream with ease, and remained comfortable with his funky thang. (This may stand as an example of what's in store for hard-core rappers such as Snoop Doggy Dogg, Ice-T, Luther Campbell, and Flavor Flav. It's possible that with enough money, the rough edges of the hard-core set can be softened, the essential nasty funk can be absorbed, packaged, and neutralized.)

## SOUL TRAIN

The most undiluted showcase of black sexuality in the country was a black enterprise that continues to this day. *Everyone* got up on Saturday mornings to watch *Soul Train,* "the hippest trip in America," the black answer to *American Bandstand*, and a cultural mecca for the entire decade of the seventies. The wild syncopated gyrations of the *Soul Train* dancers were an erotic-hypnotic revelation for most unfunky Americans. Always freshly dressed in the latest fashions, hitting the latest dances, and the right-on soul stars lip-syncing their soon-to-be classic hits made *Soul Train essential* seventies, despite the droll style of host Don Cornelius.

The cultural weight of the show was revealed when pop singer Elton John appeared in 1974 to play "Bennie & the Jets." Here, a sly turnaround of the "firsts" syndrome occurred, as John became the first white performer to appear on *Soul Train,* and everyone watched to see how he would be received (it was a warm reception, of course). The show almost lost its relevance when acts like the Captain & Tennille and the Village People performed during the disco era, but by the 1980s black music had become so juvenile and shallow that the mere survival of *Soul Train* was an exhilarating success story.

Cornelius, the show's producer, founder, and host for twenty-three years, was the single reason for *Soul Train*'s success. An ex-marine and family man raising two kids, Cornelius had been a local soul dee-jay at WVON radio in Chicago and moonlighted by working his way around a local UHF station (the practical equivalent of public access at the time), developing the idea of a dance entertainment show there. Searching for seed money, Cornelius found that most interested tak-ers wanted a black show about "culture or politics," not entertainment. Finally, George O'Hare, a merchandising manager at the largest busi-ness in Chicago—Sears—gave Cornelius the chance by forwarding him startup money. Beginning locally in the fall of 1970, *Soul Train* was an instant success. Taking his pitch to John H. Johnson of Johnson Products ("the makers of Ultra Sheen, Afro Sheen, and Ultra Sheen cos-metics!") he found a sponsor willing to underwrite the future of the pro-gram, which trickled into urban markets in syndication, city by city, until its nationwide zenith in the mid-1970s.

*Soul Train* has survived every black music trend since 1971, and it stands tall as the backdrop to black America's golden age. By 1993 the show took on another facelift, with set changes and Cornelius giving way to a series of guest hosts, but it's still here. Streetwise and savvy, *Soul Train* always made the most of its main ingredient: sexy black funk.

### BLACK ACTION MOVIES

Another outlet for the funky vibe in the mainstream was the develop-ment of black films—the so-called "blaxploitation" movies. Like *Soul Train,* the black films of the early seventies achieved a certain place in American culture—not as overtly moral parables or political mani-festos, but simply as celebrations, characterizations, and (often mis-taken) animations of the black experience. Like the original funk music, these films contained raw expressions of black reality interwoven with an assortment of Hollywood gimmicks designed to make the movies "accessible."

Melvin Van Peebles's atmospheric 1970 *Sweet Sweetback's Baadasssss Song* (which featured a soundtrack by Earth, Wind & Fire) was consid-ered by many the breakthrough. An ethereal visual tale of the sex romp of a twisted black antihero was perhaps the antithesis of Hollywood's straight-and-narrow Sidney Poitier concept of blacks in film. Gordon Parks's *Shaft* (which featured Isaac Hayes's 1971 Oscar-winning sound-track song), and his 1972 *Superfly* (featuring the powerful music of Curtis Mayfield) were also pioneers in this trend. The black cop John Shaft, played by Richard Roundtree, had to navigate black mobsters, white mobsters, white women, and the Black Panthers to get his man. This vivid new and colorful underworld was the ultimate entertainment venue for America's wild early seventies tastes. Isaac Hayes caused a pop sensation with the *Shaft* soundtrack, which was a slice of black life set to music that sold on the pop, soul, and jazz charts for months. His performance at the 1971 Oscar Awards, on a floating piano passing through a corridor of dancing dismembered limbs and dressed in nothing but a shirt made of chains, was the symbolic black macho image finally, totally revealed.

*Superfly* had perhaps more influence on the black youth of America than any other film. Following (and romanticizing) the life of a drug dealer aptly named Priest, who finally breaks from the racket, swindles whitey of his money, and escapes with his strong black woman, the film was the archetypical success story of the underground. Pimps and pushers were glorified, while the activists were portrayed as little more than marginal comic relief to the "real" world of The Hustle. After *Superfly,* the mythic battle of The People against The Man which Malcolm and the Panthers had so brilliantly rallied people toward, was washed away in favor of an effort simply to get *yours.*

The hypnotic allure of Priest was immortalized by Curtis Mayfield, who, at the peak of his career, had captured the mood on the street for a generation of lost youth:

> The aim of his role
> Is to move a lot of dough
> Ask him his dream what does it mean,
> He wouldn't know
> Can't be like the rest
> Is the most he'll confess
> But the time is running out
> And there's no happiness . . . ooh Superfly.
>                    Curtis Mayfield, "Superfly" (1972)

Only four years earlier Mayfield had been producing joyous, positive music for the Impressions. This new music wasn't happy, but it was strong (rhythmically James Brown–influenced), rich (melodically Marvin Gaye–influenced), and wide-ranging in mood. It was The Funk.

Black youngsters saw slick black gangstas in a steady stream of movies, like Goldie from *The Mack*, Fred Williamson, as *Black Caesar*, and the irrepressible karate kicks and rhymes of Rudy Ray Moore as *Dolemite*, while they saw the real-life militants Huey Newton, Bobby Seale, and Angela Davis shuttled in and out of courts and jails on the daily news.

Despite the lack of politically conscious themes in most of the blaxploitation films, there was a necessary *catharsis* in many of them. As a powerless people for generations, blacks found visualizing themselves with power, no matter how narcissistic, a thrilling, delicious turnabout, and the hunger for such material was insatiable. When Pam Grier's character grabs that white prostitute by her stringy blond hair and slams her to the wall, the crowd reaction in black theaters across the nation had more to do with exorcising the demons of segregation than with the often ridiculous plot. When Dolemite talks shit to a redneck sheriff (after having sex with the sheriff's white wife), drops *rhymes* in his face, and floors him with a karate kick, Dolemite is asserting the masculine power of the *funky* soul brotha in ways no one else could. And when the black gangsters sucker the Italian gangsters into a shootout with cops in *Across 110th Street*, or Priest suckers the white drug kingpins out of their money in *Superfly*, the shrewdness, cunning, and intelligence of the soul brothas provided a needed relief from the negativity and confusion of being black in America.

Many other more subversive black action films were produced, such as *The Spook Who Sat by the Door* and *Buck and the Preacher*, but ultimately black films dwindled into a formula: Badass brotha outsmarts whitey and takes his money; strong black sista slaps, kicks, or kills white bitch; whitey loses and the "niggas" take over. It came as no surprise to many, and a relief to some, when disco films took over the market by 1977.

The visual reality of blaxploitation films brought home bleak circumstances, but it also brought black style into the theaters. These comic, ironic black films were showcases for loud, black tastes: blue velvet furniture; green, pink, or red suits with ridiculously wide lapels, and matching hat brims; pink cadillacs, platform shoes, 357 Magnums, dashikis, Afros, hoop earrings, and more. In short, the ideology wasn't as important as the image. Black music, black fashion, black high life, black low life, black talk, black sex, black dreams, black reality, and black filmmaking were all explored, exposed, and exploited in these films.

The black film formula was a ready-made recipe for the black musician to explore the range of black American life and express it in song. Each soundtrack featured a snappy and radio-friendly intro theme, chase-scene music, romantic or sexy love scene sounds, and music for funerals, weddings, stealthy suspenseful moods, and bloody action. Starting with the *Shaft* double album in 1971, which featured the long instrumentals of the Bar-Kays backing Isaac Hayes, and followed directly by *Superfly* in 1972, the black film soundtrack found a place in black homes across the country. Prominent soundtrack albums included *Trouble Man* by Marvin Gaye, *Across 110th Street* by Bobby Womack, *Coffy* by Roy Ayers, *The Mack* by Willie Hutch, *Black Caesar* and *Slaughter's Big Rip-off* by James Brown, *Shaft in Africa* arranged by Johnny Pate, *Black Girl* by Solomon Burke, *Short Eyes* by Curtis Mayfield, *Let's Do It Again* by the Staple Singers, and *Sparkle* by Aretha Franklin (the latter two also produced by Curtis Mayfield).

The movie soundtrack was a springboard to a decade of success for Isaac Hayes; Earth, Wind & Fire; Curtis Mayfield; Roy Ayers; and many others. The soundtrack album ultimately served two extremely important functions: first, like the films in general, soundtrack albums gave *jobs* to struggling artists who may not have had the opportunity to release and distribute a record on their own. Second, and most significant, the range of the movie soundtrack allowed the artist to explore—and reflect—the diverse moods of the film and thus the diverse moods *of their people*. Soundtrack albums produced a level of variety and consistency that rivaled the great funk bands of the era, and the funky chops of soundtrack musicians brought the jams to an audience of millions.

## DOWN HOME FUNK

With the rise of the wild and unpredictable images of blacks in films came an even rowdier surge of street-smart black comics that took the nation by storm. Palatable humorists like Bill Cosby and Flip Wilson were but the tip of the iceberg of low-down and nasty folk stylists that wound up in the spotlight almost overnight. While trashy humor about winos, pimps, and prostitutes and the "fonky" ways of blacks has always been a comic undercurrent in black nightclubs for generations, truly X-rated humor began its commercial life in the 1970s. The multifaceted and utterly nasty humorist Rudy Ray Moore, a.k.a. "Dolemite," claims to be the "first X-rated comic on record, in the country," re-

leasing his comedy album *Eat Out More Often* in 1970. His equally ribald movies, in which the superhero Dolemite saves da hood from drug
dealers, and his incredibly sexually explicit comic routines are classic
cultural artifacts of the soulful black underworld.

The self-effacing, impressionistic, urbane genius of Richard Pryor
caused a storm in 1974 with the release of the bestselling record *That
Nigger's Crazy,* a comedy record that made a superstar of this street
comic from Peoria, Illinois. Pryor's graphic indulgence in sexual dialogue, and his preposterous imitations of familiar street characters in
the neighborhood, from prostitutes, pimps, and the police, to lovers,
hustlers, and addicts, provided a gut-busting, hilarious affirmation of
the black folk experience. Even with his X-rated act, Pryor's popularity landed him on television talk shows, scores of films, his own NBC
variety show (a brilliant montage of highly thematic cultural art that
lasted only four weeks in 1977), and even an appearance on the children's show *Sesame Street* in 1976.

Within a few years of Pryor's breakthrough, X-rated humor became big business. In Florida, the R&B singer Clarence Reid developed
a hilarious alter ego as a totally graphic X-rated sex-freak Blowfly. His
dirty-talking albums *Zodiac Blowfly, Blowfly Goes to College,* and others
energized the darker side of the Miami music scene, which brought us
2-Live Crew a dozen years later. The explicit Funk in its low-down,
dirtiest form was a financial boon for those with the attitude to go for
it. Much of the material of these foul-mouthed comics appears to be
the basis of gangsta rap tracks of today, although the rappers aren't
nearly as funny. This fonky new attitude of raw and low-down humor
in the seventies was just another reflection of the cultural explosion that
was occurring on the streets of black America.

The rise of The Funk coincided with the growth of a new black
identity. "Black is what's happening," George Clinton told one journalist in 1976, explaining his band's popularity. "Richard Pryor is selling a million records without being played on the radio. To me, Richard
Pryor sounds typical of everybody I grew up with. Civil rights, the
whole freedom thing has opened it up."

Funk had been elevated to an *affirmation,* in much the same way
that black had become beautiful. The loud, new look and style of black
folks—from the poorhouse to the White House—compelled black
artists to respond in ways that affirmed this sense of unity. Funk was
dirty and smelly, but it was *ours,* and it made its way into the music

mainstream. The vocal group the Dells described this new aesthetic in a series of poems on their 1973 album *Sweet as Funk Can Be:*

> Say man!
> Can you tell me what is funky
> Well uh!
> Funky used to be fonkey
> and that kind of rhyme with honk—uh, donkey
> Is that right!
> Then the word got changed
> and the scene was rearranged . . .
> Brothers paid the dues and funky gypsies played the blues
> the blues?
> Brothers paid *the* dues and funky gypsies played *the* blues
> The funky gypsies played the blues
> But funk can swing and everything
> Funk is on the case
> There is funk in outer space . . .
> Funk can be sweet
> I repeat
> Funk can be sweet . . .
> Funk can be sweet, funk can be,
> funk can, funk, funk, funk, funk
> Funk is
> sweeeet, now that we've taken it back
> Now that we've taken it back home.
> The Dells, "The Origins of Funk" (1973)

The Dells certified that black folks were ready to claim their funkiness as something to be proud of. "Brothers paid the dues and funky gypsies played the blues" is a phrase that acknowledges the depths of understanding, or historical memory, of the black struggle, while relating to it the power of "funky gypsies" to provide redemption for all who chose to identify. Funk was becoming more than simply the nitty-gritty—it was developing into a deeper understanding of the black or African self.

## MUMBO JUMBO

The Funk was not only a desirable thing; it was growing. In fact, The Funk had the power to infect the entire nation. Ishmael Reed, in his groundbreaking 1972 novel *Mumbo Jumbo,* created a freaked-out setting in which the stanky and irresistible rhythmic essence of black culture spreads through America like a disease. In this jagged, scatological treatise, a funky epidemic he calls "Jes Grew" is brought over from Haiti (initiated by the Voo Doo Generals), gains a beachhead in New Orleans, lays waste of the town (the Mardi Gras), spreads north to St. Louis and Chicago (during the Jazz Age of the 1920s), and makes its way to New York in time for be-bop to emerge by World War II.

Reed's painstaking reconstruction of a mythic black underworld (replete with slang dialects that would make Mark Twain have to excuse himself) overturned the prevailing format of black fiction. For generations, the canon of black literature had focused on the tortuous aspects of black life and culture as they are dismembered by the intrusions of white America. Reed spins this theme on its head—proclaiming the incessant, relentless, subversive nature of Jes Grew, that mystical *thang* that infects America:

> Actually Jes Grew was an anti-plague. Some plagues caused the body to waste away; Jes Grew enlivened the host. Other plagues were accompanied by bad air (malaria). Jes Grew victims said that the air was as clear as they had ever seen it and that there was the aroma of roses and perfumes which had never before enticed their nostrils. Some plagues arise from decomposing animals, but Jes Grew is electric as life and is characterized by ebullience and ecstasy. Terrible plagues were due to the wrath of God; but Jes Grew is the delight of the gods.

The rhythmic, sexual essence of black dance music is Jes Grew, and white America's insatiable appetite for it will be their downfall, according to Reed. Members of the nondancing opposition, the "Wallflower Order," which followed the ancient "Atonist Path" and were opposed to the Jes Grew, found themselves lost, for there was no vaccine for its effect. By showcasing a grand psychic confrontation between European and African value systems—encoded into the language of the underworld—Reed captured the essential purpose of jazz, and the essence of The Funk. Furthermore, as a symbolic means of total reclamation of a people's identity, Reed served to liberate his culture from centuries of oppression—dismantling the many myths of black America's powerlessness and invisibility within this country. It was, in fact, time for blacks to not only realize power, but to visualize *transformations*.

The symbolic impact of *Mumbo Jumbo* was powerful, and its practical impact was profound. George Clinton, the mastermind of the intergalactic funk movement of the later seventies, has lauded *Mumbo Jumbo* as a primary source of his inspiration. When I asked him in 1985 where he got his concepts of The Funk spreading throughout the universe, he replied "Have you read *Mumbo Jumbo*"?

### I'M FUNKY AND I'M PROUD

With the ethereal nature of funk as part of the new black identity in the early seventies, the "Negro" to "black" transformation would come full circle. What was once something to be ashamed of—a sweaty, spirited, sexually expressive lifestyle—was now becoming something to take pride in. The Funk was not a curse, it was a blessing—and it was spreading around the world like a disease. This was the final transformation that needed to take place: total self-love.

An essential aspect of the nature of The Funk is that it is *self-aware,* and comfortable with itself. Most of the original perpetrators of The Funk—Sly Stone, Hendrix, Clinton, Miles Davis—were well aware of their freaked-out image, but rather than being ashamed of their looks, they were *proud* of them: "We always been proud of it. That's what the whole P-Funk thing is all about," Bootsy Collins told me in 1994. "We always been proud of where we came from. You know, even when they said it wasn't hip . . . I always wanted to be in the most freaked-out band around."

Understanding and accepting one's African-American roots means taking an unflinching look into the dark, dangerous depths of the mutant diversity of the black American soul. For African-Americans, to truly love themselves is to totally accept their fundamental nature, which is *funky* from the start. This is why the acceptance of the funky style—as a direct result of Black Power—was in an absurd way a monumental transformation for black American culture.

# FOURTEEN

# United Funk: The Shining Star

"People all over the world, come together."
*Kool & the Gang*

### NUMBER ONE FUNK

The Decade of Funk began as it should, with monster jams from Sly and the Family Stone and the Godfather of Soul, James Brown. "Thank You (Falettin Me Be Mice Elf Agin)" was the quintessential reprise for Sly, as the ferocious bass-plucking of Larry Graham drove a new groove and a new mood into the heads of pop fans. The tight bass-line syncopation and heavy emphasis on the one-count showed a stronger James Brown influence than ever before. Released only as a single from Sly's *Greatest Hits* LP in the first week of 1970, "Thank You" was the inaugural funk jam of the decade if there ever was one. The utopian thrills of Sly's "Higher" weren't there, but the infectious, *essential* quality of the Family Stone was totally in effect. The jam revealed a direction toward his darker roots that would be explored in his next album release, almost two years away.

The Godfather would drop "Funky Drummer" on the masses in March 1970, asserting once and for all the rhythmic grip he yielded on the Black Nation. By the summer his soon-to-be-legendary sessions with Bootsy and Phelps Collins were hitting the streets: "Get Up, I Feel Like Being a Sex Machine (Parts 1 & 2)" hit in July, "Superbad" in September, and "Get Up, Get into It, Get Involved" in December all featured that signature liquid lick from Bootsy, and elevated the Godfather once again to the position of all-time black macho icon. There was no subtlety, no irony, no illusions about this dark, naked music. "Sex Machine" made a vivid and undeniable statement that *black sex* was the baddest, boldest, and nastiest on this earth. The rhythmic ferocity, infectious ego, and unbridled nastiness of the Godfather in this period is unsurpassed in music history.

Another meaningful development was laid down the following year with "Make It Funky," released in the summer of 1971, as the Godfather defined The Funk as a deep part of southern black down-home country roots. The song contains two distinct sections, one which begins with a dialogue between James and his longtime right-hand man Bobby Byrd, then the heavy horns kick loudly on the slow, nasty beat, and hit a descending line that repeats incessantly over the "Make It Funky" chant. Layers and layers of panting horns increase the heat of this heavy hump. Midway through the song the bridge turns the record inside out. The pounding horn lines give way to a prominent ascending bass triplet that kicks in—on the one—and the jam is then driven from the bottom. What was once a bar that fit a sixteen-note descending horn line was now a three-note rising thump, with the Godfather belting out names of southern foods: *"Neckbone, candied yams, grits and gravy, cracklin' bread . . ."*

With the one and only Godfather showing the way, *funky* became down-home, country-fried, tasty, desirable, and *legal*. The live recording of "Make It Funky" is one of the highlights of his third Apollo recording, *Revolution of the Mind: Live at the Apollo Vol. III,* as the long version allows James to interact with the band, asking the players about their southern hometowns, and ad-libbing on that theme. The song is a staple of Brown's performances to this day.

Most of Brown's new funk was not heard on pop radio; he was strictly a black phenomenon. "Make It Funky" reached No. 1 R&B in October 1971. It did not chart in the pop Top 100. Brown was producing some of his best work in 1972 with the *There It Is* LP and the *Get on the Good Foot* double album. He had mastered the album format; his band, now led by Fred Wesley, was cranking out the most rhythmically crisp jams; and his social consciousness was at its most visible. Jams like "King Heroin," "The Whole World Needs Liberation," "Escapism," and "Public Enemy #1" could be heard from James in 1972. His music was essentially too serious to cross over. James had managed to hit as hard as the political jazz poets Gil Scott-Heron and the Last Poets, but his repertoire of nastay funk kept him out of the jazz clubs, a visible soul star, but off of pop radio, unnoticed in terms of record sales and awards, which went to smoother soul acts such as Curtis Mayfield, Marvin Gaye, and the O'Jays. The Funk nevertheless swept the nation from 1972 to 1976 under the guise of soul music and dance music, and without one Top 10 pop radio single from James Brown. Isaac Hayes, Billy Preston, Stevie Wonder, and Sly Stone all spent part of 1972 in the pop Top 10 with music that was clearly in the mold of The Godfather.

Pop funk proliferated in the summer of 1972 as Billy Preston's instrumental keyboard workout "Outa-Space" reached No. 3 pop, followed at No. 4 pop that summer by the Jimmy Castor Bunch and their hilarious "Troglodyte." Both Preston and Castor were primed for pop success, but their novelty hits were perhaps a fluke of the times as much as a tribute to their success. Preston (born in Texas, raised in L.A.) was an energetic keyboardist who grew to fame backing the gospel greats Mahalia Jackson, James Cleveland and Andrae Crouch, and soulful superstars Sam Cooke and Little Richard. Preston then apprenticed in Ray Charles's band through a tour of Europe in 1967, worked on an early album with Sly Stone, and wound up backing *the Beatles* in 1968. His solo albums were a freewheeling mix of his soulful gospel roots and state-of-the-art synthesizer workouts. "Outa-Space," "Space Race," "Will It Go Round in Circles," and "Nothing from Nothing" reveal Preston's command of both Ray Charles soul and James Brown fonk. Preston's mastery of the clavinet and the micro Moog synthesizer influenced a generation of funk keyboardists.

Jimmy Castor was a New York–bred session man and producer of many musical styles, from fifties doo-wop, to sixties Latin pop, to dinosaur fonk in the seventies. After finally mustering his clout as a bandleader, he achieved critical success with his 1972 *It's Just Begun*. Its preposterous single "Troglodyte" was the party jam of 1972. The Jimmy Castor Bunch quickly became one of the city's tightest outfits. Castor followed with a series of ultra-fat dinosaur funk albums, typically featuring long, bass-heavy dance-funk tracks, with silly, whimsical chants to go with the beats. "The Bertha Butt Boogie" (1974), "King Kong," and "The Everything Man" (1976) are all funk classics.

Pop music in the early seventies featured a slew of off-the-wall gimmick hits, such as Tony Orlando and Dawn's "Tie a Yellow Ribbon," Paul Simon's "50 Ways to Leave Your Lover," and Jim Croce's "Spiders and Snakes," and funky jams like "Outa-Space" and "Troglodyte" slipped in as part of the joke.

When it came to The Funk, however, "Troglodyte" meant something else. When James Brown recorded "Make It Funky" in late 1971, The Funk had been officially brought back to its country roots. "Troglodyte" was perhaps the first—and certainly the most popular—of many records that took funkiness back to Africa.

The "troglodyte" was the funky man in fullest effect. "He started it all way back then," goes the lyric, as the caveman started the sayings

"Right on!" "Hot pants!" and "Sock it to me!" The *original man* was a soul brutha, and he was *fonky*.

### FUNKY WORM

Until the spring of 1973, the Ohio Players were known as little more than a freakish blues-rock band that featured a baldheaded black woman in chains on their album covers. When "Funky Worm" hit the radio, a whole new thang developed. Aside from the hilarious "granny" emceeing the affair, and the scorching keyboard riffs of Walter "Junie" Morrison, the record had a slow, pulsing swanging *hump* to it that until that time was the exclusive territory of the Godfather.

"Funky Worm" elevated the Players to national prominence, and made keyboardist and writer Walter "Junie" Morrison's talents so appealing that Westbound Records signed "Junie" to his own contract, letting the Ohio Players go. While the Ohio Players would go on to define the funk sound of the mid-seventies, "Junie" Morrison made a name for himself with a series of quirky, delectable solo albums for Westbound Records. He joined the P-Funk Mob in 1977, in time to collaborate on some of the all-time funk hits, "One Nation Under a Groove," "Aqua-Boogie," and "(Not Just) Knee Deep."

"Funky Worm" was overshadowed and almost forgotten in the wake of the Players' later hits for Mercury Records, but it has been recycled as the standardbearer for the shrill sound of urban tension in the West Coast Hip Hop sound today. The screeching synthesizer wiggle of the worm has become the primary tone from which the sparse feel of Ice-T, Dr. Dre, Ice Cube, and the N.W.A. sound is derived. The hook was looped prominently on the classic "Ain't No Future in Yo Frontin' " by M. C. Breed & the DFC in 1991, and was spliced from M. C. Breed by X-Clan in 1992, on their major rap hit "Heed the Word of the Brotha."

Funky songs proliferated into 1973 to follow the "Funky Worm"— Billy Preston's rockin' "Will It Go Round in Circles?", ex-Temptations lead singer Eddie Kendricks's Grammy-winning groove on "Keep on Truckin'," and the James Brown–produced masterpiece "Doin' It to Death," released under the name Fred Wesley and the JBs. Dance music became incredibly intricate musically, as instrumental groups such as Funk Inc., the Crusaders, Kool & the Gang, Deodato, the Meters, and others sought to interpret pop melodies and standards with R&B backdrops, making the original "rare grooves," or acid jazz sounds.

Heavier and heavier horns could be heard on the latest dance hits, as the James Brown influence grew, and an upstart hippie big band from Oakland, California, called Tower of Power, threw people for a loop, teasing listeners with the soulful brass backgrounds on the ballads "You're Still a Young Man" and "So Very Hard to Go," and kicking ass with propulsive locks like "What Is Hip?" and "Soul Vaccination." The West Coast also provided a nasty Latin-funk noise from Santana, whose incredible *Santana* and *Abraxas* sessions solidified their role as leaders of true fusion sounds; and War, whose huge pop hits "Slippin' into Darkness" and "Cisko Kid" were but hints of the band's incredible talents revealed on their albums *All Day Music* and *The World is a Ghetto*.

## KOOL & THE GANG

A powerful contribution to the funk music scene came in the fall of 1973 when the soul-jazz group Kool & the Gang kicked a deeper groove. Already well-respected for tight, upbeat funky chops like "Chocolate Buttermilk," "Pneumonia," and "Music Is the Message," the band broke it down and delivered a punishing rhythmic stomp titled "Funky Stuff." The lyrics said it all: "I can't get enough/of that funky stuff/I say wo wo wo . . . wo wo yea!" The record began with a loud party whistle, and broke into extremely tight Fred Wesley–phrased horns that rise up, hit a staccato riff, then fall in with the guitar and bass and push the groove off and rolling. The bass is thick, the pace is slow, the party-whistle vamps in and out, the rhythm guitar is locked tight, and the horns stretch and punctuate the groove in precise, mathematically placed lines. The Funk had spread to the Big Apple.

Along with the "Funky Worm," Kool & the Gang's "Funky Stuff" seemed to finally reach down into the ferocious depths of black dance rhythm that had until then been ruled zealously by James and his boys. The Godfather himself told Kool & the Gang associate Cleveland Brown at the time, "They're the *second* baddest out there."

The following single "Jungle Boogie" set an even higher standard for those who chose to challenge the Godfather. The fierce, *swanging* horn riffs charge upward—just as the chant "Get down, get down!" is repeated, and drive "Jungle Boogie" into a scorching, wide-open funk tension, which Hip Hoppers such as EPMD ("You Gots to Chill"), the Beastie Boys, and Public Enemy have looped to great effect. As if to punctuate their funk dominance, Kool & the Gang released the ruthlessly syncopated monster funk jam "Hollywood Swinging" in early 1974, yielding their first No. 1 R&B hit.

But Kool & the Gang had something else going for them besides straight funk groove. The Gang had begun to develop a subtle African spiritual theme around their music, and their accompanying album release *Wild and Peaceful* was their strongest statement to that point. The jungle-scene artwork, the nine-minute mellow African-jazz instrumental title song, and their inspirational diatribes were classy touches on a complete musical experience that expressed a black aesthetic in rhythm, lyric, and vibe. "Funky Stuff" and "Jungle Boogie" were nasty dance hits, yet the album (like their early LPs) featured elegant, thoughtful jazz compositions that drew a more mature audience into their vision.

> Cryin' babies on the doorstep
> Helpless as can be
> Lady of the evening
> Set your mind free
> Grow up in the ghetto
> Never seen a tree
> If you don't understand the words to this song,
> It's on you, it's on me.
> 
> Kool & the Gang, "This Is You, This Is Me" (1973)

Kool & the Gang had a lot to say, and a lot of music to play. " 'What are you doing to make things better?' asks a child. . . . You see we are scientists of sound, we are mathematically puttin' it down," is the refrain from the thoughtful jazz experiment "Heaven at Once." As the group matured, many of Kool & the Gang's efforts became unorthodox, quirky, and curious, yet their idealism, hip style, and musical brilliance continued to shine through each diverse song selection. Bandleader Ronald Bell (now Khalis Bayyan) described the band's experimental nature in 1974: "We are always seeking knowledge that will improve our musical ability, and we spend most of our time experimenting with ideas. Some come off, some don't, but we never tire of looking." This open-minded nature was central to the explosion of funk bands (and would soon become extinct as disco music encroached).

Kool & the Gang were ultra-hip leaders in black style, and when they dropped the popular party whistle into the pit of the groove on

"Funky Stuff," parties everywhere became shrill whistle-stops (and a Kool & the Gang jam was necessary for any legitimately hip party). When they added female vocals to the act in 1974, their new, sweet, harmonic jazzy sound influenced the entire music world. Kool & the Gang were leaders rather than followers because their deep spirituality and jazz roots grounded them. They displayed an understanding of the reverence for nature that was a part of the African heritage, and conveyed it through their popular music.

The African motif was expressed in 1975 with their *Spirit of the Boogie* LP, a record that featured a fold-out African artwork on the cover, and a number of compositions that featured the heavy bass and intricate horns of the James Brown style, yet still used prominent African percussion, and lyrics oriented toward more universal, spiritual themes. Tunes such as "Ancestral Ceremony," "Mother Earth," and "Jungle Jazz" made subtly important assertions about the reverence Kool & the Gang had toward their musical and spiritual roots—and by hitting the streets with hard funk, they brought their message to the masses.

Raised in and around the Jersey City housing projects, members and friends of the Bell family learned to play music with sticks and cans, and school instruments as youths. Meeting and playing in conga bands in the local park, the young players drew on their rhythmic roots, friendships, and a deep love for jazz and made their own group. Developing as the Jazziacs by 1964, the group was already led by big brother Ronald (Khalis Bayyan), with Robert "Kool" on bass, funky George Brown on drums, the hypnotically tight Charles Smith on rhythm guitar, and the magnificent brass of Dennis Thomas and Ronald/Khalis on saxes, with Robert "Spike" Mickens on trumpet. The group added pianist Rick West after their first album. Signed to De-Lite Records as Kool & the Flames in 1969, the group needed to change their name to avoid confusion with James Brown's group, the Famous Flames, and chose *the gang* because of the street feel of their music, which was where their roots were.

By 1972 some members of the group had converted to the Nation of Islam. The Bell brothers were given new names by the son of Elijah Muhammad himself, Wallace Muhammad. Gradually other members changed and featured their Muslim names on album liner notes, particularly on their 1976 album release *Open Sesame*. A deeply spiritual group of players, they blended as a spiritual *unit,* despite the diversity of their beliefs. The band expressed their religious orientation in universal statements of spirituality, in the same fashion as gospel-trained soul singers avoided preachiness by affirming love and God, rather than Jesus. Kool & the Gang would abandon their African imagery as the disco era beckoned, but in 1974 they were the No. 1 band in touch with the spirit of the boogie.

## AFRICAN INFLUENCE

There was plenty of support for The Funk from other parts of the world as well. There were many African music-oriented performers around who developed followings among black music listeners, such as Hugh Masakela from South Africa, the master drummer Babatunde Olatunji from Nigeria, the Afro-pop group Osibisa with members from Ghana and the Caribbean, the West Indian Afro-pop of Cymande, and the Cuban percussionist Mongo Santamaria. A more discernible funk influence could also be heard from saxophonist Manu Dibango from Cameroon, and the militant Nigerian bandleader Fela Anikulapo Kuti. A grooving African funk jazz-rock mix came from the New York City–based Afro-rock group Mandrill and the jazz-funk groups that featured African percussion prominently in their music, particularly Earth, Wind & Fire and Herbie Hancock's band, the Headhunters. These groups employed the standard electric bass, guitar, and brass section of a rhythm and blues group, while showcasing traditional percussion ensembles to accent the rhythms. The most successful of the Afro-rock groups was Manu Dibango, whose huge international 1973 hit "Soul Makossa" formalized the style. Members of Kool & the Gang admitted later that the influence of "Soul Makossa" is what drove them into the studio to record their breakthrough hits "Funky Stuff" and "Jungle Boogie." Perhaps just as important as the song itself is the fact that African musicians found their way into black music in greater numbers than ever before.

As far as The Funk was concerned, an African percussion section was an essential ingredient, musically speaking. From the earliest days of psychedelic black rock—Santana and Hendrix's six-piece Band of Gypsys at Woodstock in 1969—to the extended Norman Whitfield sessions on Temptations' albums at the otherwise stuffy Motown Records, Africa had come home to the heart of black music. Rich, percussion-filled breakdowns can be heard on many of the early seventies soul-funk standards such as Donny Hathaway's "The Ghetto" (studio and live versions), Marvin Gaye's "Inner City Blues," Curtis Mayfield's "Pusherman," Kool & the Gang's "Hollywood Swinging," and the Ohio Players' "Fire."

## EARTH, WIND & FIRE

The pop-funk formula, the African motif, and the theme of unity was expressed in grandest fashion by Earth, Wind & Fire. Founded by Maurice White in 1970, the group consisted of nine members plus a horn section, and was capable of playing everything from long Afro-jazz instruments and straight gospel-soul ballads to Sly Stone—flavored high-energy dance music. Regardless of the genre, though, their music always conveyed an infectious optimism and fresh sensuality; their lyrics were dense, poetic, and almost literary, but always accessible. It seems everything the group put out *clicked*.

White, a drummer and veteran of Chess Records' house band and the groundbreaking pop-jazz Ramsey Lewis Trio, recruited his brothers Verdine (bass) and later Fred (drums) to form the core of a wide-open percussion-filled jazz-pop act, a cross between the visuals of Sly Stone, the melodies of his Memphis roots (growing up with Booker T. Jones of the MGs), and the rhythms of Africa. Maurice was fond of the African thumb piano known as a kalimba, and featured it in all of the group's recordings. Touring through Denver in 1970, White met Philip Bailey, the drummer and singer of the opening act Friends & Love, one night. Bailey's falsetto voice brought a fantastic aural mood, as well as the musical brilliance of his own Denver buddies, keyboardist Larry Dunn and saxophonist Andrew Woolfolk.

Working out of Los Angeles, White compiled the rest of the band into what amounted to an all-star lineup, recruiting guitarist Al McKay from Charles Wright & the Watts 103rd Street Rhythm Band, vocalist Jessica Cleaves from the Friends of Distinction, and guitarist Johnny Graham from the New Birth.

The band's lyrics were rich, layered, and thoughtful, with densely packed phrases sung in syncopation over a variety of choppy rhythm breaks from the huge band. Equally at home with sentimental ballads or The Funk Bomb, sultry settings or fantastical romps, Earth, Wind & Fire elevated the standards of ensemble music as the entire world watched in amazement.

As part of Columbia Records' efforts to acquire black artists, the band was signed (away from Warner Bros.) in 1972 and was promoted heavily on both jazz and soul radio. Using the film soundtrack vehicle to their advantage (an earlier incarnation of Earth, Wind & Fire performed on Melvin Van Peebles's 1970 classic *Sweet Sweetback's Baadasssss Song*), Maurice White signed on to record the soundtrack to producer

Sig Shore's follow-up to *Superfly, That's the Way of the World*. The score for an insightful music business melodrama, the album allowed the band to take their time recording (in the Colorado mountains) and to develop a broad musical sound while remaining accessible. As a result, their ballads ("Reasons" and "All About Love") became more sentimental, their jazz-funk workouts became shorter and more coherent, and their joyous pop-soul was packaged to perfection.

"Shining Star" was the epitome of the band's idealism, infectious optimism, and incredible rhythmic mastery. A No. 1 pop and soul hit single in the summer of 1975, "Shining Star" had the pulsing throb and choppy guitars of classic James Brown fonk, an extra sweet guitar counterline that gave a Doobie Brothers' rock feel, surges of spectacular horn breaks that challenged Kool & the Gang, and furious hooks: "Shining Star for you to see—what your life can truly be!" The single opens the Grammy-winning album—a record that never lets up.

The success of the 1975 *That's the Way of the World* opened doors for the band's imagination and paved the way for a live tour that expanded the realm of black popular music. Recording live dates from around the country (and adding five studio tracks), the band's *Gratitude* double album, released in 1975, was a broad-ranging portrait of the magical essence throughout the *entire* black music tradition, and quickly became the standard by which live bands were measured.

On one of few live albums to capture the recording quality of a studio production, the band showcased their jazzy roots and African instruments on the exquisitely grooving "Sun Goddess" and the elaborate "New World Symphony," while lead singers Bailey and White expressed a genuine love to their screaming fans on live renditions of "Devotion" and "Reasons," and their showmanship sparkled through each song.

The band always kicked spirited funk tracks to drive their energetic shows. "Mighty Mighty," "Getaway," "Serpentine Fire," "In the Stone," and "Jupiter" all delivered the rich, rhythmic goods. The funky and jazzy instrumental workouts were always meticulous, with particularly *icey* funk chops on "Bad Tune," "Power," "Africano," and "Faces." The soft studio ballads were extended with long, sultry saxophone solos; the lead vocals of Philip Bailey and Maurice White soared into the skies; rich percussion draped the arrangements like a fine lace; and the audience participation and exhilaration was vivid and sincere.

Earth, Wind & Fire spent their larger budget on a larger show, wearing brightly colored skin-tight suits, platform shoes, ridiculous lapels, streamers, bellbottoms, and thousands of sequins. Stage props lifted the players to the rafters, spun the drum sets upside down, and beamed the band members out of cylinders on the stage. Wall-to-wall splash, sprints, slides, screams, sweat, and soul, Earth, Wind & Fire was a soul *christening* that every human being deserved to see. They toured every year from 1975 to 1979, creating an uproar in every town they hit. The entire package grew in size and scope year by year until by 1978 they were the most popular band in the world.

Earth, Wind & Fire represented the living fusion of traditions that had been on a collision course for a generation. The gospel love, the glitter of solid-gold soul, the informed jazz brilliance, and rooster-poot fonk at its zenith took the black music tradition to its highest heights, and still remains the standard.

### AVERAGE WHITE BAND

The universal nature and universal appeal of mid-seventies funk bands were underscored when the Average White Band, an all-white group from Scotland, scored one of the fonkiest records of 1975, "Pick Up the Pieces." The song's instrumental groove with a wicked be-bop horn riff on top and a slicing splankety guitar (which borrowed from the JBs' "Hot Pants Road") took radio listeners by surprise, but the band's workout, pulsing and grooving as saxophonist Roger Ball's masterful rolls built up the pressure, put the jam over the top.

The band betrayed its average white image when other meanly swanging, soulful hits hit the radio, and Hamish Stuart's off-key vocals hit right in the pocket. "Person to Person," "Cut the Cake," "A Love of Your Own," and "If I Ever Lose This Heaven" captured a strangely familiar soul sound that was sincere, interesting, and fresh, like a foreign guest in your house. The band covered a range of styles, locking R&B riffs in, capturing the soul ballad with surprising comfort, and by their third American LP, *Soul Searching* in 1976, the group had matured to an introspective, deeply grooving funk level. "It was the philosophy of funk, it really was," guitarist Allan Gorrie said in 1994. "We were a soul band, we could play be-bop stuff . . . there were these influences in there, but the main collision point of all the stuff was that we were a funk band."

The band's funk legacy shines brightest on one particular song, from their second LP, *Cut the Cake*—a delectably nasty begging song titled "Schoolboy Crush." A sly, metronomic drumbeat and delicately placed guitar syncopation rock the listener like a baby's crib, as the hook drives home the desperation of the situation: "She said look/but don't touch/that ain't much/it's only a schoolboy crush!" The track's beat has survived in some of today's Hip Hop hits, such as "Microphone Fiend" by Eric B and Rakim, "Grand Verbalizer, What Time Is It?" by X-Clan, and "Life Is Too Short" by Too Short. With members still performing in the 1990s, the Average White Band is another shining example of the united ethos of the times.

Unfortunately, any time white musicians get into a black thang, things can get messy. Although the Average White Band showed tremendous respect for the musical heritage they were welcomed into, they settled in America and eventually had difficulty finding a sound that rooted them—they had no blues roots or Motown roots, for example, to draw from—thousands of miles from their home. The stickiest issue they raised, however, was the notion that anyone—regardless of their background and attitude—can give up the funk. (While props should be given to Grand Funk Railroad, the Flint, Michigan, based hard-rock band—one of the first heavy metal bands that thrived on power chords and sweat to sell beer-drinking rock in the millions through the early seventies—because their funky attitude had a charming, stinky working-class irreverence, in terms of the groove it was not The Funk.) The white-led K.C. and the Sunshine Band, by contrast, was an organic, soulful band of Sly Stone clones with Florida black church roots that could be heard on every cut. They literally passed for a black band playing dance funk. Wild Cherry, on the other hand, came directly from the Pittsburgh-area rust-belt redneck rock clubs with their one and only hit "Play that Funky Music." With the tight rhythm lock, sassy vocals, and self-deprecating chant "Play that funky music white boy," the record soared to No. 1 pop, and, unbelievably, No. 1 R&B in September 1976. Doubts about the band's authenticity were confirmed when the shallow follow-up "Baby Dontcha Know (the Honkies Got Soul)" was released the following year.

While many powerful, soulful, *funky* white artists have delivered brilliant music (Frank Zappa, Edgar Winter, Eddie Money, David Bowie, Elton John, Eric Clapton, Eric Burdon, Joe Cocker, and the Beatles come to mind), the very question of America's musical identity comes into question whenever whites play black music. America's cruel history of centuries of creative exploitation is exposed by the classic turnabout. In the seventies, the funky white boy was a joke, but by the end of the decade, whites were all up into black music, disco was the sound of black America, street funk was under siege, and soul music ceased to exist. Even the success of a bona fide funk bomb like the Average White Band's "Pick Up the Pieces"—to this day one of the only No. 1 funk singles you can hear on rock and roll radio—needs to be seen partly as a function of race.

### RUFUS

With everyone getting into the picture in the mid-seventies, a female-led funk band was inevitable. One such act was Rufus, led by the sassy and stunning singer Chaka Khan. Rich robust black femininity never had a better role model than the youthful Chaka. Born Yvette Marie Stevens, she was a high school whiz, performing in student politics (Black Student Union president) and in the local Afro-Arts Theater (where Fred and Maurice White—later of Earth, Wind & Fire—used to hand out and soak up the African spirituality/free jazz/vegetarian/kalimba vibe). She took the name Chaka while working at a Black Panther Party breakfast program in Chicago. Although she isn't known to speak specifically of racial issues, Chaka nevertheless brings her roots to the forefront.

When she joined the band in 1970, Rufus was already a self-contained rhythm unit, once known as American Breed. Rufus made its own multiracial reputation in the Chicago area, featuring the intense drumming dynamics of Andre Fischer, Tony Maiden's guitar, Bobby Watson's bass, and Kevin Murphy's leadership on keyboards.

An astounding formulation of a band, even by seventies standards, the pop-rock stylists moved to L.A., and were taken literally by the hand into heavyweight contention as a funk band. After a low-key debut album that featured a cover of Stevie Wonder's "Maybe Your Baby," Stevie himself walked into the band's studio and handed the group a song he had written exclusively for Chaka's special, sensual qualities: "Tell Me Something Good." The slow, humping, heaving track was a natural showcase for the most powerful and sultry vocalist to hit the scene in years. The record also won a Grammy Award as best R&B group performance of 1974. The guitarist Ray Parker, Jr. (of Raydio fame) also brought the group a groove of his own that became "You Got the Love," the band's second hit record. The *Rags to Rufus* album became the first of five consecutive gold records. *Rufusized* followed in 1975, *Rufus Featuring Chaka Khan* in 1976, *Ask Rufus* in 1977, and *Street Player* in 1978, before Chaka went on to solo work of her own. Each record was a musical feast. Chaka's jazz-styled roots in pop format, throaty ballads that challenged Aretha Franklin's dominance, and the band's effortless range of moods made Rufus a No. 1 funk band.

More symbolically than literally, Chaka Khan provided a leadership role and a strong female image with the band, arranging songs and cowriting such monster hits as "Sweet Thing," "You Got the Love," and "Stay." Her strong identity was also revealed in the crunching rendition of "I'm a Woman (and I'm a Backbone)" from the group's *Rufusized* LP.

Her live act began in stirring fashion—dwarfing the band—as she dressed in tempting getups, and belted a furious range of sounds. The band's rhythm chops often pulsed in stuttering precision (like Tower of Power), while Chaka's voice soared over the open spaces. A string of propulsive funk splatters followed "Something Good": "Once You Get Started," "Dance Wit Me," "Ooh I Like Your Lovin'," "At Midnight," "Street Player," and many others. Their original, midtempo numbers were often their most creative. "Fool's Paradise," "Close the Door," "Somebody's Watching You," "Best of Your Heart," and "Egyptian Song" stand out as examples of a brilliant band in unison with an equally brilliant and creative singer. Leaving Rufus in 1979, Chaka's later solo works abandoned The Funk in favor of disco dance formulas and poignant jazz tributes. Songs from her solo work like "I'm Every Woman," "Papillon," and her 1984 smash "I Feel For You" all managed to transcend the music backing her up, while the group's unique chemistry was recaptured in 1983 with the monster hump of "Ain't Nobody." While few songs from Rufus contained the monster hooks used by samplers of modern beats, the band's coherent flow over a vast range of moods and textures, their exquisite rhythmic communication, and Chaka's incredible voice and delightful, sexy demeanor put a stamp on the music of the age that cannot be diluted in any form.

### FUNKY WOMEN

The fate of funky women in general, however, has been a disappointment over the years. While the number of female musicians remained fairly small (despite the success of Sly Stone's formula), there were a number of freaky, funky divas that gave up ground to no one, although they rarely had the backup Chaka Khan enjoyed. Of course the Godfather of Soul James Brown had an eye for female talent, and recruited the powerful Vicki Anderson (his favorite), the straight-talking Marva Whitney, and the hugely successful Lyn Collins. Another JBs backup singer, Yvonne Fair, was picked up by Motown Records and delivered one tasty funky pop album, *The Bitch is Black,* in 1974. The more durable Millie Jackson generated a career of low-down language and high-struttin' sass, as her aggressive sex appeal and snappy one-liners over-shadowed most of her songs, spanning a three-decade career. The lus-cious and ribald Betty Davis (the former Mrs. Miles Davis) produced a heated, funk-centered trio of underrated funk albums in the mid-seventies (check out "F.U.N.K." on the *Nasty Gal* album). She had a spicy act that was too hot for this country, and enjoyed more popular-ity in Europe. Betty had *turned out* the jazz genius Miles Davis in the 1960s, turning him on to Jimi Hendrix, showing him how to dress like a freak, and finally taking his name.

George Clinton's keen eye for female musical talent took shape in 1975, as he managed to bring Earth, Wind & Fire veteran Jessica Cleaves into the fold, and hired Sly Stone's backup singers Lynn Mabry and Dawn Silva on the spot. Mabry and Silva would become the first incarnation of the Brides of Funkenstein, sporting a strong dance hit in 1978, "Disco to Go," and a scorching live show, where Dawn Silva's one-legged Danskins predated track star Florence Griffith-Joyner's fashion statements by a decade.

Other singers such as Jeannete McGruder, Sheila Horne, Debbie Wright, Jeannette Washington, Malia Franklin, Shirley Hayden, and Janice Evans all took turns representing the "Brides," "Bridesmaids," "Parlet," and a variety of vocal chores with the P-Funk Mob.

Funky women didn't simply dress wild—they had *style.* The jazzy and snazzy Pointer Sisters began their pop careers with a forties' motif in 1973, and with the help of New Orleans producer Alan Toussaint scored huge funky hits "Yes We Can Can" and "How Long" to start their careers with a bang. Toussaint was also involved with the breakthrough of LaBelle, the scorching vocal trio of Nona Hendryx, Sarah Dash, and soon-to-be-superstar Patti Labelle. The "silver-suited space divas" had spent the late sixties in London, growing brasher and hungrier for sus-tained success from their years as the Bluebelles. Their No. 1 1975 smash "Lady Marmalade" blew the lid off of the standards of sexual in-nuendo and skyrocketed the group's star status. Sadly, their glittery image slipped into the disco undertow and was ultimately wasted as the trio broke up in search of solo star status.

One furiously hard worker who deserved solo star status was the incredible Tina Turner. Her voluptuous frame and relentless motion onstage overshadowed her compelling vocal delivery, a voice driven into bluesy sentiments by her ruthless husband, Ike. Unable to write songs that were removed from the sixties shuffle-step R&B fare, her husband, Ike Turner, resorted to blaming Tina for the band's absence from the record charts. How she endured, while delivering an electric performance nightly, is a tribute to a special spirit of a special sista. All too many brilliant female performers wound up fronting tame night-club acts, or fronting phantom disco groups that never actually recorded as a unit. If any of these women were blessed with a self-contained and creative band like Rufus was for Chaka Khan, there would have been a certain wave of funky divas on the scene, rather than the deluge of disco bimbos as the decade progressed.

## THE ISLEY BROTHERS

If Chaka Khan was the epitome of funky womanhood, the Isley Brothers were the epitome of funky black manhood, as the six heavyset brothers dropped a string of sweaty, masculine funk tracks throughout the seventies. Liberated from Motown in 1969, the group had *incorporated themselves* as T-Neck Records and signed a distribution deal with Buddha Records for four years, and finally hit paydirt when distributed by Columbia in 1973. The Isleys became the strongest proponent of hard, black funk grooves for years.

In a fascinating example of self-reliance, the older brothers, who had been recording a string of soul hits since "Shout" in 1959, put their younger siblings through music school, and introduced them on their *3+3 Featuring That Lady* album in 1973. Three singers and three musicians was all they needed. The group featured youngest brother Ernie Isley on lead guitar (and overdubs on drums) and Marvin on bass, while cousin Chris Jasper played keyboards. The slickly packaged single "That Lady" opened up a new era for the act, as Ernie's ferocious guitar solo weaved around a high-energy dance track, bringing the Jimi Hendrix heavy metal influence directly to black radio, and making yet another cover tune from their sixties years barely recognizable from the original.

The CBS contacts also provided for the production crew of Cecil and Margouleff—famous for programming Stevie Wonder's synthesizers—access to the Isleys' arrangements, laying down a churning funky bottom to the *3+3* album, and the gurgling bass on "Fight the Power." The band took it from there and delivered a series of tracks:

1974's "Live it Up" and "Midnight Sky"; 1975's "Fight the Power" and "The Heat Is On"; "People of Today" in 1976; the monsters "Livin' in the Life," "Go For Your Guns," and "The Pride" in 1977; and the phenomenal "Take Me to the Next Phase" in 1978. An assortment of interesting album cuts parlayed the younger players' talents in stunning fashion (such as the apocalyptic blues of "Ain't I Been Good to Ya" from *Live it Up*, the rocking "Hope You Feel Better Love" from *The Heat Is On,* the grooving "Tell Me When You Need It Again" from *Go For Your Guns,* and "Ain't Givin' Up No Love" from *Showdown*—and for this reason the Isleys' original albums (most are on CD) are much more revealing than any best-of compilations around.

One record more revealing than anything before was the No. 1 smash "Fight the Power." A menacing, gurgling groove of a funk jam on its own, the lyrics revealed just how much clout the Isleys held in 1975. Recording the breakdown with lyrics that went "I tried talking about it/I got the big runaround/when I roll with the punches I get knocked on the ground/by all this *bullshit* goin' down!" the brothers caused a national stir. While an edited version was given to the radios, many stations chose to let the uncut version play. People were drawn to the naked truth of the jam like a magnet, and in July 1975, the Isleys *ruled.* They took their leadership as artists seriously (for a few years, anyway) and followed up with the sentimental and socially relevant "Harvest for the World," a brilliant vision of the world's state, and the act's creative high point:

> Gather everyman, gather everywoman
> Celebrate your lives, give thanks for your children
> When will there be a harvest for all the people
> When will there be a harvest for the world . . .
> Dress me up for battle, when all I want is peace
> Those of us who pay the price, come home with the least
> Nation after nation, turning into beasts
> When will there be a harvest for the world.
>         The Isley Brothers, "Harvest for the World" (1976)

The Isley Brothers brought together their successful soul-singing background into their new sound, featuring the versatile brother Ronnie's voice, a gifted throat capable of voicing the tenderest sentiments such as "For the Love of You" and "Hello, It's Me," or scorching a manly riff along with the band, yelling in unison "been cooped up for too long/I just wanna live it up!" Their seventies act brought to life the visuals of their album covers, as the entire group was clad in freaked-out leather pants suits, parkas, boots, and bizarre studded and embroidered conquistador coordinates—red, gold, blue, yellow suede, you name it. The band's show provided a revealing juxtaposition of eras, as the younger players' theatrics fit with their musical purpose, while the older trio romped around onstage, often competing with the musical backing. As if to mirror the special, unified nature of the seventies, the band lasted as a sextet until 1984, breaking up and leaving the elder trio once again to continue their relentless hit-making vocal tradition.

By 1975, real bands not only dominated black music, they were challenging each other to ever higher standards. Stevie Wonder's brilliant, diverse works remained the centerpiece of the fluid funk mix, as his classic hits "You Haven't Done Nothin'," "Boogie on Reggae Woman," and "Creepin' " dominated black radio. The Isleys' *The Heat Is On* album featuring "Fight the Power" was a deliberate attempt to keep up with Stevie's flare for social statement and smooth sentiments. Earth, Wind & Fire's "Shining Star" and follow-up "Singasong" from the *Gratitude* album were also causing a major sensation, while the No. 1 hits by the Ohio Players ("Fire" and "Love Rollercoaster") were formidable, and the classy, jazzy riffs from Kool & the Gang ("Summer Madness," "Streetcorner Symphony," "Jungle Jazz") could not be ignored. The delicious lips logo and catchy hits "Dance Wit Me" and "Sweet Thing" from the *Rufus Featuring Chaka Khan* album provided powerful competition, while Larry Graham's tour de force "The Jam" rekindled the West Coast funk legacy, and some freaks from Detroit called Parliament were raising eyebrows with "Chocolate City" and "Tear the Roof Off the Sucker." The United Funk bands could deliver hit singles, provide a complete album-listening experience, and produce onstage in the best of the performance tradition. They were in fact redefining the hit-making tradition to reflect their own approach to the music—a synthesis of the entire African-American musical experience.

## THE OHIO PLAYERS

The new styles were represented most dramatically by the most stylish band in the land, the glamorous and gritty Ohio Players. The hit-making tradition was blown completely apart by this bunch of gutbucket funksters from Dayton, Ohio. Led on guitar and lead vocals by the blues genius Leroy "Sugarfoot" Bonner, the versatile Players took their grounded sounds in all directions. Locked in by drummer James "Diamond" Williams and Marshall Jones's bass, spread out by saxophone soloist and bandleader Clarence "Satch" Satchell, and backed up on trumpets by Ralph "Pee Wee" Middlebrooks and Marvin Pierce, the Players could tread every musical territory there was. The stomping blues of "Jive Turkey," the misty-eyed romance of "Heaven Must Be Like This," the ferocious thrash of monster funk-rock blasts "What the Hell" and "Fopp," and the thumpasaurus fonk of "Smoke" and "Who'd She Coo?" were all high points in each category. Yet it was their indescribable arrangements that set the Ohio Players even further above the rest. Their quirky, ever-changing layers of rhythms slid together into a fantastically fluid sound, heard on "Sweet Sticky Things," "I Wanna Be Free," "Contradictions," "Only a Child Can Love," "Runnin' from the Devil," and others.

Known for their scorching, high-pitched falsetto vocal hooks— "I want to be *free!*"—punctuating Sugarfoot's irresistible low-down pleading—"I will even take the blame *garl!*"—the Players kept a firm grip on the slicker, sexier standards of soul music, and smacked it together with the rowdy, down-home midwestern blues vibe to score the national No. 1 pop hits "Fire" (1975) and "Love Rollercoaster" (1976). Their string of gold albums for Mercury Records—*Skin Tight, Fire, Honey, Contradiction,* and *Gold*—delivered a luxurious and yet sassy slice of cool fonk for the masses from 1974 to 1977. Sugar's unmistakable drawl, "Oww Garl," was an instant hit maker, and became a staple of bluesy funk for a generation, as it was copied by Lionel Richie of the Commodores, Larry Dotson of the Bar-Kays, and Larry Blackmon of Cameo during the next phases of The Funk.

While the group languished on the margins as a freaked-out black rock posse for Westbound Records from 1971 to 1974, a move to Mercury brought the Players in touch with the hit-making machinery they needed. For their first move the band recruited cross-state keyboard genius Billy Beck to provide some sanity to the proceedings, as well as a satin-sheen ARP synthesizer sound, that gave the Players' music a luxurious black-mobster-lounging-in-his-penthouse feel to it. Then, in an effort to outdo their already legendary S&M image from Westbound Records—where they had hired a black model to pose baldheaded, holding whips and in chains—the group's spokesman Satch asked to have their Mercury albums feature a nude black woman on the cover of the LP. The company obliged by hiring *Playboy* magazine photographer Richard Fegley to lay out the album covers for *Skin Tight, Honey, Mr. Mean,* and *Gold.*

Predictably, controversy raged, especially after the much-anticipated *Honey* album hit the streets. After the No. 1 hit "Fire" in the fall of 1975, even America's lily-white rock and roll market was poised for the next Players set. The stunning album cover—featuring a nude model lapping up honey on the outside cover and, still nude, covered with honey on the inside cover—blew the lid off of pop standards of decency. The cover model, photographed by Fegley, was Panamanian-born Esther Stobba, the October 1974 Playboy Centerfold then known as Esther Cordet.

America's values of sex, power, race, rock, and The Funk were all affected by *Honey.* First, the *audacity* of the band—at the peak of their success—to come so hard with their flavor had a peculiar exhilaration that for many overwhelmed the obvious issues of the cover's blatant sexism; also, Fegley's ability to bring about a stylish eroticism into the most improbable of settings—and for the first time on such a scale—took the sexual allure of black women out of the closet (as far as the white mainstream was concerned) and "elevated" black women to the status of sex symbols. It was a dubious achievement—stemming from the same power trip that many so-called gangsta rappers seem obsessed with today. What *Honey* did accomplish was to break open the prevailing standards of what was an acceptable expression in cover art, creating a skin-showing precedent that was exploited by disco groups throughout the decade (the fact that Donna Summer's orgiastic wails on "Love to Love You Baby" were sweeping the radio in early 1976 along with *Honey* also helped foster the black freak mystique). When all was said and done, there was the brilliant and unforgettable music that made the record *necessary* to deal with.

Yet the controversy around *Honey* continued to grow, as rumors spread that the cover model claimed to have been burned by the honey at the photo shoot, developed a terrible skin rash, and demanded the record company pay her bills. Another rumor spread that the model was murdered during the taping of "Love Rollercoaster," as she tried to recover compensation, and her scream can be heard on the breakdown of the song. The whole thing was a hoax, of course, that the band had nothing to do with. ("We're musicians, not murderers," James "Diamond" Williams made clear in a recent interview.) Nevertheless, as is typical of rock and roll folklore, rumors spread that the Players had taken a vow of silence about the whole (entirely false) affair, and the mysteries shot record sales through the roof. The nasty, sassy Players kept music fans interested, misogynists interested, feminists interested, white rock fans interested, black teenagers *obsessed,* and Mercury Records in the black.

Life went on for the Ohio Players after their days in the sun. The mayor of Dayton, Ohio, proclaimed May 16, 1976, to be Ohio Players Day, giving each band member a key to the city. Fans followed each new release for the *album covers* as much as the music, but the hits faded. Their live concerts always had a wild look, but their act was not as large as their image, as they thrived in the smaller blues clubs where their roots were. Living the life of players to the hilt, the band began to spend their advance money faster than they could make albums. Their music became looser, longer, and less creative; debts, drugs, and a lack of hits did in the Players until a revived new incarnation in 1989 began touring again, consisting of core members Sugarfoot, Diamond, and guitarist Chet.

The end result of the Ohio Players' experience had a far-reaching impact on the packaging of black music. The plush, pristine mix of the band's totally original sound raised the standards of studio production quality that would take CDs to recapture a decade later. The lavish string arrangements on some of the band's cuts, however, helped bring about acceptance of the polished synthetic sounds of the disco arrangers. The blatant sex-freak imagery of their album art opened the doors for even cruder images by other acts, yet their music stands untouchable. Unfairly judged and masters of their craft, the Ohio Players stand out as legends of their time.

### THE COMMODORES

Perhaps the band that gave the greatest impression (outside of P-Funk) of newer changes in music was the Commodores, a self-contained sextet from none other than the Motown family, a label notorious for developing talent in the mold of the prevailing trends. The Commodores began at Tuskegee Institute in Alabama as the Mighty Mystics, led by pianist and vocalist Lionel Richie, with the chanking tones of Thomas

McClary on guitar, and William King on trumpet. Adding Milan Williams on keyboard—a penchant for loud clavinet twangs was his forte—along with drummer Walter Orange and Ronald LePread on bass gave the band their main ingredients: a close-knit family feel, a southern fonky flavor, and, with the help of Motown Records, a glittery, ostentatious image that could only be maintained through loud, swanging music.

One of the only attempts ever for the Motown family with self-contained bands, the Commodores got the greatest start any working group could ask for: *the world.* They were put on tour as the opening act for the ultra-popular Jackson 5, touring through Japan and the Philippines. After releasing their first hit single "Machine Gun" in 1974, the act opened for the Rolling Stones, Stevie Wonder, and the O'Jays before their record sales led them to top billing. By then the act had developed a mastery of size, scope, and show in their performances.

The catchy pop flavors of the band had an instant appeal, for despite the many layers of glitz, shining coordinated space-funk uniforms, crunching rhythm licks, and synthesizer-track melodies, the down-home soulfulness of their mellow vibes always came through. While it would be years before lead singer Lionel Richie would head to superstardom as a solo act, the Commodores were an ideal mix of futuristic showmanship and down-home sentiments.

Their rooster-poot fonk was evident on their first album, *Machine Gun,* which featured a number of wicked instrumentals such as "Rapid Fire" and "Gonna Blow Your Mind," and stanky ditties like "I Feel Sanctified" and "Young Girls Are My Weakness."

The *Machine Gun* album featured no ballads at all and is heavily laden with keyboardist Milan Williams's trickery on clavinet and synthesizers. The *Caught in the Act* album served up the very nasty "Slippery When Wet" dance track, but introduced Richie's softer side with the intriguing "This Is Your Life." (The *Movin' On* LP followed, with Richie's "Sweet Love" being the high point.) With each subsequent album, Richie is featured on one ballad after another, and a peculiar schizoid funkiness came from the Commodores sound: As catchy as their hits were, the Commodores literally wrote the book on album-filler funk tracks, as their hit-or-miss tonalities grabbed you one way or the other—with no middle ground—often hitting you differently each time.

The group finally came of age in late 1976 with the amazing *Hot on the Tracks* album. Busting out with hard-core grooves "Fancy Dancer" and "Come Inside," their fonk was to be expected, but by this point there was so much more to their sound. A string of playful, midtempo finger-snapping goodies (such as "High on Sunshine," "Girl, I Think the World Aboutcha," "Let's Get It Started") filled the record up, rather than the contrived synth-funk they were becoming known for. But their true breakthrough was the seven-minute ballad "Just to Be Close to You." Soaring to No. 1 R&B, the record had all of the soulful, sincere laments of the best of the southern singers, of which Lionel Richie was one, but it had something different. Instead of the posh classical string backgrounds of earlier soul slow dance tracks, the ballad used high-tech–sounding snippets to accent Richie's delivery, creating a time-warp feel, morphing from southern down-home to futuristic funky flavors.

The eventual pop success of *Hot on the Tracks* led to a massively successful follow-up, the self-titled *Commodores* album, a No. 1 pop funky soul masterpiece that featured the all-time hits "Easy" and "Zoom," and the frat-party standard "Brick House." With "Easy," Richie had found the country-funk flavor of his Alabama roots, falling in with a laid-back homespun ballad over a bouncing piano riff. "Zoom" offered his introspective spin on society and the need to escape, while "Brick House" was the engine that drove the entire Commodores train. With fans sucked in to their ballads, the accessibility of the Commodores' country-funky yet high-tech flavors, the familiarity of Richie's soulful Motown-sounding voice, and the band's monster rhythm track, "Brick House" surged to the nation's Top 5 hits, and became one of the few funk tracks to transcend the emerging disco formula in 1977.

The Commodores followed up their pop successes with many more ballads, beginning with "Three Times a Lady" in 1978, and became the first of too many funk bands to abandon their sassy style in favor of pop notoriety. Although their music *jammed* and the Commodores were a classy act, their quick change in style implies that perhaps their funk was merely a fashionable gimmick. Not saying much for a music born from the Black Revolution.

Similar shifts away from The Funk—and toward the repetitive sameness of the disco beat—occurred with other big acts. Recording a simplified dance track now and then was not the end of the world—but when an entire album featured monorhythmic drek, that group's days were numbered. Kool & the Gang, Rufus, AWB, and the Isleys were through with The Funk by 1980. Other funk groups such as Slave, Cameo, Brick, the Bar-Kays (and of course P-Funk), and Rick James would replace them, and it seemed for too many jam fans who enjoyed the total musical experience of the funk bands that by the end of the seventies, the "shining star" was burning out.

# PART FIVE

# The P-Funk Dynasty (1976–79): One Nation Under a Groove

# FIFTEEN

# *Disco Fever: The (Real) Hustle*

"With some simplification of its rhythms,
funk became the basis for disco."
*Rolling Stone Encyclopedia of Rock and Roll*

### THE CARTER ERA

The late seventies was a peculiar time for Americans. It was the period when escapist entertainment went from being an exciting sideshow to the center of the American cultural experience. The simple, catchy dance music called disco became a focal point of a culture that had lost its direction. Without war footage, riots, or tribal rock gatherings like Woodstock, the counterculture seemed to disappear, and the culture of *television* took center stage. The country was just recovering from the Watergate presidential scandal, the Arab oil boycott, and the "Energy Crisis" of the early seventies. American military strength and morale was waning in the wake of Vietnam, while at home the domestic infrastructure was gradually declining. Many local governments had become bloated with bureaucracy and filed for bankruptcy. The cosmopolitan capital of New York City suffered a crippling garbage strike, a newspaper strike, a power outage in 1977, and near total bankruptcy by 1978. Social services grew less efficient, more suspect, and finally led to what Jimmy Carter called a "malaise" that had spread through the nation in 1980.

As the seventies began to acquire the reputation of a decade devoid of social upheavals, race moved out of the spotlight. Scholars debated the "declining significance of race," while a new type of "neoconservative" emerged, one who actively socialized with racial minorities, yet harbored economic or social beliefs more consistent with the established status quo. Whites could now socialize with blacks and Latinos in the new discos that had sprung up in every city as a replacement for the live concert fare. The "color-blind" music gave the *impression* of a color-blind society, but that impression was far from the reality.

Television caricatures of blacks in the late seventies didn't help the situation. The euphoria of minorities on network television in the early seventies wore off as television shows such as *Good Times, Sanford and Son, What's Happening* and *That's My Mama* pandered to stereotypes, delivering a string of stale stories with the required fat black women and shady hustlers to bring "authenticity" to the setting. The funky and low-down humor on the shows gave the impression that it was cool to be black *and poor*. None were produced by African-Americans, and it showed.

While blacks could be found on television during the late seventies in great numbers, the trend of black action films (and films made by black filmmakers in general) was on the wane, and with them went the strong music soundtracks by black musicians. The growth of disco led to a logical and very profitable movie soundtrack experiment. The 1978 film *Saturday Night Fever,* a story about an Italian club dancer in Brooklyn played by John Travolta, became the biggest-grossing movie of the year, and the soundtrack, a compilation of new and previously released disco hits from a dozen known groups, sold over thirty million copies and became the largest-selling music album of all time. The film revived the careers of Australian pop singers the Bee Gees, Florida soul singers Tavares, and the fading funk band Kool & the Gang, while introducing a number of other disco favorites. The film also set the formula for "dance" movies distributed primarily as vehicles for soundtracks that could continue to issue singles and sell well beyond the close of the films.

### DISCO AS FANTASY

Disco fantasy became something of a fad and a formula after the No. 1 hit "The Hustle" by Van McCoy in 1975. This new sound provided a dance experience with easy-to-learn steps, taught at clean clubs typically managed by gays and white ethnics and set on the high-class boulevards (rather than dank R&B venues in da hood), and drew a middle-class white American set into the fold. The sensual dance-floor fantasies grew in scope and length as songs were extended ad infinitum—first by disco deejays lining up pairs of the same record on two turntables, and later by record companies that pressed "dance singles," records the size of twelve-inch albums but containing only one song. The endless dance, the throbbing, simple beat, the impenetrable sheen of polyester fashions, and the perpetual rush of cocaine were all a part of the escapism of the disco experience.

Every aspect of American popular culture took hold of the disco phenomenon. As a predecessor to aerobics clubs, trendy disco lessons became all the rage. A number of theme-oriented disco hits were served up for the nondancing public to consume. Disco remixes of hits by the Beatles, Sly and the Family Stone, and Motown hit medleys were popular, and themes from TV shows such as *S.W.A.T.* and *Starsky and Hutch* scored big. The intergalactic science fiction parable *Star Wars* spawned a million-selling disco album by Meco, in which dancers could be taken to "a galaxy far far away." Even the children's show *Sesame Street* recorded a disco album.

## SEXPLOITATION

The culture of disco exploited the black music experience in selective, manipulative, and ultimately racist ways. When Donna Summer was "discovered" by producer Georgio Moroder, her sensuous, strong voice was exploited in ways never before heard of. Her novelty record "Love to Love You Baby" featured a fantastic simulated sex act "performed" by Summer that scorched the radio in early 1976. Her "marathon of orgasms" prompted a wide range of reactions, not the least of which was activist Jesse Jackson's stand against what was being called "sex-rock." Jackson and his Chicago-based Operation PUSH (People United to Save Humanity) threatened to boycott records and distributors associated with the "garbage and pollution which is corrupting the minds and morals of our youth." PUSH sponsored a number of conferences on "X-rated" rock music, which included the denunciation of such gems as Johnnie Taylor's "Disco Lady" and K.C. and the Sunshine Band's "Shake Your Booty."

Despite Jackson's high-profile gambit, sexually suggestive records proliferated on the radio. The record companies basically ignored Jackson, claiming that the audience dictated their playlists and thus the morality of the airplay. It should be noted that the rise of sexually explicit music coincided with the invasion of national syndicates into black and pop radio, diminishing the local controls that were in place in the 1960s. The fact that Jackson was not taken seriously underscored the painful reality that black music was now out of the control of its practitioners.

Aesthetically, "Love to Love You" caused even more problems. As entertaining as the record was for many, it marked a symbolic demolition of the age-old black musical tradition of innuendo: of teasing, implying, and anticipating the sexual experience as a means of enriching it—through music. From this point forward, it was now more hip to express oneself in black pop *explicitly,* rather than implicitly. While any moron can state something explicitly, it takes an artist to embellish a statement with implicit meanings—not to mention subtly stimulating music. (This is one reason why "Funky Stuff" by Kool & the Gang, for example, is easily as sexy as Rick James's "Give It to Me Baby." While James demands "give it to me," Kool & the Gang imply the same impulse by simply singing "La-de-da-de-da"!) Another hallmark of great funk had bitten the dust.

### DISCO MUSIC

Many of the unique innovations in dance music made by The Funk, such as the use of African percussion, classical strings, and extended jams, were all exploited by disco. Congas, bongos, and a variety of percussion instruments could be heard on the most successful dance hits, from the Bee Gees' "You Should Be Dancin' " to Gloria Gaynor's "Casanova Brown." But African rhythms in disco were all too often used as a gimmick and did not hold the ethnic identification among disco fans that they did with funk or soul music listeners. European musical influences fared no better. The stirring synthesis of soulful R&B grooves accompanied by the sounds of an entire orchestra was perfected by Barry White and his Love Unlimited Orchestra in 1973; two years later Walter Murphy capitalized on the idea in his gimmick hit "Fifth of Beethoven," as a well-known hook from Beethoven's Fifth Symphony is repeated over and over by a keyboard on top of a disco beat. For what it's worth, the song was a catchy No. 1 pop hit.

The long-playing dance single was an innovation that should be credited to James Brown. His bands performed in the ageless African tradition of extended dance workouts, improvising along the simplest of patterns and filling up the space with lively rhythmic interplay. Brown's courageous impulse to record his songs as long dance cuts— seven minutes of "Cold Sweat," ten minutes of "Sex Machine," thirteen minutes of "Papa Don't Take No Mess"—were copied by funk bands initially, and then by disco producers who used *machines* instead of bands to extend their songs.

Studio producers took advantage of the many new recording techniques and used the drum machine—now realistic-sounding enough to simulate a real drummer throughout a song—and created endless music. To real music fans, the new developments were dreadful.

Interminable to some, and exhilarating to others, formless disco tracks became the rage. These producer-made tunes generally lacked any sense of sequence—beginning, buildup, catharsis, release—yet they were simple and catchy enough to bring rhythmless suburbanites and other neophytes flocking to plush dance clubs at strip malls from coast to coast. Silver Convention's "Fly, Robin Fly" (1976) and A Taste of Honey's 1978 "Boogie Oogie Oogie" were perhaps the epitome of the endless, brainless dance track performed by interchangeable vocalists (both records went to No. 1 soul). The "disco diva" became something of a cult phenomenon, as Donna Summer clones were "invented" with regularity by record companies banking on the gullibility of the audience. Anita Ward, Cheryl Lynn, Gloria Gaynor, Diana Ross, Patti LaBelle, Stargard, Sister Sledge, and Linda Clifford were among the best of an endless list of packaged prima donnas. By virtue of disco's lack of soulful vocalizing, the mixed-race or all-white acts sounded similar to black groups, and could score huge on the disco charts—and, unfortunately, the soul charts as well.

Universal Funk gave way to color-blind, brain-dead pop. Initially, there had been stiff criteria for white performers to succeed in black music, but disco changed that. The heavy funk of the Average White Band gave way to the lightweight, grooving dance funk of K.C. and the Sunshine Band, which opened the doors for the Australian trio the Bee Gees, the gay macho spoof of the Village People, the biggest-selling black chart hit of the Rolling Stones ("Miss You" in 1978), and finally the easy-rock duo Captain & Tennille's ironic "Do That to Me One More Time," in 1980. For the first time since the heyday of Elvis Presley in 1960, white groups made steady inroads onto the black charts, and not everyone was thrilled about it. Ken Emerson discussed the dilemma of disco in a 1977 *Saturday Review* article:

> Disco is an integrated music, probably more so than any other, and many discotheques are meeting grounds for blacks, whites, and "Hispanics." But have blacks been sufficiently assimilated into white American society (they certainly haven't been into the economy) that they can afford, psychologically, to dispense with music that is uniquely and

pridefully their own? If not, the effects of disco may well be dispiriting.

These dispiriting effects were clear: The affirmation of blackness was less and less a financially sound product. It was finally time for black music—the most primal and intimate aspect of black American culture—to integrate. Black radio stations found themselves playing "color-blind" music and assumed that their audience reflected their new perspective. A move away from black radio toward "urban contemporary" spread around the country, as the harsh realities of white ownership filtered deeper into the daily radio fare than ever before. Black flagship stations like WBLS in New York and KSOL in San Francisco were transformed overnight into the Saturday Night Fever formula, with fewer and fewer black deejays and less and less distinctively black-sounding music. In his book *The Death of Rhythm and Blues,* Nelson George described this period as nothing short of cultural suicide:

> Black radio—not everywhere, but in too many cities—
> became disco radio, just as not all but too many black artists
> made beige music. . . . In the long run, it was a march of
> folly. In the short run, it made many black artists unac
> ceptable on urban stations. Just a decade after James Brown
> cut "Say it loud, I'm black, and I'm proud," urban program
> directors began telling promoters that many black artists
> were "too black" for their format. Millie Jackson and
> Cameo: too black. The phrase echoed with the sound of self-
> hate. Too black. A retreat from the beauty of blackness. Too
> black. The sound of the death of R&B.

With the one strong, indignant exception of The Funk blasting its way through the airwaves, disco radio spread like a crippling disease on the heartbeat of a people. The once-heralded soul music aesthetic was no longer viable by the late seventies (see Chapter ten)— economically or culturally. What was really needed at the time was funk radio, a format of black music with musicality and consciousness that affirmed the values of the black community. What happened was disco radio, the death of rhythm and blues.

In the seventies the radio was always on, and black listeners were the most vulnerable to the new trends of "color-blind" entertainment.

Black radio was constantly at the upper limits of FCC federally regulated commercials-per-hour density. Over and over again mundane music would be played and people would buy it; irrelevant products would be advertised by promoters with no interest in the black community, and they would be purchased in ever greater numbers; public service announcements and public affairs programming declined along with black deejays and program directors; and black artists found themselves constantly under pressure to conform to the "format," which was not even defined by the audience.

## THE DISCO INDUSTRY

Market research studies such as the infamous "Harvard Report" on the black music industry, which is detailed by Nelson George in his book *The Death of Rhythm and Blues,* defined the soul music phenomenon in terms of its viability as a money-making *product* for CBS Records. The resulting corporate domination over the recruitment of acts, production of the music, promotion, distribution, and ultimately radio airplay and the *radio format* all served to validate the premise that black music was "taken over" by the corporations.

The late seventies was a difficult period for many musicians, for there were fewer and fewer opportunities for creativity in music within the recording industry parameters. Disco was now an integral component of popular music in general, and black music in particular. Upstart record companies like Casablanca and T.K. Records flooded the market with simplistic, accessible, often mindless, yet entertaining dance music, and the established labels were forced to follow suit. Radio stations, particularly those in national syndication, picked up on the nationwide dance craze and fueled the consumption of "dance music" as a style all its own. In 1976 the industry yardstick, *Billboard* magazine, expanded its local disco action charts to a "National Disco Action" countdown, and doubled its size in 1979 to become the "Disco Top 100," which identified the nation's most popular dance hits. Dance music was in demand, and record companies produced it by any means necessary. Fredric Dannen described what was happening in his 1991 book *Hit Men*:

> All the major labels had caught disco fever and were shipping vast quantities of dance and pop albums based more on egotism than demand. The retailers took them. Why not?

In 1979 they started to come back by the steam-shovel. The mistake made by PolyGram—and also CBS and Warner and the other majors—was shipping records and logging them as sales, never dreaming that the usual return estimates were way low.

The entire music industry learned its lesson from Casablanca Records founder Neil Bogart, who brought us disco diva Donna Summer from nightclubs in Germany, the rock band Kiss, and disco upstarts the Village People, and opened the door for George Clinton's expensive and expansive imagination to wander with the funk band Parliament. Bogart lived like a king, and perfected the art of "overhyping" acts with little talent. It was he who first took the chance of shipping unknown acts by the millions, and paying bills with imaginary record sales. With the low quality of so much disco music flooding the radio market, the necessity grew—and opportunities grew—for salespeople whose job it was to hype the worthless music for radio airplay. A network of middlemen whose sole job it was to get a product on radio stations developed, with all the requisite turf battles and dirty dealings.

By 1979 even the largest record companies were risking financial ruin by promoting mediocre music through a network of intermediaries. Concern for quality had gone through the floor, as even the most respected pop acts produced disco hits, from rock singers Rod Stewart ("Do Ya Think I'm Sexy," 1979) and the Rolling Stones ("Miss You," 1978) to jazz musicians Herbie Hancock ("I Thought It Was You," 1978) and Donald Byrd ("Sexy Dancer," 1982).

Meanwhile, record companies devised other devious ways to increase profits while undermining the cultural integrity of black music. Labels began to pass the burden of promotion on to the artists, making some new artists' profits cover the costs of promotion as well as production. A new act might cost $50,000 to make an album, but it would be another $100,000 to $200,000 to promote the group in the new climate of hype. A new act literally had to go gold before any net profits would be gained. This again increased the need for a dance single, despite the artists' format. Dance singles were nothing new for black artists, but the monorhythmic, soulless, interminable standard of disco music rendered many artists with integrity unable to remain profitable.

Record companies also began refusing to take returned merchandise, requiring retailers to make accurate judgments of their product's demand. This effectively squeezed out the small-time record stores, who rarely had the capital to take a gamble on "experimental" music and were reduced to dealing with the syndicated hit-making distributors. In short, if it wasn't on the radio, small dealers wouldn't stock it. Major labels took control of every aspect of black music at this time, from management to distribution, promotion, and *actual musical production,* leaving a perceptible void in the heart and soul of a people's collective identity.

Musicians for the most part had an awful time adjusting to the new environment of promotion and hype. A sad transition can be seen in even the most authentic bands, who were compelled to derive new formulas to remain accessible. Earth, Wind & Fire, for example, scored a No. 1 hit in 1975 with their funkiest jam, "Shining Star"—but by 1979 their spin on the pop trends landed them with the droll "Boogie Wonderland." The Isley Brothers changed pace in 1979 after an unbroken string of monster funk albums for Columbia that had started in 1973, with 1979's "It's a Disco Night," a feeble attempt at disco sales. Even the P-Funk juggernaut of Parliament could not escape the disco influence, as their self-admitted worst record ever, "Party People," was forced upon the public as a concession to airplay demands. Producer Quincy Jones revised the original flavors of the established platinum funk artists Brothers Johnson on their fourth album, *Lite Up the Nite,* in 1979, as well as Rufus and Chaka's 1979 *Masterjam* disc, both of which reeked of disco-dance folly.

With few exceptions, it was the record companies who determined which songs were to be promoted on radio, which usually meant a potential crossover hit, usually a nonethnic dance track, otherwise known as a disco single. Thus the syndrome of lame disco singles festering on the radio, with albums following months later, became part of music-industry tradition. Ultimately, this led to the success or failure of bands based on their ability to produce disco hits. This helped to destroy many black acts who failed to generate dance-single airplay and wound up with no airplay at all. While strong dance bands such as Brass Construction and Cameo could navigate this environment, the overemphasis on disco dance tracks warped the wide, rich realm of black popular music. Once again the corporate mentality had overtaken racial consciousness to the point where music was *product* rather than culture.

## DISCO SUCKS

It was becoming common knowledge that disco music was destroying the integrity of black music, but there was very little that could be done. Those who spoke out in opposition quickly became branded *too radical* for an increasingly controlled system of promotion, payola, and pale music. Jesse Jackson took the record labels to task for promoting overtly sexual songs, but who was to blame for the overtly insipid records? Everyone knew *who* was doing it—it was everyone—but nobody wanted to lose their job, either. To oppose disco amounted to taking a racial stand, such as Atlanta's legendary deejay and promoter Jack Gibson, a.k.a. Jack the Rapper, whose weekly black radio tip sheet often defiantly claimed, "Black radio shouldn't play any white records." But many artists were *told* to play "white" music in the form of disco singles, and if they wanted to keep their jobs, they were obligated to contribute to the demise of their own traditions. Ultimately there was nothing black America could do about the withering of black popular music as a voice of its people. Nothing could be done about the plethora of corporate radio stations taking over black-owned stations, about the swarm of chain-stores squeezing out mom-and-pop record stores, and the intervention of major-label managers and promoters undermining the autonomy of black performers. The only silver lining in this fiasco was the fact that white America went to war against disco as well.

It's safe to say that the average rock and roll fan was through with disco by 1979. With the absurd sales of the *Saturday Night Fever* soundtrack, disco beats had begun to sound sappy to even the most uncultured Americans. While watching many of the remaining pop and rock icons such as Elton John, David Bowie, and the Rolling Stones degenerate into disco dementia, many rock fans saw the same corporate takeover of their radio as black-music fans saw, and were just as irate. Many blamed disco for the problems of rock and roll and placed *all* black music under the guise of disco as well. Since most of the anti-disco funk music—P-Funk, Slave, Brick, Bar-Kays—never found its way to pop radio, the ignorance and the condemnation were to be expected.

Unlike black urban radio stations (whose deejays couldn't trash disco and keep their jobs), rock and pop radio stations hired deejays who claimed the integrity to respond to their audience, and went on the warpath against the disco scourge. Stations resorted to call-in contests on their most hated disco song, used slogans like "ABOLISH DISCO

IN OUR LIFETIME," featured gimmicks like a "no-disco weekend," and even resorted to smashing disco records over the air. One irate rock deejay in Chicago was so obsessed with the disco phenomenon (which was indeed taking over rock stations and putting rock deejays out of work) that he organized a promotion with the Chicago White Sox baseball team in which fans would be admitted for 98 cents if they brought along a disco record for the "disco demolition" rally in between games of a double-header with the Detroit Tigers on July 12, 1979. Between ten thousand and twenty thousand records were reportedly placed in the center of the field and blown up, to the delight of the crowd, which, according to news reports, went wild, tearing up the field and getting in fights, chanting, "Disco sucks." The field was trashed and the second game was canceled, but the deejay made his point. Disco, in fact, sucked.

Disco ultimately became a pseudonym for *any* black music to most of America's rock fans, and when the disco fad effectively was killed off, by 1982 at the latest, it was still used as a term to define black dance music. Labeling everything black as disco was a shrewd gimmick by those who did not wish competition from blacks in the business; stigmatizing black music helped to paralyze reform efforts and segregate the music even further. Unfortunately, The Funk was included in the blanket condemnation of disco by critics, rock fans, jazz fans, and trendy pop knuckleheads. But as time would prove, nothing could stop the relentless tide of grooving, meaningful music, The Funk of the late seventies.

# SIXTEEN

# Dance Funk: Do You Wanna Get Funky With Me?

*"That's the way—uh huh uh huh—I like it."*
*K.C. and the Sunshine Band*

## DANCE FUNK

Busting on the scene by 1975, a slew of heavily funk-influenced bands took the black dance impulse and deliberately stretched it into more repetitive formulas for more "accessible" consumption. Leaders of this new pack were K.C. and the Sunshine Band, the B.T. Express, Brass Construction, and Brick (all of whom scored with No. 1 R&B hits in either 1975 or 1976). Known almost exclusively as dance bands, they brought together the best of the James Brown sound and locked it in with catchy, all-purpose hooks for anyone to use. Gimmick hooks like "Do a little dance/make a little love/get down tonight" or "Go on and do it/do it/do it 'til you're satisfied" quickly became the standard for that crucial dance hit. Songs became semi-instrumentals, with only one phrase repeated over and over again. Unlike the essential, soulful James Brown chants ("Get own up") that were designed to emphasize the soulfulness of the singer, the new dance bands had a universal tone—one that anyone, from any tradition, could connect to. The fantastic, ethnic, rhythmic realm of black funk was getting whitewashed for the masses. In the same way that rock and roll grew out of rhythm and blues, only to be taken from its originators, disco was co-opting the Godfather's fundamental breakthroughs and distilling The Funk for a generation of polyester consumers. At first, the disco-dance bands burned up the floor with such energy, nobody seemed to notice the warning signs, but some funkateers could see that K.C. and the Sunshine Band was the beginning of the end.

## K.C. AND THE SUNSHINE BAND

K.C. and the Sunshine Band came up from a racially mixed Miami/ Hialeah, Florida, music culture, one in which white lead singer Harry Wayne "K.C." Casey was raised—and weaned—on gospel church music. His associations at the budding Florida dance record company T.K. Records brought Casey in touch with many performers, including the crafty R&B singer Clarence Reid (a.k.a. Blowfly) as well as his producer-to-be, Richard Finch. Their collaborations, along with T.K.'s support, brought together a high-energy band with a funky bottom, and flashy disco show up top. The combination was electric—and all too easy to imitate. The scorching grooves on "Get Down Tonight," "That's the Way I Like It," "Shake Your Booty," "Keep It Coming Love," "Do You Feel Alright," and "Do You Wanna Go Party" all brought the richness of the wide-open R&B feel into the age of mindless music, with dire consequences for the future. Casey's bouncing hair and joyous glee onstage personified the multiracial ideals of the new dance craze, and his blissful, almost spacey gaze was a symbol of the nylon fantasyland he helped create.

His almost hysterical penchant for repeating brainless hooks was an ideal gimmick for the increasingly simplified radio format. Relentlessly repeating titles like "That's the way I like it" were chanted as disco mantras in the spring of 1976. The use of traditional church-band accompaniments, the crashing sock-cymbals, percussive, energetic horn lines, a tambourine, and a relentless display of positive energy made the Sunshine Band a worldwide attraction. Despite the fact that his black competition gave at least lip service to social commentary in their music, K.C.'s energy and sincere enthusiasm for the "color-blind" music brought the band to superstar heights. From 1976 onward, black bands with anything close to a dance groove were compelled to keep up with K.C.'s spirited vibes, and drop down to the thematic oblivion of K.C.'s one-syllable, no-meaning lyrics.

### BRASS CONSTRUCTION AND B.T. EXPRESS

Two bands with furious dance-band credentials from New York, the B.T. Express and Brass Construction, were both connected by the works of producer/arranger Randy Muller, and his manager Jeff Lane. Muller's uncanny sense of catchy, melodic phrases layered onto smoking grooves became a standout in all of his productions (which also included Skyy in the eighties). Muller taught himself string arrangements while putting together the finer points of the first B.T. Express album in 1974. The Brooklyn Trucking Express, six soulful and snazzy followers of the New York funk scene, were adept at kicking dance parties and playing all of the hottest music on the radio, but it was the composition of saxophonist Billy Nichols's "Do It 'Til You're Satisfied" that got the band through the door, and with the sparse yet elegant layers of strings from young Muller, "Do It" went platinum. By 1975, two cutthroat groove tracks, "Do It" and "Express," scored No. 1 R&B, and the *Do It 'Til You're Satisfied* album remains to this day an all-time classic dance funk disc.

Muller then moved to his primary project, Brass Construction (a switch that led to the demise of B.T. Express). Brass Construction's first hit "Movin' " scored huge in Europe, drawing interest back in the United States as a dance track, busting out in the summer of 1976. The jam was a result of Muller's concerted commercial tweaking of the jazzy band's sounds, and the record seemed to float on a liquid groove. It was one of the last—and one of the best—dance jams to groove on rhythm instruments—with synthesizers dancing around *on top* of the groove—not meddling in the rhythm track. While "Movin' " is a disco classic, it truly breathes in the tradition of the best of James Brown's nine-minute-plus arrangements, and it deserves more credit. As the record pulses on and on, Larry Payton's punishing drumming rises above Wade Williamson's throbbing off-time bass riffs and Joe Wong's chanking guitars, as the horns and chants float along the hypnotic lock. The entire *Brass Construction I* album (as well as No. II) rises above commerciality and delivers a furious funk attack quotient.

New York was also known for the catchy disco dance energy of the Crown Heights Affair, a soulful eight-piece set that scored radio hits in 1974 and 1975 with such stomping delights as "Dreaming a Dream," "Dancin'," and "Foxy Lady," all of which helped to push the realms of funky-soul into an atmospheric space-disco vibe. An even more prolific New York dance troupe was the Fatback Band. A notoriously thick, pulsing groove was known to come from this East Coast favorite, founded by Bill Curtis. Fatback constantly delivered dance tracks for the latest party fads such as "Do the Bus Stop," "Double Dutch," "Soul March," and "Spanish Hustle," while dropping chunky humps of their own. Their fattest tracks came later in the decade, revealing the band's truly nastay chops on cuts like "I Like Girls" and "Backstrokin'." The band's street credentials also led them to what is often considered the first rap song, "King Tim III (Personality Jock)," released just one week before Sugarhill Gang's "Rapper's Delight" in October 1979. (The New York disco scene proved to have an irresistible pull on New York bands, as local favorites Kool & the

Gang and Cameo "went disco" in ways not heard by West Coast groups.)

## CHIC

The image of the New York disco dance band reached its zenith in the fall of 1977 when dance floors burned with the frenetic "Dance, Dance, Dance (Yowsah, Yowsah, Yowsah)" from an unknown act known as Chic. Founded and led by the rhythm duo of bassist Bernard Edwards and guitarist Nile Rodgers, Chic captured with high-class panache the sleek sounds of the disco jet set by polishing the soulful spirit and jazzy chord progressions heard in the harder funk. Smart, tightly locked riffs, accessible simple vocals, and a groove just fonkey enough to breathe through the disco beat marked the formula. Chic was a world music trend leader with the national No. 1 hits "Le Freak" in 1978 and "Good Times" in 1979. The group always dressed in the trendiest of fashions, helping to move the popular image of the black band away from the tribal freaks and space warriors that most funk bands had by 1978.

"Le Freak" started an endless string of "freak"-oriented songs, which originally referred to a disco dance, but wound up becoming references to loose women. A fad that lasted years beyond its hip usage, the "freak" became a part of America's modern folklore, and despite the sexy double entendre, *freak* eventually was used childishly to demean women in eighties black music on such sexist jibes as "I Need a Freak" and "The Freaks Come Out at Night." (It got to the point where rappers abandoned the double meanings in their music and replaced *freak* with *bitch*.) Chic was also known for unintentionally inaugurating the national popularity of the rap craze because of their No. 1 hit "Good Times." Cruising through the summer of 1979 for six weeks at No. 1 soul and reaching No. 1 pop, the syncopated, tightly grooving "Good Times" had its place in history locked up. But by October of that year an upstart trio from Harlem, Michael "Wonder Mike" Wright, Guy "Master Gee" O'Brien, and Henry "Big Bank Hank" Jackson laid down every rap riff they knew over the rhythm track to "Good Times," making "Rapper's Delight," and a new musical style was given to the nation. The obvious use of "Good Times" was a perfect example of the resourcefulness, spontaneity, and economy of Hip Hop culture. Providing the basis for Hip Hop culture to thrive was perhaps the greatest contribution disco gave to music history.

## SOUL BANDS

By 1976 dance funk bands had their hands full keeping up with the disco trends, and the powerful productions of the major bands such as Rufus and Chaka Khan's "Dance With Me," Kool & the Gang's "Spirit of the Boogie," James Brown's "Get Up Offa That Thing," Earth, Wind & Fire's incredible "Gratitude" set, Parliament's "Tear the Roof Off the Sucker," and the latest masterpieces from Stevie Wonder—"I Wish" and "Sir Duke"—were all glorious counterpoints to the hype of disco.

As a result of the skyrocketing popularity of groups such as Earth, Wind & Fire, Rufus, and the Commodores, labels were interested in the new thing—bands. The "soul band," a soft-core version of the funk band, was a new phenomenon that incorporated the large scale and thematic diversity of the self-contained and usually jazz-trained funk bands of the previous period, the United Funk Dynasty. Soul bands were complete units—singers and musicians—and could often kick up a monster funk groove. But these groups were all too often produced and developed as pop groups, with the same designs of pop formula success as young vocalists were for labels such as Motown only five years earlier. The most successful soul bands included the Brothers Johnson, Heatwave, L.T.D., Maze, Rose Royce, and the indubitable Michael Jackson.


### THE BROTHERS JOHNSON

The Brothers Johnson were a conspicuously talented bass and guitarist duo from Los Angeles that was discovered by Quincy Jones and packaged into a dynamic and very funky act for three years. Their talent was enormous, and Louis Johnson's smooth plucking bass style remains one of the hottest studio demands twenty years after his introduction to the scene. The group's solo LP *Look Out for #1* was a runaway smash in 1976 and featured the club classic "Get the Funk Out Ma Face." Platinum sales, a brilliant and diverse soul-funk album, and Quincy Jones's backing led to an even more polished follow-up, *Right on Time* (complete with twenty-four-page lyric booklet), a well-qualified vehicle for the huge pop smash "Strawberry Letter 23."

By 1978 the Brothers Johnson could play anything they wished—or so they thought. Their third disc, *Blam!,* was an unmitigated thumpasaurus funk blowout, which featured the monster jams "Ain't We Funkin' Now," "Ride-O-Rocket," "Mista-Cool," and "Streetwave," but the record unfortunately lacked a hit single. Well aware of this, Jones produced the group's fourth disc, *Lite Up the Nite,* with a decidedly synth-pop disco-flavored dance energy, and it was clear to any fan that the Brothers Johnson really did "get the funk out of their face." *Blam!* would be the last plunge into The Funk for the Brothers Johnson. Their quick turnabout was just another disappointment in a decade of music on the decline by 1979.

Heatwave, a brilliant multiracial sextet from Germany led by trumpeter, writer, and arranger Rod Temperton and Dayton-bred vocalists Keith and Johnnie Wilder captured black music much like the Average White Band four years earlier, and scored two killer LPs, *Too Hot to Handle* in 1976 and *Central Heating* in 1977. Scoring on the dance charts with "Boogie Nights," and ballads with "Always and Forever," the group still delivered punishing fonk with the much-sampled funk track "Ain't No Half Stepping" and their title cut "Too Hot to Handle." Their follow-up album featured many tasty, slick, yet sassy sides, particularly the dance smash "Groove Line" and club hits "Put the Word Out" and "Mind Blowing Decisions." Onstage, Heatwave was tight and snazzy, as they showed the strength of years of touring discos and military bases in Europe.

It was an important time for self-contained bands in the late 1970s, because many of the strongest acts had been playing since the dawn of the decade and had spent years maneuvering into position, searching for recording contracts, trying out sounds, and dropping singles in search of hits. Bands such as Sun, Con Funk Shun, the Gap Band, Lakeside, Maze, and Fatback had to endure years of struggle before scoring Top 10 soul status. For some, such as L.T.D. and Maze, it was important to surface in the 1970s, because the folksy, smooth soul band would not be in style in the eighties.

The much-traveled pop soul band L.T.D. (or Love, Togetherness, Devotion) was the vehicle for lead singer Jeffrey Osborne, producing the fresh No. 1 dance single "Back in Love Again" in 1977 and solid follow-up LP *Togetherness,* but they were a pop-oriented outfit that sought out writers and producers for their material, and after a few power struggles, Osborne went solo and took the talented technical support with him.

## MAZE

Perhaps the epitome of the well-traveled and well-oiled funky soul band was Frankie Beverly and Maze. Originally formed in Philadelphia, lead singer and founder Beverly took the group to Northern California in

1972. Years of grooving on the laid-back California rock scene influenced the band's chops, while Beverly's gravy-thick, earnest soulful voice earned him the respect of soul superstars, particularly Marvin Gaye. Gaye booked Maze on his 1976 concert tour and opened the door for their first album deal with Capitol Records.

From the outset, Maze was a magical unit. With two backup singers/percussionists Roame Lowery and McKinley Williams hitting harmonies since the Philly days as Raw Soul, the vocals of Maze had the strength of early seventies balladeers, yet their West Coast rhythm locks hooked in the melodic vibes for a charming, soothing, yet highly musical experience. While No. 1 singles were rare, the band was an album experience, and a live experience. Their first five albums—*Maze, Golden Time of Day, Inspiration, Joy and Pain,* and *Live in New Orleans*—all went gold, and deservedly so. Easy to take yet disarmingly funky cuts like "Time Is on My Side," "Working Together," "Roots," "Changing Times," and "Running Away" made it clear that Maze was a true funk original.

Then there was Rose Royce, the vehicle for Norman Whitfield's late seventies creative pursuits that scored a No. 1 disco hit in 1976 with the movie soundtrack and disco hit *Car Wash* and followed with the soulful *In Full Bloom* LP in late 1977, and *Strikes Again* in 1978. Whitfield had a hit-making knack from his days producing the Temptations, and when it became clear that a self-contained band was the best image for his songwriting skills, he developed Rose Royce. Despite the heavy-handed packaging, Rose Royce scorched the charts with dance funk like "Do Your Dance" and "Put Your Money Where Your Mouth Is," as well as spunky seventies ballads like "Ooh Boy," "Wishing on a Star," and "Love Don't Live Here Anymore." By concentrating on Rose Royce, Whitfield gave up on his black rock project, the Undisputed Truth, despite the fact that they were perhaps the most creative band under his care.

King of Pop Michael Jackson brought all the hip elements of black music together in 1979 on his Quincy Jones–produced LP *Off the Wall,* the biggest seller of 1979. Jackson used the songwriting talents of Heatwave founder Rod Temperton, Motown buddy Stevie Wonder, ex-Beatle Paul McCartney, and bass player Louis Johnson of the Brothers Johnson to provide the necessary thumps that kept the heavy funk fans interested. Jackson's own particular knack for swanging high-energy grooves reached a new level with "Don't Stop 'Til You Get Enough" and "Working Day and Night." *Off the Wall* was one of the few pop crossover albums that still dropped the heavy load of groovalistic function.

This was the era of what writer Bill Berry, in a 1978 *Ebony* magazine cover story, called the "Super Groups." Earth, Wind & Fire, the Isley Brothers, the Commodores, Rufus, and P-Funk were among the self-contained superstar bands of the time, and their live performances were lavish and entertaining. The huge arena shows created an almost religious fervor, as light shows and stage props did what stained glass and the pulpit did for the church. Berry described the super groups as bringing all of the musical traditions together as one, in which the performer became "the creator and the destroyer," the "angel and the devil," the "singer and instrumentalist," and "the composer and the poet."

New bands were held up to this revolutionary standard, and it would take The Funk to deliver the goods. Major arenas regularly sold out nationwide, featuring all funk band lineups—the Isley Brothers and Graham Central Station, or the Brothers Johnson, Brass Construction, and Rose Royce might be on the bill. Earth, Wind & Fire set up their own tours, including singer Deniece Williams and jazz-funk keyboardist Ramsey Lewis on their 1977 tour, and the Emotions on their 1979 tour. The P-Funk Earth Tours beginning in 1977 provided the greatest exposure for the most potent funk bands, giving Cameo, Slave, Rick James, and Bootsy's Rubber Band their initial exposure, and giving the tireless Bar-Kays the higher profile they richly deserved.

For the most part, the leadership of the super groups barely lasted through the decade. Radio airplay was increasingly based on disco singles or pop ballads, and the great bands slowly disintegrated as each new recording became more and more overproduced and less inspired. New bands were based in either funk or disco and were not developing in the culture of jazz-rock fusion that spawned Earth, Wind & Fire, the Ohio Players, War, or Kool & the Gang. Creativity as a band was a lost commodity, and it was only a matter of time before the lead singers went out on their own. By 1980 Lionel Richie had left the Commodores and Chaka Khan was on her own from Rufus, while Earth, Wind & Fire began to steadily lose members, the Ohio Players were off the charts, Kool & the Gang had gone totally disco, George Clinton was ready to retire, and within a few years the Isley Brothers would split up.

## MONSTER FUNK IN THE THIRD FUNK DYNASTY

The specter of disco music only increased the intensity of dance funk produced by the new breed of true funkers. For those musicians capable and determined to throw down the very heavy funk, this was the Golden Age of Dance Music, and the high point of the funk movement overall. Despite the resonance of the disco beat, hard black funk bands thrived all over the country. From New York came Cameo; Dayton, Ohio, brought Slave, Sun, and Lakeside; Vallejo, California, spawned Con Funk Shun; well-traveled Bay Area jazz keyboardist George Duke scorched the black charts with some heavy fonk; the immortal Bar-Kays continued their Memphis soul tradition into the 1980s; and two youngsters of note got their start in the late seventies—Buffalo-bred Rick James, and Minneapolis's own Prince Rogers Nelson.

The P-Funk influence was widespread among the funk bands, as the groups gravitated toward multilayered, dense funk tracks that were the foundation for outer-space concepts and outrageous characters. The Commodores kicked in with "Captain Quick Draw" in 1976, Kool & the Gang created "Big Chief Funkum" in 1977, Earth, Wind & Fire met "Jupiter" in 1977, and the Chicago funk clone Daryl "Captain Sky" Cameron scored with the funky cartoon character "Wonder Worm" in 1979. The Undisputed Truth scored a series of P-Funk–influenced albums, looking for "UFOs" on *Cosmic Truth* in 1975, flying "Higher Than High," and making "Cosmic Contact" in 1976. The Bar-Kays went to the "White House Orgy" and Brick enjoyed a "Good High" in 1976. Detroit's ADC band scored their only hit by imitating P-Funk's warped nursery rhymes on "Long Stroke" in 1978. War went to the "ninth dimension/seventh plane/out here raising solar cane" on "Galaxy" in 1977, Slave delivered a dose of "Stellar Fungk," and the Ohio Players were "Funk-O-Nots." The Brothers Johnson hit the space-funk tip with "Ride O Rocket" in 1979, and Cameo had a landing party of nine men beam down, "with phasers set on funk funk" in 1977.

### CAMEO

Cameo was the brainchild of drummer Larry Blackmon that yielded a dozen members and even more scorching dance hits (and a few ballads) well into the 1980s. A musical leader since his youth in Harlem and veteran of the New York City Players dance band, Blackmon sought to put together his own large and yet versatile band, one in which all could perform a variety of duties (make cameos). The band's first recording was the disco single "Find My Way," which got the group in the door at Casablanca Records. Once there, Blackmon was managed by Cecil Holmes, who released the gurgling funk groove "Rigor Mortis" to black radio stations, and the reaction led to a new emphasis on The Funk. Originating in the shadow of the P-Funk empire on the same label, Blackmon had to make his case for his own flavor on "Funk Funk," calling his sound the "C-Funk."

Larry Blackmon had a gift for phenomenally hot, off-key funk twangings, and he parlayed it into a career, but it would be three more years from his band's 1977 debut before pop stardom would come. Cameo's first three LPs—*Cardiac Arrest, We All Know Who We Are,* and *Ugly Ego*—are exquisite examples of the fertile, erotic realm of R&B-based funk at its most stretched out. Fat and trashy, lumpy rump funk was their legacy on cuts like "Rigor Mortis," "Funk Funk," "Inflation," "C on the Funk," "Insane," "I'll Be With You," and "Ugly Ego." By their fourth LP *Secret Omen,* in 1979, the band had slicked its sound, and tightened its chops. The single "I Just Wanta Be" was a wicked, jagged splatter of sound snippets and weird vocal chortles. It was a monster jam that seemed to be imprisoned by the tense rigidity of the beat, and the tension was delicious. The remaining LP was unfortunately all too disco-beat–oriented.

Yet Cameo would not quit. Their 1980 follow-up to "I Just Wanta Be" was the dance floor megablast "Shake Your Pants," an orgy of tight-plucking guitar strings, and spastic shrill vocalizing. Flanked by Anthony Lockett's wicked guitar chops and Gregory Johnson's freakish keyboard sense, "Shake Your Pants" showcased the ultra-tight thumpings of bassist Aaron Mills, whose jazzy sense of hump profoundly influenced the Cameo sound of the eighties. The *Cameosis* LP is often considered a masterpiece of pop moods, and Cameo certainly defined their eighties sound with it. The addition of versatile guitarist and falsetto vocalist Charlie Singleton served to focus the band's strong harmonies and rhythmic chops even further, solidifying the core of the group with vocalists Tomi Jenkins, trumpeter and vocalist Nathan Leftenant, Arnett Leftenant on sax and vocals, and the irrepressible Blackmon. Follow-up LPs *Feel Me, Knights of the Sound Table, Alligator Woman, Style,* and *She's Strange* delivered a rapid-fire dosage of beat-spanking, light-yet-heavy funk chops. Jams like "Keep It Hot," "Freaky Dancin'," "I Like It," "Just Be Yourself," "Soul Army," "Flirt," and "Talkin' Out the Side of Your Neck" kept Cameo in the upper eschelons of groovallegiance, and fended off critics of their silly disco-hype flavors. Cameo always toyed with the macho image of funk bands, pushing the envelope of eighties androgyny, while always coming with phat bottoms when the chips were down. This continued through the mid-eighties until their 1986 pop crossover "Word Up" blew them up into all-time funk band status.

Blackmon's funk mission is one of the great accomplishments in black music, and the liner notes of the *Style* LP perhaps say it all about the band: "Cameo is 21st century be-bop." Blackmon had perhaps learned an essential lesson about The Funk: that your ego trip can take you as far as you want to go.

### BRICK

Just as the major funk bands were scoring huge hits in 1976, the Atlanta-based quintet Brick blasted onto the radio with a monstrous slice of "disco-jazz," known as "Dazz." Somehow reflecting a sound with the richness of southern New Orleans–style rhythm and blues, as well as a heightened jazz sensibility, combined with smash-mouth funk chops, Brick blasted into the higher echelons of The Funk. They were driven by Ray Ransom's bass and the ultra-tight Eddie Irons on drums, serving to open up the floor for Jimmy Brown's versatility on all the brass and wind instruments. Virtually pioneering the fonky flute solo (although Maceo Parker was certainly the O.G. in this respect—check the long version of Fred Wesley and the JBs' "Doin' It to Death"), Jimmy Brown's ability to inhale and blow funky tones out of the most delicate of instruments, the flute, was fonky indeed. His ability to jump from saxophone to trumpet to flute was a visual as well as musical experience, and his locked-tight backup brought Brick instant success. "Dazz," the album title cut "Good High," the instrumental "Brick City," and the incredible follow-up monster jams "Dusic," "Ain't Gonna Hurt Nobody," and "(We Don't Wanna Sit Down) We Wanna Git Down" surged Brick to the verge of superstardom by 1977. The strength of their self-titled follow-up album was one of the true funk highlights of 1977, as a true mastery of mood, melody, and the monster jam were brought about in brilliant fashion. Their ability to weave loaded meanings into the simplest of lyrics mirrored their sound, which was an amazing fusion of simplicity and intricate interplay. "It ain't gonna hurt nobody/to get on down/don't stop me/and I won't stop you."

And while it makes no sense to say that Brick lacked any essential qualities, the absence of a charismatic lead singer kept the band somewhat anonymous as the years went by. Their third album, two years later, although noble in its grounded, blues-funk ideals, was a tragic, quirky disappointment, for Brick was one of the last bands that fans believed could master the pop formulas and still come with The Bomb. They kept their funk, but went down for the count. To their credit, despite their disco-jazz concept, Brick avoided the shameful image of a disco band (monorhythmic, inane, endless music), which, despite their low sales, is a tribute to the band's integrity. (They did come back one more time in 1981 with "Sweat ['Til You Get Wet]," a bonafide monster funk jam.)

### SLAVE

The urban Midwest was the true hotbed of seventies funk. Closely linked to their Dayton, Ohio, predecessors the Ohio Players, Slave grew out of the best of the local Dayton funk bands. Led by multitalented Stevie Washington, himself the nephew of Ohio Players sideman Ralph "Pee Wee" Middlebrooks, Slave was hooked up from the start. Grounded by the rock-hard bass thumps of Mark "Mr. Mark" Adams (who had the loudest bass thumps on black radio in the late seventies) and the atom-splitting thrashes of guitarist Mark "Drac" Hicks, there was a preposterous sense of strength coming from Slave. With bottom-heavy, jazzy, and often humorous flavors oozing through the band's inexplicable yet ice-cold rhythm notions, Slave was a monster funk band in every sense of the phrase. "With the funk, there are no rules," bandleader Stevie Washington explained. "You can put jazz with it . . . country with it, you can put classical with it, whatever the hell you feel. That's what we all are saying."

"Slide" was their first and biggest hit. A thumping, sloppy dinosaur of a jam, it featured an encyclopedia of gimmicks, but when all was said and done, it was meat-and-potatoes bass and guitar that made it work. Ghoulish laughs, bicycle horns, goofy lines like "I'll let my grandmother check that out" were all for fun, but the lumpy-hump bass, the scatological horn squeaks syncopated in drastic angular phrases, the wicked avalanche of groove at the change, and Drac's rocket-blast of a guitar solo make "Slide" an all-time funk classic.

Their albums were equally irreverent. With the help of veteran producer Jimmy Douglas, Slave delivered an almost comic assault on R&B formalities. The first self-titled Slave album never missed an opportunity to turn a riff inside out, and keep smoking. "Screw Your Wig on Tite" was one of those rhythmically assaulting funk arrangements that let you know that R&B could never go back to the "good ole days." "You and Me" and "Party Harty" also make themselves known as skull-

scraping grooves. The album cover stands out as one of the most meaningful themes in black music anywhere. A black man (a slave) holding
up a silver sphere larger than him (the world—the *white* world?) is a
visually stunning, strong, and smart symbol of what the band is about—
a strong black liberated funky vibe.

Slave followed their first LP with a run of serious funk efforts that
all seemed to capture in some way the power and subtle brilliance of
the band. "Baby Sinister," "Volcano Rupture," "Just Freak," "We Got
Your Party," and "Stellar Fungk" grooved in a class by themselves. Their
third album *The Concept* also featured the addition of vocalist Steve Arrington, whose elastic vocals captured the dog-nasty naked funk flavors
of the eighties funk styles. Arrington could be heard on the hits "Just a
Touch of Love," "Watching You," "Wait for Me," and "Snap Shot,"
among others. Still bottom-heavy in the 1980s but restrained on the guitar rock and tight with the dance funk, Slave continued to score hard,
meaningful, soulful funk as a multi-piece unit well into the late 1980s,
although the 1982 solo trip of Steve Arrington slowed the band a bit.

Dayton, Ohio, also delivered the monster thumps from the band
Sun, whose three most sinister hits for Capitol Records—"Wanna
Make Love (Come Flic My Bic)," the polyrhythmic "Sun Is Here," and
the stomping "Radiation Level"—put them on the interstellar funk
map in the late seventies. Also from Dayton, via Los Angeles, came the
dinosaur-dance funk of Lakeside, a nine-member set that was packaged
by Dick Griffey's SOLAR label after years of toiling on the scene.
Lakeside had an infectious air about their sound, a totally self-
contained unit of players with years together—the epitome of the funk
band experience. Their breakthrough was the late 1978 release of "It's
All the Way Live," a multilayered, stomping hurricane of a funk jam.
Busting out with Marvin Craig's fuzzed-out bass and Fred Alexander's
drums, Fred Lewis's percussion, and a fresh riff from Steve Shockley's
guitar kicked in the groove, the jam explodes as the group's *four* male
vocalists led by Mark Woods start yelling "It's all the way liiive, it's all
the way live!" The energy was maintained on such stanky licks as "Pull
My String," "Fantastic Voyage," "Your Love Is on the One," "Turn the
Music Up," "Outrageous," and "Raid!" Somehow the spirited sincerity
of Earth, Wind & Fire and the swamp dogg funk bottom of the P-Funk
were all wrapped into one act's flavor.

Griffey's eye for an image brought the band thematic photo lay-
outs for each album, as they were presented in medieval Robin Hood

garb on the 1978 *Shot of Love* cover; they followed that up dressed as Arabian knights on 1979's *Your Wish Is My Command*; then as cowboys on *Rough Riders*. In 1981 the band's most successful hit, "Fantastic Voyage" (yes, the source of Coolio's 1994 rap hit), featured the band in full pirate gear, on a ship. And perhaps their meanest image was for their meanest funk blast, *Untouchables,* featuring "Raid!," in which the act is dressed up as 1920s-style black gangland cops. Despite their flashy packaging, Lakeside never failed to rock the house with loud, bass-heavy country-fried dance tracks in the best tradition of The Funk.

From out West, in Vallejo, California, in the San Francisco Bay Area came the tight funk genius of Con Funk Shun, a seven-member soul-funk band that scored four consecutive gold albums, beginning with *Secrets,* the vehicle for "Ffun," the band's heaviest funk legacy. Driven by the bubbly plucking of bassist Cedric Martin and Felton Pilate's falsetto vocals, Con Funk Shun captured both ends of the funk spectrum. Founded and led by guitarist and singer Michael Cooper (who went solo in 1986) and drummer Louis McCall in 1968, the pair moved to Memphis to search for success, and almost ten years later realized it, with a Mercury Records contract. A string of hot LPs led to a series of phat jams, from "Ffun" and "Confunkshunize Ya" to "So Easy" and the monster groove of "Chase Me," while the band smoothed out on "Got to Be Enough" and the effervescent "Too Tight." With a "too tight" live act that still performs in the 1990s, Con Funk Shun is one of those hometown success stories that keeps folks dreaming they could do it, too.

## THE BAR-KAYS

Still other established acts continued to shine on in the true spirit of funkiness, such as the immortal Bar-Kays, who survived the plane crash with Otis Redding in 1967, survived the demise of Stax Records in 1975, and scored their biggest hits as a greasy, nasty eight-member funk act for Mercury Records. Their first Mercury Records album, *Too Hot to Stop,* was a reprise of the best of black funk: nasty grooves, swanging, drawling vocals, more nasty grooves, begging ballads, and more nasty grooves. It featured the snazzy "Shake Your Rump to the Funk," the sweet funk of "Cozy," and the preposterous thump of "Whitehouseorgy." The group then began to smooth out, styling themselves after the Ohio Players on the *Flying High on Your Love* LP, then sounding more like Earth, Wind & Fire on their *Light of Life* album in 1978. At the peak of their funk renaissance, their old label Stax Records packaged some of their canned material and dropped *Money Talks,* one of the thickest, stompingest funk feasts on record. Recorded around 1974, the album features the best of vocalist Larry Dodson's drawling wails, "Luscious Lloyd" Smith's backwoods guitar work, James Alexander's crunchy bass playing, Michael Beard's punishing drums, and Winston Stewart's slippery keyboard action. The single from that release, "Holy Ghost," was their show-stopper, and a dance floor *assault.* Although they received no royalties for the jam, the Bar-Kays took off with "Holy Ghost" and never looked back.

The Bar-Kays show was one of the strongest, wildest, and most polished on the scene. Larry Dotson's crackling voice and wildly cut hair fronted the band's splashy mix of high-kicking dance steps and low-down gutbucket grooving. Total entertainment was the key, as the act had years of experience, the Stax soul legacy to back them up, and some nasty, nasty chops to work with. "We held the line on the Memphis sound for over ten years," sax player Harvey Henderson told me in 1988. In the late seventies the Bar-Kays toured with P-Funk perhaps more than any other act, the ultimate sign of true groovallegiance in a funk band.

Elsewhere on the funk scene, the indomitable jazz master Herbie Hancock continued to master the funk formula as he put the latest technology to use on spectacular disco-jazz-funk recordings *Sunlight* in 1978, and *Feets Don't Fail Me Now* in 1979, the latter being one of the best records of that year. Worldly and whimsical jazz keyboardist George Duke took a leap into funk and scored the No. 1 1977 soul hit "Reach for It," and followed up in 1978 with the equally lively *Don't Let Go* LP and single "Dukey Stick." "Reach for It" was such a thumping, scandalous workout that P-Funkers George Clinton and Bootsy Collins surprised Duke onstage at a 1978 Los Angeles concert, and presented him with a "passport" to the Mothership—a tribute to his exquisite funkativity. Meanwhile, out West the perennial good-times rhythm band War kept the pressure on with monster dance singles "Galaxy" in 1977 and "Good, Good Feelin' " in 1979. Even the God-father of Soul James Brown kicked in with a string of rocking jams ("Body Heat," "Gimme Some Skin," "Jam," "The Spank," and "For Goodness Sakes, Look at Those Cakes"), but even the founder of The Funk had to step back and give it up for the new rulers in town—the single reason for the increasing funkiness of all of the previously mentioned music: THE P-FUNK MOB.

# SEVENTEEN

# The P-Funk Empire:
# Tear the Roof Off the Sucker

"Make my funk the P-Funk
I Wants to Get Funked Up!"
*Parliament*

## THE PARLIAMENTS

This fifty-plus member aggregation of geniuses, lunatics, has-beens, wanna-bes, architects, saboteurs, and hangers-on was the epitome of the loose ensemble that by sheer will and musical mastery became a collective creation greater than the sum of its many parts. The Parliament-Funkadelics, or P-Funk (short for "Pure Funk") Mob elevated funk into an ideology. Their grandiose concepts, which preached the redemptive powers of funk, their vast informal enterprise, and their powerful affirmation of common black folks, created a small-scale movement and large-scale following, that, despite their lack of prime-time exposure, P-Funk remains the strongest influence on black music since their popular zenith in 1978.

The P-Funk shockwave hit black music like an earthquake. Among their fundamental ingredients that still reign in black pop today are the electronic "clap" sound, a synthesizer-bass (a bass track played by a keyboard), a shrewdly displayed image of political (and sexual) awareness, and a penchant for elaborately layered horn and vocal lines, often creating a synthesis of European chord structure and African rhythm grooves into a large, ensemble sound. P-Funk introduced these effects along with an eminently subversive lyrical/thematic direction that challenged the apolitical pop music status quo. George Clinton, the troupe's leader, kept the forty- to one-hundred-odd musicians and creative artists focused on one grand concept after another, milking the talents of a variety of people that have yet to reach similar heights away from The Mob. Beginning in 1976 Clinton and P-Funk began producing spinoff acts on different labels, with generally the same personnel, developing what can rightly be labeled a musical empire. Clinton's mastery of the business was taken up by other artists in the 1980s such as

Rick James and Prince, who also went on to produce a number of protégés. Perhaps most importantly, Clinton and his merry band of crazies staked out new conceptual territory and asserted a postmodern black aesthetic at a time when sociologists, politicians, and writers were mired in integrationist dialectics.

With inauspicious beginnings as a doo-wop group called the Parliaments in 1956, George Clinton's Mob developed multiple identities and eventually worked their way to black pop superstardom. Born in Kannapolis, North Carolina, July 22, 1941—in an outhouse—George Clinton was well-traveled as a youth and settled in Newark, New Jersey, with his mother and eight younger siblings. He solidified his vocal group in the back room of a barbershop on West 3rd Street in Plainfield, New Jersey, with Calvin Simon and Grady Thomas, recruiting Clarence "Fuzzy" Haskins, bass singer Ray Davis, and most of the backup band through the business at the shop.

After some missed opportunities in Newark, Clinton took the band to Detroit to audition for Berry Gordy's Motown Records, often hanging around outside of the offices, singing for anyone who would listen. In typical doo-wop fairy-tale fashion, Martha Reeves, of Martha and the Vandellas, noticed the heartfelt harmonies of the ragged group hanging outside the studios, and the quintet was given an audition. But the Parliaments were only moderately received and only managed a few singles on the small Detroit-based Revilot Records. The group did score a Top 5 R&B hit with "I Wanna Testify" in August 1967, which gave the small-time outfit their first gig at the Apollo in New York. But with the demise of the Revilot label (some say due to "squeezing" from Motown), Clinton lost the group's name and a chance to play a larger role in the Motown family. Some of Clinton's irreverent songwriting made it into Motown, such as "Something I Can't Shake a Loose" to Diana Ross and "I'll Bet You" to the Jackson 5, but the Parliaments appeared done for.

The group didn't sell, but the band was *cool*. Clinton's hair conking was the hippest thang in town ("conking" was a process of melting kinky hair into a smooth, straight look, using dangerous chemicals) and only the heartiest of youngbloods frequented Clinton's barbershop after hours. Younger members of the band were often prohibited from hanging out with the cats at the shop, and word has it that when the bloods put the torch to Plainfield Avenue during the 1967 riots, George Clinton's barbershop was the only thang left standing.

Clinton's resilience would not let him quit. The genius of desperation was one of his trademarks, and facing the imminent demise of his singing group, he gave his rowdy backup band a chance, let loose on a Jimi Hendrix–style black rock image, borrowed the loudest amps they could find—something not done at R&B clubs—and let everyone loose to do their thang. The wild new band was now a mishmash of doowoppers and rockers—now called Funkadelic (a name bassist Billy Nelson insists he coined on the road with the group), and with the help of Armen Boladian of the Detroit-based Westbound Records, Clinton signed the band.

### FUNKADELIC

Funkadelic began with wide-eyed Plainfield youngster Billy Nelson strumming the guitar behind the Parliaments at gigs. After "I Wanna Testify," the group had some clout, and Nelson recruited a local session player, a childhood friend named Eddie Hazel, to play guitar. Aware of Eddie's phenomenal talents, Billy moved aside to let Eddie play lead guitar. Billy grew as a bassist and was given strong support from Motown's bass giant James Jamerson, who encouraged him to develop his own sound. The original Funkadelics consisted of drummer Tiki Fulwood, guitarists Tawl Ross and Eddie Hazel, bandleader Nelson on bass, and Mickey Atkins on organ. The band's grungy sound was accentuated by their efforts to record spacey, cosmic effects with a lack of quality recording techniques.

Funkadelic was a tough sell. Their competition on the original "heavy metal/grunge rock" circuit was the likes of MC5, the Stooges and Iggy Pop, and Grand Funk Railroad. Unlike the well-rehearsed moves of the older Parliaments crew, the band had no training, discipline, or interest in the suited-down look, and it was the youngsters in the Parliafunkadelicment Thang who influenced the psychedelic look of the act. Billy Nelson was frank about it to Rob Bowman:

> To tell you the truth, Eddie and Tiki were two trifling motherfuckers so they didn't want to be clean at all. The three of us just plain out did not want to wear them suits no more. It was all based on the theory, "Well hey, we ain't Parliaments, we're Funkadelic, we don't have to wear that. . . ." We just wore whatever we wanted to wear.

The rest of the act gradually slipped, as George was consistently raggedy from the start, and the slick look began to unravel, as each singer gave up on the suit and developed his own image: Grady had the look of a genie, Fuzzy was in long johns, Calvin donned a wizard's pointed hat, and George resorted to ripping holes in hotel sheets, poking his head through, and heading onstage. Visually, the band appeared like a group of ghetto circus clowns, with an overamped rock sound that never seemed to end. Priding themselves on playing until the crowd would leave, Funkadelics (and their Parliament vocalists) became local legends, and their first album, *Funkadelic,* was just as badly mixed, endless, and *unforgettable* as one of their concerts.

Actually, *Funkadelic* is a blues-rock classic that serves to introduce the Funkadelic concept with perfect clarity—despite the distortion. "If you will suck my soul, I will lick your funky emotions" is the intro to the first cut, "Mommy, What's a Funkadelic?", and the resulting slow throb on that jam, as well as "I'll Bet You" and "Music for My Mother" captured the gritty realism and urban blight of black rock in 1970. On side two, the eight-minute blues rock of "Good Ole Music" was actually placed as a single, and the intro-beat is now a classic Hip Hop beat sample, first made famous by the D.O.C. on "The D.O.C. & the Doctor." On "What is Soul?" Clinton explains the earliest incarnations of his mission, revealing a portent of things to come:

Behold, I Am Funkadelic
I Am not of your world
But fear me not, I will do you no harm
Loan me your funky mind
So I can play with it,
for nothing is good unless you play with it
And all that is good, is Nasty!
                    Funkadelic, "What is Soul?" (1970)

### BERNIE WORRELL

For the group's second album recording, *Free Your Mind and Your Ass Will Follow,* the band featured keyboardist Bernie Worrell, a child prodigy and occasional teenage patron of Clinton's barbershop who was trained in classical music at New England Conservatory of Music in Boston, and Juilliard in New York City. Worrell was familiar with the antics at

(*Mastahn Fanaka/Ace of Shades*)

**P-Funk Earth Tour**

*Above:* Dr. Funkenstein disembarks the Mothership.
*Right:* (l-r) Michael Hampton, George Clinton, Cordell "Boogie" Mosson, Glen Goins.

*Below left:* George Clinton and Garry Shider.
*Below right:* The Brides of Funkenstein (l-r): Dawn Silva, Jeannette Washington, Lynn Mabry.

(*Mastahn Fanaka/Ace of Shades*)

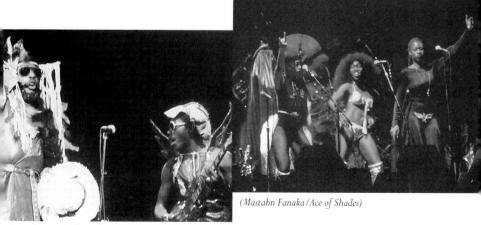

(*Mastahn Fanaka/Ace of Shades*)

(*Mastahn Fanaka/Ace of Shades*)

## *The Funk Mob*

*Above:* Parliament-Funkadelic, 1977 (l-r): George Clinton, Garry Shider, Calvin Simon, Bernie Worrell, Grady Thomas, Cordell "Boogie" Mosson, Mike Hampton, Ray Davis, Clarence "Fuzzy" Haskins, Glen Goins, Debbie Wright, Jerome Brailey, Jeannette Washington.

*Left:* Dewayne "Blackbird" McKnight performs in full gear.

### P-Funk Players

*Top left:* Eddie "Maggot Brain" Hazel (1950-1992). *Above right*: Bootsy Collins gets busy. *Below:* P-Funk Guitar Army (l-r): Lige Curry, Mike Hampton, George Clinton, Garry Shider.

(Courtesy of Polygram Records)

*Above:* The Ohio Players, *Honey*, Richard Fegley photography, 1976. *Right:* Funkadelic, *Cosmic Slop*, artwork by Pedro Bell, 1973.

## Funk Album Art

(Art direction: P. Bell and G. Clinton; Design and artwork: Pedro Bell, copyright © 1973 P. Bell)

**Deep
Funk
LPs**

*Slave*, cover design by Stevie Washington 1977;
Kool & the Gang, *Spirit of the Boogie*, cover art by Goodnight, 1975;
James Brown, *The Payback*, art by Don Brautigan, 1974;
Parliament, *Motor Booty Affair*, art by Overton Lloyd, 1978.

## Naked Funk

*(Mastahn Fanaka/Ace of Shades)*

*(Mastahn Fanaka/Ace of Shades)*

*Clockwise from top left:* The front line of Cameo (l-r): Nathan Leftenant, Larry Blackmon, Tomi Jenkins; Rick James; Roger Troutman of Zapp; The man once known as Prince.

*(Mastahn Fanaka/Ace of Shades)*

*(Mastahn Fanaka/Ace of Shades)*

## Eighties Funk Noise

*Above:* Bass player and lead singer "Big Tony" Fisher of the Go Go band Trouble Funk. *Left:* Afrika Bambaataa. *Below:* Flea Balzary and Anthony Kiedis of the Red Hot Chili Peppers raise their consciousness with George Clinton.

# Return of the Funk

**1971** James Brown, *Revolution of the Mind*.

*(Permission of Bring the Noise, Inc. / Ujama Music Inc. / Noise Songs BMI)*

**1988** Public Enemy, *It Takes a Nation of Millions to Hold Us Back*.

The Funk Age of the 1970s pioneered political themes in the music, as James Brown (above left) illustrates. Public Enemy returned to the same concept in 1988 (above right). Similarly, the Ohio Players' "gangsta" image (below left) was revisited by Ice-T (below right).

*(Courtesy of Polygram Records)*

**1977** Ohio Players, *Mr. Mean*.

*(Sire Records / Glen E. Friedman Photography)*

**1988** Ice-T, *Power*.

Clinton's barbershop and visited as often as he could without his mother finding out. Worrell's strict upbringing and formal training in music provided an eerie landscape of melodic sophistication and complexity that opened the doors for a fantastic form of fusion to occur.

In perhaps the most powerfully symbolic union of the Funk Era, Worrell's competence in classical European musical forms collided and combined with the band's twisted black urban sensibilities to generate a bizarre dichotomy of perspectives—as if Shakespeare and Stagger Lee were dropping acid together in da hood. As new keyboard technologies were made available to musicians in the 1970s, Worrell mastered a vast array of effects, almost singlehandedly producing the late-seventies sound of Parliament. His talents were observed worldwide, and in 1981 he recorded with the Tom Tom Club and toured with the Talking Heads. His solo LPs, beginning with his 1978 P-Funk extravaganza *All the Woo in the World,* are all musical adventures worth taking.

With the help of Worrell and other members, P-Funk claimed the most prized elements of the European musical tradition for its own twisted use. Clinton's operatic, layered, chanting vocals and Worrell's gothic, mystical string ensemble tones connected with the band's trashy blues and James Brownish percussive rhythms to generate the archetypical African-American aesthetic in music. More important, P-Funk confiscated European musical aesthetics as a way of symbolizing just how much of Western civilization had been internalized by African-Americans, while the streetwise sensibilities of P-Funk continued to affirm the untenable bond on black/African consciousness within the group.

Playing as two bands, Funkadelic (playing "rock," which is associated with whites) and Parliaments (soul for black radio), the notion of "double consciousness" introduced by W. E. B. Du Bois in 1903 was exposed. What appeared as two acts was actually one entity with many dimensions, as most African-Americans inevitably experience as a result of their struggle in a white country. Du Bois's reference to "two warring ideals in one dark body" has dogged the racial experience in America, as racial minorities are constantly labeled as "sellouts" when status, education, or success is realized. Yet P-Funk transcended this conundrum, as the notions of intellect, education, or sophistication were totally removed from any association with white status. Thus, P-Funk became the *ultimate* in African-American liberation.

## THE MAGGOT BRAIN

By the time of the recording of *Maggot Brain* in mid-1971, the Funkadelic lineup consisted of Worrell, Tawl Ross, Billy Nelson, Eddie Hazel, and Tiki Fulwood. Later that year rhythm guitarist Tawl Ross overdosed on LSD, and was abandoned by the ragged group. The resulting focus on lead guitar Eddie Hazel helped the band develop its balance and eventually its legendary lineup.

In one of rock and roll's legendary performances, George Clinton wrote a song so melancholy and compelling, he urged his lead guitarist "to play like your mother just died," and let Eddie Hazel loose in the studio. Hazel's nine-minute solo was a tour de force, challenging the late Jimi Hendrix (one of the few recordings ever to do so) as one of the great guitar solos of all time. A frightening concept had developed surrounding the song: While he denies it, some say Clinton was the one to find his brother's decomposed dead body, skull cracked, in a Chicago apartment—thus the Maggot Brain. "Maggot Brain," like most of Clinton's work, had to do with transcendence, in this case, the need to rise above the "Maggots in the Mind of the Universe," certainly the grimmest of realities from which to escape:

> Mother Earth is pregnant for the third time
> For y'all have knocked her up
> I have tasted the Maggots in the mind of the Universe
> and I was not offended
> For I knew I had to rise above it all,
> Or drown in my own SHIT!
> Funkadelic, "Maggot Brain" (1971)

In addition to Clinton's parable on record, he printed in the liner notes a polemic on the crux of fear, written by an obscure religious cult, the Process Church of Final Judgment, which proclaimed, "As long as human beings fail to see THEIR fear reflected in these and a hundred other manifestations of fear, then they will fail to see their part in the relentless tide of hatred, violence, destruction, and devastation, that sweeps the earth." The foreboding musical themes, the screaming black woman's head coming out of the earth on the album cover, and the similarity of the Process Church to mass-murderer Charles Manson's Church of the Final Process left Funkadelic out on their own with the image of a death-worshiping black rock band.

Emboldened by their success with *Maggot Brain,* the band produced the double album *America Eats Its Young,* which again featured liner notes from the Process Church, and an absurd dollar-bill cartoon that featured the Statue of Liberty eating babies (à la the censored version of the Beatles *Yesterday and Today* album). A wild, uneven splatter of rock noise and gospel feel, *America Eats Its Young* only increased the legend of the band.

By this time childhood barbershop homie Garry Shider came of age and joined the act. Shider's presence was integral to Funkadelic's identity, for his strong throat (his father was a preacher), versatile guitar chops, unmistakable diaper garb, and hysterics onstage made his vibe central to the Funkadelic experience. Shider's influence can be heard on the uncharacteristically optimistic ballad "Everybody's Gonna Make It This Time," and he is featured singing the dangerous high range of vocals for the title song of the band's fifth album, 1973's *Cosmic Slop.*

*Cosmic Slop* was distinctive for two reasons: As an album, no song was longer than five minutes (a first for a Funkadelic LP) and, as a result of pressure from the record label, Clinton pursued new album graphics and hired Chicago artist Pedro Bell, whose scatological landscapes are smeared over all of Funkadelic's album covers through 1981, as well as the four George Clinton solo LPs from 1982 to 1986. Bell's scandalous contributions (discussed in the next chapter) were by no means a capitulation to the censors. By 1974 the band was already aware of its ability to blast the competition, and Bell captured this sentiment on the album cover to *Standing on the Verge of Gettin' It On* with the claim: "There is nothing harder to stop than an idea whose time has come to pass. Funkadelic is wot time it is!"

By 1974 Eddie Hazel was having troubles and was arrested after a plane flight for allegedly slapping a stewardess while in flight and punching a sky marshal afterward, and landed in jail for nearly a year. Hazel was soon replaced by Cleveland-bred guitarist Michael "Kidd Funkadelic" Hampton, heir to Hazel's "Maggot Brain" in concert. In the interim, Clinton turned to a variety of other guitarists, including white Detroit-area guitarist Ron Brykowski for some of the spaced out guitar chores in the recording studio. Brykowski can be heard on the very trashy "No Head, No Backstage Pass" from the group's 1975 release, *Let's Take It to the Stage.* ("No Head" was sampled in 1990 by platinum rappers Eric B & Rakin on "Lyrics of Fury.")

Album artist Bell captured the psychedelic irreverence of the act, calling Ron Brykowski the band's "polyester, soul-powered token white devil." Bell labeled the young bassist Cordell "Boogie" Mosson "the world's only black leprechaun" and exhalted George Clinton as "the nasty and complete minister of all Funkadelia. A scrupled Heathen growth possessing the ultimate creative blasphemies, and undisputed beholder of cosmic crankrot mechanics!" For what it's worth, George managed to live up to the image, and Bell's mutant portraits of the players became part of the Funkadelic experience.

The band continued to record its own raunchy, disconcerting black rock through 1976 on Westbound Records, gaining a reputation as an outrageous live act (that nobody wanted to follow onstage) and musical iconoclasts who never sold many records. *The Rolling Stone Record Guide* (1978) put it like this: "The music of Funkadelic is an urban soundscape—not always pretty or appealing but perhaps the truest representation of urban life offered in black music."

## PARLIAMENT

Making use of his contacts with many other veterans of Motown in 1970, Clinton managed to re-sign his vocal act as Parliament for the Invictus label, the label created when Motown Records expatriates Eddie Holland and Lamont Dozier broke from Berry Gordy's stable of songwriters in 1970. The first Parliament album, *Osmium,* is a compilation of recordings performed by the entire group that combined gospel-rock, an absurd affection for country and western hooks, twisted folk-rock, and sleazy, greasy funk. The record, a masterpiece, enjoyed only a small run and was nearly forgotten, until a CD reissue in 1990.

The true success of Parliament began in 1972, when Bootsy and George Clinton finally met. While staying with family friend and show promoter Mallia Franklin in Detroit in 1972, Clinton went to see members of the band known as the Houseguests, playing at one of Franklin's locally promoted club gigs. The Houseguests featured William "Bootsy" Collins on bass and brother "Catfish" on guitar. The Cincinnati-bred brothers had played with James Brown on his hits "Sex Machine," "Superbad," and "Soul Power," but had moved on to enjoy their own brand of creative freedom.

The meeting with Clinton was a success. Both artists had fantastic imaginations, single-parent upbringings (raised by their mothers), and years of drug-induced psychedelic soul music behind them. Clinton and Bootsy quickly became an interlinked creative songwriting duo, a partnership that flourished with the social insight of Lennon and McCartney, the folksy warmth of Simon and Garfunkel, and the strength of Chuck D and Flavor Flav. Clinton has remarked of working with Bootsy, "Bootsy had a perfect personality, he had magnetism no matter what he was doing, whether it was serious funk or silly love songs." Bootsy and Phelps fell into the band so readily, they found themselves *leading* the Funkadelic band after just a couple of gigs, and left shortly afterward, but they would return only a couple of years later.

When Clinton finally signed with Casablanca president Neil Bogart in 1973, things began to change for everyone. Bogart's eye for a gimmick matched Clinton's gift of hype, and the two got things rolling for Parliament in 1974. Bogart knew Clinton in the 1960s and kept George in mind as he worked his way up through the industry at Cameo Parkway and Buddha Records until he took charge of Casablanca in 1973.

Casablanca Records was George Clinton's greatest industry ally and would be the primary reason the P-Funk was able to soar to the top. With money to back him up, Clinton began to expand, recruited Bootsy and Catfish back into the studio, and put the notion in Bootsy's head that *he* could front a band down the road. The pop success began with the Parliament single "Up for the Down Stroke" in the summer of 1974, featuring the return of Bootsy Collins's wicked bass-crunching, some absurd time changes, and a nastayness not heard on black radio since "Sex Machine." The record went to No. 10 R&B. The stirring, political *Chocolate City* hit the streets in the spring of 1975, as Clinton ranted about "Chocolate Cities and Vanilla Suburbs," warning the people that "when they come to march on ya, tell 'em to make sure they have they James Brown pass!" Clinton's absurd brand of black consciousness threw the standard gospel-soul formulas (such as "We Shall Overcome") on their heads, and made Parliament a band to reckon with. While their first two LPs were not received well at the time, *Down Stroke* is rightly becoming recognized as a classic, with *Chocolate City* not far behind.

## P-FUNK

In 1975 things really got hot for the P-Funk players. Clinton had been searching for a strong horn section, and by selling Bootsy on the idea of fronting Bootsy's Rubber Band, the pair recruited ex-JBs horn players Fred Wesley, Maceo Parker, and Richard "Kush" Griffith to join the Mob, and an entire rhythmic element of sound (from Wesley's arrange-

ments) completed the Parliament flavor. Based in the four-part harmonies as a vocal doo-wop group, and with the band inspired by Jimi
Hendrix as a black rock band, the "Parliafunkadelicment Thang" was
already representing a fusion of African-American musical and social
values well beyond the range of most black acts. With the gothic, ethereal European classical chords and spacey keyboard riffs from Bernie
Worrell; the preposterous gladiator-games horn arrangements from
Wesley; the light-saber-sharp guitar chops of Shider, Hazel, and young
Michael Hampton all stewed on top of gurgling, dinosaur stomp grooves
championed by Bootsy and Mosson; and the stable of drummers, Tiki
Fulwood, Tyrone Lampkin, and soon Jerome Brailey, a *monster sound*
developed. With Clinton's devious direction, the P-Funk sound would
come alive and deliver an all-encompassing musical experience—with
its sensibilities straight from the hood. Rhythmically deep, strong, and
seasoned, the P-Funk ensemble stretched the musical experience further and further outward.

### THE MOTHERSHIP CONNECTION

The Year of the Mothership Connection (1975) began the era of P-Funk
as a truly spiritual form of black music in the tradition of jazz, soul, reggae, or gospel. There is much lighthearted significance made about the
night in 1975 when Clinton and Bootsy were driving home from
Toronto and were "visited." As Clinton told the story to Abe Peck:

> We saw this light bouncing from one side of the street to
> the other. It happened a few times and I made a comment
> that "the Mothership was angry with us for giving up the
> funk without permission." Just then the light hit the car.
> All the street lights went out, and there weren't any cars
> around . . . I said, "Bootsy, you think you can step on it."

While nothing was said about the incident between Bootsy and
George at the time, things blew up for the band shortly thereafter. Clinton had come up with the *Mothership Connection* concept and sprung it
on their label executives Cecil Holmes and Neil Bogart, who gave them
the green light—and the greenbacks—without reservations. While
Eddie Hazel languished in jail, the phenomenal seventeen-year-old guitarist Michael Hampton joined the group on tour that summer in Cleveland. The brilliantly gifted guitarist and gospel-trained vocalist Glen

Goins was picked up back in Plainfield, and when drummer Tiki Fulwood was starting to slip into drug and health problems, former Chambers Brothers drummer Jerome Brailey was recruited just in time for the *Mothership Connection* recording sessions. Jerome Brailey; bassist Cordell "Boogie" Mosson; guitarists Garry Shider, Glen Goins, and Mike Hampton; keyboardist Bernie Worrell; and Bootsy regularly went into the United Sound studios in Detroit and jammed, as George recorded *everything,* adding horns, vocals, and concepts later. In September the band recorded a series of tracks that ultimately became Funkadelic's *Let's Take It to the Stage* LP, Bootsy's Rubber Band's *Stretchin' Out* LP, and Parliament's *Mothership Connection.*

The *Mothership Connection* LP was a motherlode of concepts and rhythm on a level never witnessed before. Lyrics spoke of "returning to claim the pyramids" and "Supergroovalistic-prosifunkstication." For what seemed like the first time ever, a popular black album succeeded with no ballads. Even James Brown's album fillers contained at least *one* down-tempo song, but *Mothership* was an entire funk record—the prototype of the Hip Hop album of the 1990s, in which *every* beat is a funk beat. Parliament had pioneered this. The P-Funk beat, characterized by Jerome "Bigfoot" Brailey's intricate patterns surrounding his throbbing bass-drum kicks, and Bootsy's now legendary rhythmic-melodic complexities, Fred Wesley's meticulous horn arrangements, Bernie Worrell's gothic, sinister keyboard work, the many guitarists, and Clinton's brand of operatic vocal hooks made P-Funk the untouchable thang it is today.

Hip Hoppers discovered the P-Funk gold mine around 1987, but an even more interesting parallel occurred in 1993. In the same fashion that P-Funk went over the top with the *Mothership,* rap star Dr. Dre became a household name with a Hip Hop interpretation of the very same ship. Dr. Dre's three-million-selling LP *The Chronic* was the rap record of the year for 1993 and his tour de force, as well as the introduction of the now infamous Snoop Doggy Dogg. Yet *The Chronic* was the most explicit sampling tribute to the P-Funk at the time, and the *Mothership Connection* was the basis. The title song of *The Chronic* uses the lines from "P-Funk: Make My Funk the P-Funk," replacing "funk" with "shit," and "P-Funk" with "chronic." Even deeper, the melodic breakdown from the title song, "Mothership Connection (Star Child)," was taken and revamped into the Grammy-winning Dr. Dre hit, "Let Me Ride."

Moreover, Parliament had pioneered the idea that The Funk was something that one cannot get enough of. "The funk is its own reward" was the chant, as the *Mothership* concept played on the black church themes of worship to claim that the more you feel The Funk, the closer you get to a transcendent level. As Star Child made clear on "P-Funk (Wants to Get Funked Up)," "The desired effect is what you get when you improve your interplanetary funksmanship." Speaking directly to black teenagers, P-Funk was in tune with the *infinite,* and brought their followers up with them.

To top it off, the band could scorch the dance floor. Before anyone knew what hit them, "Give Up the Funk (Tear the Roof Off the Sucker)" was the No. 1 soul single in the country in June 1976. While the jam was an intricate, highly complex rhythm arrangement (high school bands had an awful time playing *that* one at local dances), the vocals amounted to a wild mix of scorching screams and sinister whispers—"We're Gonna TURN—THIS MUTHA—OUT!!" was followed in a whisper by "let us in—we'll turn this mother out." "Tear the Roof Off" had so much rhythm to it that the original title, "Give Up the Funk," was just not potent enough for the jam, and very quickly after its release, the record became (and is still) known primarily by its longer name, the more appropriately rhythmic "Tear the Roof Off the Sucker." (The record also provided the basis for the breakthrough of M. C. Hammer in 1989, who sampled the jam for his first national hit "Turn This Mutha Out.")

The year 1976 was a real mutha, as P-Funk delivered five now-classic albums under four different names for three different labels. A preposterous follow-up album for Parliament, *Clones of Dr. Funkenstein,* became the vehicle for George (now known as "Dr. Funkenstein") Clinton to express his ultimate ego trips. With lyrics like "kiss me on my ego," Clinton had begun to toy with the incredible underground celebrity he was attaining, and on "Children of Production," Clinton was bold enough to give the band so much juice it was frightening: "we are deeper than abortion/deeper than the notion/that the world was flat when it was round/we're gonna blow the cobwebs out your mind!" Still with the legendary lineup of musicians, the alter-ego hard-rock band Funkadelic continued to record, and released two albums in 1976, one for their old label Westbound (*Tales of Kidd Funkadelic*) and one for Warner Brothers (*Hardcore Jollies*). "Kidd Funkadelic" was actually the newly acquired guitarist Michael Hampton, but the thirteen-minute keyboard groove instrumental title cut featured *no* guitars. The record is so strong, as was the entire album (liner artist Pedro Bell at his Daliesque best on this disc as well) that Hampton's tracks were not needed. The band made up for it on *Hardcore Jollies,* featuring Hampton and the return of Eddie Hazel on a number of ballistic rock thrashers, "Comin' Round the Mountain," "Hardcore Jollies," and a live rendition of "Cosmic Slop" for good measure. *Hardcore Jollies* indeed. Bootsy's Rubber Band hit the streets as well that year, delivering a sexy, silly style of rapping above a liquid bass, serving up a monster hit single "Stretchin' Out," a song so rhythmic, chord-heavy, noisy, and stylish that it raised one's funk expectations to a new attention.

## BOOTSY'S RUBBER BAND

The Rubber Band began in the studio, when the original "Stretchin' Out" groove finally began to cook, as Bootsy, Mike Hampton, and Garry Shider were churning out the licks. The groove moved Bootsy to say, "Man, we're stretchin' out on that one," and as usual, George Clinton heard it, snapping back, "That's it, stretchin' out *in a Rubber Band!*" The rest became the nastayest and most liberated form of P-Funk, symbolically the *exposed genitals* of the P-Funk vibe. Bootsy Collins made a name for himself quickly, releasing the *Stretchin' Out* album in early 1976 and *Aaah the Name Is Bootsy, Baby!* in the spring of 1977. With a giddy, childlike geepiness as a stage showman (listen to "Psychoticbumpschool," or "Rubber Duckie") and an erotic troubador with a "verbal rappability" and orgiastic bass effects ("Munchies for Your Love," "What's a Telephone Bill"), Bootsy's Rubber Band was the complete erotic funk experience. Supported by the amazingly soulful falsetto vocal chops of Gary "Mudbone" Cooper, who brought glee club energy to the vocals; Fred Wesley and Maceo Parker's amazing decision to leave James Brown and join the Rubber Band; and Cincinnati buddies Frankie "Kash" Waddy on drums and Joel "Razor Sharp" Johnson on keys, the Rubber Band soon took on a life of its own.

Bootsy's 1977 release featured an excellent example of P-Funk's appropriation of Western cultural references for their own use: "The Pinocchio Theory" was taken to mean: "If you fake the funk, your nose gots to grow!" The record also featured a mock-live recording introducing Casper, the bass-playing ghost, as well as a ten-minute psychedelic ballad titled "Munchies for Your Love" which set Bootsy apart from all other bass performers, with a Jimi Hendrix–style rock solo that was

drenched in erotic intensity. Bootsy took his popularity to new heights
in 1978, with *Player of the Year,* an album that featured the funk classics
"Bootzilla" and "Hollywood Squares." He called himself "The Star,"
years before Prince would claim that moniker, and (under the influence of his managers) created a mystique that kept Bootsy from the public, yet kept the public buying his mysteriously funky, sexy music.

Spinoff acts were popping up everywhere. Female vocalists Lynn
Mabry and Dawn Silva were packaged as the Brides of Funkenstein
and sang over two LPs worth of now classic material on *Funk or Walk*
and *Never Buy Texas from a Cowboy.* Guitarist Eddie Hazel recorded
*Games, Dames and Guitar Thangs* for Warner Brothers in 1978—easily
one of the best P-Funk albums ever. Bernie Worrell delivered *All the
Woo in the World* for Arista, Fred Wesley and the Horny Horns worked
out two albums of groove tracks for Atlantic, and a bevy of females
were lined up for Parlet, dropping three LPs for Casablanca.

Something happened along the way to the P-Funk circus. In the
midst of all of the chaos and clutter, P-Funk bands managed to affect
black music in at least two phenomenal ways: creative genius and financial disaster. Musically, the band introduced the electronic age into
modern black music, by incorporating the most modern forms of technology while remaining identified with the James Brown groove and
the bro on the street. Keyboardist Bernie Worrell was crucial to the
technologization of black popular music—but had he raised the standards impossibly high? As one funkateer put it, "The world can either
credit him or blame him for the synthesizer bass." P-Funk's fantastic
science fiction created a series of spectacular "otherworlds" that Africans
could inhabit freely, in which one could be loving, caring, sensual, psychedelic, and nasty without fear of cosmic retribution, and whites simply did not exist. The symbolic connections of P-Funk concepts to
one's earthly struggles for freedom were felt by many listeners, particularly black teenagers. Furthermore, the assertion of a black worldview that incorporates modern technology, the demographics of the
seventies, and a black aesthetic was a profound theoretical breakthrough, despite the silliness. Such grand visions of black people were
not found in black film, black literature, or black politics in the late
1970s.

Yet the organized mayhem led to an equally awesome magnitude
of confusion, as players came and went, the money was hard to locate,
and people rarely knew who was in charge. Manager and producer

Robert Middleman recalled his early role in the P-Funk Mob: "It was my job to tell the musicians why they weren't getting paid." Indeed, the story of "who owns the P-Funk" is deserving of a book in itself. Nevertheless, at the time, the P-Funk Earth Tour was a thing to behold.

### THE EARTH TOUR

P-Funk was challenging the established giants in the industry. While the Ohio Players, Commodores, and Earth, Wind & Fire were enormously popular, their appeal crossed racial lines, while the P-Funk Mob appeared to outsiders as some sort of disco-voodoo cult. Undaunted, and with the help of Casablanca Record executives Neil Bogart and Cecil Holmes, Clinton secured the services of Jules Fischer, the set designer who had produced the stage sets for the rock bands Kiss and the Rolling Stones. With a $275,000 budget—the largest ever for any black act—Parliament took the Mothership Connection to the people, and *landed* the Mothership on stage. Meticulously rehearsed in an airport hangar in Upstate New York (one of the few times P-Funk was deliberately rehearsed to be tight live), Clinton had a wild plan for everything, from his polyester pimpmobile entrance—a stage-prop tribute to the badass gangstas and hustlers that made up life in da hood—through Garry Shider's flight through the rafters with the Bop Gun, and the endless animated props and costumes, to the thunderous descent of the Mothership. Equal parts tribal dance ("gaa gaa goo gaa!"), church revival ("swing down, sweet chariot/stop and let me ride"), and call-and-response nightclub hype ("we love to funk you Funkenstein/your funk is the best!"), the P-Funk act drew from the ribald, uncensored entirety of the black tradition in mind-blowing ways no one had yet even attempted.

Inaugurated in New Orleans in October 1976 (voodoo cult indeed?), the P-Funk Earth Tour headed westward, and recorded their seminal P-Funk Earth Tour on January 19, 1977, at the Forum in Los Angeles and on January 21, 1977, at the Oakland Coliseum. Many of the West Coast rap stars that are so well known for incorporating P-Funk music were cloned by The Funk at these Earth Tour concerts.

The Earth Tour was the culmination of the entire musical movement of the decade toward larger shows, larger venues, and larger profits. Subsequent theme-oriented "funk operas" told the story of "Sir Nose D'Voidoffunk," "Mr. Wiggles," and "Gloryhallastupid." Interestingly, in the midst of the high-profile success in 1978, Clinton deliberately took the band on an "anti-tour," performing in small clubs, without props or costumes, avoiding the ego trips of stardom, and just *jamming*. The success continued through 1980, although there were signs of wear and tear on the group. While there were other acts in competition for dominance in black music, the release of *Parliament Live: The P-Funk Earth Tour* live recording in May 1977 set to rest any illusions that "color-blind" music could substitute for the dark realities of black funk.

### FLASHLIGHT AND ONE NATION

At the peak of the band's popularity as a far-out, ghoulish band of funk freaks in late 1977, Parliament released the first of five megahits that would take them over the top. While they were already well known to dance music fans for "Tear the Roof Off the Sucker," their follow-up hits "Do That Stuff" and "Bop Gun" appeared to sound like extra helpings for the funk clones only. "Flashlight" changed all that. Sneaking up on funk fans as the last song on the *Funkentelechy vs. the Placebo Syndrome* LP, the record obliterated the standards of dance music when it hit the radio in early 1978. It slithered along with layers of shrill, atmospheric string synthesizers, absurd vocal vamps ("Now I lay me down to sleep . . ."), a scorching, liquified guitar track (played by Phelps "Catfish" Collins, according to brother Bootsy), and an astoundingly loud clap track on the beat that drove listeners crazy when "Flashlight" hit the AM radio.

But what took the record over the top was the bass. *The* Bass. *The BASS!* Keyboardist Bernie Worrell had mastered the keyboard bass, and played with the subtle accents and walking bass line that any accomplished bass player might use—yet this bass sounded like nothing ever played before. The Moog synthesizer was capable not only of playing low notes, but of stacking a number of bass tones onto one key—creating the fullest bass sound ever played. Worrell's bass tones sounded louder than any other bass track heard on the radio because of this stacking effect, and his wizardry with freakish note-bending effects created a mind-scraping, Thumpasaurus gribble grind that forever changed the bottom groove in popular music. By the time the record faded and the chant "Everybody's got a little bit of light, under the sun" wound down, a new realm of The Funk had been discovered. Bands everywhere began playing stacked bass lines on their keyboards, often with disappointing results. Bernie Worrell was a child prodigy—a master of any keyboard—who had commanded the ultimate funk effect.

The record soared to No. 1 R&B (three weeks there), and made it to No. 16 on the pop charts in the spring of 1978. Parliament had made it big. Yet right on the heels of Parliament, riding the spastic funk explosion, was Bootsy's Rubber Band's most guttural and expressive hit, "Bootzilla"—another classic funk dinosaur that followed "Flashlight" at No. 1 soul. (Bootsy was apparently way too freaky for the pop charts, and "Bootzilla" never came close.)

Yet just as the glow of the "Flashlight" was fading from the radio in the summer of 1978, a strangely grooving, fast-paced percussive scorcher hit the radio. The record featured eerily sweet harmonies, a strange vocal tone from (their latest recruit, Ohio Players veteran keyboardist) Junie Morrison, an unrelenting splatter of percussion, and that fat, liquid bass synthesizer once again—Funkadelic had assaulted the dance floor with a monster that ripped apart the formulas for disco dance tracks. "One Nation Under a Groove" pulsed and throbbed, oozed with rhythm, slipped in subtle lyrical statements, and stood at No. 1 R&B for six weeks—the biggest seller of the year (even *Jet* magazine named "One Nation" the song of the year for 1978). For a minute, P-Funk was a pop phenomenon. Even Top 40 countdown deejay Kasey Casem delivered the P-Funk saga as one of his many trivia tales ("Can you name the act with two songs in the Top 40 this year, recorded under different names? The answer in a minute . . .").

Later in 1978, Parliament dared to follow up "Flashlight" with the preposterous "Aqua-Boogie," yet another No. 1 soul hit, and when the multilayered Funkadelic dance masterpiece "(Not Just) Knee Deep" went No. 1 the following summer, P-Funk's dominance over the dance floor was assured.

Even the average music fan was beginning to wonder about the Parliament and Funkadelic thing. Who *were* these guys? Which one was George Clinton? What's a Funkadelic? By 1977 the Casablanca Records promotions people had taken an interest in Clinton's ideas and released the *Earth Tour* album in May 1977 with a two-by-three-foot poster *and* an iron-on T-shirt transfer in each record. The next LP, *Funkentelechy vs. the Placebo Syndrome,* offered a bright pink poster of Sir Nose D'Voidoffunk and a twelve-page full color comic book describing the escapades of the "funky superheroes." The 1978 *Motor Booty Affair* LP featured a pop-up cartoon rendition of Atlantis when the album was opened, and stand-up cut-outs of even more P-Funk characters were featured. Mattel toys entered into negotiations with the group to feature a set of *toy dolls* of the main characters in the group (a Dr.

Funkenstein doll, a Bootsy doll, and a Star-Child doll!). The project was nixed because of disagreements over rights and royalties for the images. But any way you look at it, P-Funk was hot stuff. Even the often stingy Warner Brothers allowed Clinton to release an extra seven-inch single (containing a live version of "Maggot Brain" targeted at rock radio) inside the *One Nation Under a Groove* Funkadelic LP in 1978.

With Clinton's P-Funk, The Funk was elevated from a style to a way of life, but the lifestyle was only an ideal, a reality only on the stage. Before the phenomenal success, the band existed as a family, traveling, smoking, loving, creating, performing, and living together. With the success came hangers-on, stronger drugs, and lawyers. The massive entourage of the P-Funk tours ran into trouble as the industry declined, and by 1981 forces of corruption from within and without drastically reduced the group's ability to make strong music and remain on the radio. Band members who were recruited simply on the strength of the band's reputation wound up on tours or in strange towns without getting paid. Tensions were high and morale was low when Clinton "retired" in 1980, just as the band was scheduled to play a week at the Apollo Theater in Harlem—and the band played without George for the most part, although he made a few cameos.

As early as 1978 band members left the group and recorded their own music with lyrics openly critical of George Clinton. Jerome Brailey was the most vehement expatriate, leaving to produce his own band, Mutiny, whose awesome first album, *Mutiny on the Mamaship,* was wrought full of jibes at Clinton's ego, though the group's fonk was clearly in the mold of the P. The supremely talented vocalist Glen Goins left at the same time as Brailey, and recorded with Brailey the only album of the band, *Quazar,* before dying of Hodgkin's disease on July 30, 1978. Three original members of the Parliaments, Clarence "Fuzzy" Haskins, Calvin Simon, and Grady Thomas, also set out on their own in 1981 calling themselves Funkadelic, and appearing on *Soul Train,* also ripping Clinton on choice cuts of their mildly funky anachronism of an album *Connections and Disconnections.* Nevertheless the myth lived on, and Clinton persevered with a constantly changing lineup to field a band throughout the 1980s (all of these P-Funk spinoffs are delectable collector's items).

The demise of Casablanca Records and the death of Neil Bogart from cancer in 1982 eliminated one of Clinton's strongest and most generous allies. Meanwhile, Warner Brothers gave Clinton constant trouble and had his 1981 Funkadelic album *The Electric Spanking of War Babies* reduced from a two-record set to one disc and had Pedro Bell's phallic cover art censored, despite the fact that the band was following up two consecutive million-selling records. Meanwhile, Bootsy's Rubber Band found itself in a lawsuit over the "Rubber Band" name, apparently used by a country rock group in 1971. Bootsy's people incredibly lost the lawsuit, and Bootsy found himself over $275,000 in debt to his label, forced to give profits from later albums (such as the *Sweat Band* and Bootsy's *The One Giveth*) directly to Warner Brothers. It would be five years before Bootsy released himself from the contract and put out another record under his name, *What's Bootsy Doin'*, on Columbia Records in 1988.

Losing Parliament and Funkadelic almost overnight (and going out of style just as quickly) the P-Funk took a nosedive underground. While his creative input was invaluable, Clinton often brought complete legalistic and financial chaos to his projects. (Roger Troutman and his band Zapp saw the writing on the wall, and after Bootsy and George helped to bring about the first Zapp album, Roger and Zapp jumped ship, to record their own brand of monster funk—see Chapter nineteen—without the financial risks of The P.)

By the mid-1980s it appeared that anyone collaborating with George Clinton gave the impression that they were at the end of the line. Sly Stone's career never really "recovered" during his years with the P-Funk, while the band's recording with James Brown was done during one of Brown's lowest points of popularity in 1980. British rocker Thomas Dolby followed his 1983 megahit "She Blinded Me With Science" with funky duets with Clinton, "The Cube" and "Hot Sauce," and then proceeded to vanish into obscurity. Even the dethroned Miss America Vanessa Williams wound up—in the pit of her public scorn in 1988—recording with George Clinton (check out "Hey Good Lookin' " on the *R&B Skeletons* album). Clinton's collaboration with "the artist formerly known as Prince" that began in 1989 appears to have only brought him down to Clinton's underground level, and after Michael Jackson's problems with child molestation charges, his 1995 collaboration with Dr. Funkenstein seemed inevitable.

#### ATOMIC DOG

Despite being literally blacklisted from radio airplay, Clinton was able to continue the P-Funk magic show for four more years and four albums on the strength of his best hit of the 1980s—the dance-music classic "Atomic Dog." Clinton was able to sell himself to Capitol Records in 1982 with the help of Ted Currier, a funkateer at Capitol, and the fact that Clinton had hundreds of hours of music already produced and waiting for release. No record in modern black music history has had a more storied history than "Atomic Dog." The song is now a classic of black popular music, and perhaps the most sampled rhythm hook of all time.

An almost forgotten second single from Clinton's *Computer Games* LP for Capitol Records ("Loopzilla" was the first), the record was held back from the major R&B stations, and only after incredibly strong sales did stations begin to pick it up. In many cases across the country, "Atomic Dog" was the No. 1 R&B record, but was not on the playlist of R&B stations. Clinton's bad reputation with the industry, his political consciousness (as seen on his previous Funkadelic records), and a general move toward more youthful-looking acts kept him out of the loop. Lurking for six weeks at No. 2 behind Michael Jackson's "Billie Jean," "Atomic Dog" finally went to No. 1, lasted for four weeks, and in the most inexplicable turn of events, the record never made the pop Top 100—which was supposed to be automatic for No. 1 soul hits!

Meanwhile, the record became an instant classic, ripping dance floors with its backward-swinging synthesizer hooks, Clinton's characteristically absurd vocalizing ("Why must I feel like that/why must I chase the cat!"), and hilariously accurate expressions of the doglike nature of horny men (and women). The record captured the irreverent essence of the sexual drive in the electronic age. The black fraternity Omega Psi Phi (known as the "Q" dogs) claimed "Atomic Dog" as its theme song, and a slew of artists copied the hook note-for-note on their sexiest sides, from Karyn White's "Walkin' the Dog" to Teddy Riley's "Do the D.O.G.G." and Ice Cube's "The Nigga You Love to Hate," "My Summer Vacation," and "Ghetto Bird." Clinton himself recycled the hook on his 1983 rap version of "Dog Talk," his 1990 "Why Should I Dog U Out?," and his 1993 "Martial Law." "Atomic Dog" continues to thrive today as perhaps the *jam* of the 1980s.

After label difficulties, once again with Capitol, Clinton signed with the Paisley Park label, created by the black pop-rock superstar once known as Prince. The resulting collaborations ("Bob George" in 1988, "We Can Funk" in 1989, and "Tweakin'" remix in 1990) have produced only moderately stanky results, although the music of then-Prince has shown an even deeper appreciation of R&B and funk roots.

With little or no black radio airplay, Clinton found allies in the predominantly white hard rock scene (just as he did in 1970 with Armen Boladian and Westbound Records), and produced the second album for the upstart rock quartet the Red Hot Chili Peppers in 1985. Clinton appeared on and coproduced projects with British new-waver Thomas Dolby while producing a dance version of Warren Zevon's perplexing "Leave My Monkey Alone" in 1987. Clinton's band, while only a prototype for his nineties act, appeared on *Saturday Night Live* in 1986, and with the support of *Late Night* bandleader and devoted funkateer Paul Shaffer, Clinton appeared for the first of many times on David Letterman's show in 1986. The entire group performed in a chaotic bash on national television with the Red Hot Chili Peppers at the 1993 Grammy Awards, and toured with the "Lollapalooza" art-pop tour in the summer of 1994.

By 1988, when hard-core rap invaded the mainstream of music on the strength of Public Enemy's phenomenal recording *It Takes a Nation of Millions to Hold Us Back,* Clinton began to get some respect in the black music industry. The first single from the album, "Bring the Noise," was driven by the sampled loop from the 1975 Funkadelic tune "Get Off Your Ass and Jam." The militancy of rap music in 1988 was a marked turnaround from the somewhat adolescent raps of LL Cool J, Doug E. Fresh, and Run-D.M.C., who had dominated pop rap until then. The seriousness of the inner city, and the directness which Public Enemy (and other hard-core rappers such as KRS-One of Boogie Down Productions, Melle Mel, and Afrika Bambaataa) addressed the problems of their communities, recalled images of old-school funk, including Parliament's "Chocolate City," Stevie Wonder's "Living for the City," and James Brown's "Say It Loud (I'm Black and I'm Proud)."

For rap producers, the music of James Brown was the sample of the day back in 1988, but as rap music became more thematic, conceptual, and serious, straightforward braggadocio and the generic "Power to the People" chant needed more support. It was at this point that the Clinton/P-Funk loop surpassed James Brown as the jingle of choice (just as P-Funk surpassed the JBs fonk as the groove of choice in the 1970s). With the range of black rap music opening up to wider realms, the P-Funk catalog became the staple, and the standard by which stylistic breadth was conceptualized in Hip Hop sampling. Other known rap acts like Schooly D ("Saturday Nite"), EPMD ("Who's Booty," "So Whatcha Sayin'"), and De La Soul ("Me Myself and I") began to incorporate obvious and not-so-obvious P-Funk loops into their music.

The Oakland-based rap group Digital Underground went literally overboard with their allegiance to P-Funk, by first signifying on the underwater theme of the 1978 "Aqua Boogie" Parliament hit, recording a song on their platinum 1989 album *Sex Packets* entitled "Underwater Rimes." The group's third album was titled *Sons of the P* and claimed allegiance to Clinton, identifying the group as children of the "Father of Funk." The rappers also borrowed the P-Funk style of creating cartoon characters to enhance their image, and featured Dr. Funkenstein himself, George Clinton, on the title song, "Sons of the P," in 1991. Greg Jacobs, a.k.a. "Humpty Hump," recalls the "mindshattering experience" of working with the Doctor:

> I don't know whether it is good or bad, but George blew our minds wide open when we was working with him in terms of how to hear things and how to play things and how to just kind of just let it happen, rather than to control and try to make it a certain way, just let it flow out of us. . . . He led me onto a theory that we're just conveyors, we're just, you might say, the people that are directing the energy in the funk, but he seems to feel like it's a collective spirit that comes from the whole rhythm of the world, the rhythm of people. Brothers seem to have a rhythm with everything they do. One of the things George was about, was capturing that in the studio.

The Rhythm of the One was and is an operating principle of P-Funk, and it has seeped into even the most mechanical of musical forms, Hip Hop.

As the P-Funk mythology continued to grow at the dawn of the nineties, the band continued to tour. While Clinton continues to find recording difficulties, the group is gaining a new generation of followers as a result of the reissues of P-Funk material by various publishers, and recording after recording of rap music is maintained by the rhythmic, melodic, and conceptual explication of the "Parliafunkadelicment Thang."

# EIGHTEEN

# The Metaphysics of P:
# The Mothership Connection

"Funk . . . created the gods."

*Parliament*

George Clinton and his P-Funk band developed something far greater than their simple identity as a musical ensemble. P-Funk was and is more than a music style; it is a philosophy of life that for some approaches a religious creed.

Clinton himself maintains that P-Funk was never meant to be taken seriously, but its followers often did anyway. From the hard-core "maggots," "clones," and "funkateers" to the typical fan, P-Funk articulated a new worldview, often more relevant than the religious practices of their relatives in the detached decade of the 1970s. Those who chose to pay attention found that one could get deeper and deeper into P-Funk and never reach the bottom. Clinton's entourage ritualized The Funk into a metaphysical phenomenon of self-development not unlike the mystery systems of Africa and the Caribbean. Radio personality and funkateer Ashem "The Funky Man" Neru-Mesit claims that "P-Funk is a Mystery System, like the ancient Mystery Systems of Kemet (Egypt); there's a rite of passage, and a way to better yourself."

The religiosity of P-Funk has never really been taken seriously, perhaps because of the lack of religious significance Clinton himself attributes to his music. However, with the many reincarnations of P-Funk philosophies in the rap music of the 1990s, and the growing awareness of the understanding of African religious systems, the deepness of the P is more relevant than ever. (It should be understood, however, that there are as many interpretations of The Funk as there are funkateers, and what follows is just one of them.)

The cool style of P-Funk scored a series of No. 1 dance singles from 1975 to 1980, which spawned a series of platinum-selling albums, which in turn drew thousands of fans to elaborate concerts filled with black cartoon characters, painted people, million-dollar props, loud music, and a series of chants told over a nasty, nasty groove. The long jams often "spaced out," in which obscure, eerie synthesizer tones and the offbeat philosophical rantings of Clinton and others in the band compelled listeners to absorb the meanings and the feel of the sounds. Visually, the band's look suggested—and the huge show created—an alternate reality, "dressed in diapers and leotards, as genies and wolf-men . . . looking like a cross between *Star Trek* and *Sanford and Son*." The music and concepts drew listeners into a coded philosophy of black nationhood, of freedom of expression and personal salvation through the use of symbols and double meanings that had deep roots in black music and religious traditions.

### AFRO-CENTRIC

Bandleader George Clinton and writer-artist Pedro Bell were the pri-mary sources of an endless flow of offbeat black philosophy that mocked the self-importance of religious and political doctrines while subtly creating their own. Clinton's use of operatic vocals and church-based funk chants were common, but they became subversive when the lyrics reprised well-known themes in black religion, while af-firming the present-day circumstances of blacks. On "Mothership Con-nection," for example, the background vocal refrain "Swing down, sweet chariot/stop and let me ride" was a reference to the traditional black church hymn. "When Gabriel's horn blow, you better be able to go" followed at the end of the song. In this case, however, the char-iot was not an angel, but a spaceship with a funky black crew that had "returned to claim the pyramids." Without polemics, militarism, or racially charged code words, Clinton's P-Funk placed the African-American sensibility at the center of the universe, and ultimately at the center of *history*.

Presaging by a decade the controversies surrounding historical ac-counts of the African origins of civilization, Clinton's crew circulated the notion that the pyramids were not only built by Africans (probably from outer space), but that these Africans were some bad mothas who could "Tear the Roof Off the Sucker." By extension, P-Funk was claim-ing that symbolically, blacks *were responsible for civilization*:

> Funk upon a time, in the days of the funkapus, the concept
> of specially designed afro-nauts, capable of funkatizing galax-
> ies, was first laid on man-child, but was later repossessed,
> and placed among the secrets of the pyramids, until a more

positive attitude towards this, most sacred phenomenon, clone funk, could be acquired.

Parliament, "Prelude to Dr. Funkenstein" (1976)

The Mob later toyed with the notion of the Big Bang, claiming that a P-Funk party in "the Black Hole" was the cause of the *entire universe,* proclaiming, "That fuss wuz us." Parliament continued to link the story lines of every album, beginning with *Mothership Connection* in 1975, followed by *Clones of Dr. Funkenstein* in 1976, and the live recording *P-Funk Earth Tour.* A series of cartoon characters were introduced, beginning with "Star Child" (alias the long haid sucka), one of the first clones of "Dr. Funkenstein"—the body-snatching doctor of funk played by George Clinton. On *Funkentelechy vs. the Placebo Syndrome* in 1977, an evil nemesis of funk was created, "Sir Nose D'Voidoffunk" (a character first conceived by P-Funk manager Tom Vickers, and overheard as usual by Clinton). This unfunky and overdressed character refused to dance, and spread the "Placebo Syndrome" everywhere he went. "Sir Nose," along with a growing cast of characters, followed the band around the universe in liner-note stories and on the recordings of the subsequent three albums: *Motor Booty Affair* in 1978, *Gloryhallastupid* in 1979, and *Trombipulation* in 1980.

Funkadelic album artist Pedro Bell was also guilty of perpetrating a bizarre, Afro-centric mythology on long Funkadelic album cover essays, which complemented his felt-tip-marker-drawn mutant-scapes of urban black life. Bell's visual imagery had the seamless layering of twisted symbols from the unconscious that Salvador Dali was known for, while Bell's dark ghetto eroticism and hyperbolic grammar forged a new realm of black language:

AS IT IS WRITTEN HENCEFORTH . . . that on the Eighth Day, the Cosmic Strumpet of MOTHER NATURE was spawned to envelope this Third Planet in FUNKACIDAL VIBRATIONS. And she birthed Apostles Ra, Hendrix, Stone, and CLINTON to preserve all funkiness of man unto eternity. . . . But! Fraudulent forces of obnoxious JIVATION grew. Sun Ra strobed back to Saturn to await his Next Reincarnation, Jimi was forced back into basic atoms; Sly was co-opted into a jester monolith . . . and only seedling GEORGE remained. As it came to be, he did indeed, begat

Funkadelic to restore Order Within The Universe. Nour-
ished by the Pamgrierian mammaristic melonpaps of Mother
Nature, the followers of FUNKADELIA multiplied incessantly!

*Standing on the Verge of Gettin' It On,* liner notes (1974)

The fact that the entire P-Funk experience, the entire scene, the
entire thang was too preposterous to be taken seriously allowed the funk
mob to make all sorts of claims about the inherent qualities of
Africans—and reach millions of listeners without the traditional has-
sles of spokesperson status. It also kept Clinton from the pop star visibility that might have kept his band in the black countless times.

The importance of these silly stories is the fact that Parliament,
Funkadelic, and Bootsy's Rubber Band sold over ten million records in
the last half of the 1970s by hitting first with the music, then drawing
listeners into elaborate fantasyscapes that influenced a generation of
urban youth. Clinton and his associates drew such far-reaching scope
for their silly stories and cartoon characters that one can conceive of
their works as folklore, and perhaps some of the first postindustrial black
American mythology. Science fiction has often been associated with a
religion or mythology for the technological age, by posing a backdrop
for the major questions of creation and the destiny of mankind. Clinton and crew developed their own creation myths and their own black
science-fiction, which placed the streetwise homeboy in the center of
a series of intergalactic parables, in which whites did not exist and the
values and attributes alluded to by The Funk constituted the resolution
of each tale.

The mythic character of the many players in P-Funk served as
ideals—albeit freaked-out ideals—of people inhabiting an imagined
universe of total funkativity. The characters provided a framework for
young people to imagine themselves in the image of their "Super Funky
Heroes." In his 1987 thesis on "The P-Funk Aesthetic," Michael O'Neal
discusses the usefulness of the P-Funk aesthetic as positive imagery for
black children:

Sir Nose and Starchild, and Dr. Funkenstein, as animated
(as opposed to real) superheroes, give black children a sense
of animation in their own likeness that previously they have

been denied—especially by the media. These superheroes offer them a mythic sense of possibility.

The importance of inverting the negative associations with blackness, darkness, funkiness, and stoopidness cannot be underestimated. The relentless barrage of negative information about black people portrayed in the media, the absence of visible black advocates in the public eye, and the very semantic foundation of the language that associates white with "good" and black with "bad" can be overwhelming to a black child. P-Funk began to turn these notions on their heads.

## THE MOTHERSHIP

The rise of P-Funk was part of a new era in black culture that developed after the civil rights movement. The concept, and the myth, of black liberation since the days of slavery has been centered on the strong Christian-based notion of an Exodus from Babylon to the "Promised Land." The powerful speeches of Martin Luther King, Jr.,were based on this religious and cultural theme. "We Shall Overcome" was the theme song of the civil rights movement (with P-Funk the chant had become "Got to get over the hump!"); by the early 1970s, it was becoming clear that the religious imagery of the past was inadequate for many of the black youth of the day. Youngsters who grew up in the 1970s never witnessed Dr. King on television or in person, and the most prominent blacks were often sports stars, including the Muslims Muhammad Ali and Kareem Abdul Jabbar. According to record producer and funkateer Anthony "Dave-ID K-OS" Bryant, there were many blacks who could see that the conditioning of traditional religion was "not happening" for them, and also that "P-Funk was deeply religious, but also speaking to the way they are living today."

In the largest and most expensive black concert tour to date in 1977, Clinton and his entourage had a spaceship prop built, which would descend from the rafters of any large stadium. The performance preceding the descent of the Mothership was laden with funky ritualism, meditative chants, a series of massive symbolic stage props brought onstage, and a gospel churchlike invocation to bring the ship down. After a considerable frenzy had been built up, the chant "Swing down, I wanna ride" signified it was time for the landing.

The thunderous spectacle of lights, smoke, relentless music, and mystical symbolism was a profound example of black tradition in its unrestricted state. While the show was primarily designed as entertainment, and "Dr. Funkenstein" comes out of the ship to join the party, the landing of the Mothership serves as a metaphor for the "chariot" responsible for bringing "the chosen" to the Promised Land. The "chariot" is a myth, yet this chariot was *real*. The decade of the 1970s indeed represented that "Promised Land" of equality, a period of experiment in "integration" and "equality" for which the civil rights movement had worked for so long. P-Funk attempted to bring meaning and catharsis to that paradoxical realization of freedom. The Mothership was a celebration of the infinities of which blacks were now capable.

### COSMIC ONENESS

While raised with a traditional black Christian background, George Clinton was disinclined to associate with it. Clinton claims that the drug experience is what transformed his beliefs. "I didn't really believe in religion until I took acid in 1963. I didn't hear the Ten Commandments until then," he once said. Ultimately his mission was to "take rock until it becomes what the church was." By using nontraditional methods to attain a spiritual expression, Clinton used P-Funk to open the boundaries to spirituality—as a true *universalist*. Journalist Abe Peck concluded after a 1976 interview that "Clinton's spirituality has more to do with cosmic oneness than this earth's religions."

Many of the world's religions (particularly African ones) emphasize a "cosmic oneness" with everything, rather than the Western Christian concepts of man "fearing" God, man *versus* nature, mind versus body, intellect versus intuition. The African spiritual root of The Funk is important because the essence of funk music, as well as the *funk attitude,* is a return to certain traditional ways, among which are the basics of music-making; a celebration of the earthy, funky, emotionally vital way of life; and a cosmology of "oneness" in which everything and everyone in the universe is interconnected.

In ancient African cosmology—as well as in The Funk—everything lives and is connected. Locked on the one-count of the beat, Clinton's band regularly uses the chant "Every-thing-is-on-the-One" to express more than the unity of the band, the beat, and the rhythm. "On the One" means the oneness of everything. When The Funk is in full effect, every participant is a part of the Rhythm of the One.

The humanistic, inviting realm of many of the black bands of the 1970s consistently explored and advocated the idea of oneness, by maintaining large ensembles that could groove together, and by preaching songs of nondenominational spiritual and political unity. Their specific ideologies were often vague, but musically, most funk bands in the seventies had an implicit understanding of the groove, the essential *funk lock*. Funk bands accomplished rhythmically what few could say literally: that a diversity of rhythms represents a diversity of individuals, and that they all can be united—through the rhythmic groove of The Funk. Clinton's P-Funk not only grooved harder, longer, and deeper than the rest; they codified the thematic trend into an all-encompassing concept: P-Funk. By expanding the unity amid diversity concept beyond the small band—to a large band—to an entire collective—a modern tribe—a community—or a universe—P-Funk music offers a symbolic basis of organizing a *real community*. This was the idea behind "One Nation Under a Groove." Clinton described the impulse of his biggest hit "One Nation" as: "Everybody on the One, the whole world on the same pulse." Thus the Rhythm of the One is the key to a collective spirit.

### THE INFINITY WITHIN

The vision of P-Funk is clearly oriented toward uplift—of the individual, of black people, and of all people. The earliest psychedelic P-Funk work began to take on these issues. The band's second Funkadelic LP featured the following line repeated over a ten-minute pulsing groove, in the form of a chant: "Free your mind and your ass will follow/The kingdom of heaven is within." Toward the end of the song, only the second part is repeated: "The kingdom of heaven is within." By affirming the potential for transcendence, particularly in light of the graphic realism and noisy, chaotic tone of the songs, P-Funk reveals a fundamental reverence for the human capacity to overcome hardships.

When Parliament began to develop its own popularity after the breakthrough album *Mothership Connection* in 1975 the same themes surfaced, with somewhat more accessibility. On "Unfunky UFO" the following lyrics repeated in a chant: "You've got/all that is truly needed/to save a dying world/from its funklessness." What exactly this meant was up to the listener, as Clinton often has stated. However, with The Funk as the guidepost of an affirmation of soul and self, the negative image of young black teens in city streets (P-Funk's primary audience) was turned on its head. The infinite potential for growth of the listener is clearly part of the message.

One line from Parliament's 1978 "Aqua Boogie" represents perhaps the key to the P-Funk mission of redemption. The record, like the entire album *Motor Booty Affair,* is set underwater, with an endless supply of aquatic puns. On "Aqua Boogie," right before the main bridge of the song, Junie Morrison's wailing voice sings: "With the rhythm it takes to dance through/what we have to live through/you can dance underwater and not get wet." Clinton later explained the line, saying, "It's about how deep you have to be in this world and not really get funked up." Again taking on the infinity of human possibilities, this line is designed to equip a listener with a *method* of transcendence: By locking into the rhythms, one can overcome daily battles, and by extension, with further grooving, even accomplish the impossible. (It helps that the groove on "Aqua Boogie" is one of the nastayest Parliament hooks of all time.)

"The Funk is its own reward" was one of many P-Funk mantras that involved the listeners in a quest yet offered the freedom to find The Funk for themselves. It implied that finding The Funk is synonymous with finding *oneself.* Numerous P-Funk themes revolved around knowledge of self, a theme that can be traced as far back as pre-Christian civilizations. Clinton speaks/chants the following lines on "Good Thoughts, Bad Thoughts":

> The infinite intelligence within you knows the answers
> Its nature is to respond to your thoughts . . .
> You rise as high as your dominant aspiration
> You descend to the level of your lowest concept of yourself
> Free your mind and your ass will follow
> The kingdom of heaven is within.
> Funkadelic, "Good Thoughts, Bad Thoughts" (1974)

Clinton's philosophies are at least as old as the translations of the black Indian tantric scriptures, which proposed during biblical times that "each man is a Shiva (a deity: ausar) and can attain his power to the degree of his ability to consciously realize himself as such." Around the world, religious systems that are based on spiritual cultivation give power to the *individual* to attain higher realms. Clinton's funk attempts this. It is designed to empower the listener to obtain self-knowledge, rather than follow a certain lead, and the more graphic the knowledge, the more self-aware the individual. The nitty-gritty aspect of funk is thus a means of acknowledging the deeper, inner soul.

## BALANCE

In order to live a life of funk and to be able to deal with opposite forces and reconcile them—just as funk music deals with opposing rhythms and transcends them—balance is the key. There are opposing forces between males ...d females, between "good" and "evil," the sacred and profane, the mind and the body, and so on. Balance in P-Funk can be found in the childlike affection for dirty words ("Shit, goddamn get off your ass and jam!"), and in the wild appearances of the group, which serve as symbols of freedom and liberation, yet the imagery is tempered and grounded by deep traditional black family values. The Brides of Funkenstein can be heard singing "mother wit is your connection, use it for your protection" on "Never Buy Texas from a Cowboy," and the vocalists on Parliament's "Fantasy Is Reality" would bring it on home with "recollections of what granddaddy used to say/keep me hanging on/that's the only way."

It is ironic that The Funk in general, and P-Funk in particular, has been treated as a genre of music that is sexist and or disrespectful toward women. (The verbal abuse of females by certain so-called "gangsta rappers" using funk loops has perhaps implicated The Funk.) P-Funk actually portrays a reverence for women while celebrating their sexual essence in a way that is not disrespectful. The open sexuality displayed in the music and images of nude women in the visual art was often designed to emphasize broader issues—such as freedom and liberation in the case of the *Free Your Mind and Your Ass Will Follow* album cover, or in the case of the *Cosmic Slop* album cover, as a metaphor for the defilement of Mother Nature. The lyrics on "Cosmic Slop" go as follows:

> I was one of five born to my mother,
> an older sister and three young brothers
> We seen it hard, we seen it kind of rough
> But always with a smile, she was sure to try to hide
> the fact from us that life was really tough
> I can hear my momma call.
>
> Funkadelic, "Cosmic Slop" (1973)

P-Funk manages to revere the struggles of women and pursue them with open and ribald sexual aggression at the same time. P-Funk ideals incorporate, and *celebrate,* the intensity of the sexual drive, and the absurd realities of sexual attractions ("it all depends on the angle of the dangle"), while affirming the humanity of women in the process. "Red Hot Momma," "Moonshine Heather," "Freak of the Week," "Queen Freakalene," and many other females in the P-Funk pantheon are described in multidimensional, substantial—yet still ever so funky—ways. Thus, in a P-Funk fantasy, *everyone* is a freak, and women and men are both celebrated for their complete essence, including their nasty, freaky funkiness.

At the center of the P-Funk worldview is an acceptance of the instinctive, sexual nature of the individual. With mock religious fervor, Clinton is prone to chanting: "All that is good, is nasty!" While this may seem offensive to some, the behavior of P-Funk members is not one of disrespect or negativity toward women or sex. Rather, as W. A. Brower put it, "P-Funk de-fetishizes an already demeaned subject." With The Funk, the sexual being and the spiritual being are one.

## THE LIFE FORCE

The Funk is rooted in ancient African spiritual systems in which sexuality and spirituality are united in harmony with the essential *life force*. The Funk returns to that same singular orientation in which intellect, ambition, desire, and sexuality all exist as part of a greater whole. In *Muntu: The New African Culture,* Janheinz Jahn explained the origins of this unified field theory of life:

> On the basis of African philosophy, there can be no strict separation of the sacred and profane. Since everything is force or energy, the Orisha (spirit) as well as the human being, the sacred drum as well as the profane, and all force is the embodiment of a single universal life force, the boundary between sacred and profane cannot be drawn as it is in Europe.

Thus, with The Funk understood as the "life force," ethereal notions of The Funk are consistent with the ancient concepts of Ra in Egypt (or Kemet), Kundalini in India, the "Chi" in China, and other non-Western concepts that also incorporate the primacy of the sexual union. The philosopher Ra Un Nefer Amen explained the use of the "life force":

> This power which is called Kundalini by the Blacks of India, Ra by the Kamitians, Shekinah by the Canaanites, Eros by

the Greeks (though misunderstood), libido by the psycho-analysts (though misunderstood) is none other than our life force. . . .

The arousal of Ra—our life force—to the point of manifesting psychic phenomena . . . and raising conscious-ness to the higher parts of the spirit can take place when we are experiencing intense pleasure; extreme joy, heightened sexual excitement, orgasm, ecstatic trance, etc. It is of great importance to note that of all the intense pleasures that Man can experience, only two—orgasm and ecstatic trance, can be deliberately induced. This explains the fundamental na-ture of Black religious practices . . . which are centered around ecstatic trance.

It is this process of "raising consciousness to the higher parts of the spirit" through "ecstatic trance" that has such a strong lineage in the music and rituals of the Caribbean: Vodun, Santeria, Rastafari, the spiritual gospel music of the mainland, and in secular sounds of jazz and *funk*. P-Funk is thus seeking similar spiritual heights.

The unification of the mind with the body, of the spiritual with the sexual, of the intellectual with the intuitive, is a constant personal struggle for black Americans—and liberated people everywhere—to reclaim themselves from the constrictions of Westernization, and it is the clear goal of black jazz and funk. P-Funk is the music that has prop-agated these ideals to the rap music generation.

While the realities of living and performing on tour with P-Funk were much less glamorous and idealistic than implied here, the thematic content of the music and art created by the P-Funk mob has reached people far and wide. What Clinton and his funky tribe did was create an alternate worldview, complete with creation myths, funky super-heroes, and a framework for black fantasy and spiritual cultivation that could withstand the pressures of living in a white world. By reaching the audience on their terms, Clinton and his band created a center from which urban blacks could interpret conscious and unconscious reality, and operate as if they were already free. The impact of this body of work lives on today.

The modern generation has found a source of identification, faith, and fun in The Funk, while opportunities to explore higher spiritual realms have been demystified and made accessible to the average American. While P-Funk touches on many topics, it is important to understand that none of them is preached—the listeners are free to devise their own cosmology or theology as they see fit (as I have done here). The pursuit of P-Funk theology, and blending it with one's own religious background, is a part of the life of a funkateer.

Avid funkateer and philosopher Ashem Neru-Mesit has gone so far as to devise the "seven levels of funkativity" in which funk followers are "staged" along mock levels of initiation to the funk. The "seven levels" begin with the first two, in which followers are "just a little musically inclined" and presumably only know a few P-Funk hits. Somewhere between levels four and five, the true funk follower begins to do more than follow The Funk, but actively pursues The Funk as a way of life. "Funkativity" increases up to the seventh level, where the "funk masters" George Clinton, James Brown, Sly Stone, and Bootsy Collins reside. "Sly was up there at 7.9 for a while," Neru-Mesit explains, referring to Sly Stone's almost disappearance from the scene. (An eighth level was added to represent deceased funk masters, such as Eddie Hazel and Glen Goins.)

One can explore mock rituals such as these indefinitely, which can only broaden one's understanding of spirituality and religion, while not necessarily insulting either. P-Funk is designed to bring the spiritual world down to the level of its participants, so that everyone on this earth and beyond can groove together, on the One. By bringing the energies of the life force into the present, the funk brings all its listeners onto the dominant pulse, the bass line, in which all energies—sex, power, ecstasy, joy, and struggle—come together, united with The Funk, on the Rhythm of the One.

# PART SIX

# The Naked Funk Dynasty (1980–87): Dance, Music, Sex . . .

# NINETEEN

# Funk in the 1980s: Super Freaks

"Sexuality is all I'll ever need."

*Prince*

## THE NAKED FUNK DYNASTY

The Age of Naked Funk spanned the creative peaks of Prince, Michael Jackson, and Ronald Reagan's two presidential administrations. Although the naked funk sound had been played since the mid-seventies, the Naked Funk Dynasty roughly began with the election of Reagan in the fall of 1980. Reagan's conservative economic and social policies brought about a drastic shift in the society. His attack on labor unions, the gutting of "equal opportunity programs" through radical budget cuts, and the deregulation of the telephone companies, computers, airlines, and automobile industries all allowed for massive shifts in capital and jobs, uprooting families across the country. "Trickle-down economics" created a culture of greed, avarice, and abuse of the working class not seen since the Great Depression of the 1930s. Most workers in the 1980s never found work that paid as well as jobs of the previous decade. A new caste of American society—homeless people *by the millions*—became the single greatest social output of the Reagan era.

The inner city welfare rolls, which had been growing steadily as affluent minorities fled to suburbs and jobs went with them, were slashed, leaving thousands without support of any kind. After-school programs, sports programs, jobs training, counseling, prenatal care, and all nonessential government-funded programs were cut or eliminated, as the "War on Poverty" was replaced by a "War on Drugs." A fundamental policy shift—from service *to* the poor to control *of* the poor—was and is a lasting legacy of the 1980s.

The Reagan presidency relegated black America into a state of perpetual crisis. People in the inner cities hooked themselves into a syndrome of escapism. By 1982, a denser, much more addictive form of cocaine known as crack began to sweep the streets in major urban centers. What was once a "manageable" habit engaged in by thousands of disillusioned Americans was now a one-way ticket to oblivion, as crack became legendary for its ability to undermine even the strongest of family ties and moral boundaries. The well-grounded black religious themes of salvation and faith that "we shall overcome" were played out by the 1980s, and a new resignation to the realities had set in. Without a voice, without resources, and without support, blacks began to lose hope.

More than ever before, escapism was the theme of black arts and entertainment. Popular black music became more narcissistic, self-serving, and consistently shallow. Individualism and a theme of "me first" was celebrated. In music it was by the hedonistic imagery of black pop stars Prince, Morris Day, and Rick James; in politics, by the "free enterprise" and "get yours" rhetoric of the right-wing government, and by the insular high-tech toys of eighties culture: the hypnotic allure of computer games that made zombies of youth that once might have played sports or pinball games, car phones that made it easier to dial up rather than drop in on people living nearby, and perhaps the cruelest blow to a communal people, the Walkman—a tape recorder you listened to *alone* while in *public*.

Add to all this the fact that the economics of the city made the fielding of music bands a prohibitive enterprise, thus leaving the development of black bands to a more middle-class generation that was removed from the mayhem of the streets and the racial confrontations of the sixties and early seventies. Black popular music in the early 1980s shied away from the "message" song and zeroed in on issues of sex and style. This trend was encouraged by an industry that was all too eager to exploit the circumstances of any group, including and especially blacks.

### KILLER CROSSOVER

A cruel combination of industry opportunism, a virulent strand of industry racism, and a lack of leadership—political and cultural—left the black community in a quagmire and left black culture at the mercy of the whims of pop culture. Independent black art and music was marginalized during the early Reagan years, opening the doors for a swath of nostalgic trends, emphasizing the "good old days," which included the "nostalgic" stereotypes of blacks. Blacks were in fewer and fewer television shows in the 1980s, and those that were, such as Sherman Hemsley's (coon) Mr. Jefferson, Nell Carter's (mammy) Nell from *Gimme a Break,* and (pickaninny) Gary Coleman of *Different*

*Strokes,* all supported historically demeaning stereotypes of blacks.

Blacks even disappeared from the disco dance movies that continued to come out. The 1984 hit movie *Footloose* was perhaps the worst
example of this Hollywood trend of all-white American fantasies. *Footloose* was a story about a town that had banned dancing, until a quick-
footed teenager played by Kevin Bacon comes to town and turns things
around by getting everyone to dance. The theme is clearly symbolic of
the black musical presence in America, but there is not *one* single black
face to be seen in the film—not even a janitor. The smash No. 1 pop single from the soundtrack, ironically, was performed by black singer Deniece Williams ("Let's Hear It for the Boy"). It was to be her last pop hit.

Even superstar Michael Jackson, the "King of Pop," found difficulty gaining exposure on the newest form of publicity, Music Television, or MTV, the rock-oriented music video cable network. The New
York–based company apparently had a peculiar policy of no black
videos until 1982, when Jackson's ground-breaking *Thriller* album sold
more than forty million copies, and produced the "rock" video of "Beat
It," a record that featured a guest solo from rock guitarist Eddie Van
Halen. The question of crossover was of particular importance to the
industry, which based its organization on the assumption that for the
most part black artists begin on the black sales charts, and must reach
a certain sales threshold before making the grand pop scene. A few special acts, like Jackson, passed the test and were automatically let in. As
Nelson George described in the *The Death of Rhythm and Blues,* Jackson
had rediscovered his "honorary pop pass," and no longer had to toil in
black music before going "pop"; he could "now go through the checkpoints with ease."

While Jackson would take it another step, becoming a *global entertainer,* his efforts to heal the world were often misunderstood at
home. Jackson's uniquely sensitive, expressive persona appeared to
cynics as a nonracial, nonethnic, and androgynous deviation from the
black experience. The subsequent success of Prince, with his gender-
bending imagery and multiracial mystique, reinforced this new stereo-
type of black celebrity.

Outside of the controversial black male icons of Prince and
Michael Jackson (and perhaps movie star Eddie Murphy) there was a
terrible dearth of black artistic leadership as the eighties unfolded. This
was not by coincidence. The presence of Jackson as a pop superstar was
an anachronism in the pantheon of white pop, and the black rock of

Prince was an even more direct counter to the prevailing stereotypes of music and race. Black performers sang *love songs,* white players played rock—that was the formula. Prince and Jackson were pushing the limit. They were *crossing over,* but they literally set the quotas for racial crossover acts to follow.

The formalization of the black radio format in the disco era was a prime culprit in the marginalization of the black image, and it continued through the 1980s unabated. Black culture was literally being distributed and rationed out by whites. Jon Pareles described the situation in a 1987 *New York Times* article:

> Like the movie business . . . the major-label record business generally offers black performers a choice of stereotypes: nice pop band (Kool & the Gang), slick pop crooner (Luther Vandross), or nasty funk band (Cameo). Those stereotypes are self-perpetuating across the music business. It's taken for granted that what worked last year will work next year in a new suit.

Inevitably, diverse, meaningful music with a groove (The Funk) had the most difficult time reaching the population. Love songs and mindless disco records *owned* the charts in the 1980s. In 1985, for example, of the twenty No. 1 R&B singles that year, seventeen were love- and romance-oriented songs, two were straight dance hits, and only one was a message song, "We Are the World," by the collaboration USA for Africa. By contrast, of the forty-two No. 1 R&B singles a decade earlier, in 1975, thirteen were monster funk jams (five would be considered "message" songs, such as "Fight the Power" by the Isley Brothers and "Give the People What They Want" by the O'Jays), seven were disco hits, and the rest were ballads or easy dancing soul grooves. Within ten years The Funk had been removed from black radio.

### WAR ON THE FUNK

The slow dissolution of the integrity of black music cannot be considered a coincidence when so many aspects of the industry perpetuated the problems in black popular music. The massive musical juggernaut of George Clinton's P-Funk, for example, was completely destroyed in the span of only two years. Despite the fact that the band was the strongest musical unit on the scene and had recruited Sly Stone and even the Godfather of Soul James Brown to record with them, Warner Brothers was "convinced" that P-Funk was more trouble than it was worth and let Clinton go after the band's final unceremonious album release *(The Electric Spanking of War Babies)* in 1981. CBS Records sat on Clinton's P-Funk All-Stars release of "Pumpin' It Up" in 1983, despite its track record overseas, including going to No. 1 in England. "The record was selling like a motherfucker—busting out in Dallas, Houston, Chicago, L.A.—and CBS acted like it wasn't even theirs," Clinton told *Spin* in 1985. For his part, even George Clinton had burned out. Prior to a week-long set at New York's Apollo Theater in 1980 (the last concerts at the storied hall before bankruptcy shut the landmark down for three years), Clinton "retired" from touring. He was arrested along with Sly Stone for possession of cocaine the following year in California. The demise of the two icons of The Funk was symptomatic of a generation's inability to cope.

The black male performer as a symbol of strength and pride was an endangered species in the 1980s. The tragic suicide of Donny Hathaway in 1979; the fatal heart attack of Joe Tex in 1982; Spinners' ex-lead singer Phillipe Wynne's fatal stroke onstage at Ivey's in Oakland; the tragic death of Marvin Gaye during an argument with his father in 1984; the paralyzing automobile crash of sex-symbol Teddy Pendergrass, and the *musical* conversions of Reverends Al Green, Fuzzy Haskins (from P-Funk), and Larry Graham left a void in the soul music patriarchy that was filled by the likes of El DeBarge, Freddy Jackson, and Luther Vandross. Stevie Wonder, the onetime king of seventies soul music, embraced the reggae sounds of Bob Marley on his 1980 *Hotter Than July* blockbuster LP, and Stevie's political crusade to make Martin Luther King, Jr.'s birthday a national holiday was courageous and consistent with his vision, but his subsequent soul hits "That Girl" and "Part Time Lover" showed the public that even with Stevie's indomitable genius, in many ways the black soul sound was no longer the place for relevant music for the black community.

Women suffered a similar fate, as the throaty, earnest gospel-style soul singers (such as Aretha Franklin, Patti LaBelle, and Chaka Khan) were forced to compete with lighter, voiceless (and often talentless) wisps that survived on sex appeal alone. Prince protégés Vanity, Appolonia, Sheena Easton, and veteran percussionist Sheila E (Escovedo) all went for the cynical image change. Songs like "Pretty Mess," "Nasty Girl," "Sex Shooter," "Glamorous Life," and "Sugar Walls" drew erotic dance music to new levels, and with the help of videos, helped make the image as important as the music. While Janet Jackson is often credited for redefining pop music standards with her industrial-strength beats and highly choreographed videos from her 1986 album *Control,* she still had to get "nasty" to get attention. It should come as no surprise that two of the decade's most popular and deserving singers, Whitney Houston (a former model) and Vanessa Williams (beauty queen), both entered the business from careers in the glamour industry.

To her credit, even the ageless stage thriller Tina Turner escaped her southern roots, donned a *British* accent, and enjoyed a renaissance of popularity in 1984 on the strength of her rock-oriented sound, produced in Britain.

For what it's worth, the most original and unique black pop acts of the decade came from *England:* the iconoclastic Terence Trent D'Arby, the exquisitely talented and sensual (and quite funky) Sade Adu, the polyrhythmic explosion of Soul II Soul, and the multiracial acid-jazz of the Brand New Heavies brought freshness, funk, and a sense of tradition to an industry that *never* would have given them a chance had they been forced to start on "black" radio in America.

For too many black music fans, it would soon seem impossible to find an appealing and meaningful soul singer that was not androgynous, born-again, or a sex freak. In a rhythm-oriented, oral culture such as black America, singers and performers have always been given a greater clout than other traditional leaders, and the loss of strong, socially conscious artists meant a significant loss of strength and unity. In the 1970s it was first soul and then The Funk that maintained many of the values that were integral to the black community's sense of identity—but that all changed in the 1980s.

### NAKED FUNK

As recently as 1979, all of black dance music understood to be funk was derived from the P-Funk aesthetic: hard, polyrhythmic dance grooves; slick, melodic, yet nasty rock-guitar solos; the keyboard synthesizer bass; complex, methodically placed horns; moralistic, gospel-derived vocals; state-of-the-art, far-out synthesizers; and, if possible, far-out concepts. Yet for all too many acts the P-Funk standard was an unreachable one—eventually even for the P-Funk Mob—and a more diluted facsimile of The Funk emerged. Piece by piece, aspects of the organically derived funk sound were replicated by machines. The producer's medium of disco music and the promoter's medium of radio access took the black aesthetic out of the hands of artists, and the inevitable remix took more and more individuality out of each record.

Horns were the easiest to replicate with a keyboard and were the first to go. Despite the myriad patterns and hooks of even the best naked funk bands, most eighties funk horn breaks consisted of simple *notes,* rather than sustained, swinging refrains that took talent to blow. Horn solos literally disappeared from black dance music (with Rick James's Stone City Band as one strong exception). Long, sustained keyboard tones that used to vibrate, oscillate, and flow—from instruments like the Hammond B3 organ and Fender Rhodes piano—were also replaced by a more rigid, digitized keyboard sound. Within a few years the Yamaha DX7 keyboard was the standard tone for simulating all of these melodic accents in black music. Synthesizer programmer and producer Robert Margouleff was despondent about these developments:

> In the real world, no two sounds are alike. It's that randomness that we interpret as soulfulness, a certain quavering quality that we equate with some kind of humanity. . . . When the DX7 came out . . . what was happening then was every sound was so perfect, and every sound was predictably the same every time that although the pitch was correct . . . the stuff was not soulful because it was so perfect that the unconscious part of the brain got bored with it.

Drum machines and plastic-sounding "Syndrums" became all the rage during the disco era, and iconoclastic dance music drummers were forced to maintain an "accessible" beat (for nondancers) or give it up for a machine. Many of the wildest funk drummers of the early seventies—Andre Fischer of Rufus, "Willie Wild" of Graham Central Station, Dave Garibaldi of Tower of Power, and Greg Errico of Sly and the Family Stone—were replaced by drummers with a "tighter" (that is, simpler) beat. Or, in the case of George "Funky" Brown of Kool & the Gang, jazz-fusion funkmaster Lenny White, Early Young of MFSB, and others, they simplified their *own* sounds to stay accessible, and keep getting paid.

The bass player was under pressure because the gravelly, thumping sound was out of style. The bass keyboard track—as opposed to the bass *guitar*—sounded less and less like a thick, sexual instrument of rhythmic propulsion and more like a thin, fluid percussive instrument. The popping funk bass was literally an endangered species, as the fat bass solo was harder and harder to fit into the mix. Bootsy's "Body Slam" in 1982, Slave's "Just a Touch of Love," and Brick's 1981 "Sweat ('Til You Get Wet)" contained perhaps the best funk bass solos to hit black radio in the 1980s—but the competition was despairingly thin. Radio-friendly R&B bass lines popped along *(bimp bimp boom boomp, bip)* rather than stomped *(BOWM, bomp bamp, ba dum ba dum BOWM)*. Thinner, higher-pitched tones and the piercing shrills of Michael Jackson and Prince reinforced the impression that hard funk was out of style.

Only the *chanking* guitars survived relatively unscathed in black dance music. The new-sounding tones of the synth-bass made even simple rhythms sound funky when accompanied by a high-pitched, chopping rhythm guitar lick and an artificial clap track. The first efforts of the naked funk artists used these new instrumental arrangements (which P-Funk introduced), but fell short in the arena of vocals, lyrical themes, complexity, range, and historical continuity.

The tradition of subtle sexual innuendo and teasing wordplay gave way to explicit references to sex. The tender and compassionate soul-singing formula became devoid of style and grew heavy on the selfish sexual themes. Titles like "Do Me Baby," "Give It to Me Baby," "Irresistible Bitch," and "I Need a Freak" took explicitness to new levels. Yet it was the brainlessness of most of the songs that insulted the traditions from which they came. Brain-dead titles with one-syllable words became the standard. Tunes like "You Look Good to Me," "Get It Up," "Love You Down," "Hard to Get," and "Beep a Freak" became the norm. Simplicity to the point of ignorance was valued and promoted, while higher values of integrity and generosity were not. In perhaps a continuous line of disintegration from Donna Summer's explicit sex romp on "Love to Love You Baby" in 1976, images of black sexuality were exposed in the most blatant of terms. Playing on the most base emotions was only part of the package. Pimping the pleasure principle was the real deal—exploiting the natural urges of the audience, leaving them to stagger into the record store, to paraphrase George Clinton, "fat, horny, and strung out."

### RICK JAMES

Rick James was the first of the new funkers to take the hot music crown away from the P-Funk style. His tight, propulsive, sexy funk jams had a consistent theme of sex, drugs, and irresponsible behavior that combined for great record sales beginning with "You and I" in mid-1978, the very tight "Mary Jane" later that year, "Bustin' Out" and "High on Your Love Suite" in 1979, and "Love Gun" in 1980. James had a strong voice with interesting tonal inflections and could produce good ballads as well as stomping funk. He produced his best effort by far, *Street Songs,* in 1981. The first single, "Give It to Me Baby," was an excellent example of late-night naked dance funk. Capturing a propulsive bass hook with a tight spattering of horns and multilayered keyboard melodies, Rick James sang of his life as a party animal and created *new funk,* capturing the imagination of a generation with little interest in larger issues. The chorus repeated the "give it to me" hook relentlessly, using the structure of traditional "soul" songs to deliver modern themes of naked attraction. With Rick James' genius for the funky groove, "Give It to Me Baby" defined a new direction in R&B nastayness, and ultimately signalled the beginning of the end for black music in the 1980s.

The next single, "Super Freak," became a cult classic, with its distinctive, choppy "new wave" rhythm and trashy rock groupie lyrics. (M. C. Hammer reconstituted the loop of "Super Freak" on "You Can't Touch This" in 1991, Hammer's largest-selling record.) There was a ballad duet with then-girlfriend Teena Marie that made the late-night radio request line—"Fire and Desire"—and even some clear social commentary on "Below the Funk (Pass the J)" and "Ghetto Life." James predated the so-called gangsta rappers with his prophetic "Mr. Policeman," a lament on the shooting of his friend by the police. Mastering street themes that would dominate urban music ten years later, Rick James cornered the market on a bittersweet, narcissistic brand of street funk.

Born James Ambrose Johnson, Jr., and raised by a single mother in Buffalo, New York, James was a numbers runner at age fifteen and after a brief stint in the navy (allegedly going AWOL) he fled to Canada and later London. By the time he returned to the United States he had developed his trashy, intense, dangerous brand of funk and took his demos to Motown Records. His string of late seventies R&B hits, combined with his association with versatile crooner Teena Marie, endeared him to music followers everywhere. Here was an earnest performer with a mastery of melody, messages, and meaty funk and soul, singing love songs back and forth on *albums* with his equally talented girlfriend. After *Street Songs,* James became somewhat of a rock star, with his "honorary pop pass."

Yet he never quite followed *Street Songs* with music of the same relevance. James had the talent to elevate the street-bred values inherent in The Funk to a new level of notoriety, but many of those same ingredients of his success brought him—and his music—down. Living the lifestyle of a "super-freak" had its price. James was candid about this in a 1995 interview from Folsom Prison printed in the *Sacramento Bee*: "I started sinking to a point where I didn't care who I got high with, whether it was hoes or gangsters or pimps—all those people kind of found their way into my space. And when that happens, anything can happen."

James delivered a string of throbbing funk tracks in the early eighties, from "Standing on the Top" and "Hard to Get" on his *Throwin' Down* LP in 1982 to the catchy "Coldblooded" in 1983 and the trashy "17" in 1984. He had the foresight to produce a "girl group" called the Mary Jane Girls, who sold a few records, including the particularly delicious "All Night Long" in 1983, but James's flame was burning out by then. It was clear that Rick James was on the decline by 1983, if nothing else because of the meteoric rise of Prince.

### PRINCE

Born Prince Rogers Nelson in Minneapolis, Minnesota, to musical parents (both black), Prince had his own band in high school and was a perfectionist even in his first dealings with Warner Brothers in 1978, who amazingly obliged him with complete creative control as a seventeen-year-old unproven act. Their judgment proved right as Prince changed the country's music as much as any one man since James Brown.

Musically, Prince songs were arranged with stripped-down instrumentation similar to Rick James's style, but Prince had a scorching voice that he worked with the soul of a gospel singer. He played every instrument, arranged deceptively complex songs, and sang with an intense eroticism that could not be ignored, and his veiled references to mixed partners kept people guessing, and listening. Nelson George wrote that "no black performer since Little Richard had toyed with the heterosexual sensibilities of black America so brazenly." He performed in G-strings, spoke openly of oral sex, and simulated sexual motions throughout his act. His first hits were breakthroughs of sexual imagery in song: "Soft and Wet" in 1978, "I Wanna Be Your Lover" in 1979, and the remarkable "Head" from the *Dirty Mind* LP in 1980.

Prince's many daring hooks caught listeners and radio programmers by surprise and sliced apart the prevailing parameters of decency on radio. The dance single "Erotic City" was perhaps the most popular of the X-rated pop flavors: "We can fuck until the dawn/Erotic city come along" went the chorus. *Dirty Mind* was the signature album recording for Prince in the black community, while he would "cross over" later on. Warner Brothers began to promote Prince and the P-Funk spinoff band Zapp as purveyors of the "New Black Funk" in 1980.

With his fourth album, *Controversy,* Prince enamored himself of the hip white music set, and when his masterwork *1999* was released the following year, he was set for superstardom. The apocalyptic title song had to do with a party at the end of the world, while other records dealt with dance, music, and sex in gluttonous quantities, with some violent imagery thrown in. Prince continued to use a variety of rhythms, from simplistic dance rock and disco beats to heavy funk grooves ("Let's Work," "D.M.S.R.," and "Party Up").

By 1983 Prince was a phenomenon. He had earned his "pop pass" and not only went after another No. 1 pop single ("When Doves Cry"), he produced a semi-autobiographical movie starring himself, titled *Purple Rain.* The film was a well-received hit, and Prince cashed in. More significant, however, the film was a vehicle for spinoff acts from Prince that solidified his impact on black music from all ends. (Vanity, Appolonia 6, Mazerati, the Family, Madhouse, Sheila E, and Andre Cymone all owe their early eighties success—and their similar sound— to Prince.) Yet it was The Time that threatened to upstage the headliner with their own precise brand of funk.

## THE TIME

Incorporated from various Minneapolis bands to support *the image* of a hot opening act for Prince, The Time proved to be more than even The Star bargained for. The Time produced a scorching brand of tight, clean, synthesized dance funk that was accented (or ruined, depending on your point of view) by the egotistic rantings of lead vocalist Morris Day—"somebody get me a mirror, hoohaah, I'm so cool!" Their first three albums—the Prince-produced debut *The Time* in 1981, the more self-defined *What Time Is It?* in 1982, and *Ice Cream Castles* in 1984—were slick, funky soul events in the music industry. Nothing so tight had been heard on the radio, but the talented rhythm musicians slithered around the beats to make nastay, naked funk at its best. Scorching groove hits like "Cool," "Get It Up," the particularly percussive "777-9311," the monstrous "Wild and Loose," and their slick funk masterwork "Jungle Love" all set the standard for tightness in the naked funk lock.

The Time was so tight that the players were in great demand, and the band quickly spun off in every direction, with Morris Day scoring success with two solo LPs, guitarist Jesse Johnson scoring even more success with three solo LPs, and keyboard and bassist combo Jimmy Jam and Terry Lewis combining to become the hottest rhythm combo in the nation, producing massive hits for, among others, Klymaxx, Cherrelle, New Edition, Johnny Gill, the S.O.S. Band, Thelma Houston, and Janet Jackson.

The Minneapolis sound became a musical movement. The high-pitched voices, the synth-bass and nasty splinking guitar licks, the slick pop percussion, and the brazen sexual themes created a narcissistic subculture all its own for the terminally horny. Subsequent Prince records began to develop vast fantasyscapes with the ambitious scope of P-Funk or the Beatles. These records—*Around the World in a Day* in 1985, *Parade* in 1986, *Sign of the Times* in 1987, *Lovesexy* and the *Black Album* in 1988, *Graffiti Bridge* in 1990, and *Diamonds and Pearls* in 1991— were all strong examples of the genius of Prince, capable of taking the listener to another world.

What separated Prince from other artists of the 1980s was his ability to create grand visions, entire worlds of erotic indulgence and freedom. He explored with authority the range of bizarre and carnal emotions that most of us keep hidden. He told an interviewer in a 1981 *Jet* magazine story that his work is motivated by the "despair" and "loneliness" he sees around him, and that he is dedicated to addressing those feelings. Like in Clinton's "Atomic Dog," Prince's sexually charged imagery penetrated the depressing energy of the times with an exhilarating, new erotic hype.

*Ebony* magazine devoted a cover story to the Prince phenomenon in 1985 as a celebration of his incredible appeal. The magazine also recruited the psychologist Alvin Poussaint (the one responsible for designing the "positive images" for the *Cosby Show*) to critique Prince. Poussaint described Prince as a "controversial role model" and a "Pied Piper for a sexually obsessed" generation, whose music potentially steers the youth in a "shallow, misguided, and potentially destructive direction." Poussaint's concerns appeared to have fallen on deaf ears, for Prince was one of the few black artists to transcend generations, reaching the "sexually obsessed" middle-age set as well as the youth, both black and white, with his uniquely appealing music.

There is, of course, a certain fallout from the naked funk music of the early 1980s. The "sexually obsessed" generation that bought every record from Prince in the 1980s has today been forced to deal with the end of the sexual revolution and the mortal risks of AIDS. The controversial role models of the 1990s are now the newer, younger, more explicit, violent, and often mysogynist gangsta rappers, who make the controversies surrounding Prince appear somewhat tame. Yet it is indeed possible that youngsters of the eighties who spent their adolescence listening to Prince, and watched their parents do the same, may have found themselves primed for the indulgent and uncensored gangsta rap phenomenon that was down the road.

In recent years Prince has begun to approach his music with a more historical perspective. He has begun to use straight gospel styles, definitive Clinton-style funk, marginal attempts at blues, and even the new rap (the presence of gospel and R&B singer Mavis Staples and funk overlord George Clinton on his Paisley Park label have surely had an influence). In a break from his eighties look, his videos now regularly feature *black* women. His 1994 release of "Love Sign" featured Marvin Gaye's daughter Nola Gaye in a prominent acting role. Through all the titillating camouflage and controversy, Prince is an unmitigated artistic genius whose performances are lush and exhilarating, compelling in their intense, erotic flavor, and uniquely affirming of the human condition. After many image changes, a name change, and a claim to stop recording, the man formerly known as Prince has created an indisputable legacy on the development of American music—and on The Funk in particular.

Unfortunately, the vibrant energy generated by Prince and his cohorts was all too easy to imitate. Generic disco-sex music spread like an epidemic across the country at a painful rate. From Florida a style of hot electronic music, based on the Caribbean soca rhythms but produced with mind-numbing digital percussion sounds, was all the rage for years. The X-rated rap group 2-Live Crew came out of this scene. From Los Angeles came the Egyptian Lover, and his group Uncle Jamm's Army (not to be confused with the Funkadelic record of the same name), who produced an even more blatant style of egotistic, electronic, orgasmic music in which sexual sounds were looped with electronic dance beats to make nasty dance music. These records took nothing more than a microphone, keyboard, drum machine, and tape recorder (and perhaps an X-rated video for samples) to make a hit. Funk was becoming anyone's business, and it showed.

### NAKED FUNK BANDS

But the real musicians—the funk bands that survived the musical holocaust of 1979—got down and dirty with their music, and incorporated the uninhibited vibe of Prince with the polyrhythmic and fat-bottomed bass noise of the previous P-Funk Dynasty.

Cameo was the most successful. After four strong R&B/P-Funk–based records, Cameo began to stake out their own territory, with tight rhythmic breaks, silly sound effects between beats, Ohio Players–style falsetto vocals, and a rhythmic *edge* that set the band apart from the others. "That's the *bad* thing about funk, man. It can really take you a lot of different places 'cause funk basically, man, is the R&B with a real attitude," trumpeter and vocalist Nathan Leftenant explained. A relentless hit machine through the 1980s, Cameo brought the radio hits "Keep It Hot," "Freaky Dancin'," "Flirt," "Style," "Single Life," and "She's Strange." Their 1986 *Word Up,* their best seller ever, delivered a tight, sparse, stomping funk romp with just enough soul smoothness to capture synth-funk at its state-of-the-art best. It was a testament to the band's resilience that they lasted through ten of the most turbulent years of black music and are still kicking in 1995 with their latest album release, *In the Face of Funk.*

### ROGER AND ZAPP

If there was one act that consistently delivered potential for superstardom, it was Zapp. Their sound was an incredible mix of wild high-tech rhythms and old-style blues sangin' and swangin'. Zapp, with its lead guitarist and vocalist Roger Troutman, took the new electronic instruments as far out as they could swing, while still holding down a dance beat. The synth-bass became a liquid slingshot never heard before. The loud electronic clap sound was turned up to a ridiculous level. Then Troutman would twang his slick, modernized guitar in an outrageous down-home country blues style, and use an old-blues-style talk box (tweaked to sound new) that distorted his vocal style even more. The resulting mix was outer space slick meets country funk twang, and it was a perfect blend. "It's the black experience. It's the blues of the eighties," Troutman explained of his type of funk in 1995. "It has the

same purpose with black people as blues had for black people when
B. B. King started out, or Jimmy Reed."

The band's live concerts were a throwback to the old rhythm and
blues days of glittery costumes, high-kicking dance steps, and *free* concerts at local parks. While simplicity and snappy hooks are their trademarks, their fluid grooves are actually a result of years of practice and
perfectionism. Brothers Lester on drums, Larry on congas, "Zapp" on
bass, Roger on guitar, talk box, keyboards, and everything else, formed
the core of the tireless band. Their lyrics reflected the working-class
sentiments of traditional Saturday night blues and R&B, but delivered
a digitized swang that fit the new styles of the eighties.

One of many Ohio-based funk bands, the Troutmans come from
Hamilton, Ohio, a small town halfway between Dayton and Cincinnati,
where the Dayton-based Ohio Players and Cincinnati-bred Bootsy
Collins provided a steady diet of intensely funky live shows for the local
youngsters to emulate. As Troutman recalled, "It was about Bootsy, and
it was about Sugarfoot and the Ohio Players, period. That was the origin of this sound. Point blank, that's it."

With Bootsy's help, the band was signed to Warner Brothers in
1980, and with the added help of George Clinton, the No. 1 R&B single "More Bounce to the Ounce" hit the streets and became perhaps
the most sampled funk record of all time. The unmistakable thump of
the bass, the squishy, sloppy rhythm guitars, drawling talk box, and preposterous nine-minute arrangement without a bridge was an all-time
funk innovation. Used by almost every rap group at some point, *More
Bounce* qualifies as a "P-Funk" record for most funkateers.

Roger went on his own, recording a hugely successful solo album
in 1981, which scored with a preposterous, high-tech remake of Marvin Gaye's "Heard It Through the Grapevine," and unmitigated all-time
humps like "So Ruff, So Tuff" and "Do It, Roger." Like the best of
P-Funk music, Roger's brilliant musicianship carried through the electronic camouflage to take apart the common assumptions about musical formulas. And unlike most black pop acts of the time, Roger and
Zapp could be counted on to produce an entire album full of quality
material.

The band left George Clinton's musical family in 1981 (just when
Clinton's finances were declining—a long and gruesome story), and
considering Clinton's growing reputation for financial disarray, it was
probably the group's best move. Zapp and Roger went on to spectac-

ular success during the following years. The *Zapp II* LP was the band's strongest, serving up the No. 1 R&B single "Dance Floor" and the outrageous "Doo Wa Ditty" in 1982. The 1983 *Zapp III* disc was nearly as tight, lifting the massively humping single "I Can Make You Dance" and the intensely bluesy "Heartbreaker." The band's fourth album (of five) delivered the modern soul masterpiece "Computer Love" and the monster jam "It Doesn't Really Matter." Roger began to smooth out his sound on record in the late eighties, but on tour live, the Zapp/Roger show is *still* The Funk at its snazzy, bluesy, and yet high-tech best.

Another act that became extremely popular on the heels of the P-Funk sound was the Gap Band. Produced by Oklahoma-bred brothers Ronnie, Charlie, and Robert Wilson, their unique, country-fried brand of black pop was refined during the mid-seventies as a backing band for fellow Oaklahoma native, rock star Leon Russell. Determined to forge their own path, they imbued their sound with the hip black flavors of the day. Taking their name from the main streets of Tulsa's black business district (Greenwood, Archer, and Pine), and with the help of L.A.-based producer Lonnie Simmons, the group went straight for the hits. When they finally took off with "Shake" in 1979, their funky, swanging P-Funk style was clear. Their next album, creatively titled *Gap Band II,* featured the single "Oops Upside Your Head," a song that takes note-for-note a key thirty-second jazzy riff from one of P-Funk's big hits ("Disco to Go" by the Brides of Funkenstein). On "Oops," the band came up with a fresh, sparse sound driven by a synthesizer bass and Charlie Wilson's almost yodeling vocal scats, giggles, and ad libs. The formula worked like a charm and Gap Band singles spawned one huge dance craze after another. "Burn Rubber," "Early in the Morning," "Outstanding," "You Dropped a Bomb on Me," "Party Train," and the absurd "Beep a Freak" in 1984 were the most dominant in a healthy string of monster naked funk hits.

The Bar-Kays remained right on the heels of Cameo, the Gap Band, and Zapp as a state-of-the-art, old-school funk band through the mid-1980s. Recording with slick, synth-pop instrumentation, the band, led by Larry Dodson's soulful, Otis Redding—influenced style, breathed life into the eighties formula and provided heavy-hitting naked funk hits "She Talks to Me with Her Body," "Hit and Run," and "Freakshow on the Dancefloor."

Lakeside would stand strong with their heavily bass-laden stomps "Fantastic Voyage" in 1981, "Raid" in 1983, and "Outrageous" in

1984—while the steady decline of Slave was disappointing, since their monster jams were behind them by 1981. Slave veteran Steve Arrington carved out an iconoclastic niche for himself with the humbly titled *Steve Arrington's Hall of Fame,* producing some of the best of a rare breed of positive naked funk, such as 1983's "Nobody Can Be You" and "Dancing in the Key of Life" in 1985. The Detroit-based One Way and Cleveland's Dazz Band kept up a string of slick, fat, funky dance tracks through the eighties. One Way's "Cutie Pie" stands as a slow, meaty, pumping funk classic. The Dazz Band (not to be confused with the No. 1 R&B hit "Dazz" by Atlanta's Brick in 1976) was one of the most consistent sources of tight, rhythm-guitar-driven funk. "Let it Whip," "On the One for Fun," "Joystick," and "Keep It Live" were dance floor standards at the time.

For the most part, however, even the best of these funk bands were only capable of delivering dance tracks—the album experience was an almost forgotten commodity in their music. With the exception of Cameo, Zapp, early eighties Bar-Kays, and Slave, strong funk bands emphasized little else in their repertoire. The diverse, substantial funk band as it was known in the 1970s was no longer.

One band that everyone agreed continued to deliver was Earth, Wind & Fire. After ten years of success, the band still did its best to stay on top in the 1980s. After a nearly two-year hiatus from 1979 to 1981, the band released a double LP titled *Faces* that revealed more worldly wisdom and realism than their recent work, but failed to sell one million copies for the first time since 1974. The band then streamlined, replacing smooth funk guitarist Al McKay with the rowdier sounds of Roland Bautista, and returned with a vengeance. Their 1982 album *Raise!* was a smash again, although their sound had changed dramatically. The single "Let's Groove" was an international hit and spent eight weeks at No. 1 R&B, but unlike almost every other dance hit by the band, there was no meaning in the lyrics. For any other act this was not important, but Earth, Wind & Fire had literally become secular prophets, providing the moral and spiritual foundation for the integrated youth of the world.

Each new recording began to reveal just how magical the band's original lineup had been, as it slowly disappeared. Leaders Maurice White and Philip Bailey went on to do solo projects, but the band returned in 1987 for an interesting, if out of place, comeback record, *Touch the World.* As hard as they tried to make warm, happy music,

Earth, Wind & Fire in the 1980s represented more than any other act the desperate and sobering grim realities of the time; happy music was simply hard to come by.

While Kool & the Gang continued an unbroken string of entertaining pop hits with new lead singer James "J.T." Taylor, such as "Celebration," "Get Down on It," and "Take My Heart," their unbending focus on cute pop numbers over the years insulted the roots from which they came. The band had gone far beyond devoid-of-funk, to what one irate funk critic called the "sellout hall of fame." Likewise, guitarist Ray Parker, Jr., went from scorching session work for Stevie Wonder, Rufus, and Herbie Hancock in the seventies to simplistic funky pop ("The Other Woman," "Bad Boy") and wound up performing the silly 1984 theme from *Ghostbusters*.

Funky soul acts that were *actual bands* had an increasingly difficult time in the 1980s. Midnight Star's 1984 *No Parking on the Dancefloor* and Skyy's 1982 *Skyyline* were perhaps the most successful funky soul albums, yet neither sustained much hit-making strength after their initial breakthroughs. Producers Jimmy Jam and Terry Lewis created a small empire in the mid-eighties by producing a score of acts (led by Janet Jackson and New Edition) with melodic soulful hooks and metallic, hard beats to back them up. Their collaborations with Janet Jackson remain the high points of eighties funky pop, as the youthful Janet (Miss Jackson if you're nasty) took "control" of her life and redefined the standard of popular dance tracks, mixing her youthful sound with industrial-strength beats with precision. Her 1989 *Rhythm Nation* album was the boldest and most successful pop attempt to combine social commentary, celebration, and state-of-the-art dance funk since her brother Michael's efforts to be *Bad*.

By 1987 New York producer Teddy Riley extended the marriage of melodic, soulful tunes with the industrial strength of Hip Hop—making the catchy and streetwise New Jack Swing sound. New Jack vocalists such as Aaron Hall and Bobby Brown could often fill up the sparse bottoms of the New Jack beats, and rappers often got their radio airplay debuts on the tracks of Guy, Bell Biv Devoe, and Wrecks-N-Effect. Yet for the funkateers, something was missing.

Soulful, funky music had actually become an endangered species by the end of the eighties. The situation got so bad that artists actually began to *sing* about the lack of soul in popular black music. Foster & McElroy's catchy 1989 jam "Dr. Soul" sang of the lack of soulful sounds in popular music, comically pleading for help from their savior, "Dr. Soul." Likewise, George Clinton's 1988 album and title song "R&B Skeletons in the Closet" was a blanket condemnation of urban radio's failure to deliver, pleading to get the classic R&B out of the closet, because they're the ones that got the *party* started.

Even though black stars had the sense to admit that their music was not as good as it used to be, the situation continued to get worse. In 1988, British pop singer George Michael produced the R&B-oriented album *Faith,* which won so many accolades that it walked away with the 1990 American Music Award for best R&B album of the year! This prompted *Jet* magazine to produce a cover story posing the question: "Are white singers taking over blues and soul?" In it, rock superstar Rod Stewart was quoted complaining that there weren't enough "black singers for white singers to imitate."

The bottom dropped out of the R&B world in 1990 after growing embarrassment about stars playing *tapes* of their songs at concerts— and when the Grammy-winning leaders of the black pop band Milli Vanilli publicly admitted that they sang *none* of the music on their album and that it was an entire, deliberate high-tech hoax. The duo had to give back their Best New Artist Grammy and withdraw from the business in disgrace. Yet it was the entire industry that was disgraced.

In the early eighties, unless you had a sound that imitated the thin, splinking grooves of Prince and his protégés, were as brain-dead as Rick James was by 1984, or as mechanical and lightweight as the New Jack sound, radio success was not an option—so true funkers did the unthinkable: They abandoned radio. As a result, the New York City Hip Hop scene developed a life of its own based on club action, boom box play, and twelve-inch single sales; the Washington, D.C., Go Go sound flourished—at *live* clubs, rather than through record sales—as did a variety of underground styles, all of which took off without the support of radio airplay. It would be the musical *underground* that would be the driving force of The Funk through the eighties and beyond.

# TWENTY

# Hip Hop and Black Noise:
# Raising Hell

"Don't push me 'cause I'm close to the edge."
*Grandmaster Flash and the Furious Five*

With the aesthetic demise of black popular music, the *soul* of the people as it was expressed in the music went underground. The underground music of the eighties was generated by a new youth movement of deejays and emcees from every urban uptown, high-tech synthesizer wizards from around the world, and crafty old-school musicians all interpreting the impulse of The Funk. Eighties funk was a noisy, rugged, and tense interpretation of an African music and value system, fueled in part by the desperation of the inner cities. The monstrous, apocalyptic Hip Hop tracks of Grandmaster Flash and the Furious Five featuring Melle Mel, the bone-crushing bass drum throbs and hysterical yelps of Run-D.M.C., and the relentlessly thick, funk grind of Trouble Funk's live performances all reflected the intensity of eighties music—a music too desperate, too articulate, and too meaningful for so-called black radio.

The irrelevance of black radio was underscored in three major markets, the now-legendary New York Hip Hop scene, Washington D.C.'s nonstop Go Go funk clubs, and the San Francisco Bay Area's international and interracial "World Beat" fiasco. All three locales generated an authentic, people-oriented music culture from the bottom up, yet only one claimed national prominence—and even this was accomplished despite a profound lack of radio airplay.

## NEW YORK HIP HOP

The New York Hip Hop scene is now a well-oiled legend, a mythic tale that has made its way into the pantheon of rock and roll folklore. The booming sounds and break mixes of DJ Kool Herc at midsummer Bronx block parties in the mid-seventies, the turntable wizardry of Jazzy Jay, Afrika Bambaataa, and DJ Hollywood at South Bronx disco clubs, and proto-rapping styles of Grandmaster Flash, DJ Hollywood, and

Eddie Cheeba took mixing disco singles from a fad, to an art form, to a cultural symbol of resilience by the late 1970s. Youngsters in this environment abandoned their illusions of making music with bands, and instead lined up turntables and developed hyped mixing techniques such as the percussive record rotation known as *scratching,* the sound-strobe effect of *transforming,* and an ability to mix an endless supply of music onto synchronous, danceable beats. Adroit Hip Hop deejays could take the wickedest breakdowns of certain records—mixing them with identical copies—and repeat the breaks, sustaining a level of total *hype.* Craftier mixers rendered the entire history of recorded music into a scrap heap of the beat fragments at their disposal. Once just the stage-setters, the presenters of music, Hip Hop deejays became the *artists* as they took snippets of sounds, jingles, commercials, nursery rhymes, and pop standards and mixed them into a new, postmodern collage with a funky dance beat.

The culture of Hip Hop had developed to the point in 1979 where New Jersey–based producer Sylvia Robinson (of "Pillow Talk" fame) took the chance and recorded fifteen minutes of the Sugarhill Gang and took Hip Hop to national prominence with "Rapper's Delight." With catchy all-purpose rhymes that *everyone* seemed to have memorized, "Rapper's Delight" was the hippest novelty single in years. Yet members of the scene knew it was more than a fad.

Shortly thereafter, Robinson signed a seven-member set from the Bronx known as Grandmaster Flash and the Furious Five, creators of the most politically charged rap record of the early 1980s: "The Message." Lead rapper Melle Mel's scathing realism and charged animosity ("Don't—push—me—cause I'm close—to—the—*edge!*") caught the music scene off guard, for there was nothing to compare "The Message" to. It's not as if Teddy Pendergrass or Al Green had some social message of their own circulating on black radio at the time. The summer of 1982 was the heyday of the Gap Band and the much-awaited second album of slick-funk band The Time; Rick James was "Standing on the Top"; and the electric blues of Zapp, whose music was a celebration of high-tech grooves and relatively lightweight working-class lyrics, was bugging people out.

"The Message" was a window into the urban underworld that was never heard before on the radio—and unlike most rap records, it *was* heard on the radio. The despair, anger, and claustrophobia of life in the inner city was brought to the public *uncut:* "I can't take the smell/I can't take the noise/I got no money to move out/I guess I got no choice." As the voice of a forgotten social strata—poor black males from the inner city—Flash and his mates served a *political* function, by giving a voice to the voiceless. Not since Marvin Gaye's "What's Goin' On" in 1971 had social commentary been taken as seriously.

While Grandmaster Flash, lead rapper Melle Mel, and the rest of the Furious Five delivered a series of compelling, graphic, and grooving singles for Sugarhill, namely the gurgling anti-cocaine chant "White Lines," the grim "New York, New York" and "Survival (The Message II)," and the apocalyptic "Beat Street Breakdown," the group's popularity was lost in the wave of early eighties Hip Hop/break-dancing movies (such as *Crush Groove, Wild Style,* and *Breakdance*) and decidedly less political rappers Whodini, LL Cool J, and the upstart Run-D.M.C.

With the advent of powerful new machines capable of delivering concussions with electric drumbeats, a new form of funk emerged to support the rap sensation. Towering, metallic-sounding clanks became the percussion sound of choice, a crushing effect that reflected the urban soundscape of crashing cars, trash cans, and gunfire, all set against the backdrop of towering steel skyscrapers. With industrial-strength beats and yelling rap styles in vogue by 1984, a newfangled sound took hold: an industrial funk beat that thrived on minimalism. A booming electric bass "drum" (known as an 808) provided an unreal eardrum-splitting bump sound, followed by crashing symbols on the two and four counts, and a funk track was born. New York rap duo Whodini's 1984 anthem "Five Minutes of Funk" is an example of minimalist, crashing funk beats—with a simple two-note keyboard melody on top, the beat sold on its own as an instrumental.

The outrageously loud rappers Joseph (Run) Simmons and Darryl (D.M.C.) McDaniels scorched listeners with loud raps engineered over even louder beats. The pair created a stoopid-fresh sound that fit the noise of rock guitars as easily as ghetto raps. With songs like "Rock Box," "It's Like That," and "King of Rock," Run-D.M.C. began an assault on rock radio, blowing out pop notions of goofy, loud rock music that had rock buyers and music critics in a quandary. On the band's crossover 1986 album *Raising Hell,* they performed a duet with the almost-forgotten rock act Aerosmith, covering the band's earlier hit "Walk This Way," and reviving Aerosmith's stalled career. With the viciously loud riffs on Run-D.M.C. records hitting the streets, the radio, and even MTV, hard-rock fans by the millions flocked to the rap record bins in search of that elusive monster chord, the lifeblood of hard rock. (Accelerating the hype of funky rap tracks with a rock and roll sensibility was the "discovery" of three trash-talking punks that called themselves the Beastie Boys.) Even without overtly political lyrics, loud, hard-rocking rap music was threatening to overturn the music industry status quo by bringing new life to rock and roll from an urban black source. But the real instigator of the global Hip Hop movement— a true threat to the system—was a funkateer from the Bronx known as Afrika Bambaataa.

## AFRIKA BAMBAATAA

If any single player in eighties music established himself as the instigator of electro-funk, it was the New York–bred Afrika Bambaataa. Taking his (legal) name from the sixties film *Zulu,* of the South African Zulu Nation tribe, Bambaataa began his musical exploits as a deejay in the Bronx, later becoming leader of his own Zulu Nation, a street organization of break dancers, graffiti writers, deejays, and emcees. His first large-selling musical effort was a high-tech beat known as "Planet Rock," released on Tommy Boy Records in 1982. With the requisite booming bass, slick, spacey synthesizer riffs, and Bambaataa's distorted vocals, "Planet Rock" was an anthem of futuristic-minded club dancers everywhere. The record jump-started the Tommy Boy Records sound, from which flowed a stream of synthesizer beat–laden dance singles. Artists such as the Jonzun Crew, Planet Patrol, and Bambaataa became the second nationally known rap perpetrators after the successes of Sugarhill. Their works also influenced the emerging electro-disco sounds coming from Chicago known as "house" music, as well as the Miami bass grooves of bands such as Maggotron, and the digitized lechery of the Egyptian Lover in Los Angeles.

But Bambaataa had a greater scheme of things on his mind. With his 1983 single "Renegades of Funk," he began mixing African chants onto his kicking electro-funk tracks, and he presented his band, the Soul Sonic Force, as a posse of crazy black superheroes in the tradition of George Clinton's Dr. Funkenstein and Parliament-Funkadelic. Bambaataa also began a tradition of acknowledging large numbers of people as influences on his record sleeves, giving credit to Sly and the Family Stone, Clinton, Bootsy Collins, and James Brown, among others. Bambaataa would take the cycle full circle when he hooked up with the Godfather of Soul himself in 1984 to record "Unity," a rather noisy tribute to the old and new traditions of funk as they converged.

Bambaataa's cosmic concepts, historical understandings, and humility in the midst of stardom flew in the face of the ego-tripping of most airplay-friendly Hip Hop, and he remained underground, influencing such later so-called Afro-centric rap artists as the Jungle Brothers, Public Enemy, X-Clan, and De La Soul. Many of Bambaataa's efforts were simply ahead of their time, such as his duet with James Brown, recorded three years before sampling of Brown's work became the centerpiece of so many rap tracks. His incorporation of Clinton's P-Funk imagery was ridiculed by many in the eighties, yet in the mid-1990s, anything with references to Clinton's works is given instant credibility. The contemporary black music style of remaking seventies records and the showcasing of older artists on state-of-the-art beats were all pioneered by Bambaataa.

Bambaataa's crowning artistic achievement was the 1988 Capital Records LP *The Light,* in which he delivered a grand scenario of global liberation. He designed logos and symbols that represented his vision of "Peace, Unity, Love, and Fun," he wrote at length about the ills of the world on his liner notes, and he brought together a collection of artists that reflected the clout of a superstar. Guest artists on *The Light* included the reggae superstar Yellowman, George Clinton and Bootsy Collins, the pop rhythm band UB40, vocalists Boy George, Tim Hutton from the new wave act Cabaret Voltaire, ex-LaBelle singer Nona Hendryx, P-Funk vocalist Gary "Mudbone" Cooper, Bernard Fowler, and many other industry heavyweights in the production studio.

Brilliant, insightful monster jams such as "World Racial War," "Clean Up Your Act," a scorching remake of Aretha Franklin's "Something He Can Feel," and a fifteen-minute Hip Hop/Go-Go fusion set "Sho Nuff Funky" delivered the necessary humps to justify Bambaataa's bold themes—but it wasn't enough. "They were really scared of that album," Bambaataa recalled in 1994. The double-length album was stuffed into a single record for American distribution by Capitol Records (a British import of *The Light* on double album is a grand spectacle of album audiovisuals), a fight over the single release led to the record abandoning all promotion, and the record was a flop.

Afrika Bambaataa did his best to maintain the funk-oriented aspect of urban music in New York, and to this day he is revered and respected as the Godfather of Hip Hop. As the years go by, and his in-

novations have become standard aspects of modern music, Afrika Bambaataa's role in music history will be confirmed.

### INDUSTRIAL FUNK

With Bambaataa's influence, instrumental funk tracks were just as popular as New York rappers by 1984. With the demise of the P-Funk
Empire in 1980, many of the innovations in funk beats were produced
overseas. The German duo known as Kraftwerk was well known to club
deejays with their hits "Trans Europe Express," and the 1981 radio hit
"Numbers," neither of which had any "human" instruments associated
with them. The British techno-trio known as Art of Noise hit the country in February 1984 with a loud, stumbling brand of danceable beat
tracks, debuting with "Beat Box" and following with one of the all-time
industrial funk tracks, "Close (to the Edit)," in the summer.

A swarming, international funk sound came from the Talking
Heads, led by Scottish-born David Byrne, whose 1984 album and film
*Stop Making Sense* served to link the catchy new wave sound with The
Funk, providing some of the strongest and loudest funk from a white
band since the Average White Band back in 1974. A unique spinoff
group from the Talking Heads, the Tom Tom Club, led by bassist Tina
Weymouth, generated a club classic, "Genius of Love," in 1982, one
of the most sampled records of the eighties. Lyrics in the record praised
funksters such as James Brown, Bohannon, and Bootsy Collins. One reason for the oozing funk flow of the Talking Heads and the Tom Tom
Club was P-Funk keyboardist Bernie Worrell, who recorded with the
group, performed with them on *Soul Train,* toured with the Talking
Heads, and can be seen in the *Stop Making Sense* performance film.

While many early eighties pop artists dabbled in funk hooks and
funky grooves (such as the B-52s' "Planet Claire," Peter Gabriel's
"Shock the Monkey," Gary Numan's "Cars," and Queen's 1980 classic
"Another One Bites the Dust"), one master musician surfaced on a collision course through funk and Hip Hop. Keyboardist Herbie Hancock,
himself a veteran of Miles Davis's groundbreaking sixties quintet and
his own Headhunters jazz-funk innovations, continued to dabble in
electronic music. In 1982 Hancock asked his new manager, a young Bay
Area promoter and New York Hip Hop freak named Tony Meilandt,
to put together some Hip Hop tracks, and Meilandt recruited the talents of bassist and producer Bill Laswell (who would go on to become
the most important industrial funk producer of the era) and a brilliant

local New York deejay known as Grandmixer D.S.T. The resulting collaboration was a masterpiece of Hip Hop beats and multilayered keyboard tracks that hit the streets in 1983 as "Rockit." With the supporting album delivering a wicked fusion of traditional instruments, masterfully threaded chords, and melodies locked into industrial strength Hip Hop tracks and rhythms, Hancock's *Future Shock* album was much more than a Grammy-winning hit, it was a *phenomenon*. In many ways Herbie's spectacular combinations of future and past delivered a high-tech catharsis that brought the industrial funk era to its zenith, just as it was beginning. By the time of Herbie's brilliant "Hardrock" follow-up in 1984, Hip Hop was undergoing another one of its predictions of demise. Yet the beats kept coming.

While Herbie's funk legend grew, Bill Laswell's influence as a pioneer in industrial funk also expanded as a result of "Rockit." As an accomplished bass player as well as a technician, Laswell was able to extract a vast range of sounds and moods for a variety of artists—while maintaining a thick, bass-heavy musical foundation. His monster funk productions—beginning with his classic 1983 *Basslines* album, and moving on to stomping grooves for Afrika Bambaataa and punk superstar John (Johnny Rotten) Lydon's duet of "World Destruction" (under the name Time Zone), Manu Dibango's "Electric Africa," the Last Poets' gripping "Get Movin,' " and albums by Massacre and his band Material—put an indelible stamp on the eighties funk sound.

A series of independent labels began to thrive in the new noisy marketplace. Celluloid Records, On U Sound Records, Def Jam, Tommy Boy, Island, Rough Trade, World Records, and Manhattan Records delivered the sounds for artists such as African Head Charge, Afrika Bambaataa, Time Zone, Tackhead, Fats Comet, Mark Stewart and the Mafia, and others. What these acts had in common was a loud, almost scraping, rugged edge to their beats, with sound effects such as suctions, metallic scratches, or rapid-fire bass drum stutters that gurgled along under distorted voices or chants, barely recognizable melodic riffs, phased guitar solos, and a distinctly fonky bass. These ingredients all mixed into a chaotic stew that reflected the sparse feel of urban isolation and eighties Cold War tension.

The most prolific purveyors of this new fonk, the On-U-Sound collective, based in London and led by arranger Adrian Sherwood, captured the bleak, tense feel of life in the eighties by hiring the rhythm section of legendary rap label Sugarhill Records: Doug Wimbish on bass, Skip Macdonald on guitar and synthesizers, and Keith LeBlanc on an assortment of drums. The three players called themselves Tackhead and became *the* rhythm section of the underground—as central to industrial fonk as Sly Dunbar and Robbie Shakespeare were to the eighties reggae sound. With uncredited yet legendary tracks such as "Rapper's Delight," "White Lines," and "The Message" for Sugarhill; the 1984 dub track of Malcolm X, "No Sell Out," which featured the first samplings of Brother Malcolm's voice over a (killer) funky beat track; and the phenomenal Artists United Against Apartheid compilation in 1985 all featured the signature grooves of the Tackhead trio. While hits were rare from this unit, their sound was unmistakable, as bassist Wimbish had the voluminous tones to drive rooster-poot fonkiness into the most deliberately technified tracks his buddies could come up with. P-Funk album artist and music critic Pedro Bell summed up the Tackhead sound by saying that "they are the P-Funk of the eighties, they are what P-Funk should have been doing now."

The similarities between Tackhead and George Clinton's P-Funk were actually quite strong. The daring and irrepressible Clinton experimented with hypnotic hooks played in sequence backwards on his classic 1982 smash "Atomic Dog"; a backward bass line on his 1986 hit "Do Fries Go with That Shake," and bone-crushing thumps on tracks like "Double Oh Oh" and "Bullet Proof." (One of Clinton's best spin-off projects of the decade was his baby brother Jimmy Giles's Jimmy G and the Tackheads album *Federation of Tackheads*—not to be confused with the industrial band Tackhead.) But the digital direction of Clinton's work only served to remind people of the distance his music had gone from the *real fonk*. To find it in the eighties, one would have to go to *Chocolate City,* and hit the Go Go clubs.

## GO GO

At first glance looking like nothing more than large and loud R&B acts onstage, Go Go bands such as Trouble Funk, E.U., Rare Essence, Redds and the Boys, and their mentor Chuck Brown & the Soul Searchers, delivered the strongest, hottest, truest monster funk experience of the decade. Storming the Washington, D.C., club scene with long, percussion-filled jam sessions often consisting of only two or three hour-long "songs," propelled by a steady, punishing funk beat, the music at the Go Go clubs (such as the Black Hole or the Coliseum) in D.C. in the early eighties became known exclusively as Go Go music.

The Go Go beat is *hard-core* funk—a thick and slow bass groove, overlayed with a relentless counterpunching timbale or conga beat, jazzy horn breaks, chants of audience participation, and catchy lyrics or riffs from well-known dance hits, all delivered with a raw edge that rejected the digitized notions of eighties R&B heard on the radio. While the Go Go beat is an urban funk explosion, the approach to the music had more to do with the endless rhythms of Afro-Caribbean dance styles such as reggae, calypso, and salsa—all of which thrive on rhythmic energy, rather than hit records.

On his *Good to Go* compilation liner notes, writer Nelson George has described the Go Go beat as "local music with an international heart," a "ritual of black celebration" that fulfills its role "with an African beauty that connects the links between Rio de Janeiro, Kingston, Havana and Lagos." Yet the primary impulse of the Go Go beat is the outrageous irony of the proximity of the grim urban circumstances of the District of Columbia black community (the Go Go clientele) with the seat of the federal government: Congress and the *White* House. The contrast between the whitewashed political doublespeak of the capital and the heart wrenching realism of the funk tracks played on D.C.'s south side underscored the fonkiest of truths—as Nelson George put it, "that the distance between lofty American dreams and 1980s black reality is frighteningly huge."

The Godfather of the Go Go beat is Chuck Brown, bandleader of the Soul Searchers since 1968. A tireless performer, Brown made his mark playing club dates year after year, developing his particular brand of R&B, one with a simple, steady, nonstop funky groove on the bottom, with lots of room to operate and improvise on top. "I'd been trying to get drummers to play that particular groove for the longest time," Brown told journalist Adam White. "The beat is so simple most drummers don't like to play it."

With the success of his 1978 smash hit "Bustin' Loose," a groove Chuck Brown had been performing for three years before recording, the Go Go scene was finally given its spark. Inspired by Brown and the far-reaching funk of Clinton's apocalyptic P-Funk vibe (a uniquely appropriate fan base of P-Funk resides in D.C., the original "Chocolate City" referred to by Clinton in a 1975 hit, and the seat of most of black America's problems, the U.S. government), other bands began to take up their own brand of heavy, horny dance music. Locked into the endless funk groove, mimicking the dialogue on pop tunes and P-Funk hits, bands such as Trouble Funk, Rare Essence, Redds and the Boys, and E.U. were going strong by 1984. (It is important to note that anything can be played over a Go Go beat, and for three hours a night, everything was going in the mix.)

### TROUBLE FUNK

Independently producing themselves on TF Records, and later with the help (and hype) of Maxx Kidd and D.E.T.T. Records, Trouble Funk blasted ahead of the pack onto the D.C. Go Go scene. Featuring the loud and aggressive lead vocals of 250-plus-pound bass player and singer "Big Tony" Fisher, guitarist Robert "Dyke" Reed, and keyboardist James Avery, and always supporting at least *three* drummers, led by Timothy "T-Bone" David, Alonzo Robinson, and Mack Carey, Trouble Funk was a nonstop funk machine. The Trouble Funk groove was ferocious—and it never let up. Nine men strong, kicking a drum splattering, stupefying fat funk chunk from all directions, a Trouble Funk jam session burned the roof off the house. A Trouble Funk performance was a required initiation for those who wanted to be ultimate funkateers.

They were also the most adept Go Go group at capturing their sound on record. Scoring their first album deal on Sylvia Robinson's Sugarhill label in 1982, the record featured the club classic "Pump Me Up" and their anthem "Drop the Bomb." From there a series of twelve-inch singles hit the streets on D.E.T.T. Records, another one becoming a deejay's classic, the hypnotically hype "Trouble Funk Express" (a reworking of the Kraftwerk electro-hit "Trans Europe Express"). Their 1984 double album *In Times of Trouble* is a collector's item—a densely packed set of churning funk chops on one disc, while one live song covers *both sides* of the second disc.

The band was then picked up by Island Records and promoted in a variety of ways, beginning with a central role in the Island Visual Artist film *Good to Go*. Filmed in and around the D.C. Go Go scene in 1984, and starring pop singer and actor Art Garfunkel as a wayward journalist, *Good to Go* was billed as the breakthrough film for Go Go, one that would do for Trouble Funk and Go Go what *The Harder They Come* had done for Jimmy Cliff and reggae music in 1972. Power struggles and poor filmmaking delayed release and left the film—and the many bands on the soundtrack, such as Chuck Brown, E.U., and Trouble Funk's most vicious hit "Still Smokin' "—out of the spotlight. (It's still worth checking out on video under the name *Short Fuse.*) Island then reissued an earlier "live" recording for Trouble Funk recorded for D.E.T.T. (the second disc of *Times of Trouble*) and set about repackaging the group yet again.

Island's final effort with the band was the ill-fated *Trouble Over Here.* For this record, the band was given a slick, bright-colored, candy-coated angular look, with slices in their Afros—in the style of Cameo—betraying the homeboy image of the band. Many of the beats are tinny and thin, as if Big Tony left his bass at home when the set was recorded. Even guest producer Bootsy Collins couldn't salvage the band's sound on "Times of Trouble," an otherwise strong opening cut that set the slick tone for a record with monumental potential that manages to jam hard yet, like most eighties funk, still falls short.

Few Go Go hits ever scored on the charts, and even fewer were known nationally, but the driving Go Go beat persisted throughout the 1980s, infesting many classic Hip Hop dance tracks such as Curtis Blow's percussion-rich 1985 hit "If I Ruled the World," Doug E Fresh's 1985 "The Show," and Salt 'N Pepa's monster 1987 groove "Shake Your Thing," which was performed as a duet with E.U. (Experience Unlimited).

The most serious effort to "cross over" Go Go music was accomplished through Spike Lee's film *School Daze,* a fictionalized romp through a black college fraternity pledge week, in which the final party song, "Da Butt," is performed by E.U. Written by jazz performer and bassist Marcus Miller (veteran of Miles Davis's eighties efforts), the groove was slow and simple enough, yet it took the genius of E.U. lead singer Greg "Sugarbear" Elliot to bring it on home. With lyrics like "Tina's got a big ole butt/Darlene's got a big ole butt," the idea of the song caught on all too easily, but the *beat* was another thing. Slow and heavy, bass-driven and bouncy, "Da Butt" sounded like *nothing* on the radio in 1987, and filmmaker Lee struggled against enormous pressure from his label to release a different single from the soundtrack. But he stuck to his guns and scored a No. 1 R&B hit. Meanwhile, in a mysterious break from industry formula, every effort to follow up with Go Go songs fell off the charts like a brick in the water.

Despite the efforts of industry heavies such as Afrika Bambaataa, Curtis Blow, and Run-D.M.C., all of whom incorporated Go Go tracks in their music of the late eighties, the Go Go sound was all but forgotten by the time of the political upheaval of rap music in 1988. Despite the politics, missed opportunities, and industry indifference, there is a gold mine of classic monster funk from Washington, D.C., festering around record bins nationwide.

## WORLD BEAT

Another unique eighties musical phenomenon occurred across the country with the same energy and local enthusiam of the Go Go scene. The international dance music scene of the San Francisco Bay area in the mid-1980s was a thriving, compelling movement of music and politics that dared to expose the questions relating music to social movements. "World Beat," as it came to be known, was tied in part to the simmering Anti-Apartheid and Central American support movements in the Bay Area, as well as the many multicultural undercurrents in the region. Driven mostly by African and Caribbean rhythm players setting out a catchy Afro-pop rhythm, with pop stylists, activists, and rappers taking on the vocals, bands like Zulu Spear, Big City, Mapenzi, and the Looters rode the wave of Afro-pop that was spread by acts like King Sunny Ade, the Nigerian political leader and bandleader Fela Anikulapo Kuti, and the efforts of rock superstars such as Paul Simon *(Graceland)* to perform with African players. The international eighties pop trend of African music was enjoying an organic synthesis in the Bay Area with the many other cultures—Asian-Americans, Mexican-American salsa, black funk, jazz and blues, rock singers, and the struggling Hip Hop scene.

Destined for pop saturation, the World Beat scene died before it could be "crossed over," in part because of the schizoid nature of the bands (typically overqualified lifelong players on rhythm instruments and latecoming art school graduates taking lead singing roles). Ironically, some of the most potent funk in the Bay Area came from the World Beat scene. The Looters, fueled by the monstrously loud bass playing of Jim Johnson and his guitarist brother Joe and led by the almost maniacal Matt Callahan's rough voice and radical politics, sounded like a cross between the Clash and Earth, Wind & Fire, stirring up songs with catchy, accessible rhythms that were driven with strident, compelling lyrics such as this riff from "See the World": "Lady what you got in the basket/what you bringin' here to trade/is it grapefruit/is it banana/maybe it's a hand grenade." The militant group managed to score one stirring album on Island Records, *Flashpoint,* which was destined to make political rockers like U2 and Little

Steven sound like lightweights, but the disc never took off and is now out of print.

One act that never even made it to print was arguably the area's favorite, the Freaky Executives, perhaps the only truly organic funk band from the scene. The Freakys won the Bay Area's Best Ethnic Band award in 1986, the "Bammies," as they are called, smoking the stage while the other rock monoliths Journey, Huey Lewis, Santana, and the Grateful Dead looked on. "They had San Francisco locked up. They had the whole Bay Area locked up for a minute," recalled Dewayne Wiggins, bassist for Tony! Toni! Tone!. Even without a record, the Freaky Executives stirred up a storm across the bay. They were incessantly hip and funky, with the polish and theatrics of Morris Day and The Time, but kicked multilayered jazzy bridges and pace changes in their set that spoke more of a modern-day Tower of Power. The group could *jam* like Graham Central Station, smoke Latin percussion workouts like Santana, Stomp Monster Funk and break down into desparate ballads like Hubert Tubbs (who sang lead on the live version of "You're Still a Young Man" by Tower of Power). One local writer reviewing the Freakys claimed that lead singer Piero El Malo "generated enough sexuality to croon the panties off a nun." Even renowned and discriminating P-Funk scribe Pedro Bell, upon hearing demos of the band in 1987, called me to ask, "Who *are* the Freaky Executives?" Their highly percussive rhythm mix was a funk-centered total music experience, in the vein of the best Go Go, but just like the Go Go groups, they were lost in the storm in the production studio. Determined to sign on with a major label (Warner Bros.), the group's handlers pared down their sound to fit the R&B "format" until the horns were gone, the highly percussive mix was replaced by a drum machine, and the band's style was reduced to a weak imitation of the Minneapolis sound. Their furious live energy and anti-establishment irreverence that inspired acts across Northern California was wasted in an effort to "fit the format" of so-called "black radio."

While some of the players continue to perform, it is nevertheless a tragic commentary on a music industry that is so far from the realities of local communities that the best act in the area is dismantled. What's worse, it's likely that every city in the nation has its own Freaky Executives, an all-star band with the most potential for success that is only known by its imitations.

## BAY AREA FUNK

While the Freakys would go down in flames, Bay Area funk would thrive in a variety of separate forms in the eighties. Out of the blue, the Berkeley-based Timex Social Club scored an international hit with "Rumors" in 1986, with a unique fusion of soul and rap. The Oakland-based trio of Tony! Toni! Tone! produced a deceptively familiar funky soul sound in their sparse, catchy hits like "Little Walter," "Blues," and "Feels Good." With the help of producers Denzil Foster and Thomas McElroy, the homegrown trio balanced their earthy, Oakland roots feel with the dubious state of the art, and made it to the top. "We used to sit around the garage and jam fat shit like 'Hair' by Larry Graham," bassist Dewayne Wiggins recalled. Foster and McElroy's efforts also produced the crossover group Club Noveau, the ill-fated Nation Funktasia, and the "Funky Divas" themselves, En Vogue. The hard-core rock scene also produced such funk-based dinosaurs as Primus, Psychofunkapus, and the Limbomaniacs, all of whom managed eccentric records of their own in the eighties.

## FUNK ROCK

Rock bands had little trouble incorporating The Funk into their hot and heavy eighties chops. It was much easier for a funky white act to play whatever they liked and get recorded. The first album of the offbeat and whimsical funky rock band Jane's Addiction, for example, was a *live recording* of the act at a small club. (Can you name *any* black artist in the past twenty years whose first album was a live recording?) The absurd, bass-heavy stomps of Primus, led by the almost indecipherable lead singer and bassist Les Claypool, defy all the formulas of rock, pop, and funk, yet they *jam,* and their sound is their own.

Claypool's irreverent splatterings on bass are one of a kind, yet he frequently showcases the riffs of his idol, bassist Larry Graham, in concert. The San Jose–based Limbomaniacs fused hard rock riffs and go-go beats on their uniquely odorous *Stinky Grooves* LP in 1989 that featured cameos from Bootsy Collins and Maceo Parker. (Limbo's drummer "Brain" went on to record with the P-funk metal band Praxis in 1993.)

The versatile Red Hot Chili Peppers have enjoyed a vast range of styles—mixing folk, rock and blues, speed-metal, ska, and The Funk into their sound, and performing covers of such funk classics as Sly Stone's "If You Want Me to Stay," the Meters' "(Hollywood) Africa," and Stevie Wonder's "Higher Ground." Led by the cantankerous Anthony Kiedis's vocals and the preposterous chops of Flea Balzary on bass, the Chili Peppers are devout and cloned funkateers who have steadily given props to The Funk since George Clinton produced their second album, *Freaky Stylee*, in 1985. (When the Chili Peppers won a Grammy Award for their 1992 hit "Give It Away," they invited the entire P-Funk Mob to play with them onstage, and the chaotic performance is now a classic.) Their style and attitude is exquisitely funky, as their LP producer in 1985, George Clinton, put it: "rock out with your cock out, and play like you got a big dick." As white ambassadors of the contagious funk groove, the Chili Peppers have taken The Funk to new heights (and given props to the original funk along the way). Yet the original funk bands, most notably the P-Funk All Stars—bands that patented the versatile formula of funk rock—have been denied access to the exposure and freedom enjoyed by white bands.

## THE BLACK ROCK COALITION

The problems involved in the music industry's treatment of black bands that did not play stereotypical R&B came to a head in New York in 1985. The area's hottest rock band was the all-black hard rock quartet Living Colour, led by the phenomenal guitarist Vernon Reid. Despite numerous awards and a rabid fan base (which included rock and roll superstar Mick Jagger), the band could not get a recording contract. Their sound and image was defined as black rock, once again a hybrid category designed in reaction to the artificially whitened music known at the time as rock.

In the 1980s, the concept of black rock took on severe political overtones: Many artists realized the inherent racism in the industry, as MTV began its operation in 1981 with an apparent policy of airing no black videos, and the "urban contemporary" radio format was purview to disco-dance black music. It was clear that marketing a black artist in the rock format was not acceptable to the decision makers in the business. The segregation was so intense that Vernon Reid, *Village Voice* writer Greg Tate, and others founded a New York–based organization called the Black Rock Coalition, a "united front of musically and politically progressive Black artists and supporters" who produced the following manifesto that reads in part:

> The BRC also opposes those racist and reactionary forces
> within the American music industry which deny Black artists

the expressive freedom and economic rewards that cau-
casian counterparts enjoy as a matter of course. For white
artists, working under the rubric "rock" has long meant the
freedom to expropriate any style of Black music—funk,
reggae, blues, soul, jazz, gospel, salsa, ad infinitum—then
sell it to the widest possible audience. We too claim the right
of creative freedom and total access to American and international airwaves, audiences and markets. . . .

Rock and roll is Black music and we are its heirs. Like
our forebears—Chuck Berry, Jimi Hendrix, Sly Stone,
Funkadelic, and LaBelle, to name but a few—the members
of the BRC are neither novelty acts, nor carbon copies of
the white bands who work America's Apartheid Oriented
Rock circuit.

By performing concerts with experimental acts and lobbying for
their exposure, the BRC opened the door for a number of artists to gain
a foothold in their own particular flavors of funky black jazz-rock. With
the many cross-blendings of styles that occur on local stages across New
York, strong self-defined acts continue to pop up on the scene. Performers such as Steve Coleman, Me'Shell NdegeOcello, John Paul Bu-
relly, James "Blood" Ulmer, and Kelvyn Bell's Kelvynator are tireless
innovators in the hard-driving music of New York's underground jazz-
rock-funk scene. As the 1990s roll on, however, the apartheid-oriented
rock circuit continues to operate, as the majority of successful New
York bands remain on independent labels and out of the spotlight.

In the 1980s The Funk became more harsh and intense, as a di-
rect reflection of the growing intensity of oppression that fell upon
America's funky people. It would only increase in the 1990s as urban
Hip Hop became the primary medium for the rebel/funk expression.

# PART SEVEN

# The Hip Hop Nation: Amerikkka's Most Wanted

# TWENTY-ONE

# Funk in the Nineties:
# Return of the Funk

"Hip Hop saved The Funk."
*George Clinton*

The late 1980s and early 1990s brought about a radical turnabout in black American culture. An intelligent youth movement in fashion, attitude, rhythm, and rhyme spread across the country through the beats of Hip Hop. Yet beyond the stylistic change was the development of a new historical consciousness and a frank new racial dialogue among the young. In almost every perceptible way, the new movement in the music, in the proud new attitude, and in the grim, bittersweet, and almost absurd ideals of change amounted to a renaissance of the *funk movement* of the 1970s.

Top-grossing movies such as Spike Lee's 1989 *Do the Right Thing* and John Singleton's 1991 *Boyz N the Hood* provided complex, dynamic reflections of the hard, funky realities of urban life from a black perspective. Malcolm X emerged as a hero to a new generation of frustrated youth, who were rethinking their history and creating their own role models. An "Afro-centric" education movement grew in the streets, challenged local school districts, and festered in the national media. Driven by a revolution in rap music led by the funky and conscious edge of Public Enemy, an out-of-control indulgence for the sampling of seventies funk hits, and the skyrocketing popularity of MTV's highest-rated show in 1991, *Yo! MTV Raps,* the Hip Hop movement brought an entire generation into a conscious, liberated state of mind—the essence of The Funk.

Funkiness was once again in fashion, as the low-down humor of the Wayans brothers' *In Living Color* thrived in prime time on the radical new Fox network, and Arsenio Hall indulged in The Funk nightly with wacky ad-libs and banter with the band on his nationally syndicated talk show. The "New Jack Swing" sound mixed Hip Hop beats with soulful melodies to bring bite-sized portions of funk for a new generation to digest. "New Jack" singers The Boyz gave tribute to the old-school funk bands with their 1990 "Thanx 4 the Funk," and the sexy and stylish No. 1 vocal quartet En Vogue was packaged as *Funky Divas,* with their scorching 1992 pop hit "Never Gonna Get It" laced with a relentless loop of James Brown's "The Payback."

Rap music has become the focal point of the resurgence of The Funk—a continuation of The Funk in the digital age. By replicating original funk tracks, albeit in dehydrated form, Hip Hoppers have found themselves reiterating the stylistic and philosophical aspects of The Funk while repeating the groovy hooks. This should come as no surprise, since rap and funk both come from the same demographic group: the rebellious youth of the outcast urban underworld.

By 1990 rap music had grown and proliferated into a vast multitude of styles and viewpoints. The music evolved from the minimalist beats of Whodini and Run-D.M.C. into multilayered groove tracks that floated along thick bass lines and mimicked the multitrack sounds of seventies funk bands. As the music took on more political, social, and historical dimensions, an appreciation of The Funk grew at the same time. The music of the Hip Hop Nation has grown into its own subculture with its own particular historical references. Whereas their parents' generation might have revered such black cultural leaders as Duke Ellington or John Coltrane, the youthful members of the Hip Hop Nation are tuned in to their own icons, and if they follow the music of any of their elders it is the great soul singers and the legendary funk of James Brown, George Clinton, and Bootsy Collins.

Old became new when rappers Erick Sermon and Parrish Smith, known as EPMD, returned the *thump* into the rap track by looping a booming funk bass, the hump from "More Bounce to the Ounce" by Zapp, on their own 1987 hit "You Gots to Chill." The stirring release that summer of Eric B. and Rakim's "I Know You Got Soul" recaptured the smooth, tight vibe of Bobby Byrd's 1971 (James Brown–produced) original, and opened the door for the sampling frenzy of the James Brown sound. Echoes of an era—the Funk Era—began to resonate throughout the Hip Hop Nation, contributing to a renaissance of ideas of "the good old days" of black pride, culture, and history.

## POLITICAL RAP

For most of the 1980s, what was understood as "political" rap music was an obscure element of a culture whose very existence was political. With the realism of Grandmaster Flash and the Furious Five a five-year-old memory, two artists introduced themselves to the rap scene with grim, compelling streetwise rhymes and scorching beats that brought back notions of new possibilities in Hip Hop. Long Island's Public Enemy and Chris Parker (a.k.a. Blastmaster KRS-1) and his Boogie Down Productions kicked on the street scene with sinister albums in 1987. BDP's single "Poetry" was one of the first to kick a James Brown sample ("Talkin' Loud & Sayin' Nothin' ") and rhyme streetwise on top of it. Yet neither Public Enemy's *Yo! Bum Rush the Show* nor BDP's *Criminal Minded* anticipated the new directions the artists would take.

What many are hailing as a golden age of rap music began around 1988, with the release of Boogie Down Productions' *By All Means Necessary* and Public Enemy's much-awaited yet totally unexpected *It Takes a Nation of Millions to Hold Us Back.* Chris Parker's mature and broad-ranging philosophies were explored on *By All Means,* particularly on cuts like "My Philosophy," "Illegal Business," "Stop the Violence," and "Necessary." "I'm not white, or red, or black, I'm *brown*/From the Boogie Down" was Parker's take on race. Preaching the virtues of vegetarianism and delivering one of the first pleas for safe sex ("Jimmy") and to "Stop the Violence in Hip Hop," BDP was years ahead of its time.

Yet Parker's anti-violence stance was at odds with his image. The title *By All Means Necessary* brought the clear impression that violence may in fact be necessary to bring about justice, whether it was stated or not. The cover art featuring Parker posing with an automatic weapon—in the same pose as a famous Malcolm X photograph—brought cries of militarism from critics. This was the same critique of Malcolm X in the 1960s; Malcolm's charge that a man has a right to defend himself "by any means necessary" brought about virulent criticism that he was directly preaching violence. The issues KRS-1 brought up reflected just how similar the situation facing blacks on the street in the 1980s was to blacks in the 1960s. The Malcolm X renaissance in the black communities that culminated with Spike Lee's 1993 epic film of his life can be traced back to Boogie Down Productions' 1988 album.

A self-taught "intellectual" and streetwise player, KRS-1 embodied the contradictory goals that festered in the inner cities. Knowledge was important, yet the educational system was inadequate, so he taught himself. Strength is measured through force, not money or prestige, and KRS-1 paid his dues on the street, losing his deejay Scott La Rock in a street altercation in 1987. In 1988 KRS-1 used his clout in the industry to produce a collaborative recording of "Self Destruction," an anti-violence anthem and showcase of unity among a dozen of the most popular New York rappers. Further works such as "You Must Learn" and "Mr. Drug Dealer" exposed Parker's in-depth knowledge of the roots of racism and poverty—and brought the complex issues to the masses uncut. He continues to lecture at colleges while he still records. KRS-1 remains uniquely qualified to represent the viewpoints of the dispossessed, and for ten years he has continued to do so, despite a profound lack of radio exposure.

The image of rap music was turned upside down in 1988, leaving KRS-1 in the background. Building on the strength of a twelve-inch dance single "Rebel Without a Pause," Public Enemy was stirring up clubs nationwide in the fall of 1987. Their ability to make loops of pure noise, scratching, sampling tension, and hype into a collision of sensibilities brought The Funk into the digitized, postmodern age. What many thought was an abrasive exception to the rule became the standard by which aggressive rap music was measured when the album *It Takes a Nation of Millions to Hold Us Back* hit the streets in the summer of 1988.

The power, volume, and animosity delivered with this disc hit the music scene like an electric shock. The industry itself was one of Public Enemy's prime targets, as rapper Flavor Flav can be heard yelling "Who gives a fuck about a goddamn Grammy" on "Terminator X to the Edge of Panic," and on "Caught, Can I Get a Witness," lead rapper Chuck D hits the so-called black music scene, saying, "You singers are spineless/as you sing your senseless songs to the mindless/your general subject/love is minimal/it's sex for profit."

Until this point, no one had taken on the monolithic strength, status, and illusory image of the music business this boldly. The eighties was a time when pop artists were crossing barriers and performing in "Aid" concerts worldwide, giving the industry an image of cooperation and freedom. Yet the process by which acts made it to the status of star in their particular fields was just as controlled as it was before. Public Enemy was like a slap in the face to a business that had grown complacent. The group won "Album of the Year" honors from the *Village Voice* Music Poll—a music award that generally goes to rock/pop superstars—and was nominated for the very Grammy Award they claimed to despise. (Public Enemy attended the Grammys that year, but the rap award went to D.J. Jazzy Jeff and the Fresh Prince.)

Public Enemy took on a variety of controversial topics throughout the album. They challenged the deceptive practices of the media with their classic "Don't Believe the Hype"; club dancers were dealt a diatribe against the drug addictions festering in the inner cities on "Night of the Living Baseheads"; a mythic prison break was delivered on "Black Steel in the Hour of Chaos"; while black women addicted to soap operas were straightened out (fairly respectfully) on "She Watch Channel Zero." The remainder of the record featured monster jams that kicked black pride and power in your face and in your ears. Jams like "Bring the Noise," "Rebel Without a Pause," and "Mind Terrorist" packed a vicious load of shrill noise effects with maniacal drumbeats, constantly fractured with sound effects, and rappers Chuck D and Flavor Flav interspersing their own flavor of radical politics.

Even their delivery was a significant breakthrough, for the duo of Chuck D (Carlton Ridenhour) and Flavor Flav (William Drayton), both of Long Island, delivered a classic one-two punch of cultural expression from within the tradition. Chuck was the insistent orator, serious and low in the range, dropping rhymes delivered with the controlled intensity of a Malcolm X speech, while Flavor Flav delivered the comic counterpoint, acting spastic and random. He rarely rhymed, but would always accentuate and strengthen Chuck D's point. "Yea Boyeee!" was Flav's main line, yet there was an endless supply of limericks and gimmicks. What was crucial to the partnership, it should be noted, is that Flavor Flav was a clown—in the tradition of the best black comics—yet he was a clown with *consciousness,* empowered with knowledge of self, an entirely different persona from the "Stepin Fetchit" and "Sambo" stereotypes of subservient and uncouth black Americans. Flavor Flav was and is a fool, but a fool on a mission. On the cover of *Nation of Millions,* he wears a gigantic clock as a medallion— a preposterous getup—yet it is designed to illustrate, through a comic medium, that time is indeed running out.

This silly-serious dichotomy is a central part of the African-American entertainment tradition, particularly since the Black Revolution of the 1960s (the dawn of the Funk Age), when comedians such as Richard Pryor, Dick Gregory, and Flip Wilson laced their outlandish works with graphic race-conscious imagery and discussions of political issues. The silly-serious black artist was a way of life for George Clinton's Parliament/Funkadelic crew in the seventies, who were scoring No. 1 hits with off-the-wall cartoonish titles as "Aqua-Boogie" and "Flashlight" under the name Parliament, while sliding more-to-the-point messages underneath the power chords and catchy hooks. Clinton himself was an early fan of Public Enemy, and later featured Chuck and Flav in his work, on the underrated "Tweakin' " in 1989.

By that time Public Enemy had been signed to perform "Fight the Power," the theme song of Spike Lee's 1989 film *Do the Right Thing,* a record and film that brought the group even more notoriety and exposure. Lee's film, an exploration of the decline of the delicate racial and social fabric in the Bedford-Stuyvesant area of Brooklyn, New York, provided exposure to the points of view of blacks, Italians, and Koreans in a fashion never before seen. "Fight the Power" provided the requisite shrill noises and lyrics that spoke to far-ranging themes of outrage that were common in the black community, yet unspoken in public.

> Elvis was a hero to most
> But he never meant shit to me you see
> Straight out racist, that sucker was
> Simple and plain
> Mother fuck him, *and* John Wayne
> Cause I'm black and I'm proud
> I'm ready and hyped plus I'm amped
> Most of my heroes don't appear on no stamp.
> Public Enemy, "Fight the Power" (1989)

Promoting a fearless disrespect for America's institutions, Public Enemy was the embodiment of resistance for many who believed. Greg Tate wrote in 1988 that Public Enemy "wants to reconvene the black power movement with Hip Hop as the medium," and he was right. Robert Christgau concurred in a 1990 *Village Voice* editorial: "Not even in the heyday of the . . . Clash has any group come so close to the elusive and perhaps ridiculous sixties rock ideal of raising political consciousness with music." In so many ways, Public Enemy was attempting to do what rock, and The Funk, had attempted to do a generation earlier. George Clinton revered the group as truth-tellers of their generation in 1989: "To me they're like what Bob Dylan was to rock and roll when they were starting to talk about the condition of the world. That's Public Enemy now." While allegations of anti-Semitism dogged the group at their peak, their impact caused a global Hip Hop movement to rise.

The group's long-awaited follow-up album *Fear of a Black Planet* appeared to go for the jugular vein of America's racial hang-ups, and the record brought about the requisite onslaught of criticism, yet the overall work was actually more restrained than *Nation of Millions*. Indeed, the group was getting more airplay on the evening news than on "urban contemporary" radio. But their most important success was summarized by *Village Voice* writer Robert Christgau: "However mixed their motives, they have actually instigated a species of leftish Afro-centrism among kids who three years ago thought gold chains were dope." Yet on a more serious level, the opening lines of the *Black Planet* album told it all: "There is something changing in the climate of consciousness in the world today . . . Public Enemy."

### AFRO-CENTRIC RAP

Indeed a profound transformation of race consciousness took place at the dawn of the nineties, which accelerated two unique developments—the Afro-centric movement and the so-called gangsta rap phenomenon. A series of New York–based rap groups began taking on topics that spoke of African pride, historical consciousness, a respect for women, and a steady use of samples of seventies funk hits. Groups such as the Jungle Brothers hit with songs like "Done by the Forces of Nature" and "Black Woman"; Queen Latifah scored message songs "Ladies First" and "Mama Gave Birth to the Soul Children"; De La Soul created an entire cartoon landscape with their 1989 album *3 Feet High and Rising* and irreverent ditties like "Tread Water" and "Me, Myself and I"; while X-Clan appeared as tribal warriors from the East, giving out a "Funkin' Lesson," a "Tribal Jam," and warning listeners to "Heed the Word of the Brother."

By 1989 a number of essential connections were being made between the richness of African history and culture, the creative strength of seventies funk and soul, and the positive potential of Hip Hop. For a brief time, Hip Hop took the initiative to envision liberation—in a positive form. The colorful use of words brought all of these aspects of life together.

The convergence of historical consciousness, political consciousness, and a humorous spin on creativity are the central aspects of The Funk, and nearly all of the so-called Afro-centric rap groups kept the tradition alive. Producer Prince Paul, the creator of the sampling frenzy of De La Soul's *3 Feet High and Rising,* was and is an avid funkateer, whose Clinton-influenced gimmicks, game-show skits, inside jokes, nonsensical phrases, and bizarre collages of sounds represented a P-Funk aesthetic in sampling. "It's all just from listening to a lot of Parliament/Funkadelic. George Clinton does a lot of that visual, underwater stuff," he told author S. H. Fernando in 1994. "I envied a lot of George Clinton, he really bugged me out. He dogged my mentality as a child." Within the framework of Hip Hop, one could combine whimsy and humor with political education without missing a beat, just as it had been in The Funk.

### A FUNKY SPIRITUALITY

Gradually, more mystical, cerebral, and spiritual issues made their way into Hip Hop texts, as references to higher forces emerged alongside expressions of traditional religions and celebrations of The Funk. The music became the primary channeling frequency for youth of the day to remain grounded in the rhythms of their worlds, while daring to embark on higher quests, often challenging the established standards of traditional black religion. On Boogie Down Productions' 1993 chant on "The Real Holy Place," KRS-1 can be heard yelling, "If the slavemaster wasn't a Christian, *you* wouldn't be a Christian!" On "Neva Again" from the Los Angeles–based Kam, he delivers the following rip on the black church: "Lift every voice and sing/hell, lift every fist and swing/ so save that Negro spiritual/It's 1992 and niggas need a miracle." The Afro-centric rap band X-Clan appropriated some of the grandiose conceptual activity of P-Funk and expressed it—while looping numerous samples of P-Funk—in their 1991 record "Earthbound":

> Funk upon a time, in the days of vainglorious,
> the tribe-dimensional houses of energy,
> release the original powers
> to the translators to the interplanetary funk code,
> funk and religion,
> funkin' lesson,
> key bearers funk unto the east.
> Earthbound.
> > X-Clan, "Earthbound" (1991)

Creating a spiritual, mythic otherworld is perhaps necessary for a people to have faith. And for a generation unimpressed with Christianity as it is practiced in the black American community, The Funk offered new formulas for the expression of that faith. Again heavily laden with funk samples and—in the case of X-Clan and Kam—P-Funk samples, a great deal of rap music has taken on more complex issues of the heart, of the afterlife, and of faith. As might have been expected, the maturity in the rap music themes has coincided with a growth in the use of, and affection for, The Funk.

## P-FUNK HIP HOP

Ultimately, the Hip Hop Nation began to acknowledge itself as heir to a musical and spiritual legacy of The Funk. Where the soul music singers of the sixties and seventies could always look back to their days singing in the black church, artists in the Hip Hop generation look back to The Funk for guidance and inspiration. The million-selling rap band Digital Underground made it a part of their image to incorporate aspects of P-Funk philosophy, as well as the cartoon characters and humorous means of telling truths. Their 1991 release of "Sons of the P" (a concept coined by the ubiquitous Marlon "Dr. Illinstine" Kemp) revealed a deep understanding of the meanings and message of P-Funk, as the rappers exhorted the listener to "release your mind and let the funk flow." But beyond the ideal of funkiness, Digital Underground was exploring the consciousness-raising aspects of free expression. Lead rapper Shock G made it clear that those "in control" were working to "keep your natural desires in check." It is insights like these that give more power to the chorus of the song: "Most of all we need The Funk!"

By the end of the 1980s, the original funk artists had become legendary. A score of rap acts (beginning of course with Afrika Bambaataa in the 1980s) have recruited original funk masters to perform with and/or appear on their songs and videos. James Brown appeared as "The Godfather" at the beginning of Hammer's 1992 "2 Legit 2 Quit" video; George Clinton has appeared in the Latin rapper Gerardo's video of "We Want the Funk," as well as Ice Cube's "Bop Gun." Bootsy Collins is featured at the end of Eazy E's "We Want Eazy" video (the song itself is a loop of Bootsy's 1977 hit "Aah the Name is Bootsy, Baby"), as well as Ice Cube's 1994 "Bop Gun" video. Los Angeles producer and rapper Dr. Dre went so far as to take footage of "the landing of the Mothership" from a seventies performance of George Clinton's Parliament Funkadelic tours, and edit it onto his own video of "Let Me Ride." The record also won a Grammy Award as rap single of the year.

The elder statesmen of The Funk are playing important roles in the passing of traditions to a generation of urban youth that have been abandoned by so many established leaders.

### WEST COAST RAP

The West Coast has been a hotbed of outright funk-oriented rap music from the earliest days of Hip Hop. The Los Angeles–based deejay and dance music troupe, Uncle Jamm's Army, led by Rodger Clayton (Uncle Jamm) and his deejay, known as The Egyptian Lover, had been tearing up Los Angeles–area dance clubs since 1981—wearing fatigues and wild Egyptian tribal-space costumes in the vein of George Clinton's P-Funk (using Clinton's "Uncle Jam" concept). By 1984, they were generating a relentless string of Electro-Funk twelve-inch dance singles that challenged Afrika Bambaataa's domination of the early scene.

The sparse, gangsterish vibe of Oakland's veteran rapper Too Short was an inspiration for a generation of hard-core Bay Area rappers interested in that deep funky groove. After pioneering the West Coast X-rated rap sound (along with Ice-T in L.A.), Too Short also pioneered the Hip Hop/funk fusion trend, incorporating a vicious bass guitar track (played by the multitalented Shorty B, who is also the rapper on Digital Underground's crucial P-Funk/Hip Hop slam "Tales of the Funky") on his 1991 monster jam "I Wanna Be Free." Despite the funky innovations of such diverse Bay Area rappers as Hammer, Digital Underground, Too Short, and Paris, the urban rap sound that swept the country came from southern California.

An entirely different realm of rap music grew from the sparse urban landscapes of South-Central Los Angeles. Inspired in part by the aggression of Public Enemy's breakthrough *Nation of Millions*, a Los Angeles rap crew called N.W.A., or Niggaz With Attitude, scorched the scene in 1989 with their anthem "Straight Outta Compton." Dropping what appeared to be the most irresponsible attitude yet put on record, the music reeked of misogyny and rebellion. "Shoot a motherfucker in a minute/I find a good piece of pussy and go up in it" was one of the classic lines. "So what about the bitch that got shot/fuck her/You think I give a damn about a bitch, I ain't a sucker" was another refrain from Eazy E.

This was music for people who don't give a fuck—or at least people who want to feel like they don't. The tracks *smoked,* as then-unknown rappers Ice Cube, Dr. Dre, Eazy E, and Yella turned the very purpose of rap music on its head. Other songs like "Fuck tha Police" and "Gangsta Gangsta" revealed the unbridled contempt for the police force and mainstream society in general that the group had experienced in some form or another. Ultimately, their lyrics amounted to fantasies of aggression against a system that gives no ground. Yet taken out of context, they stand out as pathological adolescent ramblings of unbridled rage. Clearly, however, the crew knew that they were in a position to deliver a load of sex and violence that Americans feared in real life but came to desire in rap music.

## SEXISM AND POWER

In rap, sexual fantasies are just as common as they are in rock and roll, but the ideas are much more explicit and detailed. Schooly D's comical "Mr. Big Dick," Digital Underground's X-rated block party "Gut Fest '89," and Too Short's ideas for the pop superstars "Paula and Janet" are examples of male sex/power fantasies in rap that take the ideas of sexual conquest to absurd levels. Los Angeles rapper Ice-T's outrageous "Girls Let's Get Butt Naked and Fuck" is another example. Getting right to the point, Ice-T takes the mystique out of the attraction equation. The explicit and erotic nature of Ice-T's flavor is an undiluted, demystified aspect of sexual relations that is unique to the Hip Hop culture. (One could make the case, however, that this new dynamic of relationships is merely a result of unchecked male aggression, tempered neither by women, nor by *elders*.)

It has been said that many of the absurd and appalling violations of women in hard-core rap are merely "fantasies" put to raps. While broad sex fantasies have always been a part of pop music—and funk bands developed many of their own, such as James Brown's "Sex Machine," the Brothers Johnson's "Land of Ladies," the Bar-Kays' "White House Orgy," and Funkadelic's "Icka Prick"—the female images were celebrated rather than attacked. Eazy E defended the tone of his work in a 1991 *Spin* article by explaining that his music isn't disrespecting women in general, it is "disrespecting bitches." His (dubious) distinction was missed by many of the rappers who imitated him and the critics who condemned him outright. An almost savage treatment of women soon came from rap records across the country—both validating and perpetuating a subculture that many hoped had somehow disappeared with segregation.

Against this storm, a small cadre of female rappers has stood tall to assert a fresh and vibrant counterpoint to Hip Hop sexism. Salt 'N Pepa, Queen Latifah, MC Lyte, Monie Love, Sista Souljah, Yo Yo, and others have given a breath of life to the ideals of Hip Hop. But despite the enormous appeal of humane Hip Hop, the male power-brokers within the industry continue to ignore the calls for sanity and regularly comb the streets for the most graphic and shocking raps available.

It is ironic that a vast amount of misogynist rap music makes use of samples of the funk era, because the very purpose of the original funk was designed to bring about *unity*. There certainly was a strong thread of sexism in funky music, such as Johnny Taylor's "Cheaper to Keep Her," Joe Tex's "I Gotcha," and Funkadelic's "No Head, No Backstage Pass," but the outright humiliation and abuse of women on a large scale in black music is a phenomenon unique to the 1990s. Themes such as "Bitch Betta Have My Money," and "A Bitch Is a Bitch" reflect a powerful combination of destructive circumstances—the lack of family discipline or role models other than street hustlers; peer pressure from within as young men desperate to express their strength lash out; and the racism of the industry itself. As old-school rhymer Lonzo of the World Class Wreckin' Cru told Brian Cross: "I tried to do my positive thing. . . . To a white company, they don't want to hear that 'cause that's not what's sellin' to them—*you* talk about shooting somebody—you almost have to sell out to buy in."

### 2-LIVE CREW

When the Miami-based 2-Live Crew began in 1986, their ridiculous X-rated rhymes were not taken seriously—even by the artists themselves. Songs like "We Want Some Pussy" and "Move Something" became hilarious club chants in the local disco halls that survived in the Miami area. With a live act that consisted of juvenile beats that imitated well-known pop melodies, sexually gyrating women wearing only strips of fabric, and brain-dead graphic rhymes about sex, 2-Live Crew—led by Luther Campbell—cornered the market on X-rated musical entertainment. Their local success allowed the act to produce and distribute their own music—as well as participate in community services, such as building a housing project out of their own profits and making regular trips to Guantanamo, Cuba, to give aid to Haitian refugees there. Yet when the group released *As Nasty as They Wanna Be* in 1990, which featured the now-classic album cover photo of the three members peering between the legs of four bikini-clad women, and the million-selling single "Me So Horny," all hell broke loose.

It is likely that the group only initially went platinum as a result of the sample of the 1979 monster funk hit "Firecracker" by Mass Production. The wicked, hyped beat was a funk classic, and when 2-Live Crew reprised the hump in its entirety—which was the style at the time—national exposure on pop radio and MTV ensued. The high visibility of such completely "nasty" black men caused a national controversy. A variety of institutions took on Luther Campbell, claiming his work was "obscene," and formally took him to court. In June 1990 the record was deemed "obscene" by a federal court judge, and thus *illegal* to perform. The band was then arrested for performing the song onstage the following week. Acquitted four months later, the group's harassment represented the pinnacle of government intervention into the spread of The Funk. The chilling effect on other music cannot be calculated, but the effort was a significant one, for there is plenty of music just as "obscene" as 2-Live Crew's. Theirs is perhaps the most blatant—and most accessible—of any sexually explicit musical entertainment.

With the growth of video channels, and the seemingly lax barriers regarding sexual content in videos, 2-Live Crew and many more Miami-based (or Miami-sounding) groups, such as the Dogs, Tag Team, The 69 Boyz, and H.W.A. (Hoes with Attitude), generated explicit videos to promote their otherwise trivial songs. Anyone with access to the request-line video channel "The Box" is aware that the Miami sound videos are by far the most requested. For his part, Campbell was not slowed down, continues to record, and the notoriety brought more focus on the attack on successful black artists, particularly the explicit ones. Whether about politics, black pride, or sexuality, the nitty-gritty expressions of black reality in the 1990s have come largely from rap music, which has thoroughly sampled and incorporated aspects of The Funk, and fought the power every step of the way.

## THE FUNK WARS

With the Bush administration maintaining the apathy toward the inner cities that was established in Ronald Reagan's eight years in office, things were not getting better in the black communities nationwide in 1990. Murder rates and supplies of crack cocaine, powdered heroin, and automatic weapons all increased dramatically in the inner cities. To add to the sense of helplessness, a number of nationally renowned black figures were imprisoned or humiliated—such as the Godfather of Soul James Brown's high-speed chase through Georgia and subsequent six-year sentence in 1989, Washington, D.C., Mayor Marion Barry's videotaped arrest smoking crack with a prostitute in 1990, and heavyweight boxing champion Mike Tyson's controversial rape conviction in 1992, to name a few.

While from the outside these appeared to be isolated events involving individuals who violated the law and were punished for it, many in the inner cities made the connection with the lack of opportunities in their own communities and what appeared to be state harassment of even their most successful role models. The perception was clear: Racism was in full effect, from the bottom all the way to the top. Dr. Dre summed up the outrage on his *Chronic* album in 1993. He made it clear that "no matter how much money you got, you still ain't shit." With less and less to believe in, contempt for the system was at an all-time high. Eventually, the rage of the people could not be repressed, as the so-called Rodney King rebellion swept the nation on April 29, 1992, and frustrated citizens disrupted, burned, and looted business districts from Los Angeles to Toronto.

It is important to note that while the dimensions of the Los Angeles "rebellion" came as a surprise and a shock to the mainstream of America, the government, and the news media, the reaction was anticipated and *predicted* only a few months before by the best-selling rapper Ice Cube, on his *Death Certificate* album. "Pay respect to the black fist," he warned, "or we'll burn your store right down to a crisp." Ice Cube was addressing the simmering racial tensions between Korean shop owners and black patrons that had been festering in light of the killing of black teenager Latasha Harlins by a Korean shop owner in the summer of 1991. (Harlins was shot in the back after an altercation over a bottle of orange juice, yet the shop owner was only given probation.) While the story was not covered nationally, it simmered in the black community of Los Angeles all summer. When Ice Cube released his album in the fall of 1991—a record loaded with racial epithets directed at whites, Jews, Asians, and blacks who sell out, as well as a zeal for calling women "bitches"—Cube was labeled as the "David Duke" of rap music, a reverse racist. Yet despite his painful, stereotypical, and often shallow characterizations of his enemies, Ice Cube nevertheless emerged as a fantastically gifted street poet who to this day claims an authority among the urban set that cannot be ignored.

Indeed, while not condoning the actions that took place during that infamous week, it's important to note that the problems in South-Central Los Angeles were well known to listeners of rap music, while mainstream journalists, in both print and video, were oblivious to the situation. It was clear that the Hip Hop Nation was better informed about the plight of the inner cities than the rest of the population, and that ability to inform, educate, and empower the powerless was and is a political asset.

Hip Hop came of age as the 1990s dawned, when sampling was all the rage. After the pop success of such superstars as De La Soul, who was sued for sampling the Turtles, and Tone Loc's "Wild Thing," which looped Eddie Van Halen's "Jamie's Crying" in 1989, legal departments at record publishing houses went to war with the rap community, demanding retribution for their sound snippets. By 1993 it had become so expensive to clear samples that artists began playing the music themselves, first with digital instruments, then with bands. Dr. Dre, Snoop Doggy Dogg, Too Short, Hammer, and a variety of other acts have gathered musicians into their fold and produced Hip Hop funk, the most popular of which was Dr. Dre's 1993 *The Chronic,* the runaway rap record of the year.

By performing funk tracks with Hip Hop raps, the marriage of rap and funk came ever closer. Ice Cube's 1994 "Bop Gun" was performed as a cover of Funkadelic's "One Nation Under a Groove," in which almost *every rhyme* is a reprise of a choice P-Funk limerick. By 1995, The Funk had become an inseparable aspect of rap music, as a plethora of rappers came with funk themes in their album titles: Warren G was in *The G Funk Era,* Da Brat was *Funkdafied,* Goldie was *In the Land of Funk,* the Lords of the Underground were *Keepers of the Funk,* political rapper Paris delivered *Guerilla Funk,* and it keeps on coming.

The Funk is now the central focus in higher forms of Hip Hop. The ideals, the attitudes, and many of the riffs in hard-core Hip Hop owe their existence to the original funk masters, who paved the way by working for creative independence and delivering the truth to their people as they saw fit. Any way you look at it, Hip Hop and funk are inseparable. As George Clinton put it in 1990, "Hip Hop saved The Funk" by bringing it out of the past and into the present. Now it's time for The Funk to save Hip Hop.

# TWENTY-TWO

# *Postscript on The Funk:*
# *Sons of the P*

"The Funk is its own reward."
*Parliament*

As we have seen, there's more to The Funk than a dance fad, fashion statement, or rhythmic jam session. The Funk is an *ideal* that has thrived in the African-American community since the chant of "Black Power" served to make all things possible for a generation of second-class citizens. The Funk has served as the guiding mode of expression of the *black experience* for the past two generations. The Funk rests at the heart of the militant and rebellious notions of hard-core rap, the sexually explicit riffs of many of the most aggressive rock bands, the wicked and complex riffs of modern jazz-fusion enthusiasts, and the whimsy and idealism of eccentric jazz-rap stylists. The return of the many funk bands of the 1970s such as the Ohio Players, the Average White Band, Earth, Wind & Fire, and the Bar-Kays, and the resilience of such funk innovators as James Brown, George Clinton, Bernie Worrell, and Bootsy Collins underscores the essential regenerative qualities of the music. The impulse of The Funk rests deep in the "Souls of Black Folk" (to borrow from W. E. B. Du Bois), yet it's a vibe that anyone can tune in to.

But one key ingredient is often missing: an historical understanding of the source and purpose of The Funk. Without it, funkiness is little more than a joke. Without an understanding of its place in the black tradition, funk is little more than a rationale for antisocial behavior. What results is something "nasty" without the love (the image of hard-core rap); something ugly without the search for beauty (the image of grunge rock); something freakish without the faith in the unity of all things (the image of P-Funk); and something rebellious without a cause (the image of political rap). If one understands The Funk, however, a multitude of values are brought together—values that appear to conflict yet thrive harmoniously *in the groove*. That elusive All-American notion of unity amid diversity is embodied by The Funk.

In his groundbreaking discussion of race and society, *Race Matters,* Cornell West elaborates in his final pages about the metaphor of jazz as an operating principle of life: to flow within concurrent rhythms, working as an individual yet tuned in to the group working toward a common goal. His ideal is to identify oneself as a "jazz freedom fighter":

> I use the term "jazz" here not so much as a term for a musi-
> cal art form, as for a mode of being in the world, an impro-
> visational mode of protean, fluid, and flexible dispositions
> toward reality. . . . As with a soloist in a jazz quartet, quin-
> tet or band, individuality is promoted in order to sustain and
> increase the creative tension with the group—a tension that
> yields high levels of performance to achieve the aim of the
> collective project. This kind of critical and democratic
> sensibility flies in the face of any policing of borders and
> boundaries of "blackness," "maleness," "femaleness," or
> "whiteness."

With an understanding of the form and function of The Funk as a collective process of creating rhythmic, aggressive, danceable music with a message, it's easy to see how West's model can be adapted for a generation weaned on digital instruments and a funky beat.

Indeed, funk music is generated by the same methods as the jazz West refers to. The collective sensibilities were precisely the thrust of the many seventies bands that jammed long into the night and developed songs *as a group.* Further, the wide-open framework for The Funk was based on the universally inclusive values promoted by Sly and the Family Stone, a wild-looking outfit that included blacks, whites, men, and women operating as liberated individuals, working together as an inspired collective unit—something still rare in the packaging of what we know as jazz. With the collective improvisation (that is, long jam sessions), the rhythmic interplay, and spiritual orientation to creativity, The Funk exists as an organic evolution *from* jazz, and is perhaps the last black American musical form to be developed in *the same fashion* as jazz. Thus we might take a more contemporary spin on Cornell West's notion of a "jazz freedom fighter" and conceive of the "funky freedom fighter."

With an understanding of the values and ideals associated with The Funk—such as freedom, faith, unity, strength, creativity, and the ubiquity of the dance—we can take West's "jazz freedom fighter" to the streets. It's clear that an understanding of The Funk serves as a guidepost for understanding the graphic realities of street rap—and by extension, the graphic realities of street life. (The harsh, desperate imagery of Funkadelic's "Maggot Brain" or War's "The World Is a Ghetto" were precursors to the violent and insular "ghettocentric" words of hard-core rap.) With an understanding of The Funk, one can move and groove with the most ruthless rap tracks, and accept them as bittersweet expressions of an authentic funk flow.

Since 1988, Hip Hop has strived to emulate the musical and social values of The Funk. And since funk music rests at its core, even the rap music that has failed to represent what some would call "meaningful" values can still be analyzed in informed, useful terms. While rap has for years been dismissed as nonmusical and unworthy of serious ethnomusicological analysis, The Funk can readily be linked with the musical traditions of the black past. Thus, the birth, growth, and *strength* of rap music on the streets, with all of its seemingly inexplicable violence and despair, can be connected to a tradition of music, to a tradition of resistance, and to a timeless yearning for justice, satisfaction, and belonging that has evolved with each generation of black artists. By absorbing the past and present, empowered by the timely strength of modern rap and fortified by the rich traditions inherent in The Funk, one is given knowledge of self, knowledge of the streets—and is ready for *anything*.

### FUNKATEERS

Artists from a variety of worlds have zeroed in on the pulse of The Funk, from the late-night CBS talk show bandleader Paul Shaffer to R. U. Sirius, the editor of the groundbreaking cyberpunk magazine *Mondo 2000*. George Clinton's P-Funk All Stars constantly tour the college circuit, emphasizing the monster rock chords of Funkadelic and galvanizing a young, mostly white following that will do anything for The Funk. In addition to the many artists mentioned in this book, there are rabid funk fans—people who pursue The Funk as a way of life—from all walks of life, and the corps of funk freedom fighters is growing.

Across the country and around the world, funk fans have taken to heart the idealistic philosophies and cartoon-minded fantasies of the great funk bands and internalized them for their own use. Funkateers come from all walks of life—business and industry, entertainment, sports, the academy, the streets, and prisons. The Funk is everywhere, and people are being cloned on a daily basis. Typically, a live performance of the P-Funk Mob is necessary for such an introduction, but properly indulged recordings often are sufficient for producing the same effects. Funkateers are dedicated to the pursuit of The Funk, whether it is following the bands, buying the records, producing new music and art, or writing books.

They come up with absurd and irreverent funk names—alter egos for a cartoonish existence that perpetuates the freaky and indulgent P-Funk universe. Groovy, P-Funk-sounding names like "Liquid," "Zoot-Zilla," "Mr. P," "Satellite," "Air-Child," "Dr. Illinstine," and "The Uhuru Maggot" are but a few of the thousands of cloned funkateers who have made the pursuit of The Funk a way of life. The sage funk philosopher Patrick "Sledhicket" Norwood explained his mission of funk in this uptight world: "People in the world are acting ridiculous trying to be serious. What we need to do is get serious about being *ridiculous.*"

Others take their love for The Funk to more legitimate uses, such as screenwriter and former *Washington Post* journalist David Mills's ambitious and engaging self-published funk journal *Uncut Funk,* and German music journalist and funk fan Peter Jebsen's efforts to consolidate The Funk with the publication of the *New Funk Times.* Funk is by its very nature an active ideal, and funkateers tend to act on their groovallegiance. Indeed, Mills, Jebsen, and others have internalized the P-Funk adage: "Ask not what funk can do for you, but what you can do for The Funk!"

There is a whole universe of funk to explore, and this book is just one attempt to go "all around the world for the funk." While it would be impossible to make a comprehensive analysis of a vibe that permeates all walks of life, I hope this opening salvo has tweaked your interest. This entire project was designed not so much to *explain* The Funk, but to *indulge* in it, to savor its tangy tastes, its meaty flesh, the bitter pits, and the sweet desserts, keeping in mind that the nutrition provided in this book can energize your own pursuit of The Funk, and get you *over the hump.*

# Essential Funk Recordings

The Funk Album is a collection of grooves, jams, ballads, riffs, and attitudes that brings all of the musical forces together. While anything can be played in a funky way, there are some records that are unique and comprehensive expressions of a funk philosophy, or are simply irresistible groove sessions that must be acknowledged. Albums in this list are graded as follows:

*** = Superior—Good grooves and good ideas, but could improve.

**** = Monster—Killer grooves, *and* a total listening experience.

***** = Classic—Must listen to it, or you're faking the funk!

Some of the albums are diverse, while some are all-funk. Commentary explains the flavor of each record. Compilations and greatest-hits packages are not emphasized, and only referred to when an album extends the base of the artist's catalog. Apologies to artists left off of this list. Albums available on CD in the U.S. market as of 1995 are noted on the right.

# CHAPTER 5 / THE 1960S: IF 6 WAS 9

## Essential Funk Albums of the 1960s

| RATING | YR | ARTIST | ALBUM TITLE | COMMENTS | |
|---|---|---|---|---|---|
| **** | 63 | James Brown / | Live at the Apollo | hottest jam of all time | |
| ***** | 67 | Aretha Franklin / | Never Loved a Man | the quintessential Aretha, features "Respect" | CD |
| **** | 68 | Aretha Franklin / | Aretha Now | Aretha gets down and fonky | |
| ***** | 68 | Sly and the Family Stone / | Dance to the Music | undeniable vibe, monster grooves | CD |
| ****** | 69 | Sly and the Family Stone / | Stand! | the original funk album, a classic | CD |
| *** | 69 | James Brown / | Say It Loud . . . | breakthrough funk session, includes "Licking Stick" | |
| ***** | 69 | James Brown / | It's a Mother | scandalous proto-funk rhythms | CD |
| ***** | 69 | Isaac Hayes / | Hot Buttered Soul | extended soul/rock workouts | CD |
| ***** | 67 | The Beatles / | Sgt. Pepper's Lonely Hearts Club Band | groovy psychedelic rock and proto-funk | |

# CHAPTER 6 / THE RHYTHM REVOLUTION: TIGHTEN UP

## Essential Rhythm Revolution Albums

| RATING | YR | ARTIST | ALBUM TITLE | COMMENTS | |
|---|---|---|---|---|---|
| *** | 65 | James Brown / | Papa's Got a Brand New Bag | rhythmic madness made sense | |
| **** | 67 | The Bar-Kays / | Soul Finger | Memphis groove at its stankiest | CD |
| **** | 67 | Mar-Keys and Booker T & the MGs / | Back to Back | utterly stanky jam session | |
| ***** | 69 | The Meters / | Here Come The Meters | classic nonstop hard-core funk riffs | |
| ****** | 70 | Charles Wright and the Watts 103rd Street Rhythm Band / | Express Yourself | grooving masterpiece of soul and rhythm | |
| *** | 73 | Manu Dibango / | Soul Makossa | African funk at its best | |
| ***** | 82 | James Brown / | Can Your Heart Stand It! | one of the nastyest compilations ever | |
| ***** | 85 | Atlantic Rhythm & Blues / | Atlantic Rhythm & Blues Vol. 6 (1966-69) | all-star lineup of smelly soul | |
| **** | 88 | Stax / | Son of Stax Funk | even more stankier Stax hits | CD |
| *** | 94 | Rhino / | Roots of Funk Vol. 1/2 | worthy proto-funk selections, includes "Funky Broadway" | CD |

## Essential James Brown Funk Albums

| Stars | Year | Album / Description | CD |
|---|---|---|---|
| ***½ | 68 | Live at the Apollo Vol. II   *side two workout says it all about the birth of funk* | |
| *** | 69 | Say It Loud   *mixes proto-funk with soulful ballads* | |
| **** | 69 | It's a Mother   *primordial funk at its best* | |
| ***** | 70 | It's a New Day . . .   *churning groove tracks define the original funk* | CD |
| ***** | 70 | Sex Machine   *relentless funk workout featuring Bootsy and Catfish Collins* | CD |
| ***** | 70 | Superbad   *uneven jam session features ten intense minutes of "Superbad"* | CD |
| ***** | 71 | Hot Pants   *naked grooves that won't quit. CD has twenty-minute mix of hot pants* | CD |
| ***** | 72 | There It Is   *tight, socially conscious and ruthless grooves* | CD |
| ***** | 72 | Get on the Good Foot   *extended, uneven, but jams like crazy* | CD |
| ***** | 73 | Black Caesar   *wicked if understated rhythm session* | CD |
| ***** | 73 | Slaughter's Big Rip-Off   *instrumental teaser still packs a punch* | CD |
| ****** | 74 | The Payback   *relentless double barrel of classic funk tracks. The BOMB* | |
| ***½ | 74 | Hell   *extended, diverse selections that kick the groove* | |
| ***½ | 74 | Reality   *great arrangements. Includes "Funky President"* | |
| ***** | 75 | Sex Machine '75   *forgotten masterwork of stanky, sweaty, extended jams* | |
| *** | 76 | Get Up Offa That Thang   *hits and misses* | |
| *** | 77 | Body Heat   *James still has it, but only here and there* | |
| *** | 76 | Mutha's Nature   *quirky and not well-produced* | |
| **** | 78 | Jam 1980s   *straight dance jams get the job done—"Nature," "jam," and "Spank" all hit* | |
| *** | 79 | For Goodness Sakes . . .   *twelve-minute title jam one of the Godfather's nastayest* | |
| ***** | 72 | JBs / Food for Thought   *masters of the rhythm tracks in full effect, including the grunt* | CD |
| ***** | 73 | Fred Wesley & the JBs / Doin' It to Death   *title says it all* | CD |
| ****** | 74 | Fred Wesley & the JBs / Damn Right I Am Somebody   *funk rhythm masterpiece—taken from Payback sessions* | CD |
| ***** | 75 | Fred Wesley & the JBs / Breakin' Bread   *the last Fred Wesley sessions; complex yet loose* | |
| **** | 74 | Maceo & the Macks / Us   *complex and unrelenting funk assault* | |

CHAPTER 8 / THE FAMILY STONED: I WANNA TAKE YOU HIGHER

Essential Sly and the Family Stone Albums

## Essential Black Rock Albums

| Rating | Year | CD | Album | Description |
|---|---|---|---|---|
| ***** | 67 | CD | Jimi Hendrix / Are You Experienced? | *original psychedelic blues. The tip of the iceberg* |
| ****** | 68 | CD | Jimi Hendrix / Axis: Bold as Love | *depressing and inspiring, throbbing and floating . . .* |
| ****** | 68 | CD | Jimi Hendrix / Electric Ladyland | *time traveling, consciousness-warping opus* |
| ****** | 70 | CD | Jimi Hendrix / Band of Gypsys | *Hendrix, Billy Cox, and Buddy Miles at their funkayest* |
| | | | Jimi Hendrix / All other recordings | |
| ***** | 70 | CD | Funkadelic / Funkadelic | *spacey, grooving, nasty classic* |
| ***** | 70 | CD | Funkadelic / Free Your Mind and Your Ass Will Follow | *searing, dark masterwork* |
| ***** | 71 | CD | Funkadelic / Maggot Brain | *the ultimate Funkadelic* |
| | | | Funkadelic / All other recordings (See Chapters 17 and 18) | |
| **** | 71 | CD | Ohio Players / Pain | *twisting, swarming splatter of genius* |
| **** | 72 | | Ohio Players / Pleasure | *powerful and diverse, features "Funky Worm"* |
| **** | 73 | | Ohio Players / Ecstasy | *nasty, stomping, sizzling fonk* |
| *** | 74 | | Ohio Players / Climax | *stanky instrumental workouts* |
| *** | 68 | | Muddy Waters / Electric Mud | *electric blues at its best* |
| *** | 70 | | Buddy Miles Express / Them Changes | *left Jimi and kept kickin'* |
| ***** | 71 | | Buddy Miles Express / Message to the People . . . | *grooving, soulful, and rocking* |
| ***** | 69 | CD | Sly and the Family Stone / Stand! | *the standard for funk-rock fusion* |
| **** | 69 | | Isaac Hayes / Hot Buttered Soul | *extended brooding ballads redefine soul and rock* |
| ***** | 70 | | Bar-Kays / Gotta Groove | *awesome instrumental jam session* |
| *** | 71 | CD | Isaac Hayes / Shaft soundtrack | *defined the seventies sound, features Bar-Kays at their best* |
| *** | 71 | CD | Bar-Kays / Black Rock | *defining workouts for ex-backup act. Thick, but raggedy* |
| *** | 73 | | Bar-Kays / Coldblooded | *solid set of twisted, brooding, bluesy funk* |
| **** | 70 | | Mandrill / Mandrill | *disarming extremes of Afro-pop, rock, and funk in one package* |
| **** | 72 | | Mandrill / Mandrill Is | *stirring synthesis and thick chops* |
| **** | 73 | | Mandrill / Composite Truth | *multifaceted and memorable, on the verge of superstardom* |

| | | | |
|---|---|---|---|
| *** | 73 | Mandrill / Just Outside of Town    catchy, punchy, creative, and tight | |
| *** | 71 | Isley Brothers / Givin' It Back    all acoustic covers of rock standards. Unique and compelling | |
| *** | 72 | Isley Brothers / Brother, Brother, Brother    folksy, soulful, and meaningful | CD |
| *** | 73 | Isley Brothers / 3+3 Featuring "That Lady"    introduces younger Isleys, and jams | CD |
| ****** | 74 | Isley Brothers / Live It Up    blends rock, funk, soul, and blues brilliantly. A masterwork | CD |
| ****** | 71 | War / All Day Music    awesome latin funk mix features "Slipping into Darkness" | CD |
| ****** | 72 | War / The World Is a Ghetto    Grammy-winning masterpiece of grooves and realism | CD |
| ***** | 73 | War / Deliver the Word    no pop hits, but still hits powerful grooves | 2 CDs |
| ***** | 74 | War / War Live    brilliant live set recorded in 1972 Chicago snowstorm | CD |
| ***** | 75 | War / Why Can't We Be Friends?    catchy, charming, and diverse | CD |
| ****** | 76 | War / War's Greatest Hits    all-time jams and disc logo a cultural artifact | CD |
| ****** | 77 | War / Platinum Jazz    best of instrumental jams, plus many new ones. A monster | CD |
| *** | 70 | Santana / Santana    mind-blowing expanse of rhythm, rock riffs, and stirring vocals | CD |
| ***** | 71 | Santana / Abraxas    fierce instrumental jams, and latin rock classic "Oye Como Va" | CD |
| *** | 72 | Santana / Santana    captures west-coast rock and soul flavors while still kicking jams | |
| ***** | 73 | Graham Central Station / Graham Central Station    indescribably delicious soulful rock | |
| ***** | 74 | Graham Central Station / Release Yourself    hard, deep, gospel-flavored rock and funk | |
| ***** | 75 | Graham Central Station / Ain't No Bout a Doubt It    throbbing funk opus. Features "The Jam" | |
| *** | 76 | Graham Central Station / Mirror    crazy funk and apocalyptic gospel-rock | |
| ***** | 77 | Graham Central Station / Now Do You Wanta Dance    misnamed funk-rock blowout | |
| ***** | 78 | Graham Central Station / My Radio Sure Sounds Good to Me    old-school vibe in stellar funk age | CD |
| ***** | 76 | Johnny Guitar Watson / Ain't That a Bitch    stylish and sassy masterpiece | CD |
| ***** | 77 | Johnny Guitar Watson / A Real Mother for Ya    strong and snappy follow-up | CD |

## Essential Funky Soul LPs

| Rating | Year | Artist / Album | Description | Format |
|---|---|---|---|---|
| **** | 68 | Ray Charles / The Essential Ray Charles | works out in any format. Can't miss | CD |
| *** | 70 | Temptations / Cloud Nine | stirring breakthrough of psychedelic Motown | |
| *** | 72 | Temptations / Psychedelic Shack | spacey, deep, and grooving | CD |
| *** | 72 | Temptations / All Directions | grooving, kicking, and deep | CD |
| *** | 75 | Temptations / Song For You | monstrous. Features P-Funkers E. Hazel and B. Nelson | CD |
| ***** | 70 | Undisputed Truth / Undisputed Truth | underrated psychedelic soul masterpiece. Features "Smiling Faces" | CD |
| *** | 71 | Stevie Wonder / Music of My Mind | oozing, subconscious exploration | CD |
| ***** | 72 | Stevie Wonder / Talking Book | liquid soul-funk genius | CD |
| ****** | 73 | Stevie Wonder / Innervisions | the all-time funk-soul album | CD |
| ***** | 74 | Stevie Wonder / Fulfillingness' First Finale | meticulous, masterful creation | CD |
| ****** | 76 | Stevie Wonder / Songs in the Key of Life | endless, elaborate opus | CD |
| ****** | 71 | Marvin Gaye / What's Goin' On | political, moral manifesto of soul | CD |
| ***** | 73 | Marvin Gaye / Let's Get It On | erotic, exquisite manifesto of sexuality | CD |
| ***** | 75 | Marvin Gaye / I Want You | breathy package of grooving genius | CD |
| ***** | 79 | Marvin Gaye / Here, My Dear | bittersweet palate of sweetly layered groove | CD |
| ***** | 70 | Donny Hathaway / Everything Is Everything | flowing, strong, and deep. Features "The Ghetto" | |
| ****** | 75 | Barry White / Greatest Hits | sexy, strong, and thick. Awesome | |
| *** | 72 | Aretha Franklin / Young, Gifted and Black | inconsistent but daring. Includes "Rock Steady" | |
| ***** | 72 | Curtis Mayfield / Superfly Soundtrack | definitive funky soul soundtrack | CD |
| ***** | 73 | The New Birth / Birth Day | grooving and raw | CD |
| *** | 73-78 | MFSB / Best of Phase I | compilation of catchy instrumental grooves | |
| ***** | 72 | O'Jays / Back Stabbers | intricate and compelling soul manifesto | CD |
| ***** | 74 | O'Jays / Ship Ahoy | powerful, artistic, consciousness-raising session | CD |
| *** | 75 | O'Jays / Survival | punchy and street-smart package of soul-funk | |
| **** | 76 | O'Jays / Family Reunion | heartfelt synthesis of Gamble & Huff brilliance. Also jams | |

## Essential Jazz-Funk Albums

| | | | | |
|---|---|---|---|---|
| *** | 70 | Miles Davis / Bitches Brew | oozing, primordial proto-funk | |
| ***** | 71 | Miles Davis / Jack Johnson | hard rock under the label of jazz | |
| ***** | 71 | Miles Davis / Live at Fillmore | scorching, thrashing splatter | |
| *** | 73 | Miles Davis / On the Corner | Miles doing his best to reach the kids. Dissonant, irreverent jam session | |
| *** | 74 | Miles Davis / Big Fun | Miles trying again to reach the youth. Spacey and slick | |
| ****** | 75 | Miles Davis / Aghartha and Pangea | Live masterwork from Japan. His last for over five years | |
| *** | 81 | Miles Davis / The Man with the Horn | underrated comeback album for Miles. Features "Fat Time" | |
| *** | 83 | Miles Davis / You're Under Arrest | flashes of brilliance, flashes of the end to come | |
| ****** | 93 | Miles Davis / Doo Bop | original hip hop jazz. Slickest, tightest, hardest jam session of 1993! | CD |
| ****** | 73 | Herbie Hancock / Headhunters | magnificent and defining fusion of jazz and funk | |
| *** | 74 | Herbie Hancock / Thrust | grooving and experimental workouts | |
| ***** | 75 | Herbie Hancock / Man-Child | well-packaged, with slick and sharp funky jams | CD |
| ***** | 76 | Herbie Hancock / Secrets | diverse masterwork of moods, grooves, and jazz-funk riffs | CD |
| *** | 77 | Herbie Hancock / V.S.O.P. | Very Special Onetime Performance includes nasty funk sides | |
| *** | 78 | Herbie Hancock / Sunlight | somewhat digitized treatment of jazzy dance music | |
| ****** | 79 | Herbie Hancock / Feets Don't Fail Me Now | underrated masterpiece of disco and funk | CD |
| ****** | 75 | Headhunters / Survival of the Fittest | vicious, scandalous, twisted funk stew | |
| ***** | 74 | Crusaders / Southern Comfort | vast and intensely creative two-disc set of funky jazz | |
| ***** | 75 | Crusaders / Chain Reaction | tight, thumping liquid flow | |
| *** | 73 | Donald Byrd / Blackbyrd | pioneering grooving jazz session with R&B backup | |
| *** | 75 | Donald Byrd / Places and Spaces | tight package of slick funk and easy jazz | |
| ***** | 74 | Blackbyrds / The Blackbyrds | brilliant, fluid groove session introduces instant stars | |
| ***** | 75 | Blackbyrds / Flying Start | smoothly packaged set includes pop hit "Walking in Rhythm" | |
| ****** | 75 | Blackbyrds / City Life | wild and highly creative set of Monster Jams. Essential | |
| *** | 76 | Blackbyrds / Unfinished Business | slicker and smoother. Kicks but doesn't elevate | |

| Rating | Artist / Album | Description | CD | Year |
|---|---|---|---|---|
| **** | Ramsey Lewis / Sun Goddess | wild flavors of jazz, funk, and percussive groove | CD | 75 |
| *** | Ramsey Lewis / Don't It Feel Good | thumping, focused set of thick funk-jazz | | 76 |
| **** | Ramsey Lewis / Salongo | elegant and diverse | | 77 |
| **** | Minnie Riperton / Adventures in Paradise | warm and joyous, deceptively funky and sexy | | 75 |
| **** | Quincy Jones / Body Heat | steamy, gurgling swamp of funky soul and jazz | | 74 |
| **** | Quincy Jones / Mellow Madness | varied and rich, with touches of nastayness | | 75 |
| **** | Grover Washington, Jr. / Mr. Magic | exquisitely groovy; definitive funky soul-jazz | CD | 75 |
| ***** | Grover Washington, Jr. / Feels So Good | monstrous. Hard and thick | CD | 76 |
| ***** | Grover Washington, Jr. / Reed Seed | blends with band Locksmith to bring funky jazz to its peak | | 77 |
| ***** | Grover Washington, Jr. / Live at the Bijou | an elevated level of warmth, technique, and funk groove | | 77 |
| **** | George Duke / Reach for It | smorgasbord of styles, topped off with monster jam "Reach for It" | CD | 77 |
| **** | George Duke / Don't Let Go | slicker, smoother, and even nastayer | CD | 78 |
| **** | Stanley Clarke / School Days | most thoroughly thumpalistic funk sessions | CD | 76 |
| *** | Return to Forever / No Mystery | elaborate and spastic set of funky jazz-fusion | | 75 |
| *** | Weather Report / 8:30 | best example of bassist Pastorious's mutant grooves and band's warped senses | CD | 78 |
| *** | Tower of Power / East Bay Grease | sloppy and raggedy horn-heavy R&B. Smelly | CD | 70 |
| **** | Tower of Power / Tower of Power | unbridled mastery of funk, jazz, and soul styles | | 73 |
| *** | Tower of Power / Back to Oakland | inspired workouts | | 74 |
| *** | Tower of Power / Urban Renewal | can't miss session of catchy jams | | 74 |
| *** | Tower of Power / Live And In Living Color | out of control workouts still jam | | 76 |
| ****** | Pleasure / Joyous | forgotten masterpiece of flavors and styles | | 77 |
| *** | Pleasure / Future Now | rugged and thumping jam session. Features "Glide" | | 78 |
| ***** | Ornette Coleman / Virgin Beauty | twisted, grooving, harmolodic funk | CD | 88 |
| ****** | Defunkt / Defunkt | propulsive and stinky | CD | 80 |
| **** | Defunkt / Thermonuclear Sweat | scandalous, rugged riffs. Features Vernon Reid's guitar | CD | 82 |
| *** | James "Blood" Ulmer / Black Rock | spastic and irreverent guitar noise | | 81 |
| *** | Mike Clark and Paul Jackson / The Funk Stops Here | the funk kicks here | CD | 92 |

CHAPTER 12 / POWER TO THE PEOPLE: IT'S JUST BEGUN

Essential Black Power Albums

| | | | | |
|---|---|---|---|---|
| ****** | 71 | James Brown / Revolution of the Mind | *quintessential live LP of Brown's political era* | CD |
| **** | 70 | Curtis Mayfield / Curtis | *scorching, purposeful, and rich* | |
| *** | 70 | Curtis Mayfield / Roots | *heartfelt and somber* | |
| **** | 71 | Curtis Mayfield / Curtis Live | *powerfully hopeful* | |
| **** | 73 | Bill Withers / Bill Withers Live | *radical, yet touching* | |
| **** | 69 | Gil Scott-Heron / Small Talk at 125 St. & Lenox | *vicious anti-establishment rap* | CD |
| **** | 70 | Gil Scott-Heron / Pieces of a Man | *from sentimental jazz to revolutionary poetry* | CD |
| **** | 74 | Gil Scott-Heron / The First Minute of a New Day | *richly musical, and deeply political* | |
| **** | 75 | Gil Scott-Heron / Winter in America | *bittersweet and introspective* | |
| ****** | 81 | Gil Scott-Heron / Reflections | *cutthroat assault on Reagan* | CD |
| ****** | 70 | The Last Poets / The Last Poets | *as nasty and truthful as it gets* | CD |
| ***** | 71 | The Last Poets / This Is Madness | *thematic, truthful, and balls to the wall* | CD |
| *** | 72 | Lightnin' Rod / Hustler's Convention | *the original gangsta rap track* | |

CHAPTER 14 / UNITED FUNK: THE SHINING STAR

Essential United Funk Albums

| | | | |
|---|---|---|---|
| **** | 72 | Jimmy Castor Bunch / It's Just Begun | *brilliant, grooving, and diverse* |
| *** | 74 | Jimmy Castor Bunch / Butt, of Course | *silly, thick groove sessions* |
| *** | 75 | Jimmy Castor Bunch / The Everything Man | *ruthless stomp-fest, like all his later LPs* |
| **** | 70 | Kool & the Gang / Kool & the Gang | *rhythmic, horn-heavy instrumental jam blowout* |
| **** | 71 | Kool & the Gang / Live at the Sex Machine | *grooving, meaningful, meticulous funk session* |
| **** | 72 | Kool & the Gang / Music Is the Message | *catchy and polyrhythmic set of lovable jams* |

| Rating | Year | Artist / Album | Description | CD |
|---|---|---|---|---|
| **** | 73 | Kool & the Gang / Good Times | tight, snappy, soulful, and brilliant | |
| ***** | 73 | Kool & the Gang / Wild & Peaceful | masterful package of grooving funk, jazz, and messages. All-time | |
| ***** | 74 | Kool & the Gang / Light of Worlds | jazz and funk fused with finesse. A classic, including "Summer Madness" | CD |
| **** | 75 | Kool & the Gang / Spirit of the Boogie | ruthlessly creative, deceptively spiritual. A crime it's not on CD | |
| ***½ | 76 | Kool & the Gang / Love and Understanding | classy jam sessions from New York and London. Icy | |
| **** | 76 | Kool & the Gang / Open Sesame | spiritual, avante-garde, deep funk | |
| ***** | 80 | Kool & the Gang / Spin Their Top Hits | best available package of KG favorites | |
| **** | 70 | Earth, Wind & Fire / Earth, Wind & Fire | snappy, well-balanced teaser of what's to come | CD |
| **** | 73 | Earth, Wind & Fire / Head to the Sky | extended, layered grooving and meaningful jams | CD |
| **** | 74 | Earth, Wind & Fire / Open Our Eyes | the complete package of soul, funk, and jazz | CD |
| ***** | 75 | Earth, Wind & Fire / That's the Way of the World | has everything. The ultimate seventies album | CD |
| ***** | 76 | Earth, Wind & Fire / Gratitude | the ultimate live sessions. An all-time classic | CD |
| **** | 77 | Earth, Wind & Fire / All & All | complex and intense package. Their funkayest | CD |
| ****** | 74 | Average White Band / AWB | pulls it all together from the start. A classic | CD |
| *** | 75 | Average White Band / Cut the Cake | snappy hits, here and there | |
| ***** | 76 | Average White Band / Soul Searching | underrated masterpiece of moods, soul, and funk | CD |
| *** | 76 | Average White Band / Person to Person | loose live sessions do the trick, but could have done more | |
| *** | 74 | Rufus featuring Chaka Khan / Rags to Rufus | wild, clumsy mix that includes classic Rufus funk | |
| **** | 75 | Rufus featuring Chaka Khan / Rufusized | total package of soulful funk, warm snappy grooves | CD |
| **** | 76 | Rufus Featuring Chaka Khan / Rufus Featuring Chaka Khan | brilliant jam sessions and ballads | CD |
| ***** | 77 | Rufus Featuring Chaka Khan / Ask Rufus | classy and subdued work of art | CD |
| ****** | 74 | Isley Brothers / Live It Up | underrated masterpiece of rock, blues, soul, and funk | |
| **** | 75 | Isley Brothers / The Heat Is On | deserving classic. All jams on side A, ballads on B | CD |
| ***** | 76 | Isley Brothers / Harvest for the World | classy package of some of their best material | CD |
| ***** | 77 | Isley Brothers / Go for Your Guns | non-stop barrage of open-fire funk | CD |
| **** | 78 | Isley Brothers / Showdown | grooving, locked-tight package of A-1 funk tracks | |
| *** | 79 | Isley Brothers / Winner Takes All | extended workouts still fill two LPs with jams | |
| **** | 72 | Ohio Players / Pleasure | powerful and diverse. Features "Funky Worm" | CD |

| Rating | Year | Artist / Title | Description | Format |
|---|---|---|---|---|
| ***** | 74 | Ohio Players / Skin Tight | *fantastic fusion of slick and nasty, standard and strange jams* | CD |
| ***** | 75 | Ohio Players / Fire | *even more originality, catchy licks, and killer jam factors* | CD |
| **** | 75 | Ohio Players / Honey | *intensely creative set of classic jams* | CD |
| *** | 76 | Ohio Players / Contradiction | *inconsistent but shows genius* | |
| **** | 76 | Ohio Players / Gold | *essential compilation of the best of the last four years* | CD |
| **** | 77 | Ohio Players / Angel | *inspired, slightly looser mix of band's magical vibe* | CD |
| ***** | 74 | Commodores / Machine Gun | *unknown, brilliant package of vicious funk* | |
| **** | 76 | Commodores / Hot on the Tracks | *catchy, varied mix of uniquely funky soul jams* | CD |
| **** | 77 | Commodores / The Commodores | *tight, funky tracks with pop appeal, featuring "Brick House"* | CD |

# CHAPTER 16 / DANCE FUNK: DO YOU WANNA GET FUNKY WITH ME?

## Essential Dance Funk

| Rating | Year | Artist / Title | Description | Format |
|---|---|---|---|---|
| *** | 74 | K.C. and the Sunshine Band / K.C. and the Sunshine Band | *energetic breakthrough dance track sessions* | CD |
| *** | 75 | K.C. and the Sunshine Band / Part 3 | *brain-dead boogie at its best* | CD |
| **** | 75 | Brass Construction / Brass Construction | *surprisingly stanky. Classic jams "Movin'," and "Changin',"* | |
| ***** | 76 | Brass Construction / II | *even more surprisingly diverse and original* | CD |
| ***** | 75 | B.T. Express / Do It 'Til You're Satisfied | *utterly awesome dinosaur funk* | |
| *** | 74 | Fatback / Yum Yum | *stirring mix of funk and disco at the crossroads* | |
| *** | 80 | Fatback / Hot Box | *best session includes biggest hits "Backstrokin'," and "Gotta Get My Hands On Some Money"* | CD |
| *** | 79 | Chic / C'est Chic | *slick and tight. Too slick* | CD |
| *** | 80 | Chic / Good Times | *massive and influential at the time. Useless musically* | CD |
| **** | 79 | Michael Jackson / Off the Wall | *original and awesome funk sessions reclaim pop throne* | CD |
| *** | 75 | Rose Royce / Car Wash | *prototype of disco-dance soundtrack record, still kicks* | |
| *** | 77 | Rose Royce / In Full Bloom | *well-packaged funky soul* | |
| **** | 77 | Maze / Maze featuring Frankie Beverly | *stirring, down-home sound* | CD |

| Rating | Year | Entry | CD |
|---|---|---|---|
| **** | 79 | Maze / Inspiration   best funky soul since Marvin Gaye | CD |
| ***** | 80 | Maze / Joy and Pain   flowing, inspired funky soul masterwork | CD |
| *** | 76 | Heatwave / Too Hot to Handle   snazzy, soulful, and sharp | CD |
| **** | 77 | Heatwave / Central Heating   complete package of high-energy riffs and soulful snippets | CD |
| ***** | 76 | Brothers Johnson / Look Out for #1   unmitigated masterpiece | |
| **** | 78 | Brothers Johnson / Right on Time   well-produced session of lite-funk | |
| **** | 79 | Brothers Johnson / Blam!   thick and phat | |
| **** | 77 | Cameo / Cardiac Arrest   stanky, unique, and very happening | CD |
| **** | 78 | Cameo / We All Know Who We Are   meanly grooving, original sessions | |
| **** | 79 | Cameo / Ugly Ego   exquisitely stanky mess of throbbing funk licks | |
| *** | 80 | Cameo / Secret Omen   disappointing disco mishmash does salvage itself with "I Just Wanta Be" | |
| **** | 76 | Brick / Good High   catchy, creative, and quirky cuts support all time monster jam "Dazz" | |
| ***** | 77 | Brick / Brick   delectable set of massively thumping funk classics | |
| **** | 77 | Slave / Slave   ruthless groove workouts and outrageous effects | |
| ***½ | 78 | Slave / The Hardness of the World   subdued yet lethal in parts | |
| ***** | 79 | Slave / The Concept   awesome scorching workouts and brooding, hypnotic groove tracks | |
| *** | 80 | Slave / Just a Touch of Love   slick and uninspired, yet still kicks in places | |
| **** | 76 | Bar-Kays / Too Hot to Stop   non-stop session of all-beef funk and soul tracks | |
| *** | 77 | Bar-Kays / Flying High on Your Love   smoother mix still gets rough here and there | |
| **** | 78 | Bar-Kays / Money Talks   resurrected from Stax vaults delivers deadly dinosaur funk licks | |
| **** | 78 | Bar-Kays / Light of Life   tight mix of catchy and upbeat grooves | |
| *** | 77 | Con Funk Shun / Secrets   uneven showcase for first hit "Ffun" | |
| **** | 78 | Con Funk Shun / Loveshine   smooth, delicate masterpiece of sweet funky soul | |
| *** | 79 | Con Funk Shun / Candy   rougher, thicker, and stankier set | |
| **** | 75 | Undisputed Truth / Cosmic Truth   out the box, Funkadelic wanna-bes still hit | |
| **** | 75 | Undisputed Truth / Method to the Madness   inspired lunacy | |
| **** | 77 | Undisputed Truth / Higher Than High   sloppy and comically nasty | |
| *** | 77 | War / Galaxy   unrelenting thump-fest proves band's resilience | CD |

## Essential P-Funk Hit Albums

| | | | | |
|---|---|---|---|---|
| ***** | 74 | Parliament / Up for the Down Stroke | unheralded erotic adventure | CD |
| **** | 75 | Parliament / Chocolate City | twisted, scalding sessions of harmony and groove | CD |
| ****** | 75 | Parliament / Mothership Connection | divine funk | CD |
| ****** | 76 | Parliament / Clones of Dr. Funkenstein | the resurrection of divine funk | CD |
| ****** | 77 | Parliament / Funkentelechy vs. the Placebo Syndrome | new age has dawned | CD |
| ***** | 78 | Parliament / Motor Booty Affair | divinely inspired, drug-infested underwater fantasy | CD |
| ***** | 79 | Parliament / Gloryhallastupid | preposterous | |
| ***** | 80 | Parliament / Trombipulation | twisted and irreverent, yet wearing thin | |
| ****** | 76 | Bootsy's Rubber Band / Stretchin' Out | rhythmically assaulting debut of number-one funkateer | |
| ****** | 77 | Bootsy's Rubber Band / Aah The Name Is Bootsy, Baby | nastayest record ever made | |
| ***** | 78 | Bootsy's Rubber Band / Bootsy? Player of the Year | bizarre and tight at the same time | |
| ***** | 79 | Bootsy's Rubber Band / This Boot Is Made for Fonkin' | subdued and ill, yet underrated | |
| ****** | 80 | Bootsy's Rubber Band / Ultra Wave | preposterous | |
| ***** | 81 | Bootsy's Rubber Band / The One Giveth . . . | rarely heard gems. A lost classic | |
| ****** | 78 | Funkadelic / One Nation Under a Groove | funk-rock opus | CD |
| *** | 79 | Funkadelic / Uncle Jam Wants You | wild and ragged setup for fifteen minutes of "Knee Deep" | CD |
| ****** | 81 | Sweat Band / Sweat Band | non-stop liquid Bootsy throb. Unbelievable | |
| ***** | 79 | Mutiny / Mutiny on the Mamaship | scandalous manifesto of anti—P-Funk P-Funk! | |
| *** | 80 | Mutiny / Funk Plus the One | working, ripping rhythm session | |
| ***** | 79 | Quazar / Quazar | utterly obnoxious funk chops from spinoff band featuring Brailey & Goins | |
| ***** | 83 | P-Funk All-Stars / Urban Dancefloor Guerillas | underrated package of premo P | CD |
| ****** | 82 | George Clinton / Computer Games | surprisingly groovalistic comeback for the Doctor featuring "Atomic Dog" | CD |
| **** | 83 | George Clinton / U Shouldn't Nuf Bit Fish | ridiculous | CD |
| **** | 85 | George Clinton / Some of My Best Jokes Are Friends | packaged synth-funk at its stankayest | CD |
| *** | 87 | George Clinton / R&B Skeletons in the Closet | brilliant concepts, not brilliant music | CD |

## CHAPTER 18 / THE METAPHYSICS OF P: THE MOTHERSHIP CONNECTION

### Essential Cosmic P-Funk Albums

| | | | |
|---|---|---|---|
| ***** | 70 | Parliament / Osmium *trashy country funk and apocalyptic gospel-rock anthems of salvation* | CD |
| ***** | 77 | Parliament Live / P-Funk Earth Tour *stanky and sanctified, the ultimate live P-Funk recording* | CD |
| ***** | 70 | Funkadelic / Funkadelic *spacey, grooving, nasty classic* | CD |
| ***** | 70 | Funkadelic / Free Your Mind & Your Ass Will Follow *searing, dark masterwork* | CD |
| ***** | 71 | Funkadelic / Maggot Brain *the ultimate Funkadelic* | CD |
| **** | 72 | Funkadelic / America Eats Its Young *crunchy and country-fried filth* | CD |
| **** | 73 | Funkadelic / Cosmic Slop *coherent package of sick, twisted flesh* | CD |
| ***** | 74 | Funkadelic / Standing on the Verge of Gettin' It On *inspired and anthemic* | CD |
| ***** | 75 | Funkadelic / Let's Take It to the Stage *massive groovallegiance. Ultimate P-Funk* | CD |
| ***** | 76 | Funkadelic / Tales of Kidd Funkadelic *swarming liquid stinkfest* | CD |
| **** | 81 | Funkadelic / Electric Spanking of War Babies *politically charged rhythm riot* | CD |
| ***** | 93 | Funkadelic / Music for Your Mother *compilation of warped Westbound 45s includes great notes* | 2 CDs |
| ***** | 78 | Eddie Hazel / Games, Dames and Guitar Thangs *forgotten slab of divine funk* | CD |
| ***** | 95 | Eddie Hazel / Rest in P *unearthed posthumous guitar grooves* | |
| ***** | 79 | Bernie Worrell / All the Woo in the World *eclecticism at the height of P-Funk popularity* | CD |
| *** | 92 | Bernie Worrell / Funk of Ages *creative yet meandering comeback project* | |
| *** | 94 | Bernie Worrell / Blacktronic Science *clumsy mix of jazz and digital funk is still memorable* | CD |
| ***** | 92 | Praxis / Transmutation *modern funk fusion masterpiece, features Bootsy, Bernie, and others* | CD |
| **** | 94 | O.G. Funk / Out of the Dark *Billy "Bass" Nelson goes for his* | CD |

## Eighties Funk

### Essential Naked Funk Albums

| Rating | Year | Artist / Album | Description | CD |
|---|---|---|---|---|
| **** | 78 | Rick James / Come Get It | monstrous debut of a funk dominator | CD |
| *** | 79 | Rick James / Bustin' Out of L-7 | stomping showcase for hit singles | |
| *** | 80 | Rick James / Fire It Up | nasty and on target | CD |
| ***** | 81 | Rick James / Street Songs | inspired anthems of street smart eighties funk | |
| *** | 82 | Rick James / Standing on the Top | uninspired, yet hard-driving | |
| **** | 83 | Rick James / Coldblooded | well-packaged and uniquely arranged | |
| **** | 86 | Rick James / The Flag | surprisingly deep and hard comeback album | |
| **** | 79 | Prince / Prince | subtly titillating exploration of identity of little-known artist | CD |
| **** | 80 | Prince / Dirty Mind | wicked and wild, definitive naked funk | CD |
| *** | 81 | Prince / Controversy | overtly political, overtly nasty | CD |
| ***** | 82 | Prince / 1999 | epic album of social unrest and self-expression | CD |
| **** | 84 | Prince / Purple Rain | pop standards, absurd and incoherent riffs all in one | CD |
| **** | 85 | Prince / Paisley Park | quirky, consistent fantasyscape | CD |
| *** | 86 | Prince / Sign O' The Times | grooving, licking, churning, grinding | CD |
| ***** | 88 | Prince / Lovesexy | stirring, stunning, and sharp | CD |
| **** | 91 | Prince / Diamonds and Pearls | daring diversity, deeper funk. Features "Gett Off" | CD |
| *** | 80 | The Time / The Time | locked tight. As simple as they wanna be | CD |
| *** | 81 | The Time / What Time Is It? | redefined tightness in a band. Introduces Morris Day's persona | CD |
| ***** | 84 | The Time / Ice Cream Castles | surprisingly complete and kicking | CD |
| *** | 89 | The Time / Pandemonium . . . | works, but times have changed | |
| *** | 85 | Jesse Johnson / Jesse Johnson's Revue | slick, liquid, nasty nasty nasty licks | |
| *** | 86 | Jesse Johnson's Revue / Shockadelica | standard set features Sly Stone duet "Crazay" | |
| *** | 88 | Morris Day / Color of Success | ridiculous, pretentious, and totally grooving | |
| *** | 80 | Zapp / Zapp | quirky and cute grooves. Features "More Bounce to the Ounce" | CD |
| ***** | 81 | Zapp / Zapp II | monstrous hooks, ruthless licks. A masterpiece | CD |

| | Year | CD | Artist / Album | Description |
|---|---|---|---|---|
| *** | 82 | | Zapp / Zapp III | stanky and swanging digitized blues |
| *** | 83 | | Zapp / Zapp 4 U | original and energetic. Features "Computer Love" |
| ***** | 81 | | Roger / The Many Facets of Roger | brilliant artist packages, brilliant album |
| *** | 80 | | Slave / Just a Touch of Love | slick and uninspired, yet still kicks in places |
| **** | 81 | | Slave / Stone Jam | thumpasaurus jam session puts it all together |
| **** | 82 | | Slave / Showtime | awesome package of grooving, nastay dance funk |
| *** | 83 | | Steve Arrington / Hall of Fame | ex-Slave singer deservedly kicks his own flavor |
| *** | 85 | | Steve Arrington / Feel So Real | born-again funk in full effect |
| *** | 94 | CD | Slave / Best of Slave | features Arrington solo hits, but not enough stomping Slave jams |
| ***** | 80 | CD | Cameo / Cameosis | complete package of band renewing itself and redefining funk |
| ***** | 81 | CD | Cameo / Knights of the Sound Table | masterful, unrelenting groove session |
| ****** | 82 | | Cameo / Alligator Woman | underrated stroke of new-wave funk genius |
| *** | 84 | CD | Cameo / She's Strange | catchy rap flavor and hard riffs on inconsistent album |
| ***** | 86 | CD | Cameo / Word Up | sparse, swanging monster hit parade |
| *** | 94 | | Cameo / Best of Cameo Funk Essentials | tired mix of eighties funk only |
| *** | 81 | | Lakeside / Fantastic Voyage | thumping, grooving, smelly set |
| *** | 83 | | Lakeside / Untouchables | thumping, grooving, smelly set |
| *** | 84 | | Lakeside / Outrageous | thumping, grooving, smelly set |
| **** | 81 | CD | Bar-Kays / Nightcruising | slick, new, nasty sound elevates ageless band |
| *** | 82 | CD | Bar-Kays / Propositions | assertive, soulful package of naked funk |
| *** | 84 | CD | Bar-Kays / Dangerous | derivative even by Bar-Kays' standards |
| ***** | 89 | CD | Bar-Kays / Animal | surprisingly tight and energetic comeback of funk Methuselahs |
| ***** | 94 | | Bar-Kays / Best of Bar-Kays Funk Essentials | comprehensive and entertaining package |
| ***** | 81 | | Earth, Wind & Fire / Raise! | rough and rugged no-nonsense comeback |
| *** | 83 | | Earth, Wind & Fire / Powerlight | still strong, but running on fumes |
| *** | 87 | | Earth, Wind & Fire / Touch the World | quirky, digitized comeback yet again |
| *** | 82 | | S.O.S. Band / S.O.S. Band | tight and catchy funky pop |
| **** | 84 | | Midnight Star / No Parking on the Dancefloor | polished, pumping funky pop |

## CHAPTER 20 / HIP HOP AND BLACK NOISE: RAISING HELL

### Essential Eighties Underground Funk

| | | | | |
|---|---|---|---|---|
| ***** | 88 | Various / Celluloid Trilogy | awesome cross-section of best underground grooves of the decade | CD |
| **** | 88 | Gettovetts / Missionaries Moving | thoroughly noisy and conceptual industrial New York rap | CD |
| ***** | 92 | Praxis / Transmutation | modern funk fusion masterpiece, features Bootsy, Bernie, and others | |
| *** | 83 | Art of Noise / Who's Afraid Of . . . | best and most thumping industrial funk beats from Britain | CD |
| *** | 82 | Kraftwerk / Numbers | quirky and ethereal digitized funk beats from German trio | CD |
| **** | 81 | Talking Heads / Remain in Light | scandalous, offbeat, nasty new-wave funk | CD |
| **** | 84 | Talking Heads / Speaking in Tongues | deeply thumping funk disguised as modern rock | CD |
| *** | 85 | Talking Heads / Stop Making Sense | live session features keyboard work of guest Bernie Worrell | CD |
| **** | 82 | Tom Tom Club / Tom Tom Club | complex, silly, and cute mix of grooves. Features "Genius of Love" | CD |
| ***** | 82 | Trouble Funk / Drop the Bomb | relentless and totally hype percussion overload | |
| **** | 84 | Trouble Funk / In Times of Trouble | awkward mix of studio efforts and vicious live tracks | |
| ***** | 85 | Trouble Funk / Saturday Night Live | incredible live session. Absolutely essential | CD |
| *** | 87 | Trouble Funk / Trouble Over Here | overproduced disappointment | |
| **** | 85 | Various Go Go bands / Paint the White House Black | strong and stirring set of nasty funk | CD |
| **** | 85 | Various Go Go bands / Good to Go soundtrack | scattered samplings of Go Go from movie Short Fuse | |
| **** | 88 | Looters / Flashpoint | unheralded political funk rock of the future | CD |
| *** | 85 | Red Hot Chili Peppers / Freaky Stylee | wicked and ridiculous. Produced by George Clinton | |
| ***$^{1/2}$ | 88 | Red Hot Chili Peppers / Mother's Milk | tight and yet still preposterous | |
| **** | 92 | Red Hot Chili Peppers / Blood Sugar Sex Magik | deep, strong, and stanky | |
| *** | 88 | Primus / Suck On This | grungy and thick, like all their stuff | |
| *** | 89 | Fishbone / Truth & Soul | tight and spastic, like all their stuff | |
| *** | 88 | Living Colour / Vivid | tight and noisy black-rock breakthrough | |
| *** | 91 | Brand New Heavies / Brand New Heavies | noble effort to bring back real funk and soul | CD |
| **** | 94 | MeChell NdegeOchello / Plantation Lullabies | ruthless bass-driven rap and funk | CD |

Essential P-Funk Hip Hop Albums

| | | | | | |
|---|---|---|---|---|---|
| **** | 86 | Schooly D / Saturday Night, The Album | *loud and comical. One of the original P-funk samplers* | CD |
| ***** | 87 | EPMD / Strictly Business | *icy and thick. Devastating breakthrough LP, first Zapp sample* | CD |
| *** | 88 | EPMD / Unfinished Business | *monster jams and nasty samples* | |
| ***** | 88 | Boogie Down Productions / By All Means Necessary | *brilliant and funky political manifesto* | |
| **** | 89 | Boogie Down Productions / Ghetto Music: The Blueprint of Hip Hop | *crucial political education* | |
| | | All Boogie Down Productions | | |
| **** | 87 | Public Enemy / Yo Bum Rush the Show! | *crucial rock-hard street beats* | CD |
| ***** | 88 | Public Enemy / It Takes a Nation of Millions to Hold Us Back | *anthem of conscious Hip Hop* | CD |
| **** | 90 | Public Enemy / Fear of a Black Planet | *scandalous issues sensibly delivered* | |
| **** | 91 | Public Enemy / Apocalypse '91: The Empire Strikes Black | *sinister and smart* | |
| | | All Public Enemy | | |
| ****** | 89 | De La Soul / 3 Feet High and Rising | *psychedelic hard-core hippie trip of the highest order* | CD |
| *** | 90 | Jungle Brothers / Done by the Forces of Nature | *accessible Afro-centric rap* | CD |
| ***** | 90 | X-Clan / To the East, Blackwards | *assaulting Afro-centric raps and killer funk loops* | CD |
| **** | 93 | Digable Planets / A New Refutation of Time . . . | *eccentric, streetwise, and jazzy, but deep into funk* | CD |
| ****** | 93 | Miles Davis / Doo Bop | *original hip hop jazz. Slickest, tightest, hardest jam session of 1993!* | CD |
| *** | 93 | Arrested Development / 3 Years, 5 Months & 2 Days in the Life of . . . | *liberated, southern-fried rap and country funk* | CD |
| ***** | 89 | Ice-T / Power | *brilliant, historically minded package of nasty L.A. attitude* | CD |
| ****** | 90 | Digital Underground / Sex Packets | *indescribable cartoon-minded funk genius rap* | CD |
| **** | 92 | Digital Underground / Sons of the P | *powerful, far-reaching statement of funk authority* | CD |
| **** | 88 | The D.O.C. / No One Can Do It Better | *scandalous Dr. Dre produced tracks put west coast on the map* | CD |
| **** | 93 | Dr. Dre / The Chronic | *apocalyptic niggerish manifesto, the dominant rap record of '93* | CD |
| **** | 91 | Too Short / Life Is Too Short | *breakthrough pimp-rap from Oakland's own* | CD |
| **** | 89 | N.W.A. / Straight Outta Compton | *devastating gangsta rap showcase* | CD |

**** 91 N.W.A. / NIGGAZ4LIFE  *cuthroat tracks and rhymes*
*** 90 2-Live Crew / As Nasty As They Wanna Be  *ridiculous, filthy, and uneven, but historically important*
**** 91 Paris / The Devil Made Me Do It  *articulate, grooving debut of "Black Panther of Hip Hop"*
***** 92 Kam / Neva Again  *politically charged yet street strong and funky masterpiece*
***** 91 Ice Cube / Death Certificate  *the ultimate in urban indignation*
*** 94 Ice Cube / Lethal Injection  *well-packaged and deeply funk-centered*

Essential Funk Compilations

****** 91 K-Tel "Superbad" *One of the earliest pkgs gets it right the first time.*
****** 91 Priority "All Star Funk" *out of print ace of rare extended P-funk goodies.*
**** 94 Priority "All Star Funk vol. 1" *well-known humps, little p*
***** 94 Priority "All Star Funk: Vol. 2 *Thumpasorus tracks for all occasions.*
****** 93 Polygram "Best of Funk Essentials" *One of the strongest packages ever.*
*** 94 Polygram "Funk Funk: Best of Funk Essentials" vol.2 *lots of leftovers*
****** 93 Rhino "History of Funk" Vol 1 *All-purpose early funk starter kit*
***** 93 Rhino "History of Funk" Vol 2 *Much stanky all-time early 70's classics*
***** 93 Rhino "History of Funk" Vol 3 *Clumsy mix and edits, but still rocks*
***** 93 Rhino "History of Funk" Vol 4 *Tasty, outrageous mix of late 70's jams*
****** 93 Rhino "History of Funk" Vol 5 *Monster pile of raw-dog rare & classic shit*
***** 94 Rhino "Phat Trax Vol 1 *Awesome lineup and rocking mix*
**** 94 Rhino "Phat Trax Vol 2 'One Nation' 12" and other monsters*
**** 94 Rhino "Phat Trax Vol 3 *Hits getting too thin*
**** 95 Priority "Da Funk" *Some bombs, some quirky misses*
**** 95 Priority "Funkdafied" *Crazy splatter of oldies. Who did those notes?*

# Sources and Notes

## 1 INTRODUCTION TO FUNK: THE BOMB

PAGE

3   "If You Got Funk, You Got Style," Funkadelic. Written By G. Clinton, B. Collins, B. Worrell. Tercer-Mundo, Inc. Used by permission.

3   "nothing but sensation" Barry Walters review of George Clinton's *Some of My Best Jokes Are Friends* LP, "Learning to Funk the Bomb," in *The Village Voice,* August 16, 1985, p. 63.

4   "whatever it needs to be, at the time that it is" Interview with George Clinton at KALX radio, 1985.

5   "The dreadful funkiness" *The Bluest Eye,* Toni Morrison, Washington Square Press, New York, NY, 1970, p. 68.

6   "the most natural force in the universe" *The Roots of Soul: The Psychology of Black Expressiveness,* Alfred Pasteur and Ivory L. Toldston, Anchor Press/Doubleday, Garden City, NY, 1982, p. 145. Although out of print, this book was an essential resource.

## 2 FUNK MUSIC: DANCE WIT ME

13   "If it makes you shake your rump it's The Funk." Interview with George Clinton at KALX radio, 1985.

13   "Heaven at Once," Kool & the Gang. Written by Robert Bell, Ronald Bell, George Brown, Dennis Thomas, Robert Mickens, Claydes Smith, Richard Westfield. Copyright © 1973 Warner-Tamerlane Publishing Corp. (BMI) and Gang Music Ltd. All rights administered by Warner-Tamerlane Publishing Corp. (BMI). All rights reserved. Used by permission.

13   "you can construct The Funk." Interview with Fred Wesley, "Lenny Henry Hunts the Funk" episode of *South Bank Show,* Bravo Network, 1992. Used by permission. This was an excellent summation of the history of Funk.

14   "can you do it with feeling, *all night long?*" Interview with Fred Wesley by the author, 1995.

15   "togetherness in motion" *The Complete Book of Composition, Improvisation and Funk Techniques,* Howard Harris, De Mos Music Publications, Houston, TX, 1980, p. 114.

PAGE

16  "Funkadelic conceived the notion of being in the stratosphere and at the same time . . ." "The P-Funk Aesthetic," thesis submitted to UCLA by Michael O'Neal, 1985, p. 8.

17  "an entire school of horn-based . . . groups" Alan Light's liner notes to Earth, Wind & Fire's compilation, *The Eternal Dance,* Columbia Records, 1993.

18  "we used to go in there and *jam groove*" Interview with James "Diamond" Williams of the Ohio Players by Gary Baca of KPFA radio, June 10, 1992.

18  "we were very free, very spontaneous" Maurice White of Earth, Wind & Fire, in liner notes to compilation *The Eternal Dance,* Columbia Records, 1993.

18  "Nobody . . . knew what was going on except the horn players" Clyde Stubbefield on "Lenny Henry Hunts the Funk" episode of *South Bank Show,* Bravo Network, 1992.

18  "rewind the tape and get something out of that" Dr. Dre quoted in *The New Beats,* S. H. Fernando, Jr., Anchor Press/Doubleday, Garden City, NY, 1994, p. 238.

19  "the seventies provided the freedom for black performers to interpret and present . . ." Interview with Portia Maultsby. "The P-Funk Aesthetic," thesis submitted to UCLA by Michael O'Neal, 1985, p. 13.

20  "the strength of the music has been destroyed . . ." D'Angelo Stearnes, in self-published 1990 essay, "The Funk Age." Used by permission.


## 3  MYTHS ABOUT FUNK: ALL THAT IS GOOD IS NASTY

24  "Nasty? I didn't make the rules" Funkadelic, "Mommy What's a Funkadelic," Westbound Records, 1970, Bridgeport Publishing, used by permission.

25  "She's a big freak . . . " Funkadelic, "Freak of the Week." Written by G. Clinton, P. Bishop, D. McKnight. Tercer-Mundo, Inc. Used by permission.

27  "as long as you get great musicians who will play them right" Quoted from Davis, Miles with Troupe, Quincy, *Miles: The Autobiography,* Simon & Schuster, NY, 1989, p. 295.

29  "A lot of them just kind of lost interest when the soul music era ended" Telephone interview with John Morthland, August, 1994.

30  "just listen to your 'Loose Booty' " Quoted from Tate, Greg, *Flyboy in the Buttermilk: Essays on Contemporary America,* Simon & Schuster, NY, 1992, p. 17.


## 4  ROOTS: WHERE'D YOU GET YOUR FUNK FROM?

31  "funk is 'a term of uncertain origin' " Quoted from Morehead, Philip D., *The New International Dictionary of Music,* Meridian, New York, NY, 1991, p. 178.

31  "more positive attitude towards this most sacred phenomenon, clone funk" Parliament, "Prelude to Dr. Funkenstein," 1976. Written by Clinton/Worrell. Tercer-Mundo, Inc. Used by permission.

PAGE

32    "such a funke in the night" Quoted from *Webster's New International Dictionary of the English Language,* unabridged. 1970 ed. Edited by Philip Babcock Gove, et al. Merriam-Webster, Springfield, MA, p. 742. A thorough etymology of the word "funk" is offered here, from 14th century usage to present definitions.

32    "style derived from early blues" ibid.

33    "a return to fundamentals" Quoted from Thompson, Robert Farris, *Flash of the Spirit,* Vintage, NY, 1983, p. 104–5. Also supported by telephone interview, January 1995.

33    "this lingo involved the substitution of English for West African words" Quoted from Smitherman, Geneva, *Talkin' and Testifyin': The Language of Black America,* Wayne State University Press, Detroit, MI, 1986, p. 5.

34    "Heterogenous Sound Ideal in African American Music" Adapted from Wilson, Olly, "The Heterogenous Sound Ideal in African American Music," 1992. Edited by Josephine Wright, *New Perspectives in Music: Essays in Honor of Eileen Southern*, Warren, MI: Harmonie Park Press. Points were rearranged for emphasis.

36    "when he dance it's always on the one" Parliament, "Mr. Wiggles," written by G. Clinton, B. Worrell, M. Hampton. Tercer-Mundo, Inc. Used by permission.

36    "no distinction between . . . music and dance" An idea presented by UC Berkeley Professor Roy Thomas in during one of many consultations in preparation for early editions of the book. His guidance and insight were immeasurable.

40    "the disco music of the 1930s." One of many opinionated historical insights from series of consultations with Ted Vincent, author of *Keep Cool: The Black Activists Who Built the Jazz Age,* Pluto Press, London, England, 1995.

41    "Its very vulgarity assured its meaningful emotional connection" Quoted in Jones, LeRoi, *Blues People,* William Morrow & Co., New York, NY, 1963, p. 174.

41    "I realized that what I was doing was something special" Interview with Fred Wesley by the author, February, 1995.

41    "You'll never enjoy R&B if you need a pencil and a scorecard" Liner notes to "The Black Rhythm Revolution" LP by Idris Muhammad. 1971 BGP Records.

43    "the object of praise for its specifically black qualities" *Black Nationalism and the Revolution in Music,* Frank Kofsky, Pathfinder Press, New York, NY, 1970, p. 43. This book, along with an interview with Ishmael Reed, gave me particular insights on the "funk" phenomenon in jazz.

44    "perhaps the profoundest change within the Negro consciousness" Jones, op cit. p. 218.

## 5  THE 1960S: IF 6 WAS 9

47    Gospel chants on civil rights buses. Ideas given to me during interview with Ted Vincent, historian, and veteran of several rides.

48    "schools . . . still underfunded and all-black" Most of this information is taken from Berry and Blassingame's "Long Memory," but it is available in many places.

PAGE

48   "spontaneously combusts from within itself" *The Autobiography of Malcolm X,* Malcolm X with assistance from Alex Haley, Ballantine Books, New York, NY, 1964, p. 366.

49   "It Was a Funky Deal" *The Essential Etheridge Knight,* Etheridge Knight, copyright © 1986 by Etheridge Knight. Reprinted by permission of the University of Pittsburgh Press.

50   "many large-scale riots" Detailed accounts of the urban unrest in the 1960s include the Kerner commission report, and *Black Violence: The Political Impact of the 1960s' Riots,* James Button, Princeton University Press, Princeton, NJ, 1978.

50   "origins of 'black power' " Discussed in Berry, Mary Frances and Blassingame, John W., *Long Memory: The Black Experience in America,* Oxford University Press, New York, NY, 1982, p. 418–420.

50   "call for black people . . . to unite" Quoted in *Black Power,* Stokely Carmichael and Charles Hamilton, Vintage Books, New York, NY, 1967, p. 45.

51   *"time has come for Black people to arm themselves" Revolutionary Suicide,* Huey P. Newton, Ballantine Books, New York, NY, 1973, p. 166.

52   "It was a rebellion" Telephone interview with Claude "Paradise" Gray of X-Clan in January, 1995.

53   "No Viet Cong ever called me a Nigger" Well-known reference, available from *Muhammad Ali: His Live and Times,* Thomas Hauser, Simon & Schuster, New York, NY, 1991, among other sources.

53   "next thing I know, I'm caught up in it . . ." Telephone interview with Marshall Jones in January, 1995.

53   "We was goin' for *all* of it" Telephone interview with Bootsy Collins in September, 1994.

53   "When you're from the street, everything is a gamble" Telephone interview with Gary "Mudbone" Cooper in January, 1995.

54   "motivated by the truest/of the oldest/lies" "Black Panther," from *Collected Poems* by Langston Hughes. Copyright © 1994 by the Estate of Langston Hughes. Reprinted by permission of Alfred A. Knopf, Inc.

54   "can you kill the nigger in you . . ." Giovanni, Nikki "The True Import of Present Dialogue, Black vs. Negro (For Peppe, Who Will Ultimately Judge Our Efforts)" from *Black Feeling, Black Talk, Black Judgement* by Nikki Giovanni. Copyright © 1968, 1970. Reprinted by permission of William Morrow & Company, Inc.

55   "Say It Loud! I'm Black and I'm Proud" James Brown, "Say It Loud, (I'm Black and I'm Proud)," written by James Brown and Alfred James Ellis. Copyright © 1968 Dynatone Publishing Co. All rights administered by Unichappell Music Inc. All rights reserved. Used by permission.

57   "black music was my life and still is" John Lennon quoted in *Jet* magazine, Oct. 26, 1972. Story reprinted on Dec 25, 1980, after Lennon's death, p. 57.

## 6  THE RHYTHM REVOLUTION: TIGHTEN UP

60   "I invented that thing, Get On The One" Telephone interview with James Brown in August, 1993.

60   "I also took gospel and jazz and defied all the laws" ibid.

61   "the real important thing that changed" Telephone interview with Lee Hildebrand in February, 1995.

62   "now free to dance themselves" Liner notes to "Roots of Funk" CD compilation, Rhino R271615, notes by Sarah Brown and John Morthland, 1994.

64   "You can't overdub on a one-track machine" The 1968 interview was first printed in *Rolling Stone* on January 20, 1968 (after Redding's death) and found in *Rock and Roll Is Here to Pay*, Steve Chapple and Reebe Garafalo, Nelson Hall, Chicago, IL., 1979, p. 251.

67   "it's not what you say, but what you don't say" Telephone interview with George Porter in March, 1995.

69   "In New Orleans roots music" *Under a Hoodoo Moon*, Max (Dr. John) Rebenak, St. Martin's Press, New York, NY, 1994, p. 186.

69   "The New Orleans funk scene" Porter, op cit.

## 7  THE GODFATHER: SOUL POWER

72   "they'll know where the funk come from" James Brown, "Dead On It," written by James Brown and Fred Wesley. Copyright © 1975 Dynatone Publ. Co. (BMI). All rights administered by Unichappell Music Inc. (BMI). All rights reserved. Used by permission.

73   "We were it . . . and everybody went" Ellis quoted in *Living in America: The Soul Saga of James Brown*, Cynthia Rose, Serpent's Tail, London, England, 1990, p. 52.

73   "you just had to throat it" Maceo Parker quoted in Rose, ibid, p. 49.

73   "You see funk and soul is really jazz" Telephone interview with James Brown by Chuy Varela of KPFA radio in July, 1987.

73   "Fred Wesley . . . always claimed to be a 'frustrated be-bop trombonist' " Interview with Fred Wesley in 1994.

74   "you need freedom to create" *James Brown: The Godfather of Soul*, James Brown with Bruce Tucker, Macmillan, New York, NY, 1986, p. 159.

74   "I could tell from looking at the speakers that the rhythm was right" Ibid, p. 158.

75   "But it wouldn't be nothing, without a woman or a girl" James Brown, "It's a Man's Man's Man's World," written by James Brown and Betty Newsome. Copyright © 1966 (Renewed) Dynatone Publishing Co. (BMI) and Clamike Records Music (BMI). Unichappell Music administers all rights o/b/o Dynatone Publishing Co. All rights reserved. Used by permission.

75   "where black people move in almost absolute openness and strength" *Blues People "Black Music,"* LeRoi Jones, William Morrow & Co., New York, NY, 1967, p.186-7.

PAGE

77 "We're outgunned and we're outnumbered" James Brown, op cit., p. 174–5.

78 "machine gun toting Black Panthers" Interview with Ballard found in Cliff White's jacket notes to "James Brown: CD of JB II," Polydor 831-700-2.

78 "Say It loud, I'm black and I'm proud" James Brown, "Say It Loud (I'm Black and I'm Proud)." Written by James Brown and Alfred James Ellis. Copyright © 1968 Dynatone Publishing Co. All rights administered by Unichappell Music Inc. All rights reserved. Used by permission.

79 "Suppose James Brown read Fanon" "The Social Background of the Black Arts Movement," Larry Neal, 1987, Black Scholar Vol 18, No. 1, p. 19.

79 "The song cost me a lot of my crossover audience" James Brown, op cit., p. 200.

80 "The kind of energy he (Bootsy) brought to the funk was infectious" Fred Wesley interviewed by Lenny Henry on the *South Bank Show* in 1992. Used by permission.

81 "When he started playing, man . . . *everything* moved." Clyde Stubbefield interviewed by Lenny Henry on the *South Bank Show* in 1992. Used by permission.

81 "you just had to figure it out" Telephone interview with Bootsy Collins in June, 1994.

81 " 'young and single and loved to mingle' " Telephone interviews with Alan Leeds and Bootsy Collins in September, 1994.

82 "I saw a lot of spunk in Bootsy. A lot of life" James Brown, op cit., p. 218–9.

82 "He ran it through my brain" Telephone interview with Fred Wesley in 1995.

83 "Ladies and Gentlemen, without *no* doubt, *these* are the JBs" Fred Wesley & the JBs. "Doin' It to Death," by James Brown. Copyright © 1973 Dynatone Publishing Co. (BMI). All rights reserved. Used by permission.

83 "President . . . Albert Bongo of Gabon paying for Brown to fly to Africa." *Jet* magazine, April 25, 1975, p. 19.

83 "He'll free them if he talks to James Brown" Headline in story in *Jet* magazine, October 25, 1975, p. 52.

84 "James shot back 'Don't *touch* this' " "The Payback: Sample of the Moment," Harry Weinger, in *Vibe,* September, 1992, p. 40. Also discussed with Weinger and Wesley during several interviews.

86 "Dead On It," written by James Brown and Fred Wesley. Copyright © 1975 Dynatone Publishing Co. (BMI). All rights administered by Unichappell Music Inc. (BMI). All rights reserved. Used by permission.

88 "without the four-letter words it makes sense . . . but when you add all that . . . " Telephone interview with James Brown in August, 1993.

## 8  THE FAMILY STONED: I WANNA TAKE YOU HIGHER

90 "If Sly is as good as he is described" Jacket notes to "Life," Epic E 30333, by John Gabre, 1968.

92 "There was an enormous freedom to the band's sound" *Mystery Train,* Griel Marcus, E. P. Dutton, New York, NY, 1975, p. 91.

93 "the most widely imitated of his innovations" Jacket notes to "Small Talk," Epic PEQ 32930 by Steve Lake, 1973.

PAGE

94    "We got this encore . . . " Radio interview with Larry Graham, KPFA, Berkeley, July 7, 1995.

94    "massive human tidal wave of approval" Lake, op cit.

95    "the thumb of Larry Graham" Taken from cover story in *Bass Player*, September, 1992, p. 34.

95    "when I started to thump the strings with my thumb" Larry Graham quoted in *Bass Player*, ibid.

97    "portrait of what lay behind the big freaky black superstar grin" Griel Marcus, op cit., p. 89.


## 9  BLACK ROCK: GIVIN' IT BACK

103    "Funk is just speeded-up blues." George Clinton quoted during interview at KALX radio in 1986.

104    "But you see blues, it's tone, deep tone with a heavy beat . . . " Muddy Waters interview in David Henderson's book about Hendrix, *'Scuse Me While I Kiss the Sky: The Life and Times of Jimi Hendrix*, Bantam Books, New York, NY, 1981, p. 60.

104    "Nothing fancy—just a straight and heavy beat with it" Muddy Waters, ibid.

104    "started reaching that elusive white audience." *The Death of Rhythm and Blues*, Nelson George, Pantheon Books, New York, NY, 1988, p. 107.

107    "Go ahead on Mr. Business man you can't dress like me" Jimi Hendrix Experience, "If 6 Was 9," written by Jimi Hendrix. Copyright © 1969 Bella Godiva Music, Inc. Used by permission.

107    "let me live *my* life/the way I want to" ibid.

108    "The sound the African drums made was lost" *'Scuse Me While I Kiss the Sky: The Life and Times of Jimi Hendrix*, David Henderson, Bantam Books, New York, NY, 1981, p. 267.

109    "Sly brought [James] Brown's funk to the rock masses almost uncut" Nelson George, op cit., p. 109.

110    "Both him and Sly were great natural musicians" *Miles Davis: The Autobiography*, with Quincy Troupe, Simon & Schuster, New York, NY, 1989, p. 293. Used by permission.

115    Rebirth of the Bar-Kays. Telephone interview with Larry Dotson in March, 1995.

115    "turned black music fans from singles to album buyers" *Top of The Charts*, Nelson George, New Century Publishers, Piscataway, NJ, 1983, p. 73.


## 10  FUNKY SOUL: EXPRESS YOURSELF

121    "What I think I got from Ray Charles was the soul" Maceo Parker interviewed in *Terminal Zone*, July, 1988, issue No. 1.

121    "*What I Say* probably got to be the most funky record ever made" George Clinton, interviewed in *Terminal Zone*, July, 1988, issue No. 1.

122    "Singing gospel's a good way to learn about music in general" *James Brown: The Godfather of Soul*, James Brown with Bruce Tucker, Macmillan, New York, NY, 1986, p. 43. Used by permission.

PAGE
123 " 'Cause we're movin' on up" The Impressions, "We're a Winner," written by Curtis Mayfield. Copyright © 1967 Warner-Tamerlane Publishing Corp. All rights reserved. Used by permission.

125 "cause sam cooke said 'a change is gonna come' " "Revolutionary Music" from *Black Feeling, Black Talk, Black Judgement*, Nikki Giovanni. Copyright © 1968, 1970. By permission of William Morrow & Company, Inc.

127 "My feel was always an Eastern feel" *Buppies, B-Boys, Baps & Bohos: Notes on Post-Black Culture*, Nelson George, Harper Collins, New York, NY, 1992, p. 172.

128 "I wrote it by watching her move" Ibid.

128 "It was time to stop playing games" Marvin Gaye quoted in David Ritz, *Divided Soul: The Life of Marvin Gaye*, Da Capo, New York, NY, 1991, p. 140. Used by permission.

## 11  JAZZ-FUNK FUSION: THE CHAMELEON

138 "I paint pictures of infinity with my music" Sun Ra quoted in *Encyclopedia of Jazz in the 70s*, Feather, Leonard and Gitler, Ira, Da Capo Press, New York, NY, 1976, p. 319.

138 "it was sacrilegious to involve any other kinds of music, especially R&B, with jazz" Ramsey Lewis quoted in *Jazz-Rock Fusion, The People, The Music*, Julie Coryell and Laura Friedman, Dell, New York, NY, 1978, p. xi.

140 "I was beginning to listen to a lot of James Brown" Quoted from *Miles Davis: The Autobiography*, with Quincy Troupe, Simon & Schuster, New York, NY, 1989, p. 288.

141 "The trick about this music is that its textures" *Flyboy in the Buttermilk: Essays on Contemporary America*, Greg Tate, Simon & Schuster, New York, NY, 1992, p. 78.

143 "I got funk cats who knew how to play jazz" Herbie Hancock quoted in Coryell, op cit., p. 162.

144 "The funk band—now that music has such strong roots in the Earth . . . " Hancock, Herbie. Jacket notes to Herbie Hancock: VSOP Columbia PG 43688, 1977.

148 "Sure, Blood is pimping the funk," Greg Tate, op cit., p. 19.

149 "While many hail the rebirth of so-called jazz" Text of speech by Harry Allen delivered to New Music Seminar, New York, NY, July 13, 1987. Text delivered to seminar participants.

149 "Jazz was invented for people to dance." *To Be or Not to Bop: Memoirs of Dizzy Gillespie*, Dizzy Gillespie, Da Capo, New York, NY, 1979, p. 484–5.

149 "There's a long distance between that and playing jazz." Wynton Marsalis in *Goldmine*, June 28, 1991, p.10.

## 12  POWER TO THE PEOPLE: IT'S JUST BEGUN

153 "Get Down" War. Written by Sylvester Allen, Harold Brown, Morris Dickerson, Leroy Jordan, Charles Miller, Lee Oskar, Howard Scott, Jerry Goldstein. Copyright © 1971 Far Out Music, Inc. Used by permission.

PAGE

154   "don't be surprised if Ali is in the White House" "Chocolate City," Parliament. Written by G. Clinton, W. Collins, B. Worrell. Tercer-Mundo, Inc. Used by permission.

154   "We gotta fight the powers that be" "Fight the Power," Isley Brothers. Written by R. Isley, R. Isley, M. Isley, O. Isley, E. Isley, C. Jasper. Used by permission.

155   "You have more power over my seven kids than I do." Dick Gregory quoted in Arnie Passman's "Ethnic Radio—White Ownership of Black Media," in *Scanlans*, 1970, p. 13, vol. 1, no. 1.

156   "they will have to make us part of it if they wish to stay in business" Del Shields quoted in *Sweet Soul Music*, Peter Guralnik, Harper & Row, New York, NY, 1987, p. 383.

156   "I was there when the nitty went down with the gritty" Telephone interview with Jack Gibson in February, 1995.

156   "Maybe the record companies were a little more sensitive . . . after that" Isaac Hayes quoted in Peter Guralnik, op cit. p. 283.

156   "If we could have succeeded" Telephone interview with Jack Gibson in February, 1995.

158   "extremist views and philosophies" *Jet* magazine article, October 25, 1975, p. 8, pointed out James Brown's name in a list that was made public in 1975.

159   "I Plan to Stay a Believer" Curtis Mayfield, written by Curtis Mayfield. Copyright © 1971 Warner-Tamerlane Publishing Corp. (BMI). All rights reserved. Used by permission.

162   "The Revolution Will Not Be Televised" Gil Scott-Heron, "The Revolution Will Not Be Televised." Copyright © 1971 Bienstock Publishing Company. Used by permission. All rights reserved.

163   "Niggers Are Scared *of Revolution*" The Last Poets. Written by Umar Ben Hassan. Copyright © 1971 Douglas Music Corp. Used by permission.

164   "the revolutionaries were synchronizing their watches" Interview with Toni Vincent, my mother, in March, 1994, about the demise of the Black Panthers.

165   "When the Revolution Comes" The Last Poets. Written by Abiodun Oyewole. Copyright © 1971 Douglas Music Corp. Used by permission.

## 13  THOSE FUNKY SEVENTIES: LIVIN' FOR THE CITY

168   "funk is the conscious adoption of value systems previously considered antithetical" "Funk is in the eye of the Beholder," Henry Allen, *The Washington Post*, Washington, DC, January 11, 1971, B1.

171   "But time is running out / And there's no happiness" "Superfly," Curtis Mayfield. Copyright © 1972 Warner-Tamerlane Publishing Corp. (BMI). All rights reserved. Used by permission.

174   "the whole freedom thing has opened it up" "A Funky View of the Universe, courtesy of a band of wierdos," Abe Peck, *Oakland Tribune*, December 26, 1976 (AP).

175   "Funk can be sweet" The Dells, "The Origins of Funk—Segue 3," Terry Callier and Charles Stepney. "Segue 3: The Origin of Funk," by Terry Callier and Charles Step-

PAGE

ney. Copyright © 1973 Chappell & Co. (ASCAP), Last Go Round Music (ASCAP), Butler Music (ASCAP), & Eibur Music (ASCAP). All rights administered by Chappell & Co. (ASCAP). All rights reserved. Used by permission.

176   "Jes Grew is the delight of the gods" "Mumbo Jumbo," Ishmael Reed, Atheneum, New York, NY, 1972, 1989, p. 6.

177   "Have you read *Mumbo Jumbo?*" George Clinton interviewed at KALX radio in 1986.

177   "I always wanted to be in the most freaked-out band around." Telephone interview #2 with Bootsy Collins in September, 1994.


### 14  UNITED FUNK: THE SHINING STAR

182   "They're the *second* baddest out there." James Brown discussion with Cleveland Brown found in liner notes to *Funk Essentials: The Best of Kool & the Gang,* Polygram Records, 1994.

183   "Cryin' babies on the doorstep" Kool & the Gang, "This Is You, This Is Me," by Robert Mickens, Robert Bell, Dennis Thomas, Claydes Smith, Richard Westfield, George Brown, Ronald Bell. Copyright © 1973 Warner-Tamerlane Publishing Corp. (BMI), Gang Music Ltd. (BMI). All rights o/b/o Gang Music Ltd. administered by Warner-Tamerlane Publishing Corp. All rights reserved. Used by permission.

183   "but we never tire of looking" Ronald Bell (Khalis Bayyan) quoted from passage found in *Billboard Book of #1 R&B Hits,* Adam White, Billboard Books, an imprint of Watson-Guptill Publications, New York, NY, 1993, p. 147.

188   "we were a funk band" Allan Gorrie of AWB in telephone interview in November, 1994.

194   "I get knocked on the ground/by all this *bullshit* goin' down!" The Isley Brothers, "Fight the Power." Written by R. Isley, R. Isley, M. Isley, O. Isley, E. Isley, C. Jasper. Used by permission.

194   "When will there be a harvest for the world . . ." The Isley Brothers, "Harvest for the World." Written by R. Isley, R. Isley, M. Isley, O. Isley, E. Isley, C. Jasper. Used by permission.

198   "We're musicians, not murderers" Telephone interview with James "Diamond" Williams in December, 1994.

199   Discussion of the Commodores, and many other acts taken from *Illustrated Encyclopedia of Black Music,* Harmony Books, New York, NY, 1982.


### 15  DISCO FEVER: THE (REAL) HUSTLE

207   "garbage and pollution which is corrupting the minds and morals of our youth." Passage of Jesse Jackson speech at 1977 Media Ethics conference. Taken from *Anti-Rock: The Opposition to Rock and Roll,* Linda Martin and Kerry Segrave, Da Capo Press, New York, NY, 1988, 1993, p. 252.

210   "the effects of disco may well be dispiriting." *Saturday Review,* Ken Emerson, November 12, 1977, p. 48.

PAGE

210   "The sound of the death of R&B." Quoted in *Death of Rhythm and Blues,* Nelson
      George, Plume, New York, NY, p. 161.

211   "All the major labels had caught disco fever" *Hit Men,* Frederic Dannen, Vintage,
      New York, NY, 1991, p. 176.

214   "Black radio shouldn't play any white records." Telephone interview with Jack Gib-
      son in February, 1995.

215   "Disco, in fact, sucked." *Anti-Rock,* Martin and Segrave, op cit., p. 231.


## 16   DANCE FUNK: DO YOU WANNA GET FUNKY WITH ME?

223   "the 'Super Groups.' " "The Super Groups," Bill Berry, *Ebony,* July, 1978, p. 36.

226   "Cameo is 21st century be-bop." *Style* LP liner notes, 1983.

227   "With the funk, there are no rules" Telephone interview with Stevie Washington
      in August, 1994.

230   "We held the line on the Memphis sound for over ten years" Harvey Henderson of
      the Bar-Kays interviewed in April, 1989.


## 17   THE P-FUNK EMPIRE: TEAR THE ROOF OFF THE SUCKER

231   "P-Funk (Wants to Get Funked Up)" Parliament. Written by G. Clinton, B. Collins,
      B. Worrell. Tercer-Mundo, Inc. Used by permission.

232   "George Clinton's barbershop was the only thang left standing." "George Clinton:
      Ultimate Liberator of Constipated Notions," W. A. Brower, *Downbeat,* April 5,
      1979, p. 17.

233   "Eddie and Tiki were two trifling motherfuckers" Billy Nelson quoted in Rob Bow-
      man, liner notes to *Music for Your Mother,* Westbound Records, 1993.

234   "Behold, I Am Funkadelic" Funkadelic, "What is Soul?" George Clinton, Jr./William
      "Billy" Nelson/Eddie Hazel. Copyright © 1970 by Bridgeport Music Inc. (BMI) and
      Southfield Music Inc. (ASCAP) All rights reserved. Used by permission.

236   "Maggot Brain" Funkadelic. George Clinton, Jr./Eddie Hazel. Copyright © 1971
      by Bridgeport Music Inc. (BMI) and Southfield Music Inc. (ASCAP) All rights re-
      served. Used by permission.

236   "As long as human beings fail to see THEIR fear" "Process Church of Final Judge-
      ment" liner notes to *Maggot Brain,* LP, Westbound Records, 1971.

237   "Funkadelic is wot time it is!" Pedro Bell liner art, Funkadelic LP, *Standing on the
      Verge of Gettin' It On,* Westbound Records, 1974.

238   "the truest representation of urban life offered in black music." *The Rolling Stone
      Record Guide,* 1977 ed.

239   "Bootsy had a perfect personality" George Clinton quoted in *Terminal Zone,* July,
      1988, issue no. 1.

240   "We saw this light bouncing from one side . . . to the other." "A Funky view of the
      universe, courtesy of a band of weirdos," Abe Peck, *Oakland Tribune,* December 26,
      1976, 13-E.

PAGE

242 "P-Funk (Wants to Get Funked Up)" Parliament. Written by G. Clinton, B. Collins, B. Worrell. Tercer-Mundo, Inc. Used by permission.

242 "we are deeper than abortion" Parliament, "Children of Productions." Written by Bootsy Collins, George Clinton, Jr., and Bernie Worrell. Copyright © 1976 Rubber Band Music, Inc. Tercer-Mundo, Inc. Used by permission.

244 "The world can either credit him or blame him for the synthesizer bass." Interview with Teo Barry Vincent in June, 1994.

246 "Flashlight" Parliament. Written by Bootsy Collins, George Clinton, Jr., and Bernie Worrell. Copyright © 1978 Rubber Band Music, Inc. Tercer-Mundo, Inc. Used by permission.

249 "Rubber Band" name lawsuit info courtesy of Pedro Bell and *Jet,* April 17, 1980.

252 "George blew our minds wide open" Telephone interview with Greg "Shock G" Jacobs in October, 1993.

## 18  THE METAPHYSICS OF P: THE MOTHERSHIP CONNECTION

253 "P-Funk is a Mystery System" Taken from interview with Ashem Neru-Mesit in January, 1993.

254 "looking like a cross between *Star Trek* and *Sanford and Son.* " "A Funky view of the universe, courtesy of a band of weirdos," Abe Peck, *Oakland Tribune,* December 26, 1976, 13-E.

254 "Funk upon a time" Parliament, "Prelude to Dr. Funkenstein," written by Clinton/Worrell. Tercer-Mundo, Inc. Used by permission.

255 "AS IT IS WRITTEN HENCEFORTH . . ." Taken from Pedro Bell's *Standing on the Verge of Gettin' It On,* liner notes, 1974.

257 "These superheroes offer them a mythic sense of possibility." Michael V. O'Neal; Master's thesis on "P-Funk aesthetic" at UCLA, 1987, p. 89.

257 "P-Funk was deeply religious" Interview with Anthony "Dave-Id K-OS," Bryant, 1993.

258 "I didn't really believe in religion until I took acid" Clinton interviewed in "A Funky view of the universe, courtesy of a band of weirdos," Abe Peck, *Oakland Tribune,* December 26, 1976, 13-E.

258 "more to do with cosmic oneness than this earth's religions." Ibid.

259 "Everybody on the One, the whole world on the same pulse." George Clinton interviewed by Lenny Henry on the *South Bank Show,* 1992. Used by permission.

259 "Unfunky UFO" Parliament. Written by G. Clinton, B. Collins, G. Shider. Tercer-Mundo, Inc. Used by permission.

260 "Aqua-Boogie" Parliament. Written by Bootsy Collins, George Clinton, Jr., and Bernie Worrell. Copyright © 1978 Rubber Band Music, Inc. Tercer-Mundo, Inc. Used by permission. All rights reserved.

260 "It's about how deep you have to be in this world" Clinton quoted in "George Clinton: Ultimate Liberator of Constipated Notions," W. A. Brower, *Downbeat,* April 5, 1979, p. 17.

PAGE

260 "The infinite intelligence within you knows the answers" Funkadelic, "Good Thoughts, Bad Thoughts," George Clinton, Jr./Grace Cook. Copyright © 1974 by Bridgeport Music Inc. All rights reserved. Used by permission.

260 "each man is a Shiva" "The Serpent Power," Woodrofe, John George, Sir (a.k.a. Arthur Avalon) Ganesh & Co. (Madras) Private, Ltd. 1964.

261 "Cosmic Slop" Funkadelic. George Clinton, Jr./Bernie Worrell. Copyright © 1973 by Bridgeport Music Inc. (BMI). All rights reserved. Used by permission.

262 "P-Funk de-fetishes an already demeaned subject." Brower, op cit.

262 "the boundary between sacred and profane cannot be drawn as it is in Europe." *Muntu: The New African Culture,* Janheinz Jahn. Translated by Marjorie Greene. Faber and Faber, London, England, 1961, p. 83.

263 "The arousal of Ra—our life force—" *The Metu Neter,* Ra Un Nefer Amen, Khamit Corp, Bronx, NY, 1990, p. 145.


## 19  FUNK IN THE 1980S: SUPER FREAKS

267 "Sexuality" written by Prince Nelson. Copyright © 1981 Controversy Music (ASCAP). All rights o/b/o Controversy Music administered by WB Music Corp. (ASCAP). All rights reserved. Used by permission.

269 "he could 'now go through the checkpoints with ease.' " *The Death of Rhythm and Blues,* Nelson George, Plume, New York, NY, p. 169.

270 "the major-label record business generally offers black performers a choice of stereotypes" "Racism in the music business," Jon Pareles, in *The New York Times,* May 17, 1987, II, p. 32.

271 "The record was selling like a motherfucker" "The Atomic Dog: George Clinton interview by Greg Tate and Bob Wisdom," found in Tate, Greg, *Flyboy in the Buttermilk,* op cit., p. 34.

273 "the unconscious part of the brain got bored with it." Telephone interview with Robert Margouleff in February, 1995.

276 "I started sinking to a point where I didn't care" Rick James quoted in J. Freedom du Lac, "Free Fall," in *Sacramento Bee,* February 19, 1995, p. 18.

276 "no black performer since Little Richard" Nelson George, op cit., p. 174.

278 "shallow, misguided . . . direction" Poussaint quoted in *Ebony* magazine, June, 1985, p. 170.

280 "funk . . . is the R&B with a real attitude" Telephone interview with Nathan Leftenant in May, 1995.

280 "It's the black experience" Telephone interview with Roger Troutman in February, 1995.

281 "It was about Bootsy, and it was about Sugarfoot" Ibid.

284 "sellout hall of fame" The irate funk critic is Chris Williams, veteran staffer at Casablanca Records and WWRL radio in New York.

285 "Are white singers taking over blues and soul?" *Jet* magazine, "Are white singers taking over blues and soul?" issue March 6, 1989, p. 61.

## 20 HIP HOP AND BLACK NOISE: RAISING HELL

PAGE

287 "The Message" Grandmaster Flash & the Furious Five. Written by E. Fletcher, M. Glover, S. Robinson, J. Chase. Sugarhill Music. Used by permission.

290 "They were really scared of that album" Telephone interview with Afrika Bambaataa in February, 1995.

293 "they are the P-Funk of the eighties" Telephone interview with Pedro Bell in 1987.

294 "ritual of black celebration" Nelson George quoted from liner notes to *Good to Go* soundtrack, Island Records, 1986.

294 "the distance between lofty American dreams and 1980s black reality" Ibid.

294 "The beat is so simple most drummers don't like to play it." Chuck Brown quoted from *Billboard Book of #1 R&B Hits,* Adam White, p. 252.

297 "maybe it's a hand grenade" "See the World" by the Looters. Written by the Looters, 1985. Used by permission.

299 "jam fat shit like 'Hair' by Larry Graham" Telephone interview with Dewayne Wiggins in June, 1995; "they had the whole Bay Area locked up for a while," telephone interview with Dewayne Wiggins in August, 1995.

300 "rock out with your cock out, and play like you got a big dick" George Clinton quoted in Tower *Pulse,* June, 1985, p. 30. Thanks to Linda Tosetti for her research.

301 "America's Apartheid Oriented Rock circuit." BRC manifesto, courtesy of Greg Tate.

## 21 FUNK IN THE NINETIES: RETURN OF THE FUNK

308 "Terminator X to the Edge of Panic" Public Enemy. Rodgers/Ridenhour/Drayton. Ujamaa Music. Used by permission.

308 "Caught, Can I Get a Witness" Public Enemy. Ridenhour/Shocklee/Sadler. Ujamaa Music. Used by permission.

310 "Elvis was a hero to most" Public Enemy, "Fight the Power," Shocklee/Sadler/Ridenhour, Ujamaa Music. Used by permission.

310 Public Enemy "wants to reconvene the black power movement" "The Devil Made 'Em Do It," Greg Tate, *Village Voice,* July 19, 1988, p. 71.

310 "ridiculous sixties rock ideal of raising political consciousness with music." Robert Christgau in *Village Voice* editorial, January 16, 1990, p. 84.

310 "To me they're like what Bob Dylan was" Telephone interview with George Clinton in May, 1989.

311 "they have actually instigated a species of leftish Afrocentrism" Christgau, op cit.

311 "There is something changing in the climate of consciousness" Public Enemy, "Contract on the World Love Jam," Shocklee/Sadler/Ridenhour. Ujamaa Music. Used by permission.

312 "It's all just from listening to a lot of Parliament/Funkadelic." Prince Paul quoted in *The New Beats,* S. H. Fernando, Jr., Anchor Press, New York, NY, 1994, p. 230.

PAGE

312  "Neva Again" Kam. Written by Bootsy Collins, George Clinton, Jr., Bernie Wor-
     rell, Roger Troutman, Larry Troutman, and Craig Miller. Copyright © 1993 Saja
     Music Co./Songs of Lastrada/Tercer-Mundo, Inc./Rubber Band Music, Inc./Right-
     song Music Inc./I-Slam Music/Street Knowledge Music. Used by permission. All
     rights reserved.

312  "Earthbound" X-Clan. Written by Jason Hunter, Lumumba Carson, George Clin-
     ton, Jr., Garry Shider, Walter Morrison, and David Spradley. Copyright © 1990
     Songs of Polygram International, Inc. and Vanglorious Music. Tercer-Mundo, Inc.
     Used by permission. All rights reserved.

314  "Straight Outta Compton" N.W.A. O. Jackson, L. Patterson, E. Wright, A. Young.
     Ruthless Attack Music (ASCAP). Used by permission.

314  "So what about the bitch that got shot" Ibid.

316  "you almost have to sell out" Lonzo quoted in Brian Cross, *It's Not About a Salary:
     Rap, Race, and Resistance in Los Angeles,* Verso Press, London/New York, 1993,
     p. 123–4.


## 22  POSTSCRIPT ON THE FUNK: SONS OF THE P

321  "jazz freedom fighter" *Race Matters,* Cornell West, Beacon Press, Boston, MA, 1993,
     p. 105.

323  "get serious about being *ridiculous.*" Interview with Patrick "Sledhicket" Norwood,
     Los Angeles, CA, 1989.


All chart positions courtesy of Joel Whitburn's Top R&B Singles; compiled from
Billboard Rhythm & Blues charts. Record Research Inc., Menomonee Falls, Wisconsin, 1988.

# *Index*